Film Noir

By the same author in this series:

COEN BROTHERS

virgin
film

FILM NOIR

Eddie Robson

For Catherine

First published in Great Britain in 2005
by Virgin Books Ltd
Thames Wharf Studios
Rainville Road
London
W6 9HA

A catalogue record for this book is available from the British Library.

ISBN 0 7535 1086 3

Typeset by TW Typesetting, Plymouth, Devon
Printed and bound in Great Britain by Mackays of Chatham PLC

Contents

Acknowledgements	vi
Introduction	1
Background	5
Stranger on the Third Floor (1940)	7
The Maltese Falcon (1941)	17
Double Indemnity (1944)	32
Murder, My Sweet (1944)	46
Detour (1945)	60
The Big Sleep (1946)	70
The Killers (1946)	84
Out of the Past (1947)	99
The Lady from Shanghai (1948)	110
Force of Evil (1948)	123
Gun Crazy (1949)	135
Sunset Boulevard (1950)	149
The Big Heat (1953)	163
The Big Combo (1955)	173
Kiss Me Deadly (1955)	184
The Night of the Hunter (1955)	197
The Killing (1956)	210
Touch of Evil (1958)	223
The Wider World of Film Noir	239
Index of Quotations	251
Bibliography	279
Picture Credits	289
Index	291

Acknowledgements

Thanks to Kirstie Addis, Mark Clapham, Ben Felsenburg, Simon Guerrier, Steve O'Brien, Catherine Spooner, Jim Smith, the BFI Library, Lancaster Public Library, Lancaster University Library, www.imdb.com and www.wellesnet.com.

Special thanks to Lee Horsley, whose vast resources of film, print and knowledge were invaluable in the writing of this book.

And, as always, thanks to Mum, Dad, Helen and Gran.

Introduction

Upon seeing the contents page of this book, your reaction may have been to cry, 'What? No *La Bête Humaine*? No *Shoot the Pianist*? No *The Third Man*? No *Chinatown*? No *The Usual Suspects*?' Different critics have their own ideas about what is and isn't film noir. Undoubtedly the noir movement was prefigured in France shortly before it emerged in America; there was a comparable and contemporary movement in Britain and there have been noir films produced ever since the form emerged (and particularly after it was identified, named and written about). However, I have chosen to restrict the scope of this book to Hollywood films of the 1940s and 1950s, because in order to give each film adequate consideration from factual and critical angles in the Virgin Film format there was only space to accommodate so many films. It was absurdly easy to compile a list of eighteen essential noirs from the 'classical' American period alone, and even this regrettably excluded some fine works (I have covered as many of these as possible in the sections between chapters). In addition, because the 'classical' period can be identified as a cycle of Hollywood filmmaking which came to an end, this lends the book coherence. Through these examples we can watch noir develop and in some cases the desire to demonstrate this development has influenced my selections. The selection is a balance between personal favourites and what I feel to be the most significant examples.

Another reason for sticking to 'classical' Hollywood noir is that many of the 'neo-noirs' which might have featured are covered in other Virgin Film books: *The Conversation* is in *Coppola*; *Blue Velvet* and *Mullholland Drive* are in *Lynch*; *Taxi Driver* is in *Scorsese*; *Blade Runner* is in *Ridley Scott*; and *Blood Simple* and *The Man Who Wasn't There* are in my own *Coen Brothers*. As there is unlikely to be a volume on Robert Siodmak or Joseph H Lewis, it seems fair to make space for them in *Film Noir*. (The exception is *The Killing*, which is also in *Kubrick* – but within the parameters of the 'classical' period it demands inclusion here.) A section at the end of the book discusses examples of neo-noir, as well as noir from other countries. This book's focus on the 'classical' period should not then be seen as a claim that 1940s and 1950s films are definitively superior to those produced subsequently. It is not my intention to nostalgically sigh that they don't make 'em like this any more. I deliberately use the term 'classical' (referring to the 'classical' era of Hollywood and relating to the regularity of form which was a feature of the studio system) in preference to 'classic' (meaning 'of the highest class' and therefore incorporating a value judgement).

In the format established by previous entries in the Virgin Film series, I have ordered information and criticism under category headings to aid the reader in locating what they want to know. Each chapter is headed with the title of the film and year of release, followed by the main production credits (transcribed in the order that they appear on-screen) and the credited cast. From there on, the following headings are used as appropriate.

SUMMARY: A brief account of the film's plot. Obviously it is advisable to watch the film before reading the entry, but it can be difficult to track down copies of some of the films covered in this book and it is reasonable to expect that many readers will not have seen them all. Additionally, for some of the more tortuous plots a recap may refresh the memory.

DIRECTOR: A profile of the film's director. It is worth noting that the Hollywood film director of the 1940s and 1950s did not possess the level of creative influence that he or she enjoys today. In 1939 Frank Capra noted that 'there are only half a dozen directors in Hollywood who are allowed to shoot as they please and who have any supervision over the editing.' Under the 'studio system' (see **Background**) the director was a hired hand like any other, employed for their ability to handle actors and produce shots that would flow smoothly when edited together. Development work, casting and set management would frequently fall within the producer's remit and the director's daily work would often be scrutinised by the producer.

Auteurist film criticism has had a huge influence on the way we think about films. This school of thought, originated by French film critics ('auteur' being French for 'author') but widely disseminated by Andrew Sarris, looked for a single creative force upon which it could confer authorship and found the director. This was an attempt to make cinema an object of study alongside literature and can be traced to a belief that it was a prerequisite of great art to be personal, and that art produced by many people would be less personal and contain less of value: however, a skilled and distinctive director could break through and stamp his personality on a film. Sarris stated that auteurism 'values the personality of the director precisely because of the barriers to its expression. It is as if a few brave spirits had managed to overcome the gravitational pull of the mass of movies.' Orson Welles was auteurism's poster-boy – an actor-writer-producer-director who repeatedly clashed with the Hollywood system.

Yet film is inescapably a collaborative medium, and if a critic prizes the single author so much then they should probably write about something else. In cinema the 'single author' is a myth often encouraged by venerated directors such as Welles, who habitually took credit for the contributions of others. Furthermore, auteurism has less time for genre products, which films noirs generally are: it prizes a few special films, while genre criticism recognises the importance of an overall system of production and wider film culture (the 'mass of movies' of which Sarris is so dismissive). Since we are dealing with a cycle of films which tended to deviate from classical Hollywood style, the director is often an important figure and some of the studies in this book are quite director led, but it is necessary to recognise the strong roles played by other personnel.

WRITER: A profile of the writer(s) – there's usually more than one. Many of these films are based on novels or short stories, and I have also profiled the writer of the source material. I generally haven't profiled writers who did uncredited redrafting work unless they're quite notable, as this happened all the time in Hollywood and it can be difficult to gauge how much they actually contributed. (It can also be difficult to establish whether or not somebody worked on a film at all.)

DEVELOPMENT: Focusing on the film's progress from initial concept to shooting script. This sometimes overlaps with the production process, but I have attempted to divide as sensibly as possible.

CASTING: Profiles of the main cast members, and any pertinent details relating to their being cast in the film. The standing and established personality of the stars is often useful in establishing the context in which a film was made and originally seen. (Note that if any profiled person – director, writer or actor – worked on more than one film covered in this book, their profile will be split across those films.)

PRODUCTION: An account of the production process.

RECEPTION: How the film was received upon release, mainly looking at the contemporary critical response but also in terms of the response from audiences, major awards and the reaction from Hollywood itself.

ASPECTS OF NOIR: Analysis of the film in question, looking at a selection of the many critical perspectives that have been brought to bear on film noir. I have aimed to use each film as an example of a different aspect of noir: for example, *The Maltese Falcon* discusses the detective figure, *Double Indemnity* the femme fatale and so on.

AFTERLIFE: Notable developments following the film's release, such as remakes or director's cut versions.

AVAILABILITY: Notes on what editions of these films are available on DVD: if no UK DVD is available, the VHS is noted.

Background

In discussing the Hollywood movies of the 1940s and 1950s it is useful to possess some knowledge of how the industry operated at that time: what is referred to as the 'studio system'.

During the 1910s and 1920s the American film industry became dominated by vertically integrated companies: consortiums which owned not only the studios which produced the films, but also the distributors and the cinemas. This began in 1919 when Famous Players-Lasky, already involved in production and distribution, opened a cinema chain and soon after adopted the name Paramount Pictures (previously the name of its distribution wing). This prompted the cinema chain First National Pictures to found a studio, and in the late 1920s the company was absorbed into Warner Bros. Loew's Incorporated took over Metro Pictures in 1920 before fusing it with Goldwyn Co. and Louis B Mayer Productions Incorporated in 1924 to form Metro-Goldwyn-Mayer; in 1929 the Keith, Albee and Orpheum Theater Chain, American Pathé, Joseph P Kennedy's Film Booking Office of America and Radio Corporation of America formed Radio-Keith-Orpheum, or RKO; and finally in 1935 Twentieth Century Pictures bought a controlling share in Fox Film Corporation to form Twentieth Century-Fox.

These companies became known as the 'Big Five', and their control over all stages of a film's journey from commission to première resulted in a degree of security that was invaluable during the Depression. While they only owned around 15 per cent of American cinemas between them, these cinemas were located in the major urban centres and were by far the most profitable and influential. At that time a film would have a much longer life than today, opening first on a few screens in major cities before moving out to second- and third-run urban cinemas and eventually coming to small towns several months later. This was less risky than modern large-scale openings, which require more prints to be struck and allow little time for the distributor to modify its strategy. The first-run cinemas therefore set the agenda, and these were largely owned by the Big Five: as they could charge more for tickets, they also accounted for almost 70 per cent of American box-office revenue. Any film which did not play in the Big Five's theatres would not be successful. Competition between the Big Five was mild, since each exhibited the products of the others in its cinemas and so a hit film would make money for all of them, regardless of which studio had produced it.

The ranks of the major studios were completed by the 'Little Three': Universal (founded 1912), Columbia (founded 1924) and United Artists (formed in 1919 by the actors Charlie Chaplin, Douglas Fairbanks and

Mary Pickford and the director DW Griffith). These were producer-distributors which owned no cinemas (Universal acquired some in 1929, but sold them after going into receivership in 1933), and, while the personalities behind United Artists ensured that its output was high profile, Universal and Columbia produced mainly mid- and low-budget features. At the bottom end of the scale were 'Poverty Row' studios such as Monogram, PRC, Republic and Tiffany, which largely produced B-movies to be bought by the majors for filling the bottom end of double and triple bills.

What developed was a system whereby a studio would produce a wide range of movies, with the intention of building a package around a successfully realised 'quality' picture, attaching several 'programme' pictures to it and forcing the exhibitor to buy the whole package or nothing at all. The 'programme' pictures would typically be lower-budget, more conventional product. This made good financial sense, as the overall costs of running the studio could be spread over all the films while the top producers' attention could be focused on producing the handful of hit films necessary to sell the rest. In 1937, the major studios produced 408 films (as a point of comparison, in 1986 the figure was precisely one-quarter of that amount). Exhibitors, meanwhile, were more interested in encouraging regular attendance than pulling in big audiences for the major films, and the best way of doing this was with a bill of entertainment produced to a reliable standard. It is not difficult to see how this fostered the development of genres in Hollywood, particularly among lower-budget features – if the main attraction fell flat with audiences, a B-picture based on a tested formula might still allow them to derive enjoyment from their evening.

The studio system came to an end when the Supreme Court declared in 1948 that Hollywood's vertically integrated companies were illegal under monopoly laws, forcing the producer-distributors to divorce from their exhibition chains. This led to the development of Hollywood as we recognise it today. Movies had to compete with each other for space in cinemas, meaning that every movie had to be sold on its own terms. The majors abandoned economies of scale, instead putting their resources into fewer movies designed to stand out from a reduced crowd, and rather than operating their own 'production line' they increasingly provided studio space and financial backing for independent companies which came to them with projects. Previously, much of the creative and technical talent would be contracted to the studio (hence, the use of terms such as 'contract players' and 'contract directors' in this book); now everybody worked freelance, hugely reducing the majors' fixed costs. The majors retained power in their crucial middleman role of distributors, while the independent cinemas which had pushed for an end to the studio system floundered without its secure (if oppressive) network: the cheaper movies that had been their bread and butter were no longer being made, and many of those exhibitors closed down.

The old system of production was phased out during the 1950s: the 'classical' period of film noir, which this book covers, petered out over the same period. These two facts are connected, but we're getting ahead of ourselves. Our starting point is 1940, and the movie usually agreed to be the first film noir: *Stranger on the Third Floor*.

Stranger on the Third Floor (1940)

Black and White – 64 mins

RKO Pictures, Inc. Presents
Stranger on the Third Floor
Produced by Lee Marcus
Story and Screenplay by Frank Partos
Musical Score by Roy Webb
Director of Photography: Nicholas Musuraca, ASC
Special Effects by Vernon L Walker, ASC
Art Director: Van Nest Polglase (Associate: Albert D'Agostino)
Wardrobe by Renié
Recorded by Bailey Fesler
Edited by Harry Marker
Directed by Boris Ingster

CAST: Peter Lorre (*The Stranger*), John McGuire (*Mike Ward*), Margaret Tallichet (*Jane*), Charles Waldron (*District Attorney*), Elisha Cook, Jr (*Joe Briggs*), Charles Halton (*Albert Meng*), Ethel Griffies (*Mrs Kane*), Cliff Clark (*Martin*), Oscar O'Shea (*The Judge*), Alec Craig (*Defence Attorney*), Otto Hoffman (*Police Surgeon*)

SUMMARY: Ace newspaper reporter Mike Ward gives evidence at the trial of petty criminal Joe Briggs. Joe stands accused of the murder of coffee-shop owner Giuseppe, and although the evidence is circumstantial he is found guilty on the basis of Mike's testimony (Mike found Joe standing over the body, and had previously heard Joe threaten Giuseppe). Mike returns home with doubts in his mind, then develops a

suspicion that his neighbour, Albert Meng, is dead. Meng has indeed
been murdered in a similar way to Giuseppe, and suspicion falls upon
Mike (he and Meng did not get along, and had a number of angry
confrontations). Mike is arrested, protesting that the crime must have
been committed by a stranger he saw fleeing the building earlier. His
girlfriend Jane searches tirelessly for the stranger, and eventually finds
him. The Stranger is an escapee from an asylum: both Giuseppe and
Meng had discovered this and he killed them both to avoid going back.
He realises that Jane means to turn him in and chases her, only to be run
over by a truck. As he dies, he confesses, and both Mike and Joe are
released.

DIRECTOR: Boris Ingster (1903–78) was an expatriate Russian who
had worked as a writer on such movies as *I'll Give a Million* (Walter
Lang, 1938) and *Miracle on Main Street* (Steve Sekely, 1939). *Stranger
on the Third Floor* was the first of three films he directed, the others
being *The Judge Steps Out* (1949) and the noir *Southside 1-1000* (1951).
He continued to write and moved to TV in the 1960s with episodes of
Rawhide, before becoming producer of the hugely successful
tongue-in-cheek spy show *The Man from U.N.C.L.E.* (1964–68),
including four theatrical films.

WRITER: Frank Partos (1901–56), originally from Hungary, started
working in Hollywood in the early 1930s and made his screenwriting
debut at Paramount with *Guilty as Hell* (Erle C Kenton, 1932). He
generated many story ideas, and in the mid-1930s came up with *Stranger
on the Third Floor*. His other writing credits include *Thirty Day Princess*
(Marion Gering, 1934), *She's No Lady* (Charles Vidor, 1937) and *Rio*
(John Brahm, 1939) – the last of which has been argued to be an even
earlier noir than *Stranger*. He was Oscar-nominated for *The Snake Pit*
(Anatole Litvak, 1948) and scripted two further noirs, *The House on
Telegraph Hill* (Robert Wise, 1951) and *Night without Sleep* (Roy Ward
Baker, 1952).

DEVELOPMENT: Producer Lee S Marcus read Partos's story in 1936
'and was deeply impressed by its drama and possibilities for unique
filming: however, I was not then in a position to go ahead with its
production.' Marcus kept it on file and eventually convinced RKO to
give it the green light in 1940. 'We engaged Partos to adapt his own
story to the screen,' noted Marcus shortly before the film's release, 'and I
believe the script is even more powerful in story and treatment than the
original. It is an "out of the groove" story and told in an entirely new
manner.' In addition, novelist Nathanael West, author of *Miss*

Lonelyhearts (1933) and *Day of the Locust* (1939), was engaged to perform uncredited rewrites.

CASTING: Peter Lorre (1904–64, born László Löwenstein) was born in Rosenberg, Hungary, and educated in Vienna, before running away at the age of seventeen to join the theatre. His stage work eventually brought him to Berlin, where he started to appear in films and became famous via the role of Hans Beckert in *M* (Fritz Lang, 1931). Although he worked extensively in German cinema over the next two years, the rise of the Nazis forced him to leave for Britain, where he was immediately cast in Alfred Hitchcock's *The Man Who Knew Too Much* (1934). The director asked him back for *Secret Agent* (1936), but not before Lorre had won his first Hollywood role, as an archetypal insane surgeon in *Mad Love* (Karl Freund, 1935). Having signed a contract at Twentieth Century-Fox, he made *Think Fast, Mr Moto* (Norman Foster, 1937) – the first of eight light-hearted B-features in which Lorre played the eponymous Japanese detective. RKO had Lorre on a short contract when *Stranger on the Third Floor* entered production: realising that he was not booked to work on his final two days, the studio assigned him the murderer's role. As befitted his standing, he was billed first. (See **The Maltese Falcon** for more Lorre.)

The players who filled out the main roles of *Stranger on the Third Floor* were less distinguished. Margaret Tallichet (1914–91) was the wife of director William Wyler: despite promising roles in this film, *It Started with Eve* (Henry Koster, 1941) and *The Devil Pays Off* (John H Auer, 1941), she retired after the birth of her second child to concentrate on her family. John McGuire (1910–80) had some reasonable roles in B-features such as this and *The Invisible Ghost* (Joseph H Lewis, 1941), but was often among those not credited; he can be glimpsed in the noirs *Shadow of a Doubt* (Alfred Hitchcock, 1943), *White Heat* (Raoul Walsh, 1949) and *Where the Sidewalk Ends* (Otto Preminger, 1950). More successful in his later career was Elisha Cook Jr (1903–95). Cook acted on Broadway in the 1920s and made his film debut in *Her Unborn Child* (Albert Ray, 1930), reprising the role he had played in the stage version. He didn't move decisively into movies until 1936, initially playing juveniles due to his small stature (he was five feet six), but quickly revealed an intense quality which lent itself well to the portrayal of criminal lowlifes and neurotic cowards. Like Lorre, after *Stranger on the Third Floor* he took a role in *The Maltese Falcon*.

PRODUCTION: As a B-feature, *Stranger on the Third Floor* was assigned a budget of $171,200 and filming took place in July 1940. The cinematographer, Nicholas Musuraca (1892–1975), would go on to become arguably *the* definitive noir cameraman through his work on this, *The Fallen Sparrow* (Richard Wallace, 1943), *The Locket* (John Brahm, 1946), *Out of the Past*, *Clash by Night* (Fritz Lang, 1952) and *The Hitch-Hiker* (Ida Lupino, 1953). Ingster prepared for the shoot by commissioning sketches of its 243 scenes and then, from these sketches, ordered miniature models of all the sets to be built. On these miniature sets Ingster and Musuraca developed and tested the lighting effects he intended to use during shooting, as well as establishing his camera angles. As he worked with the models he modified them to suit his plans, then photographed them as a basis for the full-size sets. This meant that the sets could be tailored to Ingster's visuals rather than the other way around. 'The advance work saves time when shooting begins,' Ingster said, 'and, in addition, it leaves the director's mind free from most of the mechanical problems and permits him to devote his time and energy to the players.'

Most of the work went into designing the central dream sequence. For this, the studio floors were painted with a new type of paint developed by RKO, which had the effect of rendering the floor 'invisible' to the camera so that anybody walking across the floor would appear to float: this was the paint's first use on an RKO production. The effect was aided by the use of a fog machine. Ingster deployed small pieces of scenery on a large and otherwise empty stage, throwing reflections of sets on walls to use as backgrounds and closely lighting figures and props so that they would cast large shadows. The prop newspaper whose headline reads 'MURDER' was specially made; as the letters were nineteen inches high, and no metal type in this size was available, the type had to be made to order and carved from wood blocks.

The courtroom scenes during the dream were achieved by setting the various components of the set – the witness stand, the two attorneys' tables, the jury box, the judge's bench and the spectator benches – on movable platforms. These could be repositioned, as well as raised and lowered, to exaggerate distances depending upon the shot. A crew was on stand-by to move the components around for each new set-up while Ingster and Musuraca established lighting and angles. The most challenging set-up was the shot of the judge (Oscar O'Shea) as he is replaced in a crossfade by a figure combining elements of Justice and Death: a skeleton posed as Justice, holding the scales in one hand but a scythe in the other. The problem was that the figure was much larger than O'Shea. This took over an hour to complete, as the crew attempted to mathematically establish an angle from which both figures would match.

There was also some location work, including an entire day spent trailing Margaret Tallichet around Los Angeles, gathering footage to be used in the montage sequence in which she attempts to locate the Stranger after her fiancé has been arrested. Tallichet walked about ten miles during the filming of this. 'I was supposed to look more and more tired as the search progressed,' Tallichet said, 'and I didn't need any make-up for that effect by the time I got near the end.'

From a film noir viewpoint, it is interesting that contemporary publicity for *Stranger on the Third Floor* clearly demonstrates that RKO knew it had an unusual movie on its hands, and rather than play this fact down the studio used it as a selling point. The press book describes it as 'a genuinely "different" picture' and 'a crime drama novelty', featuring 'light-and-shadow effects and unique angle treatments said never before to have been seen on the screen'. A justification of the dream sequence was also included. 'LET'S BE FRANK! This picture has a dream in it, and in show business there is a common belief that dream pictures are box office poison! *But this isn't that kind of a picture!*' It was stressed that the dream sequence was not used for plot convenience: it did not gift information to a character, or paper over gaps in the story's logic, or act as an easy explanation for lurid events. 'The dream is used merely as an excuse to pointedly emphasize a character's mental disquiet, and as a device for some of the most novel and effective photography ever shown on the screen.'

RECEPTION: *Stranger on the Third Floor* was released on 16 August 1940. 'They haven't done right by Peter Lorre in this picture,' wrote *Variety* on 4 September 1940. 'He's so subordinated in the story that his character amounts to a bit.' More accurately, RKO hadn't done right by the audience, who would be entitled to expect to see more of the ostensible star. 'For the box-office it is extremely mild dual fare,' continued the review. 'It's a film too arty for average audiences, and too humdrum for others.' The visual interest which RKO had attempted to play up was greeted with apathy, assuming that the film 'doubtlessly cost more than necessary for fancy camera effects, lighting and trick dubbing, [yet] still remains a desultory "B" . . . Boris Ingster's direction is too studied and, when original, lacks the flare to hold attention.' As a B-feature it does not appear to have been reviewed anywhere in the press, and went largely unnoticed until noir critics 'rediscovered' it in the 1970s.

ASPECTS OF NOIR: As critic Andy Klein notes, 'When the first film noir – whatever you might consider that to be – was released, nobody yelled, "Hey, let's go on down to the Bijou! The first film noir is out!" ' So, what is film noir and why is *Stranger on the Third Floor* one while the movies which came before it are not?

The movement was first identified by French critics as something distinct from the usual crime pictures, hence its French name. This has often been attributed to the intensity with which these films arrived in France. In July and August of 1946, as the country caught up with the Hollywood product it had missed during the war, its moviegoers saw *The Maltese Falcon, Laura* (Otto Preminger, 1944), *Murder, My Sweet, Double Indemnity* and *The Woman in the Window* (Fritz Lang, 1944) for the first time. The noir term was coined by the critic Nino Frank, drawing upon the name of the publisher Gallimard's crime-novel imprint Série Noire (which had been founded in August 1945 and had published French editions of Raymond Chandler and Dashiell Hammett; the name was a play on words, also meaning a sequence of misfortunes). The pattern in American crime films was made more obvious to the French by these films being released in such close proximity. However, in his highly influential 1972 essay *Notes on Film Noir*, Paul Schrader also suggested that, unlike European critics, 'American critics have always been slow on the uptake when it comes to visual style. Like its protagonists, film noir is more interested in style than theme.'

In the same *Notes*, Schrader asserted, 'Film noir is not a genre. It is not defined, as are the western and gangster genres, by conventions of setting and conflict, but rather by the more subtle qualities of tone and mood.' Other critics have disagreed: Michael Walker claims, 'Film noir is not simply a certain type of crime movie, but also a generic field.' However, if noir is a genre it is an unusual one. The notion of genre is rooted in audience recognition and, while the hallmarks of other genres are generally agreed upon, those of noir are perpetually in dispute. Intense debate surrounds whether or not certain films 'count' as noirs (e.g. *Citizen Kane, Key Largo, Strangers on a Train*). Furthermore, noir is generally bracketed in the 1940s and 1950s: similar films made since that period tend to be labelled 'neo-noir' (a term coined by critic Todd Erikson) or 'noirish', and, as Andrew Spicer notes, film noir has acquired 'high cultural capital . . . connotations of sexy, chic, "artiness", visual sophistication and "adult" subject matter'. Generic terms do not generally carry such connotations.

The need to identify film noir as a genre is perhaps indicative of its status as a Hollywood product. Richard Maltby points out that, while Hollywood cinema 'is normally understood in terms of its genres, the history of the European film is conventionally written as a series of movements: German Expressionism, Italian Neo-Realism, the French New Wave, for example'. Maltby also notes that these 'movements' are constructed and discussed in a similar way to movements in more 'respectable' media (such as Pre-Raphaelitism or Modernism). Spicer's identification of film noir's 'artiness' is pertinent here: although it seems clear that noir's filmmakers were not consciously creating a new type of film (unlike, say, Modernist writers, who had very self-conscious objectives), they did note, copy and develop innovations in each other's work. It seems more useful to regard film noir as a Hollywood movement, one which inspired similar work in other countries and has since been self-consciously referred back to by other filmmakers who recognise its value. But, as Walker recognises, 'The issue of whether the noir cycle constitutes a genre is not very interesting.'

The factors which contributed to the development of film noir are numerous. The cinema of Germany's post-war Weimar Republic has been seen as a key influence, principally because so many noir directors (Wilder, Ulmer, Siodmak, Lang, Preminger, Maté) worked in Germany in the 1920s and 1930s. Expressionism in particular was significant: a movement, which encompassed all the arts, concerned with communicating emotional states rather than accurately depicting the physical world. In an Expressionist artwork, certain details of the subject might be exaggerated or modified to demonstrate how the artist prioritises those details over others, or to place associations with other things in the mind of the audience. (The dream sequence in *Stranger on the Third Floor* uses Expressionist ideas, such as the giant newspaper headlines: Mike is a reporter, so newspapers are a large part of his life.) In film, which required the presence of a physical world in which shooting could take place, this stylisation was achieved principally through the use of high-contrast photography (which could alter the emphasis of the image through light patterns) and unusual camera angles (which distorted the relationship between objects in the frame). The most famous Expressionist film is *The Cabinet of Dr Cagliari* (Robert Wiene, 1919). Another German influence was the 'street film', which commenced with *The Street* (Karl Grune, 1923) and typically pitched its protagonist into a threatening urban environment. Both movements are reflected in Fritz Lang's *M* (1931) and *The Last Will of Dr Mabuse* (1932). That so many Weimar luminaries moved to Hollywood is not solely attributable to the rise of Adolf Hitler – Hollywood had always sought to poach talent from other countries as a means of weakening other film industries while strengthening itself – but his appointment as Chancellor in 1933, and Joseph Goebbels's desire to use the film industry for propaganda ends, hastened the departure of many personnel.

A number of those filmmakers came to Hollywood via the French film industry, where another influential movement was developing: Poetic Realism. The term emerged in 1933 and referred to works focused around ordinary (lower-middle and working class) people and ordinary settings, locating intrigue, strangeness and poetry in these places. Its worldview was generally pessimistic; crime and romance were central themes and the femme fatale was a common figure. Although it was less stylised than Expressionist and 'street' cinema, Poetic Realism strove to create a distinctive atmosphere from shadow and neon, and the employment of German filmmakers made the influence direct. These were sometimes described by contemporary reviewers as film noir, and prime examples are Marcel Carné's – *Port of Shadows* (1938) and *Daybreak* (1939). Many films drew upon the work of French crime writers, principally Georges Simenon who, like Ernest Hemingway, was both hugely popular and critically respected. American 'hardboiled' fiction also made its way to France: James M Cain's *The Postman Always Rings Twice* was filmed by Pierre Chenal in 1939 as *The Final Twist*, years before its Hollywood adaptation.

The hardboiled tradition is the most immediately recognised literary influence on film noir, because so many hardboiled novels were adapted during the movement. Michael Walker identifies three types of American crime fiction which established the main noir narratives: the hardboiled detective story from Dashiell Hammett and Raymond Chandler (see **The Maltese Falcon**), which concerns a 'seeker-hero' who delves into the noir world to resolve a problem; Cain's stories of seduction and then betrayal by a femme fatale, which generally involve a 'victim-hero' (in *Mildred Pierce*, Cain also provided a version with the genders reversed); and Cornell Woolrich's paranoid noir, in which the central character is plunged into a dangerous and frequently illogical world. In some sense the hero will be a victim, perhaps of bad luck, of a bad decision which causes events to spiral out of control, or of the actions of another person: they may also be a seeker, searching for whoever has caused their misery, as in *D.O.A.* (Rudolph Maté, 1950).

Another influential strand of literature, often overlooked in favour of the hardboiled tradition, is the Gothic romance. Although Gothic is primarily connected with horror, it is a complex aesthetic and the term's definition is even more contested and debated than 'film noir'. The Gothic romantic tradition dates back to Horace Walpole's novel *The Castle of Otranto* (1764) and characteristically revolves around a victim-heroine who feels threatened by dark secrets or enclosed in a decaying environment: the narrative may be disordered, with the result that the reader shares her disorientation in a fatalistic nightmare (which bears similarities with Woolrich's fiction; see also **The Lady from Shanghai**). The entire detective-fiction tradition has its roots in a Gothic novel, Wilkie Collins's *The Woman in White* (1860). The definition of Gothic given by Chris Baldick is a useful one: the Gothic narrative combines 'a fearful sense of inheritance in time with a claustrophobic sense of enclosure in space, these two dimensions reinforcing one another to produce an impression of sickening descent into disintegration'. This description fits *The Killers* and *Out of the Past*, the heroes of which are afraid of the past and find themselves with nowhere to run (note the Swede's declaration 'I feel kinda sick' when he realises his number is up). Noir's urban setting is often depicted as sinking into decay (appropriately, the ultimate example is *Touch of Evil*). Some critics have made the case for *Rebecca* (Alfred Hitchcock, 1940), adapted from Daphne du Maurier's Gothic romance novel, to be considered one of the earliest noirs.

The films adapted from and inspired by these novels drew upon existing types of Hollywood film, chiefly the gangster movie (again, see **The Maltese Falcon**), but also prison movies such as *The Criminal Code* (Howard Hawks, 1930) and 'social-problem' films like *I Am a Fugitive from a Chain Gang* (Mervyn Le Roy, 1932). The development of all these genres was tempered by the introduction of the Production Code in 1934 (see **The Big Sleep**), although there were still some social-problem films which have a bearing on noir, such as Lang's Hollywood debut, *Fury* (1937). Visually, horror movies had a bigger influence on film noir; Universal dominated the genre in the 1930s, hiring much German talent (such as Ulmer) via its German-born studio head Carl Laemmle. Expressionism was an effective way of translating Gothic horror to the screen, and Universal horrors were among the first Hollywood films to bear Expressionist influences (Spicer identifies Robert Florey's *Murders in the Rue Morgue* and Karl Freund's *The Mummy*, both released in 1932, as the most notable examples). RKO tried to challenge Universal's supremacy in the early 1940s, producing work that was equally influential on noir (see **Murder, My Sweet**).

The influence of visual arts is often understated, but it is impossible to look at Gilberte Brassai's nighttime, high-contrast photographs of 1930s Paris without thinking of film noir. There was also America's 'Ashcan' school of painting and subsequently the Realists exemplified by Edward Hopper, who produced many bleak urban scenes during the 1920s, 30s and 40s, and was fascinated by light and shadow (his most famous painting, 1942's *Nighthawks*, has a definite noir ambience). This had a direct influence on *Force of Evil*. Later in the cycle, the photojournalism of Arthur H Fellig ('Weegee') became significant.

Numerous social factors had a diffuse effect. For example, many psychoanalysts settled in California after fleeing Europe, and the influence of Freud can be seen in the emphasis on sexually motivated actions and the use of sexual symbolism. The aggressive efforts of Joseph McCarthy and the House Un-American Activities Committee (HUAC) to smoke Communists out of Hollywood may have contributed to the development of noir's hounded, suspicious heroes, and many personnel on these films were victims of HUAC. Existential themes have been identified, and later in the cycle nuclear paranoia emerges (*The Lady from Shanghai*, *Kiss Me Deadly*). The most frequently identified social factor is W.W.II, although it is too simplistic to characterise film noir purely as a post-war hangover – not least because the cycle began before America entered the war and was in full swing by the time the war ended. It undoubtedly had an effect, but it was a complex and multifaceted one – for example, an upper limit of $5,000 for new materials for set construction was set by the War Production Board in 1942, and some filmmakers disguised their shabbier sets with underlighting. This popularised the high-contrast style which is a noir hallmark.

Noir should not be regarded purely as having thrived under limitations; in other aspects, the movement was spurred on by the *removal* of limitations. Whereas scenes set at night had previously been shot in daylight and underexposed ('day for night'), the development of faster film stock meant that good results could be achieved at night ('night for night'). Innovations in lenses made lighting more flexible – there had always been a risk that a single light source would swamp the camera and throw the image out of focus, so scenes tended to be flat-lit. This was no longer a problem with the new lenses, and interior scenes set at night could be more realistically and powerfully achieved as a result. Cameras were also becoming lighter, allowing for greater movement (longer takes became common), a wider variety of angles (including low angles and the 'Dutch tilt', in which the camera deviates from the vertical) and shooting in unusual and cramped spaces (adding to the sense of claustrophobia). The development of the 'crab dolly', a wheeled camera platform which could move smoothly sideways as well as forwards and backwards, further assisted fluid camera movement.

Some have disputed *Stranger on the Third Floor*'s status as the first noir: critic Arthur Lyons suggests that three obscure B-movies from 1939 – Charles Vidor's *Blind Alley* and John Brahm's *Let Us Live!* and *Rio* – all qualify and precede *Stranger*. However, *Stranger* is a clearer example because it ticks so many of the noir boxes. It has high-contrast lighting, stylising the image in the frame by encouraging the viewer to look at it as two-dimensional, what critics call the 'graphic' qualities of the image. The construction of cinema is a balance between this and the attempt to map a three-dimensional space sufficiently that the viewer feels comfortable with it, appreciating its 'architectural' qualities. The arrangement of objects in the frame creates 'expressive' space, in which the relationship between those objects creates its own meaning in addition to that signified by action and dialogue. Film noir tends to favour 'expressive' space: as Mike wonders whether Meng is dead, his apartment ceases to become a comprehensible 'real' space. The lighting robs Mike of authority within the frame, emphasising that he is no longer in control of the narrative as he was when condemning Briggs.

The construction of the narrative is not chronological and favours disorientation (which is just as well, because the plot relies on some pretty big coincidences). Crucial information about Mike's past actions towards Meng is held back until the flashbacks, after which we see him in a different light, and the narrative is further disrupted by the dream sequence. Mike becomes the victim-hero in a paranoid nightmare, in which he finds himself wrongly accused in the same way that he wrongly accused Briggs; Jane is then placed in the role of seeker-heroine (giving her a level of control over the narrative that could be viewed as gender-subversive). Noir's criminals are often ambiguous, and the Stranger is surprisingly sympathetic: the escaped inmate of an asylum, he is depicted as mistreated and afraid, killing only those who threaten to send him back. He buys fresh meat for a stray dog and is nice to Jane until he realises her intentions (Lorre's wounded performance aids this – without him, the meaning might have been quite different). Notably, he is not recaptured and dies defiant: 'I'm not going back.' A number of criminals in noir, particularly femmes fatales, retain a power in death which they would lose if caught. This has the effect of tempering the otherwise upbeat ending, in which even Joe cheerily greets the man who helped sentence him to death. Order has been restored, but it is the darkness at the film's centre which lingers.

AVAILABILITY: At the time of writing *Stranger on the Third Floor* is not commercially available anywhere in the world and has not been for quite some time, a 1980s VHS release having been deleted long ago.

The Maltese Falcon (1941)

Black and White – 101 mins

Warner Bros. Pictures, Inc. Presents
The Maltese Falcon
A Warner Bros.–First National Picture
Executive Producer: Hal B Wallis
Associate Producer: Henry Blanke
Screenplay by John Huston
Based upon the Novel by Dashiell Hammett
Director of Photography: Arthur Edeson, ASC
Dialogue Director: Robert Foulk

Film Editor: Thomas Richards
Art Director: Robert Haas
Sound by Oliver S Garretson
Gowns by Orry-Kelly
Make-up Artist: Perc Westmore
Music by Adolph Deutsch
Musical Director: Leo F Forbstein
Directed by John Huston

CAST: Humphrey Bogart (*Samuel Spade*), Mary Astor (*Brigid O'Shaughnessy*), Gladys George (*Iva Archer*), Peter Lorre (*Joel Cairo*) and Barton MacLane (*Lt. Of Detectives Dundy*), Lee Patrick (*Effie Perine*), Sydney Greenstreet (*Kasper Gutman*), Ward Bond (*Detective Tom Polhaus*), Jerome Cowan (*Miles Archer*), Elisha Cook Jr (*Wilmer Cook*), James Burke (*Luke*), Murray Alper (*Frank Richman*), John Hamilton (*Bryan*)

SUMMARY: Brigid O'Shaughnessy hires the detective agency Spade and Archer to shadow a man named Floyd Thursby, who is involved with her sister. Miles Archer volunteers for the duty ahead of his partner, Sam Spade. Archer and Thursby turn up dead the next day and the police suspect Spade. Brigid admits to Spade that her story was untrue: she was involved with Thursby and became afraid of him. She asks Spade to protect her. Spade is visited by Joel Cairo, who believes Spade may be in possession of a valuable statuette in the form of a black bird. When Cairo discovers that Spade doesn't have it, he hires Spade to find it for him. Brigid claims that Thursby hid it and it will come into her possession soon. Spade then meets Kasper Gutman, who is also in pursuit of the bird and explains that under its coating of black enamel it is the Maltese Falcon, a priceless jewelled tribute to Spain from the Knights of Rhodes dating back to the 16th century. Gutman drugs Spade's drink and goes in search of the Falcon. Later, Spade awakens and returns to his office, where a man hands him a parcel and dies. This is Captain Jacobi of the *La Paloma*, the ship on which the Falcon came in. Brigid had instructed him to bring it to Spade, but he was shot by Gutman's henchman on the way. Spade makes a deal with Gutman and Cairo to get the police off his back and hands over the Falcon, but it turns out to be a fake. Gutman and Cairo escape, but Spade tips off the police about them and gets Brigid to admit that she killed Archer to frame Thursby, so that he would be arrested and she could collect the Falcon herself. When Gutman's henchman killed Thursby, Brigid sought Spade's help, hoping that he would become infatuated with her and take the fall for her crimes. Spade hands her over to the cops.

DIRECTOR: John Huston (1906–87) won the California amateur lightweight boxing championship at the age of eighteen before his journalist mother Rhea got him a reporting job on the *New York Graphic* newspaper. He submitted a number of stories with horrendous factual errors and was fired. In 1931 his actor father Walter got him a job as a screenwriter in Hollywood. Two years later he left the industry and drifted, but returned in 1937 with a new sense of purpose and scripted films for Warner Bros. including *Sergeant York* (Howard Hawks, 1941) and *Jezebel* (William Wyler, 1938). On the latter he gained his first directing experience, overseeing a location shoot. Eventually Warners agreed to let him direct one of his own scripts and the result was *The Maltese Falcon*, in which he cast Walter in the uncredited role of Captain Jacobi. During the war Huston joined the army and made documentaries, one of which (1943's *Report from the Aleutians*) won an Oscar. *The Treasure of the Sierra Madre* (1948) netted further Academy Awards for Huston as writer and director, plus Best Supporting Actor for Walter. Huston made two other crime thrillers, *Key Largo* (1948) and *The Asphalt Jungle* (1950), and oversaw Bogart's Oscar-winning performance in *The African Queen* (1951). Angered by the activities of HUAC, Huston moved to Ireland in 1952. Thereafter his output varied, taking in Marilyn Monroe and Clark Gable's final film *The Misfits* (1961), the James Bond spoof *Casino Royale* (1967) – undertaken in return for paying off a large gambling debt – and *Prizzi's Honour* (1985), for which his actor daughter Anjelica won an Oscar. He made an acting appearance in *Chinatown* (Roman Polanski, 1974). The last film he directed was *The Dead* (1987).

WRITER: Huston's script was based on the work of Dashiell Hammett (1894–1961, born Samuel Dashiell Hammett). Born in Maryland, Hammett grew up in Philadelphia and Baltimore, and after miscellaneous jobs became an operative for Pinkerton's Detective Agency. He spent time away from the profession when service in W.W.I took its toll on his health, but eventually returned to detective work and in the 1920s began writing. Drawing upon his own experiences and developing a tough, economical, detached prose style, he quickly found work at *Black Mask*, the most significant of the pulp crime-fiction magazines. Editor Joseph T Shaw held up Hammett as an example to the magazine's other writers, and encouraged him to move from short fiction to novels. Some of Hammett's earlier longer magazine stories were reissued in hardback, including *The Maltese Falcon* in 1930. Hammett's other novels include *Red Harvest* (1929), *The Dain Curse* (1929), featuring his oft-used anonymous detective 'The Continental Op', *The Glass Key* (1931) and *The Thin Man* (1932). *The Thin Man* turned out to be his final novel, as he subsequently moved to Hollywood to be a screenwriter, rarely working from his own ideas. A film of *The Thin Man* (WS Van Dyke, 1934) spawned five sequels starring its husband-and-wife detective duo, Nick and Nora Charles (Nora was based upon the playwright Lillian Hellman, with whom Hammett had a lengthy relationship). In 1951 he received a jail sentence for 'un-American activities'.

DEVELOPMENT: The film rights to *The Maltese Falcon* were pursued almost immediately upon its serialised appearance in *Black Mask* in 1929. Paramount expressed an interest but abandoned its proposed adaptation following casting difficulties. Subsequently, Warner Bros. picked up the property for $8,500 and in 1931 produced its first film version, a reasonable success directed by Roy del Ruth and starring Ricardo Cortez and Bebe Daniels (in the wake of the 1941 success it acquired the alternative title *Dangerous Female*). Five years later the novel was produced again under the title *Satan Met a Lady*, this time directed by William Dieterle and pitched as a comedy vehicle for Bette Davis. (Warren William played Spade.) A third version was mooted in 1939 and would have been called *The Clock Struck Three*, but ran into scripting problems.

In 1941 Huston was able to suggest material for his directorial debut. He was a fan of Hammett's and, aware that Warners still held the rights, asked to make a new version of *The Maltese Falcon*. Howard Hawks (see **The Big Sleep**) later claimed that he had suggested *The Maltese Falcon* to Huston, stressing his belief that a better film could be made by faithfully adapting the material (Hawks had been thinking about doing a new version of the book himself). Huston's script is indeed highly faithful; more or less every scene is lifted from Hammett's novel, with its meaning and plot function intact, and much of the dialogue survives. Huston mainly endeavoured to cut down the novel and reduce the cast; scenes are often shortened and characters such as Rhea, Gutman's daughter, have been excised. The police's suspicion that Spade shot Archer is given more emphasis in the novel, and Spade is seen visiting the scene of the crime. There is also more of a role for Effie.

There is a section in the middle of the novel which Huston reduced dramatically. In the novel, after Spade's first meeting with Gutman, Spade meets with his lawyer, then discovers that Brigid is missing. He attempts to trace her, then meets Gutman again. After being drugged, he wakes up outside his own office. He gets Luke to help him ransack Cairo's room and discovers which ship the Falcon came in on, then evades questioning by Polhaus and the District Attorney. When Spade returns to his office, Captain Jacobi arrives. Because the last of these events was not initiated by Spade, Huston was able to cut much of what led up to it. The scene with the DA was shortened and used to break up the two Gutman scenes, and leaving Spade in Gutman's apartment after the drugging gave him a way of discovering the shipping information. A phone call to Effie allowed him to discover that Brigid was missing, and then Jacobi's arrival allowed Huston to skip directly to the end sequence at Spade's apartment. From there the novel and film are much the same, although, when Gutman accuses Brigid of having stolen one of the bills from the envelope, in the novel Spade takes her into the bathroom and demands that she strip so that he can search her clothes (it is fairly clear that they have already had sex). Cairo is explicitly a homosexual, and infatuated with Wilmer. A final scene, based on the final scene of the novel, was scripted but never shot (see **PRODUCTION**).

CASTING: Humphrey Bogart (1899–1957) had worked on Broadway in the 1920s and become a contract player at Twentieth Century-Fox, making his feature debut in *A Devil with Women* (Irving Cummings, 1930). However, Fox struggled to find suitable roles for him and he had to make do with bit parts in B-movies. Brief spells at Columbia and Warners were similarly unsuccessful and he returned to Broadway convinced that a film career was beyond him. However, after he reprised his role in Robert Sherwood's play *The Petrified Forest* (1935) for its film version (Archie Mayo, 1936), Warner Bros. put him under contract and used him effectively in crime pictures, alongside Bette Davis in *Marked Woman* (Lloyd Bacon, 1937) and *Kid Galahad* (Michael Curtiz, 1937), and supporting James Cagney in *Angels with Dirty Faces* (Michael Curtiz, 1938) and *The Roaring Twenties* (Raoul Walsh, 1939). A role in the Huston-scripted *High Sierra* (Raoul Walsh, 1941) opposite Ida Lupino (later to become the only female director of a classical-period noir, *The Hitch-Hiker* (1953)) set his career on track, and in spite of a subsequent dispute with Warners he was cast in the lead of *The Maltese Falcon*.

The events which led to this demonstrate how studios would use stars, directors and even entire projects as bargaining tools. George Raft, who had been billed above Bogart in *Invisible Stripes* (Lloyd Bacon, 1939) and *They Drive by Night* (Raoul Walsh, 1940), was assigned the role by Warners on 19 May 1941, but did not want to work with a first-time director on what he considered a minor film. Huston gave Warners its due for backing him ('I must take my hat off to them – [they] stuck by their guns and stuck by me') but an examination of Warners' motives reveals that they did not want Raft in the movie either. Fox was interested in 'borrowing' Raft, while Warners wanted to cast Fox's Henry Fonda in their college comedy *The Male Animal* (Elliott Nugent,

1942). An exchange could be agreed, but the notoriously difficult Raft was contractually able to object to loan deals. Hence, Warners placed Raft in *The Maltese Falcon* and, when he voiced his objection as expected, they offered him the alternative of doing a movie for Fox. Raft was given until five o'clock on 3 June to make his decision. Even before Raft notified the studio of his intent, Bogart was already on set.

Mary Astor (1906–87, born Lucile Vasconcellos Langhanke), born in Illinois to German parents, was a highly experienced actress whose first screen appearances had been in her early teens. After a number of bit parts, her big break came with *Beau Brummel* (Harry Beaumont, 1924) and she possessed a strong enough voice to remain a star following the switch to talkies. She appeared in *Don Juan* (Alan Crosland, 1926), *Red Dust* (Victor Fleming, 1932) and *The Prisoner of Zenda* (John Cromwell, 1937), and won the Best Supporting Actress Oscar for *The Great Lie* (Edmund Goulding, 1941). After *The Maltese Falcon* (during which she had an affair with Huston, which was far from unusual for either of them) her career started to wind down, although she appeared in several other films including *The Palm Beach Story* (Preston Sturges, 1942). She later wrote five novels and two bestselling memoirs.

After *Stranger on the Third Floor*, Peter Lorre had worked at Columbia and MGM before landing the role of Joel Cairo ('Don't try to get a nancy quality into him, because if you do we will have trouble with the picture,' Wallis told Huston). This commenced a fruitful period which saw him opposite Bogart again on *All Through the Night* (Vincent Sherman, 1942) and *Casablanca* (Michael Curtiz, 1942), and, when Lorre's high-rolling lifestyle and morphine abuse outstripped his earnings, Bogart often 'lent' him money without expecting to be repaid. In the late 1940s Lorre was asked by HUAC to name anybody suspicious he had met while in America, and he responded with a list of every single person he knew. In post-war Germany he wrote and directed *The Lost One* (1951). In the 1950s he made a successful career in television; notably he played the first ever James Bond villain in the TV adaptation of *Casino Royale* (1954), as part of the anthology series *Climax!* He died from a stroke in 1964.

The Maltese Falcon was the first film to pair Lorre with Sydney Greenstreet (1879–1954): they went on to appear in eight other films together, most notably *Casablanca* but also *Three Strangers* (Jean Negulesco, 1944), *Passage to Marseille* (Michael Curtiz, 1944) and *The Verdict* (Don Siegel, 1946). Indeed, *The Maltese Falcon* was Greenstreet's first film. The British actor had been working on the stage for more than forty years, but Gutman was the first film role to interest him. He also made a highly memorable trailer for the movie. His other films include *Devotion* (Curtis Berhardt, 1946) and *The Woman in White* (Peter Godfrey, 1948). Elisha Cook Jr had been in a handful of movies since *Stranger on the Third Floor*; more details on him can be found under **The Big Sleep**, although it is worth noting here that Cook was later a semi-regular in *Magnum, P.I.* and in the 1986 episode 'A.A.P.I.' he played a criminal called Wilmer in a black-and-white dream sequence, in which Magnum imagines himself as a Spade-like detective in 1941 San Francisco.

PRODUCTION: The budget of *The Maltese Falcon* was set at $381,000, towards the lower end of A-picture budgets, and Huston was allotted a 36-day shoot. Given the notoriously tight purse strings of studio head Jack L Warner, it was imperative that the untried Huston did not exceed either of those numbers. Huston's plans for the film were not unambitious and so to ensure confidence he produced his own storyboards, preparing hundreds of sketches to which he referred his actors and technicians prior to and during production. 'This method of "designing" motion pictures in advance . . . is not a new one in Hollywood,' noted the publicity materials for the film. 'But this is the first time that the whole operation of preparing the screenplay, designing it, and directing it, has been left to one man.' Huston's explanation of his intent reveals a continued desire to faithfully adapt the source material. 'I attempted to transpose Dashiell Hammett's highly individual prose style into camera terms: i.e. sharp photography; geographically correct camera movements; striking if not shocking set-ups.' Although executive producer Hal B Wallis supported Huston's notion of remaining faithful to the novel (he had recommended this himself during development of *Satan Met a Lady* and been ignored), he had a habit of intervening with the films he oversaw; producer Henry Blanke came into his own here, convincing Wallis to minimise his interference.

Huston shot most of the film in script sequence, so production commenced with the very first scene in Spade's office, on Monday, 9 June 1941. He kept production ahead of schedule for the duration of the shoot, often by letting takes run on for the duration of the scene and thereby getting extra material in the can. 'There was the understanding that we were attempting something purely cinematic, never tried before,' said script supervisor Meta Wilde, 'and everyone – stars, camera operators, and cablemen – worked industriously to bring it off.' Outsiders were kept away from the set, encouraging the company to work more closely and consistently. The tortuous plot began to cause disagreements on set between the actors, who were not always sure of their characters' motivations or whether they were lying at any given moment. Astor noted that Huston would intervene at these points to 'shut us up and quietly explain it'. Although Hammett's novel had not used first-person narration, it did stick close to Spade, and Huston was determined to retain this. 'The audience knows no more or less than [Spade] does,' he commented. However, he did not seek to plunge the audience into Spade's predicament; the viewer was to be placed in the position of a 'silent and disinterested spectator'.

Wallis viewed the initial dailies, identified that Bogart had modified his acting style for *The Maltese Falcon* and decided that he didn't like it. This was not the quick-fire Bogart who had so suited the house style of Warners' crime pictures: instead, 'Bogart . . . has adopted a leisurely suave form of delivery. I don't think we can stand this all through the picture, as it has a tendency to drag down the scene.' Huston reshot the opening scenes accordingly. However, Bogart was continuing to impress Huston. 'He was forever surprising me with how good he was,' the director recalled. 'Practically no direction was required – he was just *excellent*. Two little things that I suggested – I can't recall them now – he picked up and instantly used.'

Production was ahead of schedule going into July, and Huston asked for an extra rehearsal day for the 25-minute, dialogue-heavy final sequence, which Warners reluctantly granted (the studio would have preferred the film to wrap sooner and free up resources). The sequence started shooting on Thursday, 3 July, paused the next day for the Independence Day holiday, then continued for the following week. The Falcon itself was actually a plaster cast rather than lead; as Greenstreet would be required to damage it, seven of the prop were made. The final confrontation between Spade and Brigid took up the final three days and Huston didn't shoot a satisfactory version until after midnight on Saturday, 12 July. The following Monday covered the arrival of the police.

Following this, Huston went back and covered everything that had not been accounted for in his sequential shoot, concluding with further Spade and Gutman material on Friday, 18 July; the film wrapped at two o'clock in the morning, with two days and $54,000 to spare. Huston had saved a little extra time by dropping his scripted final scene, which would have seen the action return to Spade's office. In the script Effie regards Spade coldly for his treatment of Brigid, then Ida arrives at the office and Spade asks Effie to send her in. Although losing this scene meant that Ida vanished from the narrative two-thirds of the way through, Huston and Blanke thought the final confrontation as filmed a better ending, following Bogart's addition of two extra lines – Polhaus's query about the Falcon and Spade's description of it as 'The stuff that dreams are made of'. The contribution of a Shakespeare quote saw the real Bogart – a literate man who quoted Plato and subscribed to the *Harvard Law Review* – creeping in around his screen persona.

Jack Warner subsequently approved the decision to drop the scripted ending, although after seeing the final cut he instructed that the first scene be reshot in September, with some script changes to clarify Brigid's reasons for employing Spade and Archer. ('Why be so clever,' asked Warner in a memo, 'as we have a hell of a good picture.') Post-production saw Huston work with composer Adolph Deutsch to produce a minimal score that would not disturb the rhythms of the dialogue. This version was previewed under the dreadful title *The Gent from Frisco*, an alteration made by Wallis for unknown reasons (possibly to differentiate it from the 1931 version). The feedback from the preview was highly positive and Warner had the title changed back, perhaps anticipating that this version of Hammett's novel would easily eclipse its predecessors.

RECEPTION: *The Maltese Falcon* was released on 4 October 1941. On that date the *Motion Picture Herald* noted that it had attended a preview 'in the Warner projection room in New York where an audience comprised of trade press reporters and exhibitors generally conceded that it was an excellent production'. Praise was slightly qualified by genre, however. 'In its class, in which several similar productions have proved box office attractions, it is an exceedingly good picture.' A few days before, on 1 October, *Variety* had been equally enthusiastic, calling it, 'One of the best examples of atmospheric and suspenseful melodramatic story telling in cinematic form . . . a prize package of entertainment for widest audience appeal. Due for hefty grosses in all runs.' The reinvention of its star was a key point of interest. 'Of major importance is the stand-out performance of Humphrey Bogart, an attention-arresting portrayal that will add immeasurable voltage to his marquee values.' The review concluded with a piece of advice, 'To secure utmost in audience reaction, exhibs can take advantage of the surprise finish by publicizing starting times of the picture, and advising patrons to get maximum entertainment by seeing it from the start.'

'The Warners have been strangely bashful about their new mystery film, *The Maltese Falcon*, and about the young man, John Huston, whose first directorial job it is,' noted Bosley Crowther in the *New York Times* on 4 October 1941. Crowther wondered whether this was due to the novel having been filmed before: 'Maybe – which is somehow more likely – they wanted to give everyone a nice surprise', as he declared the film 'the best mystery thriller of the year'. There was certainly an impression that this was, if not something wholly new, a fresh take on an old tradition. 'Hollywood has neglected the sophisticated crime film of late, and England, for reasons which are obvious, hasn't been sending her quota in recent months . . . we had almost forgotten how devilishly delightful such films can be.' Huston was thought to show 'promise of becoming one of the smartest directors in the field', having 'worked out his own style, which is brisk and supremely hardboiled'. Although Crowther was unacquainted with the 1931 version, 'We'll wager it wasn't half as tough nor half as flavored with idioms as is this present version, in which Humphrey Bogart hits his peak.'

The reaction from the British press was no less enthusiastic. 'The Maltese Falcon has nearly everything a mystery film should have,' noted William Whitebait in the New Statesman on 20 June 1942, including 'admirable photography of the sort in which black and white gives full value to every detail, every flick of panic. Who can imagine a detective story in Technicolor?' The film was associated with the previous decade's gangster tales, Whitebait describing it as 'rich in sardonic revelation and belong[ing] to the vintage period of American gangsterdom'. In the Sunday Times of 21 June, Dilys Powell called it 'the most interesting and imaginative detective film to come out of America, or anywhere else for that matter, since the first Thin Man', relating this back to the author of the source material. 'Yes, the film owes much to the performance of Bogart; and not a little to Mary Astor's frightened beauty . . . But beyond this, it is from the start ingeniously conceived and tellingly translated to the screen.'

ASPECTS OF NOIR: Often cited as the first film noir until the reappraisal of Stranger on the Third Floor, The Maltese Falcon only partly conforms to most definitions. Critic John Blaser notes that the film 'prefers balanced, low-contrast lighting to the high-contrast lighting and deep shadows of film noir', which is true – although he goes on to state, 'Camera angles tend to be at eye level, with the exception of the subjective camera used when Spade is drugged.' Actually Huston's camera often moves below eye level, most notably when framing Gutman from a low viewpoint to emphasise his bulk. This was possible because the sets had been constructed with complete ceilings, rather than being open-topped and lit from above; this in turn meant that lighting came from 'natural' sources, such as lamps and windows. However, as Blaser says, visually the film largely conforms to classical Hollywood style – as one would expect from a novice director under the watchful eye of Hal Wallis. The real noir aspects of The Maltese Falcon are located in Huston's writing and Bogart's performance, as between them these two brought the hardboiled detective to the screen. It is a mistake to think of the private eye as the noir standard, but The Maltese Falcon did create an important archetype – not necessarily a professional detective, but what studies of noir have dubbed the 'seeker-hero'.

The detectives written by Hammett were distinctly different from the existing detective tradition, initiated by Edgar Allan Poe and then taken up by many British writers. The likes of Sherlock Holmes and Hercule Poirot treat their endeavours as a kind of intellectual sport, and the 'whodunnit' format invites the reader to join this pursuit. The story must be carefully ordered, revealing all the pertinent facts without indicating any of the suspects too strongly. Meanwhile, the detective usually endeavours to remain detached and objective; Moriarty is Holmes's nemesis largely because his intellect is comparable to Holmes's, rather than because the two are morally opposed. ('If I could beat that man,' comments Holmes in 'The Final Problem', 'if I could free society of him, I should feel that my career had reached its summit, and I should be prepared to turn to some more placid line in life.') Maintaining objectivity often involves the detective adopting the status of the 'talented amateur', motivated not by money, but by the challenge and the satisfaction of having removed a rogue element from society. Accordingly, the detective may be somebody who does not need to work for a living: a gentleman.

Hammett's detective figure is not generally considered respectable, as he essentially profits from the misfortune of others and this mercenary aspect to his character leads the rest of society to view him as corruptible. John Cawelti notes that the detective 'finds that the process of solving the crime involves him in the violence, deceit and corruption that lies beneath the surface of the respectable world'; this may render him distasteful to those who manage to avoid that dark underbelly, while those who inhabit it will tend to regard the detective as an unwelcome intrusion – unless he can be corrupted, of course. At some point in this type of story the villain will usually try to make the hero complicit, and the author will draw both characters in such a way that a collaboration seems possible. However, as Michael Walker states, 'As [the detective] unravels the often labyrinthine plot and uncovers the layers of deception, it is as much his incorruptibility as his intelligence which enables him, finally, to emerge safely.'

In *The Maltese Falcon* Spade locates this honourable streak when Archer is murdered, despite his antipathy towards Archer and the affair he was having with Ida. 'When a man's partner is killed he's supposed to do something about it. It doesn't make any difference what you thought of him.' (Considering the climate in which the film was made and released, Spade's dilemma resonates with America's deliberation over joining the war.) He also indicates that his apparently flexible morality is an act. 'Don't be too sure I'm as crooked as I'm supposed to be. That kind of reputation might be good business – bringing in high-priced jobs and making it easier to deal with the enemy.' The desire for money is explicitly not equated with immoral practices – the *appearance* of corruptibility makes money for Spade while allowing him to maintain a sense of personal integrity. The introverted nature of the noir hero can be seen here too, as he does not care what others think of him and sees people as unknowable, untrustworthy. In fact, Spade does not appear to form emotional attachments of any kind. Unlike Chandler's 'man who is not himself mean', Spade cares less about justice and more about order; according to Blaser, Spade's personal code 'is his first and only line of defence against a hostile world – an artificial structure designed to provide some meaning and order to an otherwise chaotic existence'. Because most people would rather live in a world of order than a world of chaos, Spade becomes a hero.

Previous adaptations of *The Maltese Falcon* failed to reflect this, retaining the structure but changing the hero's nature. Their detective figure was closer to the gentleman adventurer and their tone more light-hearted, but Huston adapted the novel with Spade and his worldview intact. Casting Bogart in the lead enhanced this, and built upon the actor's recent work in *High Sierra* (Raoul Walsh, 1941). AM Sperber and Eric Lax's biography of Bogart identifies that, prior to *High Sierra*, Bogart suffered from a particular typecasting problem; the Production Code (see **The Big Sleep**) had called for an end to what it saw as the glorification of criminals in Warners' popular crime pictures, and so the studio slightly modified its formula. The criminal anti-hero (played by the likes of James Cagney and Edward G Robinson) became more decent, so he could be redeemed by the end – usually by way of a noble death – while the real punishment was meted out on a supporting character who was crooked through and through. 'By the late thirties, the notion had become a concept and the concept had a name: the "Bogart role".' His laconic, inscrutable style created characters who seemed to be lacking in humanity, in contrast to the heated, emotionally engaging performances of Cagney and Robinson. Warners valued Bogart in such roles and could not see him playing A-picture heroes.

Arguably the roles did not exist for him to play. It was Huston who created a heroic Bogart role with his script for *High Sierra*, and as with *The Maltese Falcon* he achieved this by sticking to the original novel (engaging its author, WR Burnett, to work on the final draft with him). This created a character who did not come from gangster-film stock: 'an embattled man equally at odds with public morality and himself', as described by Sperber and Lax. 'He was a strange mix of ambiguity and integrity, someone who might be on both sides of the law, but whose true allegiance was to the man within, and whose world had neither ideals nor absolutes.' (This prefigured the existential noir gangster of the 1940s, exemplified in Walsh's 1948 film *White Heat*.) The performance transferred to *The Maltese Falcon*, bringing the hardboiled hero of 1930s crime fiction to the cinema for the first time. As the publicity materials said of Bogart's performance here, 'The last of the bad men has joined the forces of law and order.' Although Bogart later employed his cynical but decent and distantly romantic persona in non-noirs such as *Casablanca* (Michael Curtiz, 1942) and *To Have and Have Not* (Howard Hawks, 1944), it would become identified as a noir archetype.

However, although Spade's adherence to his code while he maintains a cynical outlook is characteristic of noir, the tactic is a little too effective. 'Sam Spade is not a true film noir hero,' claims Blaser, 'because he is able to control himself, his destiny, and his obsessions.' Even when Spade isn't entirely sure what's going on, he improvises effectively and trusts nobody – including Brigid, which denies her the status of a true femme fatale. There is therefore no nightmarish aspect to the film, no moment when the circumstances threaten to overwhelm Spade, an impression confirmed by the balanced and uncluttered visual style. The uncertainty for the audience mainly lies in wondering whether Spade will accept Gutman's offer rather than wondering if Spade will escape unscathed from his experience, whereas in the best noirs the hero is plunged into chaos and frequently isn't allowed out again. 'The hero becomes more deeply implicated in an all-inclusive guilt, and . . . even a partial victory over the evil and hostility of the world seems impossible.'

AFTERLIFE: Warners attempted to replicate the film's success with *Across the Pacific* (1942), a light thriller directed by Huston and starring Bogart, Astor and Greenstreet. The studio also considered making a direct sequel entitled *The Further Adventures of the Maltese Falcon*. Hammett was requested to write a story on which the film could be based, and he agreed, but lacked confidence as he had not written an original work since *The Thin Man*. A concerned Warners decided to abandon the idea after Hammett demanded an advance of more than $5,000. George Segal played Sam Spade Jr in the spoofy follow-up *The Black Bird* (David Giler, 1975), a film chiefly notable for return performances by Lee Patrick and Elisha Cook Jr.

In 1986 media magnate Ted Turner had *The Maltese Falcon* colourised for broadcast on his WTBS channel. An ill Huston slammed the decision, demonstrating against it from his wheelchair. 'It would almost seem as though a conspiracy exists to downgrade our national character. Yes, bring it down to the lowest common denominator.' Other films ruined by Turner in this way include *Out of the Past*.

One of the falcon props was given to actor William Conrad (one of the killers in *The Killers*) by Warner as a gift in the 1960s. In 1994, by which time it was one of only two left in the world, it was auctioned at

Christie's in New York. The reserve price was \$30,000 but it ultimately sold for \$400,000, the highest price yet paid for a film prop.

AVAILABILITY: The Region 2 (D065012) and Region 1 DVDs include the original trailer, plus a feature on Bogart's other trailers.

I Wake Up Screaming (1941)

A Twentieth Century-Fox B-picture directed by Bruce Humberstone, *I Wake Up Screaming* (also known as *Hot Spot*) stars Victor Mature as a sports promoter, Frankie Christopher, who is suspected of the murder of Becky Lynn, a waitress whom he was building into a starlet. As he seeks to prove his innocence, romance blossoms with Becky's sister Jill (Betty Grable). The film is something of a generic mix, incorporating a rags-to-riches story along the lines of *A Star Is Born* as well as some scenes of light comedy, but is marked out as a noir by its intriguing use of flashback, impressive chiaroscuro work on the scenes of Christopher being interrogated and the character of corrupt cop Ed Cornell (Laird Cregar), whose unrequited love for the victim leads him to frame Christopher for her murder. As an early example of noir it arrives surprisingly close to fully formed, and Cregar is superb. *Released on 14 November 1941*

This Gun for Hire (1942)

Based on Graham Greene's novel *A Gun for Sale* (1936), this was the first film to pair Veronica Lake and Alan Ladd. The narrative follows hit-man Raven (Ladd), who kills a blackmailing scientist only for his employers to pay him in cash which they then report stolen, setting the police on Raven's trail. The film gradually evolves from underworld thriller to W.W.II flag-waver, as the corporate mogul who hired Raven is revealed to have sold a chemical weapon formula to the Japanese. Although Raven ultimately has to pay for his crimes, he is briefly positioned as a patriotic vigilante – a highly unusual tactic to say the least. With his dual motives of revenge and justice, and his emotional detachment explicitly traced to a traumatic childhood, he is a classic morally ambivalent noir anti-hero. (He also has a soft spot for cats.) It is also notable as an early example of Hans Dreier's influence at Paramount; Dreier, who had previously worked at UFA in Germany, was supervising art director at the studio and in October 1941 drew up a response to wartime limitations, suggesting the adoption of more stylised techniques. In the case of *This Gun for Hire*, visual interest was limited by the small number of sets and Dreier suggested that director Frank Tuttle and cinematographer John Seitz could combat this with an array of unusual angles and compositions. Lake and Ladd would later star together in the noirs *The Glass Key* (Stuart Heisler, 1942) and *The Blue Dahlia* (George Marshall, 1946). It probably helped that Lake was one of the few leading ladies who didn't show up how short Ladd was. *Released on 13 May 1942*

Phantom Lady (1944)

The first noir to be produced at Universal, this B-feature also marked the first Hollywood success of Robert Siodmak (see *The Killers*). Based on a 1942 novel by Cornell Woolrich (published under the pseudonym of William Irish), the predicament of its hero is typical of the author and highly influential on noir; architect Scott Henderson (Alan Curtis) meets a mysterious woman in a bar and they spend the evening together, although she insists upon not telling him her name. He returns home to find his wife – whom he was trying to divorce – murdered. Unable to track down the woman, he is unable to provide an alibi and everybody he met that evening denies seeing him. Thus, the innocent man is made to seem absurdly guilty in the eyes of everybody except the viewer and Scott's faithful secretary, Carol Richman (Ella Raines). Thereafter, scriptwriter Bernard Schoenfeld does away with the 'whodunnit' structure of the novel and reveals the identity of the killer to the audience halfway through, but the paranoia of Woolrich's work is strongly apparent in the early scenes and the depiction of the city at night, as Carol investigates the 'witnesses' of Scott's activities, is particularly significant. The New York sets were studio bound and, as Michael Walker notes, this 'works particularly well for film noir, with its pervasive sense of claustrophobic menace. The action takes place almost entirely at night, with the German Expressionist influence clearly visible.' Carol is a rare example of a seeker-heroine, taking an expanded version of Jane's role in *Stranger on the Third Floor*. *Released on 17 February 1944*

Double Indemnity (1944)

Black and White – 107 mins

A Paramount Picture
Double Indemnity
Screenplay by Billy Wilder and Raymond Chandler
From the Novel by James M Cain
Music Score: Miklos Rozsa
Director of Photography: John Seitz, ASC
Editorial Supervision: Doane Harrison
Art Direction: Hans Dreier and Hal Pereira
Process Photography: Farciot Edouart, ASC
Costumes by Edith Head
Make-up Artist: Wally Westmore
Sound Recording by Stanley Cooley and Walter Oberst
Set Decoration: Bertram Granger
Directed by Billy Wilder

CAST: Fred MacMurray (*Walter Neff*), Barbara Stanwyck (*Phyllis Dietrichson*), Edward G Robinson (*Barton Keyes*) with Porter Hall (*Mr Jackson*), Jean Heather (*Lola Dietrichson*), Tom Powers (*Mr Dietrichson*), Byron Barr (*Nino Zachetti*), Richard Gaines (*Edward S Norton*), Fortunio Bonanova (*Sam Gorlopis*), John Philliber (*Joe Peters*)

SUMMARY: Insurance salesman Walter Neff comes to his office in the middle of the night, picks up a dictation machine and confesses to murdering a man named Dietrichson. In flashback we see Neff meet and flirt with Dietrichson's wife Phyllis. She wants to insure her husband against accidents without telling him, and Neff realises that she wants to kill him. Infatuated with her, Neff concocts a plan to get away with the murder and the money. They trick Dietrichson into signing the policy and Phyllis tries to convince her husband to take the train to a school reunion instead of driving (a 'double indemnity' clause in the policy pays out double for unlikely deaths, such as on a train). Fortunately, Dietrichson breaks his leg and cannot drive. Phyllis drives Dietrichson to the station; Neff hides in the back and kills Dietrichson in a quiet spot. Then Neff disguises himself as Dietrichson, gets on the train and surreptitiously drops off the back a few minutes into the journey. Phyllis meets him and they leave Dietrichson's body on the tracks, creating the appearance that he died falling from the train. It looks like they will get away with it until Neff's colleague Barton Keyes realises that, if

Dietrichson knew about his accident insurance, surely he would have claimed for his broken leg. He suspects Phyllis, and Neff has to stay away from her, instead spending time with her stepdaughter Lola. Neff realises that Phyllis is plotting against him with Lola's ex-boyfriend Nino; he tells Nino to go back to Lola, then confronts Phyllis. They shoot each other and we realise that Neff has been dying throughout his confession. Keyes arrives at the office and allows Neff to leave, but Neff collapses on the way to the elevator.

DIRECTOR: Billy Wilder (1906–2002, born Samuel Wilder) was born in the Austro-Hungarian Empire (although his birthplace is now part of Poland). In the 1920s he worked as a journalist in Vienna, then in Berlin, where he became a screenwriter in the flourishing German film industry. As he came from a Jewish family, he was forced to leave in 1933 for France, where he co-directed *Mauvaise Graine* (1934), but after a year he moved to Hollywood. He shared an apartment with Peter Lorre and learned English so that he could continue screenwriting. There's a story that he got his first studio job by blackmailing a studio executive whom he had discovered was having an affair in the apartment next door. He formed a highly successful collaborative partnership with staff writer Charles Brackett (see **Sunset Boulevard**) at Paramount, and received Oscar nominations for *Ninotchka* (Ernst Lubitsch, 1939) and *Hold Back the Dawn* (Mitchell Leisen, 1940). Following this, Paramount agreed to let Wilder direct. *Double Indemnity* was his third film, after the Ginger Rogers comedy *The Major and the Minor* (1942) and *Five Graves to Cairo* (1943), both of which he co-wrote with Brackett. (See **Sunset Boulevard** for more Wilder.)

WRITER: Born in Maryland, James M Cain (1892–1977) initially desired to become a professional singer as his mother had been. He skipped so many school grades that he graduated from college at eighteen and, after a spell selling insurance, embarked on a journalistic career in Baltimore and New York. In 1927 he covered the trial of Ruth Snyder and her lover Judd Gray, who had conspired to murder her husband and collect the insurance; this would later form the basis of *Double Indemnity*. Cain had made an abortive attempt to become a novelist in his early thirties (and had written unsuccessful plays), but it wasn't until he started writing stories in a first-person 'common' voice that he began to find success. In 1931, with newspapers suffering from Depression decline, Cain moved to California to become a screenwriter after receiving a contract offer from Paramount. Finding the vernacular of Californians an appealing one, he began to write prose in that voice and produced a bestselling debut novel, *The Postman Always Rings Twice* (1934).

Cain continued to produce prose throughout his Hollywood period, and *Double Indemnity* was published as an eight-part serial by *Liberty* magazine in 1936 (it was reprinted as one of a trio of novellas, *Three of a Kind*). *Postman* was first adapted for the screen in France and Italy as *The Final Twist* (Pierre Chenal, 1939) and *Ossessione* (Luchino Visconti, 1943), the latter of which was unauthorised. There had not been a Hollywood adaptation because MGM had acquired *Postman* in 1935, only for Production Code administrator Joseph Breen to declare the novel utterly unsuitable for cinematic treatment. The same applied to *Double Indemnity*. Cain's next three novels were all subsequently adapted: *Serenade* (1937 – filmed by Anthony Mann, 1956), *Mildred Pierce* (1941 – filmed by Michael Curtiz, 1945) and *Love's Lovely Counterfeit* (1942 – filmed as *Slightly Scarlet* by Allan Dwan, 1956). The subsequent historical dramas *Past All Dishonour* (1946) and *The Butterfly* (1947) set a pattern for the rest of his career, as he abandoned hardboiled fiction and moved away from Hollywood.

Raymond Chandler adapted the novel for the screen; at the same time, his novel *Farewell, My Lovely* (1940) was being adapted as *Murder, My Sweet* (see his biography under that entry and **The Big Sleep**).

DEVELOPMENT: Producer Joseph Sistrom approached Billy Wilder in 1943 and asked him, 'Look, do you know James M Cain?' Wilder replied, 'Certainly. He wrote *Postman Always Rings Twice*.' Sistrom said, 'Well, we don't have that, Metro has that, but as an afterthought, and to cash in, he wrote a serial in the old *Liberty Magazine* called *Double Indemnity*. Read it.' Sistrom had judged Wilder's taste well; the director loved it. 'Terrific,' he told Sistrom. 'It's not as good as *Postman*, but let's do it.' Wilder gave the book to Charles Brackett so that they could commence work, but Brackett thought the book was awful. An argument ensued, they threw things at each other and Brackett stormed out, dissolving their partnership. In need of a new collaborator for *Double Indemnity*, Wilder's first thought was Cain himself, but the writer was contracted to work on another movie. Sistrom said he knew of a novelist with a similar style and gave Wilder *The Big Sleep*. Wilder read it and, although Raymond Chandler had never written a script before, Wilder invited him to the office.

They hated each other immediately. Wilder had been expecting a hard-bitten guy with a smart turn of phrase, but instead found a mild, cultured man who wore tweed and smoked a pipe. Chandler found Wilder's fidgety manner distracting and wondered why the director never took off his hat, even indoors. In addition, Chandler disliked Cain's work. ('He is every kind of writer I detest. Such people are the offal of literature, not because they write about dirty things, but because

they do it in a dirty way.') However, Wilder needed a writer and
Chandler needed the money, so they agreed to work together. Chandler
was put on a salary of $750 per week and finished the script in a
fortnight. In order to make more money he waited another three weeks,
then delivered the script to Wilder. Wilder read it, declared, 'Mr
Chandler, this is *shit*!' and threw it at him. The script was full of camera
instructions, which Wilder explained were not Chandler's department,
and began to lecture the novelist on the art of screenwriting. Wilder
recalled that at this point Chandler became 'bad-tempered – kind of acid,
sour and grouchy'.

For six months Wilder and Chandler wrote together, working in an
office on the fourth floor of Paramount's writers' block. (This kind of
close collaboration, with greater independence permitted for directors
and writers, was characteristic of the innovative Paramount.) Wilder was
irritated by Chandler's arrogance about writing and his pipe-smoking
(exacerbated by Chandler's refusal to open any windows), and he would
go to the toilets every fifteen minutes just to get away. Wilder seemed
brash and abrasive to Chandler, who found it difficult to concentrate
with the director pacing up and down the office. The fact that Chandler
was a recovering alcoholic didn't help. 'I was a lot younger,' said Wilder.
'I knew many pretty girls, and I could drink without it ever getting in
control of me.' Eventually Chandler quit the project; according to
Wilder, this was because Chandler had asked him to draw the venetian
blind, and Wilder had refused because Chandler hadn't said please.
Chandler sent Sistrom a list of his grievances with Wilder and set
conditions under which he would agree to return to work.

However, the collaboration produced good results. 'We worked well,'
said Wilder. 'We would discuss a situation. Once we had the broad
outline, we added to and changed the original story and arrived at
certain points or orientation that we needed.' Each scene was then
written purely as dialogue, then the transitions between scenes were
added. 'And he was very good at that, just very, very good.' One notable
aspect of the script was that it ended differently to the book. In Cain's
version Keyes allows Walter to escape on to a boat to Mexico, but
Phyllis catches up with him there and, after realising that they are going
to be arrested before they can land, the couple commit suicide by
jumping overboard into shark-infested waters. Wilder and Chandler's
ending saw Neff arrested and sentenced to the gas chamber, in
accordance with the Production Code's demand that movie criminals
must pay for their crimes. Even so, it was remarkable that the script was
passed in September 1943 by Joseph Breen, who in 1935 had considered
the novel to possess a 'low tone and sordid flavor'. Although he
described this script as 'a blueprint for crime', he was appeased by the

writers' efforts in adding a clearer moral dimension. Furthermore, the novel featured less overt sexuality than *Postman* (and had been further toned down by Chandler) and was easier for Breen to sanction. The script headed into production, despite Paramount's lack of confidence in the project.

Chandler told his publisher, 'Working with Billy Wilder . . . was an agonizing experience and has probably shortened my life, but I learned from it about as much about screen-writing as I am capable of learning, which is not very much.' By all accounts Chandler was treated better than most writers, but he still felt the need to publish a bitter attack on the industry for *Atlantic Monthly* magazine, entitled 'Writers in Hollywood'. Wilder was aggrieved by the myth that sprang up around this. 'Don't fall for that dreck – what Hollywood did to Raymond Chandler,' he said. 'What did Raymond Chandler do to Hollywood? . . . He gave me more aggravation than any writer I ever worked with.'

CASTING: Fred MacMurray (1908–91) started out as a saxophonist in the 1920s, and was signed up by Paramount while on Broadway in the musical *Roberta* (1933). He made several romantic comedies with director Mitchell Leisen, playing opposite Carole Lombard: examples include *Hands across the Table* (1935) and *Swing High, Swing Low* (1937). After Lombard's departure from Paramount, MacMurray's career was in danger of stagnating. Afraid of tarnishing his image – which was so clean cut that the comic-book character Captain Marvel was visually based on him – he turned down the role of Walter Neff, despite being Wilder's first choice.

Wilder approached numerous others, all of whom rejected the part. 'I tried up and down the street, believe me, including George Raft,' said Wilder. 'Nobody would do it; they didn't want to play this unsympathetic guy.' Raft turned the film down on the grounds that he didn't understand it (another triumphant career move from George; see **The Maltese Falcon**). 'That's when we knew we had a good picture,' Wilder later noted (he had ignored Raft's suggestion that Neff might turn out to be an FBI agent trying to bring Phyllis to justice). The only man who wanted to play Walter Neff was Dick Powell (see **Murder, My Sweet**): 'He volunteered to do it,' said Wilder. 'He told me, "I'll do it for nothing." He knew that was the way out of those silly things – you know, where he was singing smack into Ruby Keeler's face.' However, Wilder couldn't see it working (with hindsight the director noted that 'he was damned good, you know, in *Murder, My Sweet*'). Eventually Wilder returned to MacMurray and harassed him. To get Wilder off his back, MacMurray accepted the role, thinking that Paramount would probably veto his participation. However, he was coming to the end of his contract and had accepted an offer to move to Twentieth Century-Fox, and Paramount endorsed MacMurray's acceptance in the private hope that *Double Indemnity* would dent his image shortly before he went to another studio. His anxiety shows through in contemporary publicity. 'I could have turned down the part, I guess . . . You sort of hate to spring such a sudden surprise on your fans when they are accustomed to seeing you in a certain type of part over a period of years.'

The move paid off. Although MacMurray returned to comedy afterwards, he now found that he was also offered dramatic roles such as *The Caine Mutiny* (Edward Dmytryk, 1954) and Wilder's *The Apartment* (1960). After *The Shaggy Dog* (Charles Barton, 1959), he became a significant Disney star, including in *The Absent-Minded Professor* (Robert Stevenson, 1961) and twelve years starring in the TV comedy *My Three Sons* (1960–72).

Barbara Stanwyck (1907–90, born Ruby Catherine Stevens) was orphaned when very young and raised in New York by her older sister. She became a chorus girl at seventeen and worked up to leading roles on Broadway. She married vaudeville star Frank Fay in 1928 and went to Hollywood, where she regularly worked with Frank Capra (including in *Ladies of Leisure* (1930) and *The Bitter Tea of General Yen* (1933)). Her tough image drew her to a contract at Warner Bros., where she gradually became successful enough to go freelance; she divorced the resentful Fay and received an Oscar nomination for *Stella Dallas* (King Vidor, 1937). Other notable roles included *The Lady Eve* (Preston Sturges, 1941) and *Meet John Doe* (Frank Capra, 1941). By 1944 she was America's highest-paid woman, with earnings of $400,000 a year.

Like MacMurray, she was reticent about taking the role in *Double Indemnity*. 'I realized that I had never played an out-and-out killer,' she recalled of her reaction upon reading the script. 'I had played medium heavies, but never an out-and-out killer. And because it was an unsympathetic character, I was a little frightened of it.' She told Wilder that, although she thought the script was very good, she wasn't sure that the role was for her. 'Mr. Wilder looked at me and resolutely declared, "Are you an actress or a mouse?" "Well, I hope I'm an actress," I lamented. To which he bluntly replied, "Then take the part."' Wilder claimed that she initially prevaricated about the role, and he spent some time taunting her and claiming that she was afraid to play Phyllis until eventually she gave in. 'He used the right sales approach, I guess,' said MacMurray.

Stanwyck went on to make further noirs, such as *The Strange Love of Martha Ivers* (Lewis Milestone, 1946), *The Two Mrs Carrolls* (Peter Godfrey, 1947), *Cry Wolf* (Peter Godfrey, 1947), *Sorry, Wrong Number* (Anatole Litvak, 1948), *The File on Thelma Jordan* (Robert Siodmak,

1949) and *Clash by Night* (Fritz Lang, 1952), among many other screen appearances. She moved to television in the 1960s, with an Emmy-winning role in *The Big Valley* (1965–69), and then went into retirement. She revived her career for TV guest appearances in the 1980s. 'She was as good an actress as I have ever worked with,' said Wilder. 'Very meticulous about her work. We rehearsed the way I usually do. Hard. There were no retakes.'

Edward G Robinson (1893–1973, born Emanuel Goldenberg) was born in Bucharest. His family came to New York when he was ten: he studied at the American Academy of Dramatic Arts and started acting on Broadway in 1915, making occasional silent films in the days when production was still part-based in New York. *The Hole in the Wall* (Robert Florey, 1929) was his first notable role and led to a contract at Warner Bros., where he became a star following the success of *Little Caesar* (Mervyn Le Roy, 1930). An unlikely leading man (he was just five feet five inches tall), Robinson became strongly identified with the new wave of Warners gangster movies, of which *Little Caesar* had been the first; although he played a variety of roles, his gangster persona informed them all. In the late 1930s Warners started to feel that Robinson was past his commercial peak and they parted company following the crime comedy *Larceny, Inc* (Lloyd Bacon, 1942).

Double Indemnity was a turning point for Robinson. 'I debated accepting it,' he said of the good-guy role. 'Emanuel Goldenberg told me that at my age it was time to begin thinking of character roles ... The decision made itself ... It remains one of my favourites.' He subsequently played victim-heroes in Fritz Lang's *The Woman in the Window* (1944) and *Scarlet Street* (1945), and an FBI agent in Orson Welles's *The Stranger* (1946). In the late 1940s and 1950s he was offered fewer roles due to the 'grey-listing' which arose from unfounded suspicions over his political affiliations. His last great gangster role came in *Key Largo* (John Huston, 1948); he also appeared in the noirs *The Night Has a Thousand Eyes* (John Farrow, 1948), *House of Strangers* (Joseph L Mankiewicz, 1949), *The Glass Web* (Jack Arnold, 1953), *Black Tuesday* (Hugo Fregonese, 1954), *Tight Spot* (Phil Karlson, 1955), *A Bullet for Joey* (Lewis Allen, 1955), *Illegal* (Lewis Allen, 1955) and *Nightmare* (Maxwell Shayne, 1956). He continued to work through the 1960s and early 1970s, even after being diagnosed with cancer, and died two weeks after completing *Soylent Green* (Richard Fleischer, 1973).

PRODUCTION: Shooting commenced on 27 September 1943, with a budget of $927,262. On-set, Wilder was heard to say to his crew, 'Keep it quiet, fellows, keep it quiet. After all, history is being made.' At

Wilder's request, Chandler was kept on full salary for the duration of the film and given approval of any changes.

A great deal of publicity would be focused around Stanwyck's shift in hair colour for this film. 'I had always visualised murderesses as brunettes,' Stanwyck said, 'but apparently blondes are considered harder and more unscrupulous, this season at least.' This was in accordance with the novel, in which Phyllis is described as having 'dusty blonde' hair, and the wig was designed to complement her anklet. Wilder noted, 'I wanted to make her look as sleazy as possible.' However, the wig just didn't look very good. 'I was the first one,' said Wilder, 'to see the mistake after we were shooting.' Unfortunately, this realisation came halfway through the shoot. 'After I shot for four weeks with Stanwyck . . . I can't say, "Look, tomorrow, you ain't going to be wearing the blonde wig." . . . I can't reshoot four weeks of stuff. I'm totally stuck.' The wig was too thick; as Buddy DeSylva, Paramount's Head of Production, commented, 'We hired Barbara Stanwyck and here we get George Washington.' Production had to continue, and in retrospect Wilder felt that 'Fortunately it did not hurt the picture . . . when people say, "My god, that wig. It looked phony," I answer, "You noticed that? That was my intention. I wanted the phoniness in the girl." '

John Seitz commented, 'The film was shot in newsreel style. We attempted to keep it extremely realistic.' In order to achieve the diffuse quality of light in the Dietrichson home, Seitz fed a light mix of smoke and silver dust into the set and lit it low. Exteriors of the house were shot at 6301 Quebec Street in the Hollywood Hills (Neff's apartment was in the Normandie-Wilshire section of the city), and the sets were modelled on the real interior for a close match. Stanwyck's first scene saw her sunbathing on a balcony, and, while the script had originally called for her to wear a sun suit for this (the novel has her in pyjamas), Wilder decided that sun suits were too commonplace and not seductive enough. He changed it to a bath towel, which designer Edith Head fitted and pinned around Stanwyck to ensure that she would be properly covered at all times.

Exteriors for the grocery-store scene were shot at Jerry's Market on Melrose Avenue, just around the corner from Paramount Studios, while the interior was built on a sound stage. As the story was supposed to be set in 1938, the shelves had to be fully stocked in a way that wartime supermarkets were not – and this meant borrowing goods to the value of 72,000 ration points, or $20,000, to line the set. This included such delicacies as tomatoes, tinned pineapple and chocolate. The meat counter proved too difficult to fill and Wilder framed all shots to disguise the fact that it was empty. Four policemen guarded the food 24 hours a day, and Paramount would be held responsible for anything that went missing. When the goods were returned, four bars of soap and a tin of peaches were unaccounted for.

Shooting wrapped on 24 November 1943. Wilder attended a preview screening of the film, then cut twenty minutes from it – the bulk of which made up the closing sequence as Neff is sent to a gas chamber, with Keyes solemnly looking on. This had cost around $150,000 and taken five days to shoot. 'We were delighted with it at first,' said Wilder, praising MacMurray's performance. 'I shot that whole thing in the gas chamber, the execution, when everything was still, with tremendous accuracy. But then I realized, look this thing is already over.' Neff's fate was sealed when he failed to run from the office, 'where he can't even light the match. And from the distance, you hear the sirens, be it an ambulance or be it the police, you know it is over. No need for the gas chamber.' Additionally, the confession, originally introduced as a narrative device, confirmed Neff's fate: it has all been recorded, he *will* be found guilty. The sequence was dropped in its entirety, despite Wilder's belief that it was 'one of the two best sequences I ever did'. (The footage belonged to Paramount, so he didn't get to keep it – it is unclear whether the sequence still exists.) The director also stated that, although 'I never look at my old stuff', he still rated *Double Indemnity* as one of his best films, 'because it had the fewest takes, and because it was taut and moved in the staccato manner of Cain's novel'.

RECEPTION: *Double Indemnity* was reviewed early by *Variety* on 26 April 1944, where it was dubbed 'certain boxoffice insurance' with a plot that was 'rapidly moving and consistently well developed. It is a story replete with suspense, for which credit must go in a large measure to Billy Wilder's direction.' MacMurray was judged to have 'seldom given a better performance. It is somewhat different from his usually light roles, but is always plausible and played with considerable restraint', while Stanwyck was 'not as attractive as normally with what is seemingly a blonde wig, but it's probably part of a makeup to emphasize the brassiness of the character'. The film was released on 6 September 1944. Cain was delighted by the result and waited in the lobby to congratulate the screenwriters, but Chandler had already ducked out of a fire exit and Wilder had not turned up at all, preferring to spend the evening drunk under a table at Lucey's, a popular Hollywood restaurant.

'The cooling system in the Paramount Theater was supplemented yesterday by a screen attraction designed plainly to freeze the marrow in the audience's bones,' wrote Bosley Crowther on 7 September 1944 in the *New York Times*. Wilder was felt to have filmed the novel 'with a realism reminiscent of the bite of past French films . . . but the very

toughness of the picture is also the weakness of its core, and the
academic nature of its plotting limits its general appeal'. James Agee (see
The Night of the Hunter) echoed this judgement when writing in *The
Nation* dated 14 October 1944. '*Double Indemnity* is quite a gratifying
and even a good movie . . . smart and crisp and cruel like a whole type of
American film which developed softening of the brain after the early
thirties.' He did, however, note that it was 'essentially cheap' and
professed disappointment that the material had not been exploited to its
full potential.

Writing on *Double Indemnity* for *The New Yorker* dated 16
September 1944, John Lardner was fascinated by 'the nature of its
treatment of the insurance industry and the predatory types among us
who buy insurance'. Lardner considered that 'the picture, without so
much as blinking, shows insurance as a deadly war between
beneficiaries, felonious to a man, and the company, which fights tooth
and nail in defense of its capital holdings'; he further noted, 'When Mr
Robinson, told that the police are giving up their investigation of the
death of a policy holder, says scornfully, "Sure, it's not their money," he
sounds the keynote of the struggle.'

The British press reception was generally more enthusiastic. 'A
Brilliant New Thriller' was the title of Campbell Dixon's review in the
Daily Telegraph on 18 September 1944, describing the film as 'one of
those cynical, brutal things which Hollywood does so well'. Dixon
dismissed the 'blueprint for murder' moral panic over the film. 'It is safe
to say that few horrible crimes will be caused by *Double Indemnity*.
Punishment dogs the criminals too ineluctably.' He also went some way
towards pinpointing what had been added to the crime film in the
transition to noir. 'For suspense *Double Indemnity* compares with
gangster thrillers like *Angels with Dirty Faces*, for ingenuity with *The
Maltese Falcon*: but psychologically it is more complex than either, and
more nearly universal.'

Edgar Anstey thought *Double Indemnity* recalled 'the heyday of the
crime-film' in the *Spectator* of 22 September 1944: 'an idiom which
Hollywood thoroughly understands, and a wildly improbable world of
melodrama into which Hollywood has always been able to infuse quiet
probabilities of characterisation denied to its more pretentious dramas of
real life.' The film was not considered to be a great work of cinema – but
it was worthy of comparison with one. 'The drama concentrates on
everyday occurrences, illuminating them with horror, and *Double
Indemnity* has points in common with *Le Jour se Leve* [Marcel Carné,
1939] without however reaching the level of that masterpiece.' William
Whitebait, writing in the *New Statesman* dated 23 September 1944, was
more willing to praise. 'Good murders on the screen are not so rare;

what is rare is to find a film that has ... the atmosphere of crime but characters and a plot as solid as that of a novel.' Whitebait also implied that the filmmaking process had improved the source material. 'If the novel is anything like the film, it must be a cut above *The Postman*, who rang rather too often for my taste.'

The film garnered seven Oscar nominations (Best Picture, Screenplay, Director, Score, Cinematography, Sound Recording and Leading Actress) but won none. It was said that the Academy thought *Double Indemnity* the outstanding film of the year but was nervous about its Production Code transgressions and compensated Paramount by giving Best Picture, Director and Screenplay to one of its other releases, *Going My Way* (Leo McCarey, 1944).

ASPECTS OF NOIR: The most famous hallmark of film noir is surely the femme fatale, and rightly so; although the figure of a 'dark lady' whose transgressive desire and willingness to use her sexuality to achieve that desire is not ubiquitous, it unites more of the movement's films than any other feature.

As critic Janey Place notes, the 'spider woman' was by no means germane to film noir; rather, she 'is among the oldest themes of art, literature, mythology and religion in Western culture. She is as old as Eve.' Stating that 'Film noir is a male fantasy, as is most of our art', Place identifies that it defines women by their relationship to men and therefore by their sexuality; the woman who attempts to adjust that definition is a threat to men. As Neff eventually realises in *Double Indemnity*, Phyllis has no intention of freeing herself of one man only to become subordinate to another. Once Neff has exceeded his usefulness, she will 'take care' of him, and if necessary engage another man to 'take care' of the man who got rid of Neff. Accordingly, she must be destroyed. 'Film noir is hardly "progressive" in these terms,' notes Place, 'it does not present us with role models who defy their fate and triumph over it.' However, it does depict women who 'are active, not static symbols, are intelligent and powerful, if destructively so, and derive power, not weakness, from their sexuality'. In other words, fear is a degree towards respect (and the transgressive criminal female's inability to triumph did not necessarily originate with the filmmakers but with the Production Code, which demanded that criminals pay for their crimes).

Double Indemnity is identified by Michael Walker as being the paradigm film for one of his three noir narrative types, the type which is specifically based around a femme fatale and the hero who falls victim to her manipulation. This is not to say that the femme fatale does not feature in the other narrative types. Brigid in the original noir private-eye narrative *The Maltese Falcon* operates like a femme fatale, her status only compromised by her eventual neutralisation. The figure is stronger in *Murder, My Sweet*, which privileges the plottings of Helen/Velma to a greater degree than the novel and features a contrasting 'good girl', Ann. (The repositioning of Ann as Helen's stepdaughter, which she is not in the novel, suggests the influence of *Double Indemnity* – although the film had not been released when Paxton wrote the script, he may have read the novel.) Likewise the 'nightmare' noir makes use of the figure; *Detour*'s Vera does not manipulate Al via her sexuality but he is caught up in her transgressive bid for financial independence, which ultimately destroys her and condemns him.

However, in the other narrative types the femme fatale is chiefly a disruptive element who blocks the hero's attempts to resolve the plot, whereas in the Cain version she is the instigator of events and the objective of the hero, who has been led to believe that he can 'keep' the woman via his actions. Her power is more significant in such narratives because it is sufficient to draw the hero into the noir world, unlike the seeker-heroes who enter it of their own volition. The ordinariness of the victim-hero, emphasising that no man is safe from the femme fatale, is of central importance and enhanced in *Double Indemnity* by the casting of MacMurray. The sexualised presentation of the femme fatale is crucial to the male viewer's identification with the victim-hero (see the *Daily Graphic*'s review of **Out of the Past**), and in *Double Indemnity* she is coded as sexual from the first shot: hence the type could not fully emerge on-screen until the Production Code had slackened. Wilder and Chandler's triumph in getting the sexual aspect of *Double Indemnity*, as well as the extreme nature of Neff's crime, past the Code accounts for its impact on release and the subsequent prevalence of the femme fatale. The Cain adaptations are among the most extreme examples of the 'destructive femme fatale' films; as Walker notes, 'it is only occasionally in these films that the hero is driven to murder, but the power of the femme fatale is such that he has only about even chances of surviving the film.' *Sunset Boulevard* is a good example.

In addition to the exciting portrayal of the femme fatale, noir is frequently subversive in its depiction of her opposite – the 'domestic' or 'nurturing' woman. The opposition of 'good' and 'bad' girls is by no means unique to noir. *It's a Wonderful Life* (Frank Capra, 1946) employs the same tactic, contrasting domestic woman Mary Bailey with Violet Bick (played by Gloria Grahame – see **The Big Heat**): Violet is highly aware of her sexuality and causes a minor scandal by her dependence on George Bailey. However, the film ultimately sees George appreciate the pleasures of domestic life and Violet's path is not depicted as desirable. Noir often goes against the grain of this; although *Murder,*

My Sweet leaves Marlowe with Ann, *Double Indemnity* never presents Lola as a realistic alternative for Neff, which he acknowledges by sending Nino back to her. Other films, such as *The Woman in the Window* (Fritz Lang, 1944), start with the hero in a domestic context and dramatise his temptation towards the more exciting femme fatale, while *Out of the Past* presents the hero with a direct choice between the 'good' and 'bad' girls; 'the lack of excitement offered by the safe woman is so clearly contrasted with the sensual, passionate appeal of the other that the detective's destruction is inevitable,' notes Place. She also points out that the occasional appearances of the domestic world depict it as 'either so fragile and ideal that we anxiously anticipate its destruction (*The Big Heat*), or . . . so dull and constricting that it offers no compelling alternative to the dangerous but exciting life on the fringe'. In this sense, film noir depicts a male crisis of identity which may be a reaction to wartime upheaval – many commentators have drawn a parallel between the femme fatale and women who had taken over men's positions in the workforce during the war.

Additionally, a sociological study made in the late 1940s by Martha Wolfenstein and Nathan Leites looked at Hollywood A-features which were set around the present day and in an urban milieu, taking particular interest in the play of false identities such as in the 'wrong man' thriller; 'the theme of looking guilty but being innocent, recurs persistently in various forms throughout American films.' This led them to identify a type they dubbed 'the good-bad girl', who possesses the exciting promise of dangerous sexuality but is not detached from her feelings towards men as Phyllis is and lacks the desire to destroy. Although the type is not unique to film noir, Andrew Spicer notes, 'Her importance to the noir cycle is difficult to overestimate. She can appear to be cynical, wilful and obsessed with money, but this stems from disillusionment with men and the frustrations of a circumscribed life.' It is here that noir comes closest to a progressive portrayal of women, although the notion frequently remains that she must ultimately return to the control of a man (note the closing lines of *The Big Sleep*, in which Bacall plays a classic 'good-bad girl': 'What's wrong with you?' 'Nothing you can't fix').

However, Andrew Britton has used the 'good-bad girl' of *Gilda* (Charles Vidor, 1946) to refute blanket accusations of misogyny towards film noir; 'the fact that a work of art contains a female character who is represented as vicious and destructive cannot *in itself* be used as evidence that the work in question is either misogynistic or anti-feminist.' Like *Double Indemnity*, *Gilda* presents a married woman desired by a man younger than her husband, but Britton describes it as 'a film *about* misogyny. Both Johnny and Ballen desire Gilda and wish to possess her, but her sexuality appals as much as it attracts them because they experience it as an irresistibly powerful, independent force.' A disturbing and at times unpleasant film, *Gilda* nevertheless presents male sexuality as contradictory and destructive while Gilda herself is not; the very thing which makes Gilda attractive to the men is what they wish to eliminate in her. By offering *The Lady from Shanghai* as a misogynist alternative, Britton suggests that film noir's depiction of women is not as simple as has often been assumed.

AFTERLIFE: 'Since Paramount's *Double Indemnity* became one of Hollywood's box office smash hits last year,' noted the *Daily News* on 6 December 1945, 'all the studios have gone in for making pictures based on realistic murder stories. The tougher and gorier the better.' The film's success made a large contribution towards the erosion of the Production Code's authority and its formula was much imitated; the most shameless rip-off was PRC's *Apology for Murder* (Sam Newfield, 1945), starring *Detour*'s Ann Savage. This was directly based upon the case which inspired *Double Indemnity*, and although the story could not be copyrighted (given that it was true) Paramount successfully sued, preventing the film from being shown. Years later, *Body Heat* (Lawrence Kasdan, 1981) recycled the story.

In 1973 the film was remade for TV by ABC, and Wilder was approached to direct. 'Can you believe that I was asked to make a remake of my own picture?' he said. 'Not a sequel – a remake . . . What would they call it? *Triple Indemnity*?' The remake was eventually directed by Jack Smight and faithfully scripted by Steven Bochco (creator of *Hill Street Blues* and *NYPD Blue*).

AVAILABILITY: *Double Indemnity* is available on Region 2 and Region 1 DVD.

The Woman in the Window (1944)

Fritz Lang's first film noir (see *The Big Heat* for more about him) saw Edward G Robinson cast in another atypical role, that of a married, mild-mannered professor of criminology who spends an evening with a mysterious woman (Joan Bennett) whose portrait he has seen in a window. Attacked by a jealous boyfriend, he kills to defend himself and tries to cover up the crime. A good example of the ordinary man who is caught in the nightmarish noir world, although (stop reading now if you don't want to know the ending) it is rather literal about this as Robinson's character wakes up to discover that it was all a dream. Your opinion of the picture very much depends upon whether or not you view this as a massive cop-out; Lang, whose idea the coda was, told Peter Bogdanovich that 'you know as well as I that a gimmick like the dream is so old that you practically shouldn't use it any more', but he felt that the storyline had become implausible and he liked the notion of revealing the people who had entered the character's subconscious. Many critics have suggested that the possibility of this crime exists in the character's mind, thereby revealing a dark side to his psyche – although the killing is self-defence, so he's not exactly entertaining wild murder fantasies. The team of Lang, Robinson, Bennett, supporting actor Dan Duryea and cinematographer Milton Krasner made a follow-up, *Scarlet Street* (1945). *Released on 10 October 1944*

Laura (1944)

Directed by another Weimar notable, Otto Preminger, at Twentieth Century-Fox, *Laura* is one of the most disorientating of the 1944 noirs with its flashback structure, narrative voice which commences the film with authority but then disappears, and the twist which initially seems like a dream sequence. The plot centres around cop Mark McPherson (Dana Andrews) and his investigation into the death of Laura (Gene Tierney), who turns out not to be dead at all halfway through the film. The fact that she appears just as McPherson has fallen asleep throws confusion over whether or not McPherson has imagined her return, an impression reinforced by the fact that he is explicitly infatuated with her even before they meet. The fact that he loves her when he believes she's dead is disquieting in itself. It is this ambiguity, and the obsessive quality of McPherson's investigation, that lends the film its noir quality, as it is otherwise a society murder whodunnit in the Agatha Christie style. Vincent Price is surprisingly camp as a Deep South ladykiller. *Released on 11 October 1944*

Murder, My Sweet (1944)
A.K.A. *Farewell, My Lovely*

Black and White – 95 mins

RKO Radio Pictures, Inc. Presents
Murder, My Sweet
Executive Producer: Sid Rogell
Screenplay by John Paxton

Based upon the Novel by Raymond Chandler
Director of Photography: Harry J Wild, ASC
Special Effects by Vernon L Walker, ASC
Art Directors: Albert D'Agostino and Caroll Clark
Set Decorations: Darrell Silvera and Michael Ohrenbach
Recorded by Bailey Fesler
Montage by Douglas Travers
Music by Roy Webb
Musical Director: C Bakaleinikoff
Gowns by Edward Stevenson
Edited by Joseph Noriega
Assistant Director: William Dorfman
Rerecording by James G Stewart
Dialogue Director: Leslie Urbach
Produced by Adrian Scott
Directed by Edward Dmytryk

CAST: Dick Powell (*Philip Marlowe*), Claire Trevor (*Helen Grayle*), Anne Shirley (*Ann Grayle*) with Otto Kruger (*Jules Amthor*), Mike Mazurki (*Moose Malloy*), Miles Mander (*Mr Grayle*), Douglas Walton (*Lindsay Marriott*), Don Douglas (*Lt Randall*), Ralf Harolde (*Dr Sonderborg*), Esther Howard (*Jessie Florian*)

SUMMARY: Private detective Philip Marlowe is accused of murder, and tells his version of events to the police while recovering from an accident which has left him blind. In flashback, he is seen being hired by recently released criminal Moose Malloy to find a woman named Velma. He is also hired by Lindsay Marriott, who is about to act as a go-between for a lady who needs to buy back a jade necklace and asks Marlowe to accompany him. Upon arriving at the rendezvous Marlowe is knocked unconscious; the money is stolen and Marriott is killed. Marlowe is contacted upon his return by Ann Grayle, the daughter of the man who owned the necklace. Mr Grayle's young second wife, Helen, claims she was wearing it when it was stolen. Helen hires Marlowe to get it back. Marlowe is brought to see Jules Amthor, a therapist who also wants the necklace and thinks that Marlowe knows where it is. He drugs Marlowe and spends three days trying to get the information out of him. Marlowe escapes. Helen tries to convince Marlowe to help her kill Amthor, claiming that he has been blackmailing her over her extra-marital affairs. However, Marlowe realises that Helen is Velma and Amthor was actually blackmailing her over her criminal past with Moose. Helen has been in possession of the necklace all along; she promised it to Amthor as a pay-off, then set up Marriott's rendezvous and killed him, allowing her to keep the money and conceal the necklace. She also knew that Marlowe had been hired by Moose and told Marriott to hire him in the hope of drawing him off the case and disposing of him. Marlowe brings Moose to Helen's beach house and tells him to wait outside while he extracts the information he needs from Helen. However, he is interrupted by the entrance of Mr Grayle and Ann. Grayle shoots Helen, then Moose enters and he and Grayle shoot each other. Marlowe is blinded by a pistol flash. The police tell him that Ann has corroborated his story and the couple leave together.

DIRECTOR: Edward Dmytryk (1908–99) was born in Canada, the son of Ukranian immigrants, and raised in California. As a teenager he sought a variety of junior jobs at the studios, eventually rising to become an editor in the early 1930s. In 1935 he directed *Trail of the Hawk*, a B western, but the switch to directing was not permanent until he was given the last-minute assignment of completing *Million Dollar Legs* (1939). Columbia signed him up, but he was still stuck making B-pictures and in 1942 moved to RKO. His breakthrough was the propaganda film *Hitler's Children* (1943), notable for not portraying the Nazis in the ridiculous fashion common to Hollywood at the time. After this he graduated to superior projects such as *Murder, My Sweet*. The noirish revenge thriller *Cornered* (1945) reunited him with Dick Powell. The director was Oscar-nominated for his noir *Crossfire* (1947), credited as the first Hollywood movie to confront racism (it concerns an anti-Semitic murder). Unfortunately, Dmytryk's rise was immediately cut short by HUAC; as a left-wing liberal he was questioned about any Communist affiliations but refused to answer and was blacklisted, becoming one of the 'Hollywood Ten'. RKO fired him and he continued his career in England. (*Give Us This Day* (1949) is a real oddity, set in New York but shot in England and populated with actors such as Sid James.) During a return visit to the USA he was arrested and imprisoned for six months, after which he agreed to 'name names' and was taken off the blacklist. He went on to direct the noir *The Sniper* (1952) as well as *The Caine Mutiny*, *The End of the Affair* (both 1954) and *Walk on the Wild Side* (1962). He later taught and wrote about filmmaking.

WRITER: Raymond Chandler (1888–1959) was born in Chicago, grew up in Ireland and was public-school educated in England. He gave up a civil service career to write book reviews and poetry, but with limited success. In 1912 he moved to Los Angeles. Serving in W.W.I, he was the only survivor when his unit was caught in a bombardment. In the 1920s he married Cissy Pascal, eighteen years his senior, and worked in the oil industry. In 1932 he was fired for erratic, drunken behaviour.

Wandering up the coast, he happened to read an issue of *Black Mask*. 'It struck me that some of the writing was pretty forceful and honest, even though it had its crude aspect,' he later recalled. 'I decided that this might be a good way to try to learn to write fiction and get paid a small amount of money at the same time.' After taking a correspondence course (living off friends he'd assisted in a lawsuit against his former employer), he wrote 'Blackmailers Don't Shoot', which was published by *Black Mask*. A slow and studious writer, he decided that the way to make money was to write a novel. Recycling parts of his *Black Mask* stories 'Killer in the Rain' (January 1935) and 'The Curtain' (September 1936), as well as scenes from 'Finger Men' (October 1934) and 'Mandarin's Jade' (from *Dime Detective*, November 1937), he came up with *The Big Sleep* (1939). It sold well enough for him to give up writing for magazines. *Farewell, My Lovely* (1940) was his second novel; he was dissatisfied with it ('More than three-quarters done and no good,' he told his editor in the midst of writing) and started working on another, *The Lady in the Lake* (1943), as a distraction. The sales of *Farewell* and the follow-up *The High Window* (1942) were disappointing, and the movie rights had not sold for much, and when Billy Wilder asked him to work on *Double Indemnity* he had little choice but to accept.

John Paxton (1911–85) was a staff writer at RKO with few notable credits to his name when he was assigned *Murder, My Sweet* – he had just come to the studio following some success in New York theatre. Producer Adrian Scott would have preferred to work with Chandler himself, but the novelist had signed a $1,250-per-week contract with Paramount after *Double Indemnity*. Paxton's successful adaptation resulted in him collaborating with Dmytryk again on *Cornered*, *Crossfire* and *So Well Remembered* (1947). His most celebrated work was *The Wild One* (László Benedek, 1953) and *On the Beach* (Stanley Kramer, 1959).

DEVELOPMENT: *Farewell, My Lovely* had been acquired by RKO for about $2,000 and filmed in 1942, but this version removed Marlowe and used the plot as the basis for the third adventure of the studio's popular B-movie detective, The Falcon. The character was a gentleman adventurer in the mould of The Saint and therefore more light-hearted in his sleuthing, but the producers had still intended to be reasonably faithful to Chandler's novel until Production Code censors refused to pass the script until it was made a lot less hardboiled. It was released as *The Falcon Takes Over* (Irving Reiss, 1942). (A similar fate befell *The High Window*, which was quickly filmed as *Time to Kill* (Herbert I Leeds, 1943) by Twentieth Century-Fox; again, Marlowe was replaced by an existing character, private eye Michael Shayne.)

In 1944 Adrian Scott (1912–73) became a producer in RKO's B-movie department. Like Paxton, he had come in from the New York theatre; like Dmytryk, he would later become one of the blacklisted 'Hollywood Ten', although his politics were further to the left (he spent time in prison for this, which ruined both his health and his career, and he never worked in film again). Scott started looking through the studio's discarded properties for material nobody else was interested in; happening upon *Farewell, My Lovely*, he decided that it might make a 'good, gritty movie' and convinced RKO to give it the green light. He gave the novel to Paxton, who read it in a morning and got to work. Both men needed to justify their employment at RKO by producing a solid programme picture, entertaining and story driven, and they collaborated to create a script that was a condensed, more straightforward, but ultimately more intense version of the novel.

Paxton cut some of the longer passages, considering them 'too narrative, too aimless, too unresolved for the film [we] had in mind'. However, he and Scott were keen to retain the spirit of the novel and this motivated the inclusion of passages as voice-over from Marlowe. In an effort to make this hackneyed and frequently unsubtle device fresher, the narration was used 'not so much for the purposes of direct story-telling, [but] in a subjective way', according to Paxton, 'what I chose to think of as syncopated narration, or narration that is not directly related to the images one is seeing on the screen at the time'. The plot was refocused and given a clearer direction, driven by the acquisition of the jade; the novel contains much material concerning friction between Marlowe and the police of both Los Angeles and Bay City, and there is also rivalry between those police departments. Paxton considered that 'This is too complex to handle in ninety-odd minutes of film,' and largely removed the LAPD from the proceedings. Several minor characters were also dropped (notably some black characters who were not flatteringly depicted by Chandler), as well as the major figure of Laird Brunette, a gambler and major player in Bay City. The roles of other characters were enhanced; the greater emphasis on the jade meant that Ann's father had a larger role. In addition, Moose Malloy – one of the film's most memorable characters – became more prominent during scripting. 'We liked him and wanted to use him more, so he took on some of the functions of some of the other assorted cop-goons hanging about the story,' Paxton said later. 'I made him more simple-minded than Chandler did, less articulate, more monosyllabic – and consequently, I think, more menacing.'

The completed script was titled after the novel: *Farewell, My Lovely*. During development the project was slated as a B-picture, but when studio head Charles M Koerner read the script he passed it to Dmytryk with a view to upgrading it. 'I was on my way into A-pictures,' Dmytryk recalled, 'and he wanted to know if I would make the thing. And I got together with Adrian and Johnny and decided that I would love to make it.'

CASTING: Scott, Paxton and Dmytryk wanted to borrow Bogart for the Marlowe role but he was unavailable, so they were willing to settle for John Garfield and met with Koerner to discuss this. However, Koerner asked them, 'Could you use Dick Powell in the role?'

In the 1920s Powell (1904–63) had been a crooner, bandleader and theatre MC, and it was through such work that he was given a Warner Bros. contract in 1932. For the rest of the decade his career was dominated by musicals such as *42nd Street* (Lloyd Bacon, 1933), *Stage Struck* (Busby Berkeley, 1936), *The Singing Marine* (Ray Enright, 1937) and *In the Navy* (Arthur Lubin, 1941). Bored of these flimsily written characters, he bought out his Warners contract and went in search of non-singing roles such as *Christmas in July* (Preston Sturges, 1940), but still could not free himself from typecasting. After being turned down for the lead in *Double Indemnity* Powell gave up the freelance life, and signed a contract with RKO in May 1944. According to Dmytryk, Koerner 'believed that musicals were due for a comeback and was trying to put together a stable of singing stars'. Accordingly, he had pursued Powell, but Powell would only agree to the musicals if he could do a tough-guy part first. 'He had seen our script and liked it,' said Dmytryk, '[and] would not sign unless he could make *Farewell, My Lovely* as his first picture of the deal.' Scott and Dmytryk were reticent, but Koerner told them he would appreciate the favour and they agreed. Powell 'figured it would be my best or my last picture . . . It turned out to be the best.'

Powell never did make the musicals Koerner signed him for, as he became more valuable to RKO in tough-guy roles. These included Dmytryk's *Cornered* and the noirs *Johnny O'Clock* (Robert Rossen, 1947), *Pitfall* (André de Toth, 1948) and *Cry Danger* (Robert Parrish, 1951). In 1954 he reprised the role of Marlowe in a TV adaptation of *The Long Goodbye* (the first-ever episode of the anthology series *Climax!*). He moved into directing with the noir *Split Second* (1953), following this with *The Conqueror* (1955), *You Can't Run Away From It* (1956), *The Enemy Below* (1957) and *The Hunters* (1958). *The Conqueror* was shot near an atomic testing site in Utah, and it is thought that this caused many of the cast and crew – including Powell – to develop cancer.

Claire Trevor (1910–2000), a New Yorker, was known for her 'bad girl' roles and spent most of the 1930s under contract to Fox, playing assorted western saloon girls and crime-picture floozies. She portrayed an undercover insurance investigator in *Fifteen Maiden Lane* (Allen Dwan, 1936) and was top-billed in *Stagecoach* (John Ford, 1939), by which time she had gone freelance. In the 1940s she appeared in noirs such as *Street of Chance* (Jack Hively, 1942), *Johnny Angel* (Edwin L Marin, 1945), *Crack-Up* (Irvin Reis, 1946 – another Paxton script), *Born to Kill* (Robert Wise, 1947) and *Raw Deal* (Anthony Mann, 1948); she won the Best Supporting Actress Oscar for *Key Largo* (John Huston, 1948). She made few noirs in the 1950s – *Hoodlum Empire* (Joseph Kane, 1952) is a notable exception. Instead, she appeared in dramas such as *Hard, Fast and Beautiful* (Ida Lupino, 1951) and more of the westerns for which she originally became known. She went into semi-retirement in the 1960s.

Anne Shirley (1918–93, real name Dawn Evelyn Paris) was a child star who initially acted under the name of Dawn O'Day. Early notable roles included *Rasputin and the Empress* (Richard Boleslavsky, 1932), but her career gained momentum when she played the eponymous *Anne of Green Gables* (George Nichols Jr, 1934) and adopted the character's name as her stage name. *Stella Dallas* (King Vidor, 1937) brought her a Best Supporting Actress Oscar nomination. RKO signed her up but she was largely wasted in programme pictures and retired after this film, having been in continuous film work since the age of four. Any possibility of a comeback was scuppered by the blacklisting of her husband, producer Adrian Scott, in the late 1940s.

PRODUCTION: With Dmytryk and Powell on board, *Farewell, My Lovely* was now intended as a modest A-picture. 'The budget,' noted Dmytryk, 'instead of being a hundred and fifty thousand, was jumped up to around four hundred thousand.' Other sources state as much as $500,000. Koerner appears to have backed this film quite heavily, suggesting that the picture's style resonated strongly with the studio head (see **ASPECTS OF NOIR**). The shoot was completed over a relatively comfortable 44 days.

'I felt Powell was quite nervous at the start of photography,' said Dmytryk, who came up with some notions on how the star's self-confidence could be boosted. 'One was to involve him in the technical aspects of the film, some of which were unique. I would ask him to look through the camera while it followed Dick's stand-in.' Powell observed a few of these test run-throughs, but, 'After humouring me a few times, he finally pulled me aside and said, "Eddie, just tell me what to do, and I'll do it." ' (Of course, Powell himself later became a director, so there must have been some flicker of interest in the production process.) Dmytryk rated Powell as 'the best of all the Philip Marlowes', and although scarcely impartial he made a good case for his star – who would later be overshadowed by Humphrey Bogart's work on *The Big Sleep*. 'Spade was tough,' noted Dmytryk, 'and that's what was wrong with Bogey doing Marlowe. He made him Spade.' Dmytryk saw Marlowe as 'kind of an Eagle Scout in the wrong business. I think all Eagle Scouts are weak, and that's exactly what I patterned him on.' Aware of this essential weakness, 'He tries to make up for it by getting all the goddamned merit badges he can possibly get and getting all the things on his chest to prove he's a man.' Dmytryk also saw Marlowe as 'a very American character', duty-bound to continue with the case because he has accepted money. 'Even though it's a couple of hundred bucks and no more than that. It's not ten thousand dollars or fifty thousand dollars, or something of that sort. He believes he's got a job.'

One problem that arose from Powell's casting was that he was surprisingly tall at six feet two, which made it difficult to emphasise the looming figure of Moose Malloy (ex-wrestler Mike Mazurki, who played the part, was six feet four). 'So Dick walked in the gutter while Mike walked up on the curb,' said Dmytryk, 'or Dick stood in his stockinged feet while Mike stood on a box.' A more complex trick was used for the reflection of Moose in the window, one of the film's most commented-on shots. 'We staged it and shot it normally,' said Dmytryk, 'but when we looked at the rushes the next day, the effect was not there – the image was not in the least menacing.' The problem was that Mazurki was standing further from the glass than Powell, resulting in a smaller and fainter image. The only way to fix this was to move the reflection closer to the camera. 'I couldn't move the window – so we put in an invisible one.' This involved the positioning of a large piece of plate glass between the desk and the camera, while Mazurki stood off-camera with a spotlight trained on his face. The spotlight was synchronised with the flashing of the neon sign. 'This was reflected in the plate glass in front of the camera, but since the plate glass is clear, the reflection seems to be in the window in the background,' said Dmytryk. 'The effect of size and menace was more than we had hoped for. I never heard from anybody who felt cheated.'

The same piece of glass came in useful later, when Mr Grayle's gun goes off in Marlowe's face. Even though the gun was loaded with blanks, the pistol flash was still very dangerous at that range. 'We put Powell on the far side of the glass,' said Dmytryk, 'and [Miles] Mander's hand, holding the gun, on the camera side.' Mander held the gun in his left hand, projecting a reflection into the glass which looked like his right hand, and Powell was given a mark to dive at which 'had to be carefully calculated so that Marlowe would appear to be diving directly through the line of fire, which was actually only the reflection'. This technique eliminated the need for a stunt double or a cut-away. 'Not only was

Powell several feet away from the gun, but the intervening plate glass
gave him double safety.' Another trick shot of Marlowe was used in the
dream sequence, as he falls away from the camera into blackness. 'The
technique for filming this effect is standard,' said Dmytryk. 'We
projected the standard falling shot on a screen and reshot it with a
camera moving away at an ever-increasing speed.' The director cited FW
Murnau as an influence on the film's Expressionist stylings, including the
use of forced-perspective sets.

The title was changed at a very late stage; according to Paxton, the
film had been 'produced, previewed, and even advertised under' the title
of *Farewell, My Lovely*. Dmytryk went as far as to say, 'They released it
as *Farewell, My Lovely* in New England states, in a few theaters, and
everybody thought it was a musical because of Dick Powell and nobody
went to see it.' RKO's market research confirmed this and the title was
altered to the structurally similar but more clearly hardboiled *Murder,
My Sweet*. In Britain the film retained the novel's title, and is screened on
television as *Farewell, My Lovely* to this day.

RECEPTION: The film was released on 18 December 1944. Chandler
wrote to Paxton to congratulate him, commenting that he had
'considered the book untranslatable to the screen', but was much
impressed with the result.

Time considered the film 'as good a piece of melodramatic
20-minute-egg sentimentality as the famous *Double Indemnity*', in a
review on 14 December 1944. 'In some ways it is more likeable, for
although it is far less tidy, it is more rigorous and . . . more resourcefully
photographed.' Rather surprisingly, the single 'glaring fault' concerned
the film's fidelity to the book; 'it is far too fond of reproducing, by direct
quotation, samples of the worst of the careful but uneven prose in which
Raymond Chandler wrote the original thriller.' Nevertheless, in all other
aspects, 'it handles Chandler's extremely cineadaptable story so well
that, if anything, it improves it in the retelling.' *Variety* was more
enthusiastic, describing the film as being 'as smart as it is gripping' on 14
March 1945. 'Ace direction and fine camera-work combine with a neat
story and top performances. It should pay off plenty.' The review
conceded, 'Plot clarification may not stand up under clinical study . . .
But interest never flags, and the mystery is never really cleaned up until
the punchy closing.' In addition, 'Dick Powell is a surprise as the
hard-boiled copper. The portrayal is potent and convincing.'

Writing in the *New York Times*, Bosley Crowther made an
observation not dissimilar to that which would be made by Parisian
critics around eighteen months later. 'Murder and assorted violence
continue to be the order of the day at the Palace, where a superior piece

of tough melodrama called *Murder, My Sweet* arrived yesterday,' he wrote on 9 March 1945, noting that the film had followed *The Woman in the Window* (Fritz Lang, 1944) which had itself followed the noir melodrama *Experiment Perilous* (Jacques Tourneur, 1944). 'Three such hit pictures in a row is enough to turn any respectable theater into a chamber of horrors, so there's no telling what sort of black magic the Palace might come up with next.' Crowther endorsed the star's attempt at reinvention. 'While he may lack the steely coldness and cynicism of a Humphrey Bogart, Mr Powell need not offer any apologies. He has definitely stepped out of the song-and-dance, pretty-boy league with this performance.'

Over in Britain, Chandler fan Dilys Powell begged to differ. 'Some of the poetry (for poetry, I insist, is there) has been lost in the passage from one medium to another,' she wrote in *The Sunday Times* of 15 April 1945. 'But whatever has been subtracted, a brilliantly hard, fast film comes out at the end.' She considered *Farewell, My Lovely* to be 'not the very best of [Chandler's] streamlined thug novels, but good enough to be going on with', and expressed approval of the casting. 'Dick Powell, not until now one of my favourite players, gives us the graduation from constrained watchfulness to blonde trouble with an economy of facial expression which is a delight to follow.' In the *New Statesman*, William Whitebait did not rate the film quite as highly, feeling that it 'belongs in the same class of *Double Indemnity* and *The Glass Key* [Stuart Heisler, 1942], though not quite up to either', in his review of 21 April 1945. 'But there are consolations in excitement – blonde for excitement, brunette for keeps – and the atmosphere of toughness, hard drink, insomnia, sourcracks, incipient murder and fifth degree seems highly stimulating.' Additionally, 'Dick Powell makes a good realistic hero who has to hack his way through a jungle to the solution where Lord Peter Wimsey would stroll across a lawn.'

ASPECTS OF NOIR: 'As for that style which you've been talking about as noir,' said Edward Dmytryk in later years, 'as far as RKO is concerned, I think I had a very definite part in it, I think in a way, we started that style.' While this statement is undeniably self-glorifying, it is not unjustified; of all the majors, RKO is the studio most associated with film noir. Critic Andrew Spicer (whose summary of RKO's significance in his own *Film Noir* book was invaluable in compiling this section) has broken down a number of noir filmographies by studio to establish which was most involved in the movement and RKO comes out well ahead of the others (with the exception of United Artists, which acted as a distributor for independents which were drawn to noir for the same budgetary reasons described below).

Each of the major studios had its own characteristics and its own approach to film noir. MGM's involvement was initially limited owing to studio head Louis B Mayer's hatred of 'fancy photographic effects'; this attitude is apparent in MGM's rather flat version of *The Postman Always Rings Twice* (Tay Garnett, 1946). Likewise, both Paramount and Twentieth Century-Fox tended towards glossier fare and so produced fewer noirs. Paramount, however, had a reputation for innovation and can lay claim to key early noirs such as *This Gun for Hire* (Frank Tuttle, 1942), *Street of Chance* (Jack Hively, 1942 – the first adaptation of Cornell Woolrich) and *Double Indemnity*. Fox's main contribution was to give rise to the 'docu-noir' (see **Force of Evil**). The noir style appealed more to the cost-conscious studios such as Warner Bros., whose noirs were an extension and modification of the studio's existing line of gangster pictures. However, this depends on one's definition of noir, as Warners produced numerous crime films which are excluded in some accounts (certainly the examples covered in this book, *The Maltese Falcon* and *The Big Sleep*, have a relatively traditional visual style). Similarly, many of Universal's were noirish melodramas such as *The Dark Mirror* (Robert Siodmak, 1946) and *Secret beyond the Door* (Fritz Lang, 1948). Columbia was a bandwagon-jumper, starting late but making up for lost time when it realised noir's cost-effectiveness. 'Columbia's noirs specialized in brooding, interior narratives which "outnoired" other studios' product', in Spicer's words, and *Gilda* (Charles Vidor, 1946), *In a Lonely Place* (Nicholas Ray, 1950) and *The Big Heat* are all notably bleak.

Formed from several smaller companies, RKO was always the poorest of the 'Big Five' and the only one to go out of business after divorcement (it was wound up in 1957). It has been suggested that one reason why noir became so influential was that RKO's library, with its large stock of noirs, was sold to General Teleradio in 1955 and the films ran on the company's TV stations many times. Like Warners and Columbia, RKO was drawn towards lower-budget, black-and-white genre-based product but lacked the distinctive style of its rivals and in the 1930s was perceived as producing movies that were rather, well, generic. In 1938 George Schaefer took over as studio head and determined to improve RKO's reputation (he was replaced by Koerner in 1942 – RKO's high turnover of studio heads partly accounts for its struggle to carve out an identity). Central to Schaefer's plan was his signing of Orson Welles, whose infamous *War of the Worlds* broadcast in 1938 had attracted the interest of Hollywood. To secure Welles's services ahead of other studios, Schaefer offered him an unprecedented level of freedom (see **The Lady from Shanghai** for further details).

The result, *Citizen Kane* (1941), saw Welles and cinematographer Gregg Toland make extensive use of deep-focus photography, which combined wide-angle lenses with recent innovations noted under **Stranger on the Third Floor** (faster film stock, superior lens coating and more powerful lighting) to keep as much of the frame in focus as possible. The lighter camera was used to create audacious tracking shots and long takes, and the use of high-contrast lighting, unusual angles and unbalanced compositions came directly from Expressionist cinema, as did the fragmented flashback structure (see **The Killers**). Many of these techniques were not new (other filmmakers had been experimenting with deep-focus), but Welles and Toland developed them and found new ways to apply them. Other techniques had been used in European cinema, but were new to Hollywood. The film was not a box-office success (newspaper magnate William Randolph Hearst, on whom the character of Kane was partly based, took offence and sent out negative publicity) but it fascinated other filmmakers and its techniques were widely absorbed. 'Anybody who says they did not gain from that film is either a damn fool or is not telling the truth,' said *Gun Crazy* and *The Big Combo* director Joseph H Lewis. 'I ran that film fifty times . . . if you want to call that stealing, fine.' Nowhere was the film more influential than at RKO itself, which continued to produce its black-and-white genre-based programmers, but making increasing use of unusual visual and narrative approaches.

As *Stranger on the Third Floor* demonstrates, the studio had produced interesting work in this vein before *Kane* and so Welles and Toland's work can be seen as accelerating an existing tradition. With the appointment of Val Lewton as head of the B-movie unit in 1942, the combination of genre product and unusual photography became part of RKO policy. The unit was set up with a brief to rival Universal's dominance of the horror genre, and, rather than simply copy Universal's monster-dominated output (pointless, since Universal owned the rights to all the best monsters), Lewton decided that his films would exist on the edge of the supernatural, hinting at strange explanations for events but focusing more around dark passions and insane killers. The first three films were directed by Jacques Tourneur (see **Out of the Past**), two of which arguably merit inclusion in the noir canon; *Cat People* (1942) has a femme fatale-like central figure who believes she can turn into a panther, while *The Leopard Man* (1943), based on a Cornell Woolrich story, follows a serial killer who tries to blame his murders on an escaped leopard. The horrors of Lewton's films are psychological and have much in common with the nightmare world of paranoid noir; furthermore, each one displays a uniformly dark, Expressionist aesthetic. For those who worked at Lewton's unit, noir style became the norm. It is easy to see how critic Robert Porfirio arrived at the conclusion that 'RKO developed the quintessential noir style of the 1940s due to a unique synthesising of the expressionistic style of Welles and the moody, Gothic atmosphere of Lewton.'

Dmytryk, who had recently directed a dumb Universal horror called *Captive Wild Woman* (1943) about a scientific experiment to transform an ape into a beautiful woman, was receptive to this style and later claimed credit for *Murder, My Sweet*'s low-key lighting. 'A cameraman contributes what you ask him to,' he said. 'Harry Wild had been doing westerns and B-pictures with pretty flat lighting. I made a low-key cameraman out of him, and after that he did a lot of low-key work.' This is unfair, as Wild had lately lit *Mademoiselle Fifi* (Robert Wise, 1944) for Lewton. Regardless, *Murder, My Sweet* stands out as an early example of RKO applying these techniques to a crime thriller – and an A-picture at that.

The low-key lighting is apparent from the first scene of Marlowe being interrogated, but stranger and more interesting is the transition to the following scene: as Marlowe starts to tell his story, the camera pans left and out of the window, taking us into the city at night. A short montage of similar city shots brings us to Marlowe in his office several days earlier, and we realise that at some point we have been taken back in time – but when did this happen? (The effect is not dissimilar to a transition in *Kane*, when Kane poaches the staff of a rival newspaper.) The confusion of time and space highlights the fact that these events are not occurring within the timeframe of the film, but are presented to us retrospectively by Marlowe. The film is frequently subjective, most notably the black pool which closes over him when he is unconscious and the haze after he is drugged. This is not what an observer would have seen had they been there, nor is it Marlowe's own point of view; it gives the audience its own viewpoint but subjects it to Marlowe's experience. The sequence after he is drugged is also interesting; it initially seems to be a dream sequence, but afterwards when the audience sees Dr Sonderborg they realise that it was Marlowe's distorted impression of what was happening to him. Marlowe's recovery also calls into question the origin of his voice-over, as when he orders himself to walk the audience assumes that he is not saying this to the cops back in the interrogation room. Marlowe has drifted into his own story, confusing time and space for the audience again.

There are further Expressionist influences in the framing of Moose Malloy, who is shot from above when standing with Marlowe (as this makes Marlowe look tiny by comparison) and from below when framed on his own (so as to appear larger), and the mirror shot when Helen enters Marlowe's apartment, in which she manages to push him to both sides of the frame to dominate it herself. In its treatment of Helen, the film eschews the flattering close-ups common to Hollywood style but which were unsuited to the wide-angle lens. In the first shot of Helen, her body describes a line from one corner of the frame to its diagonal opposite and the camera's concentration on her entire figure, rather than just her face, is unmistakably lustful and anti-romantic. Later, her beach house is made into an appropriately ambiguous space by the use of multiple light settings; at the flick of a switch, Helen alters its dimensions. This foreshadows the chaos that will occur there at the end.

'There's no question,' stated Dmytryk, 'that *Murder, My Sweet* started a trend, set a style, that was continued up to the present day.' This claims a little too much credit for the film, but it was undeniably significant in its synthesis of so many of the noir elements that had been present in other films up to that point.

AFTERLIFE: The novel was filmed again in 1975 by Dick Richards as *Farewell, My Lovely* and was generally well received, although in retrospect it has been considered gauche in its deliberate transgression of 1940s taboos and its location of corruption in the female characters. Robert Mitchum played Marlowe for the first time (see **The Big Sleep**) in spite of his advanced age.

AVAILABILITY: *Murder, My Sweet* is presently only available on Region 1 DVD with no extras. The PAL VHS has been deleted but, if you can still find it, it goes under the title of *Farewell, My Lovely* (0555523).

Mildred Pierce (1945)

The second of Hollywood's James M Cain adaptations, *Mildred Pierce* is interesting for several reasons. It was one of the most successful noirs of the 'classical' period and received six Oscar nominations, for Best Picture, Script, Cinematography, Leading Actress (Joan Crawford) and Supporting Actress (Eve Arden and Ann Blyth) – although only Crawford won on the night. It is one of the few noirs directed by Budapest-born Michael Curtiz (1886–1962, real name Manó Kertész Kaminer), an exemplary studio director who was prepared to match his style to any genre, accepted whatever assignment Warner Bros. gave him and never appeared to desire greater control over his projects, ultimately notching up over a hundred Hollywood productions to add to the sixty-plus films he helmed in Europe. This has led to Curtiz being neglected by auteur-centred film criticism – Andrew Sarris dismissed him as an 'amiable craftsman' – yet Curtiz oversaw some of the finest films of the studio era, including noir antecedents such as *20,000 Years in Sing Sing* (1932) and *Angels with Dirty*

Faces (1938), as well as Casablanca (1942). It is also an inversion of Cain's usual femme fatale plots, with a struggling female protagonist (Mildred Pierce) caught between a good man and an 'homme fatal' who is shot in the opening scene, leading to the film being narrated in flashback by Mildred. In turn, the 'homme fatal' has fallen victim to a femme fatale in the form of Mildred's ungrateful daughter Veda. *Released on 20 October, 1945*

Detour (1945)

Black and White – 68 mins

PRC Pictures, Inc. Presents
Detour
Screenplay and Original Story: Martin Goldsmith
Musical Score: Erdody
Direction of Photography: Benjamin H Kline, ASC
Production Manager: Raoul Pagel
Assistant Director: William A Calihan Jr
Art Director: Edward C Jewell
Set Decorator: Glenn P Thompson
Director of Make-up: Bud Westmore
Wardrobe Designer: Mona Barry
Sound Engineer: Max Hutchinson
Dialogue Director: Ben Coleman
Film Editor: George McGuire
Produced by Leon Fromkess
Associate Producer: Martin Mooney
Directed by Edgar G Ulmer

CAST: Tom Neal (*Al Roberts*), Ann Savage (*Vera*) and Claudia Drake (*Sue*), Edmund MacDonald (*Haskell*), Tim Ryan (*Diner Owner*), Esther Howard (*Waitress*), Pat Gleason (*Joe the Trucker*)

SUMMARY: A drifter named Al Roberts gets into an angry altercation with a man in a diner who has put a particular song on the jukebox. Having calmed down, Roberts explains for the viewer that this song was one that his girlfriend Sue used to sing when they performed in a New York club, with Roberts accompanying her on the piano. Sue became frustrated and left for Hollywood; later, Roberts decided to hitch-hike to Los Angeles and join her. Eventually he got a ride with a man named

Haskell who was going all the way to LA, but Haskell died in his sleep while Roberts was taking a turn driving. Reckoning that the police would assume that he had killed Haskell, Roberts hid the body and assumed Haskell's identity for the remainder of the journey. Unfortunately, Roberts then picked up a hitch-hiker himself, Vera, who had met Haskell before. Vera attempted to profit from her knowledge by taking the proceeds when Roberts sold Haskell's car, but then saw an opportunity to collect a substantial inheritance that Haskell was due. Roberts, desperate to drop Haskell's identity and distance himself from the man's death, refused. During a drunken argument, Vera threatened to call the police, shutting herself in her bedroom with the telephone; Roberts pulled on the phone cord to try and break it, but the cord had become wrapped around Vera's neck and strangled her. Roberts fled the city, leaving him as we originally found him, a drifter evading the law. As he walks away from the diner, he says that he knows the police will catch up with him one day; sure enough, a highway patrol car pulls up alongside him.

DIRECTOR: Edgar G Ulmer (1904–72) was born in Olmütz (then in the Austro-Hungarian Empire, now part of the Czech Republic) and worked as a production designer in theatre, moved to Broadway in 1923, then worked at Universal before returning to Germany to work in cinema. His impressive CV from this period includes *People on Sunday* (1929, co-directed with Robert Siodmak and Fred Zinnemann) and set design for *Metropolis* (Fritz Lang, 1927) and *M* (Fritz Lang, 1931). On returning to Universal, he directed the horror *The Black Cat* (1934). Unfortunately, he antagonised the studio's owner Carl Laemmle by having an affair with Shirley Kassler Alexander, whose husband was Laemmle's nephew ('Uncle Carl' was notorious for employing his relatives at the company). Laemmle used his influence to 'grey-list' Ulmer, making it difficult for him to find work (although he was already talked of as difficult to work with, so some may have found his indiscretion a convenient excuse to avoid him). He spent some time in New York making films aimed at ethnic groups, such as the African-American *Moon over Harlem* (1939), the Yiddish *The Light Ahead* (1939) and the self-explanatory *Cossacks in Exile* (1939). In the early 1940s he returned to Hollywood on 'poverty row', making B westerns under the pseudonym of John Warner. He did most of his work at Producers Releasing Corporation (PRC), directing a series of noirs that were probably the studio's most interesting films: *Bluebeard* (1944), *Strange Illusion* (1945, a reworking of *Hamlet*) and *Detour*. The next year Ulmer directed a rare A-feature for United Artists, *The Strange Woman* (1946), but he will be remembered for directing just about every kind of cheap movie there is. He made the noirs *Ruthless* (1948) and *Murder Is My Beat* (1955) and became an early director of sci-fi B-movies, such as *The Man from Planet X* (1951) and *The Amazing Transparent Man* (1960), before moving back to Europe to make the low-budget epic *Journey Beneath the Desert* (1961) and a number of nudist films.

WRITERS: Martin Goldsmith was a New York-based writer of short crime stories. *Detour* (1939) was his first novel, and the screenplay led to further work with PRC and then with superior studios. He was later Oscar-nominated for writing the scenario of RKO's celebrated B noir *The Narrow Margin* (Richard Fleischer, 1952), but eventually quit screenwriting when he moved into political activism.

Making uncredited contributions to the script was Martin Mooney (1896–1967), a prolific writer of hardboiled fiction who had generated stories for movies such as *Mutiny in the Big House* (William Nigh, 1939) and *Millionaires in Prison* (Ray McCarey, 1940). He joined PRC in 1943, and his other films included the comedies *Danger! Women at Work* (Sam Newfield, 1943), the notion of women working apparently being a hilarious one at the time, and *Shake Hands with Murder* (Albert Herman, 1944). His novel *Crime, Inc.* was filmed by Lew Landers in 1945.

DEVELOPMENT: 'At that time I was called "the Capra of PRC",' Ulmer later recalled. '[Leon] Fromkess became head of the studio, and he would listen; when I would say, "Let's make *Bluebeard*," that's what we would make.' Accordingly, it was Ulmer who read *Detour* and suggested it to PRC as his next project. Although the director considered it 'a very bad book', he did see potential in it. 'I was always in love with the idea, and with the main character – a boy who plays piano in Greenwich Village and really wants to be a decent pianist.' He saw Roberts's inability to exist with anybody other than Sue as a '*Blue Angel* kind of thing' and was attracted to the fatalistic aspect of the journey; 'the idea to get involved on that long road of fate – where he's an absolute loser – fascinated me.'

When PRC acquired the rights to *Detour*, Goldsmith was hired to adapt the novel himself, although he had no screenwriting experience. The motivation for this appears to have been speed, as Goldsmith knew the novel better than anybody else. The writer spent a week reading film scripts to see how it was done, then set to work on his own draft, a predictably faithful interpretation with a few added touches (which many have assumed were written in by Ulmer, probably because the director later claimed to have substantially rewritten the script).

Unfortunately, when Ulmer received the screenplay it was 130 pages long and somewhat overburdened with detail. Realising that he had a script for a two-hour movie, Ulmer set about cutting it down with the help of associate producer Martin Mooney; when it was reduced to a satisfactory length, however, the director followed Goldsmith's script closely.

CASTING: *Detour* was the last of four films to pair Tom Neal (1914–72) and Ann Savage (born Bernice Maxine Lyon, 1921), although their working relationship was uneasy due to his unwelcome sexual advances towards her. Without wishing to undermine their fine performances in *Detour*, it must be said that this tension is apparent on-screen.

Neal had acted on Broadway in the 1930s and graduated from Harvard with a law degree in 1938, but moved to Hollywood to seek film work in the 1940s. He made a few notable films, appearing opposite Savage in *Klondike Kate* (William Castle, 1943), *Two-Man Submarine* (Lew Landers, 1944), *The Unwritten Code* (Herman Rotsten, 1944) and *Detour*. He starred in the horror *The Brute Man* (Jean Yarbrough, 1946). In 1951 a romance with the actress Barbara Payton ended very badly, as he became frustrated with her affections wavering between him and fellow actor Franchot Tone; he violently confronted Tone and, as a former member of Northwestern University's boxing team, was capable of inflicting a good deal of damage. Tone received a broken nose, a shattered cheekbone and a brain concussion. Neal found himself ostracised in Hollywood, and gave up acting to become a landscape gardener. In 1965 he received a ten-year jail sentence for involuntary manslaughter after shooting his wife in the head. The prosecution attempted to convict him for murder and apply the death penalty, while Neal (like his *Detour* character) maintained that the killing had been accidental. He served six years, and died within a year of his release.

Savage adopted her stage name while training at Max Reinhardt's acting school in Los Angeles. She acted in films for Columbia in the early 1940s such as *Two Senoritas from Chicago* (Frank Woodruff, 1943) and *Saddles and Sagebrush* (William A Berke, 1943). While *Detour* was her best role to date, it consolidated her typecasting as an abrasive femme fatale, as in the *Double Indemnity* knock-off *Apology for Murder* (Sam Newfield, 1945) and the noir *The Last Crooked Mile* (Philip Ford, 1946). She retired from acting in the early 1950s to travel the world on her husband's money (and why not?), but upon his death in 1969 found herself broke and had to return to work. She made one further acting appearance, in a film called *Fire with Fire* (Duncan Gibbins, 1986).

PRODUCTION: The original press notes for *Detour* belie the film's drastically reduced circumstances; for example, they quote $70,000 as a price put on Goldsmith's script, yet the entire budget (including the novel rights) was just $30,000. Elsewhere, it is claimed, 'For days, [Tom] Neal trudged uncounted miles in the blazing sun, as the cross-country hitch-hiker of the story,' suggesting that this process went on for quite some time. In fact, the entire film was shot in six days, which seems astonishing today but was unremarkable to Ulmer at the time. 'Most of my PRC productions were made in six days,' he later recalled. 'Just try to visualise it – eighty set-ups a day.' This was nothing compared to the westerns Ulmer had worked on for Universal in the silent era, of which he reckoned they made 24 a year. 'Monday and Tuesday, you wrote your script and prepared the production; Wednesday and Thursday, you shot; Friday, you cut; and Saturday, you went to Tijuana, gambling with the old man [Laemmle].' By comparison, production on *Detour* was quite relaxed.

Detour began with a small amount of location shooting on US Highway 101 (including the California drive-in), in the Mojave desert outside Las Vegas. The car carrying the publicity-stills photographer to the location broke down, so the versatile Ulmer obtained a camera and took the stills himself. Ann Savage got separated from the crew on the day she was supposed to film the scene in which Roberts picks up Vera, and was lost in the desert for three hours. Prior to filming, Savage didn't wash her hair for ten days, while Neal avoided shaving for four and, when he got back into the studio, the company shot scenes of him shaving off his stubble for real. Neal also suffered during the scene in which he carried the limp body of Edmund MacDonald down the slope, as the six-foot-two MacDonald weighed around 200 pounds and Neal was struggling under the effects of a wind machine and rain effects.

The other parts of the scene, as Roberts struggles to put the convertible's roof up, were shot back at the PRC studio on Stage 4. The water tank on the lot held five hundred gallons, and was emptied on to Neal four times before the sequence was completed. Most of the rest of the movie was shot in the car, which was filmed in front of a process screen, and on the hotel-room set. During retakes of the strangling scene, Savage lost her voice. On the final day, Ulmer brought his finely honed 'quickie' skills into play to finish off the movie. 'I had a perfect technique worked out,' he later said. He would always ensure that one wall of every set was clear of decoration and painted grey. 'I would shoot my master scene, but left the close-ups for the last day: they would play against that one flat blank wall, and I would say "Look camera left; look camera right." ' Instead of a clapperboard he would place his hand over the camera lens, which not only speeded the process but saved wasting film stock on material that would not be used in the finished movie.

RECEPTION: The film was released on 30 November 1945. 'Based on a novel story idea that could have raised this film out of the run-of-the-mill category,' said *Variety* on 23 January 1946, '*Detour* falls short of being a sleeper because of a flat ending and its low-budgeted production mountings.' However, it was generally regarded as 'OK for the duals' (meaning double bills) and there were many good things to be said for it, such as, 'Ulmer achieves some steadily mounting suspense' and 'Kline contributes some outstanding camera work that helps the flashback routine come off well . . . Erdody's score, revolving around some Chopin themes, aids in backing up the film's grim mood.' However, the paper's contention that it would not be commercially successful was accurate. Like *Stranger on the Third Floor*, it does not appear to have received any press reviews; writing in the 1990s, critic Andrew Britton concluded, 'No-one noticed its existence when it was released.'

ASPECTS OF NOIR: The term 'B-movie' has come to have a different meaning since the 1950s. The B-movie in the proper sense died out with the studio system (see **Background**); the economies of scale which had made the double bill a popular method of exhibition were no longer viable, and the production of quick, cheap supporting features died out. Today 'B-movie' is a more flexible term, taken to simply mean a cheaply made and often genre-based movie, and its roots in a system of double bills featuring primary and secondary attractions are part of the past. The term was always quite flexible; movies intended for B-picture status might be upgraded if they performed well on the first run, and disappointing A-pictures might be trimmed down and used as B-material (as happened to *The Lady from Shanghai*). Most films noirs, in fact, can be classed in a middle tier between 'A' and 'B', identified by Andrew Spicer as the 'programmer' – films that were intended to form part of a package but their position in that package was left open. Their budgets were reasonable but they were not expected to be major attractions. There is no doubt that a film like *Detour*, with its minuscule budget and short running time, was always intended as a B-movie. This was very much the stock in trade of PRC, a studio whose product made Republic (the studio for whom Orson Welles made a version of *Macbeth* on secondhand western sets) look lavish. What's notable about the B-movie in relation to film noir is that the genre worked particularly well with the format – arguably even better than horror or sci-fi, the genres with which B-movies are most closely aligned.

B-movies were heavily dependent on genre. This is best demonstrated by a story about (and often told by) Bryan Foy, head of B-movie production at Warners in the late 1930s and one of many men to adopt the title 'keeper of the Bs'. Foy is said to have worked from a pile of about twenty scripts on his desk, comprising the last twenty movies he had made; he initiated the development of each new project by taking a script off the top and giving it to a writer to rewrite. The writer might alter the genre, location or character types, but ultimately the story and structure were already provided, speeding the process and giving Foy confidence that the finished product would be what he wanted. The new script would then go into production, while a copy was placed on the bottom of Foy's pile. Around a year later the script would have worked its way back to the top of the pile, and would be rewritten again. (Foy claimed to have made the same film eleven times.) Not only is this a microcosmic example of how Hollywood genres work, as the plot and characters would gradually mutate as they were rewritten to accommodate different genres (one imagines that the eleventh version of Foy's legendary script was quite different to the original), but it also offers a simple insight into what was required of B-movies.

Studio films strove to supply a mix of familiar and unfamiliar elements, drawing audiences in with the promise of the familiar but then showing them something new as well, so they wouldn't be bored. A-features tended to rely on stars to provide the familiar, partly because the A-features could afford stars and partly because the films played in cinemas for a percentage of the box-office takings. The studios could best maximise the profitability of an A-feature if it enjoyed a long run in theatres; a movie that was perceived as 'out of the ordinary' had a good chance of doing this. The B-feature was not an attraction in itself, but merely represented added value by its presence on the bill, and so it played in cinemas for a flat fee. The main interest of the B-movie producer was therefore that the exhibitor was supplied with a reliable product, and would keep buying movies from them. Often, the 'poverty row' studios and the B-units of the majors strove to carve out a distinctive identity for themselves, supplying a standardised product that could not be bought anywhere else. With the studio heads and the most powerful producers busy overseeing the A-features, those producing B-movies would often have a free hand and could enjoy working without interference. Ulmer was a director who'd had very bad experiences with studio heads and, although his 'grey-listing' gave him little choice other than to work on B-movies, he professed to be happier working independently. 'It had a nice family feeling,' he later recalled of his time at PRC, 'not too much interference – if there *was* interference, it was only that we had no money, that was all.' As B-movies tended to use formulaic stories in established genres, the area which gave producers and directors the greatest freedom was often visual style – good conditions for the production of noir over other types of film.

The B-movie was drawn to noir for other reasons. The noir was character driven rather than action driven, so time-consuming set pieces were not always necessary. Night shooting was common on B-movies, because tight production schedules resulted in long hours, and priority over the stages and backlots was often given to A-films during the day. As has already been noted, noir's lighting contrasts and visual stylisation partly evolved from wartime budgetary constraints which led to sparsely decorated sets; this was frequently true of B-movies even before the war, and B-unit crews had developed techniques to conceal their limited means (they used the same equipment as the A-feature crews, so they would often have access to the latest lighting and camera technology). Examples of this approach in *Detour* include the early scene in which Roberts walks home from the club with Sue (largely achieved with heavy use of fog effects and lighting), and the scene in which Roberts is admonished by a cop for stopping in the middle of the road (which avoids using much of a backdrop by its combination of darkness and rain). Scripting would often be done very quickly and some scenes might not be shot if the company ran out of time, sometimes resulting in an incoherent finished product; this could ruin a mystery or a romance, but a noir could turn such narrative chaos to its advantage. Furthermore, the use of a flashback structure like *Detour*'s meant that plot holes could be covered by narration (and, in the case of *Detour*, gaps in the plot might support the notion, postulated by many critics, that Roberts is an unreliable narrator).

Even those aspects of the cheap B-movie which could not be concealed by noir's visual and narrative tricks could still contribute to an ultimately successful product. Today the viewer can recognise *Detour* as a road movie; a genre which only really emerged in the post-war era, and this recognition is likely to be filtered through the notable road movies that have followed it. Road movies tend to feature some attempt to claim the freedom promised by the road. Long shots emphasise the landscape and place the travellers in context; a variety of locations emphasise the distance travelled and the story will be characterised by encounters with interesting people and/or places. *Bonnie and Clyde* (Arthur Penn, 1967), *Vanishing Point* (Richard Sarafian, 1971) and *Thelma and Louise* (Ridley Scott, 1991) all conform to a pattern in which the journey ends when the film ends and the protagonists, prevented from moving, die (see **Gun Crazy**). While *Detour* had the means for some location filming, there was no time for expansive landscape shots or journeys to different places, and the cast was too small for many incidental characters. The car is mainly shot in front of a process screen, with a loop of the desert running behind.

The effect of these restrictions on *Detour* is that the film does not depict the road as a place of freedom, despite Roberts's intent to leave

behind his unsatisfactory life in New York and join his girlfriend's bid
for stardom in Hollywood. His journey is interminable from the very
start, with the road never seeming like anything other than an obstacle
which Roberts cannot quite overcome. Because the movie is largely shot
in small spaces, Roberts restricts his own perception to a small space,
thinking only of his destination and never enjoying the road for its own
sake. The sparseness of the New York scenes and the blandness of the
process-screen scenery mitigate against any place having an individual
character and, because everywhere seems like everywhere else, the
journey becomes meaningless. When Roberts finally gets on the right
track, the death of Haskell and his reaction to it send him into an endless
detour, and the one person he meets along the way merely deflects him
further from his intended path. The result is that his arrival in Los
Angeles does not feel like an arrival at all – 'It struck me that, far from
being at the end of the trip, there was a greater distance between Sue and
me than before I started out' – and indeed it turns out to be just another
stop on his endless journey. The road seems open, but somehow Roberts
has become trapped on it just as Haskell and Vera seemed to be (the
former is depicted as a feckless wanderer who ran away from his family,
while the latter shows no interest in where her hitch-hiking takes her). It
is this that makes Roberts a true noir protagonist, as he is oppressed by a
sense of claustrophobia that seems to have no logical point of origin.

Meanwhile, the artificial look of much of the film collaborates with
the defensive nature of Roberts's narration to highlight the idea that he
is an unreliable narrator. If the film looks uneasy and contrived, this can
be ascribed to the nature of Roberts's story. The ending is interesting to
consider in this light; it is a Production Code-fulfilling coda, showing
Roberts paying for his crime, but the narration gives it an abstract
quality. The narration is located in the present, and Roberts is talking
about his arrest as something he expects to happen, so the final scene
must take place in the future; accordingly, it feels more like a depiction
of Roberts's conjecture, just as most of what we've been watching was a
depiction of his story – and if we can view him as an unreliable narrator
then we can certainly view his prediction as nothing more than a
possible ending. One can equally imagine Roberts continuing to live on
the road in perpetual fear of this final event which he can visualise so
clearly.

It would be inaccurate to suggest that all B-movie noirs thrived on low
budgets; if handled by less perceptive talents, a small budget can just as
easily result in a stagey, underdeveloped film. It is also true that these
effects were not always intended, and the viewer may have to find their
own way of watching the movie that accommodates faults and converts
them into virtues. However, the stylised nature of film noir allows for

this kind of flexibility, and in the case of a film like *Detour* the low production values can create their own meaning.

AFTERLIFE: Ulmer remembered *Detour* as a favourite among his own films, alongside *The Black Cat* and *The Naked Dawn* (1955). In 1992 it was selected for preservation by the Library of Congress National Film Registry, the first 'poverty row' production to be so honoured. In the same year a highly faithful (and equally cheap) remake was directed by eccentric sci-fi archivist Wade Williams, sticking to the original script and reinstating some material which Ulmer's tight shooting schedule had not permitted. The most peculiar thing about this version of *Detour* was that Tom Neal Jr reprised his late father's role.

AVAILABILITY: Most DVD editions of *Detour* are no longer available. The easiest to find at the time of writing is in the Region 0 *Film Noir Thrillers* box set (SIRE1002), alongside *D.O.A.* (Rudolph Maté, 1950) and *The Fast and the Furious* (John Ireland and Edward Sampson, 1954). The disc has been transferred from a poor print and looks pretty nasty, with lots of dirt, 'sparkle', scratches, missing frames, picture jumps and gaps in the sound evident, but it is better than the film not being available at all.

Gilda (1946)

One of the most remarkable explorations of male–female relationships in the noir canon, Charles Vidor's *Gilda* is uncomfortable to watch. Its three characters are Ballin Mundson (George McCready), who owns a casino in Buenos Aires and whom it eventually transpires has collaborated with Nazi businessmen to protect their interests, Johnny Farrell (Glenn Ford), a gambler who comes to work at the casino, and Mundson's wife Gilda (Rita Hayworth), who knew Johnny back in America. The two men both attempt to possess Gilda, applying increasingly harsh restrictions on her, and although Johnny emerges as the nominal hero he has behaved quite appallingly and been closely identified with Mundson, the nominal villain. Whether it is a misogynist film or a film about misogyny is open to debate (see Double Indemnity), but it is notable that the film explicitly absolves Gilda of her supposed crimes, indicating that all along she was trustworthy and not destructive. Yet her acceptance of Johnny at the end is unconvincing and, although clearly added only to provide a happy ending, it does make the film more problematic. Amazingly it was a box-office hit and encouraged Columbia to make more noirs. *Released on 15 March 1946*

The Postman Always Rings Twice (1946)

With Paramount having got a version of *Double Indemnity* past the Production Code, MGM finally felt able to press ahead with its adaptation of James M Cain's bestseller *The Postman Always Rings Twice* – a book which it had optioned back in 1934 – in which drifter Frank Chambers is goaded by his lover Cora Papadakis to murder her husband and make it look like an accident. The director was Tay Garnett, responsible for a number of box-office hits – few of which have stood the test of time. 'It was a real chore to do *Postman* under the Hays Office,' commented Garnett, 'but I think I got the sex across.' Although the novel of *Postman* is somewhat lustier than that of *Double Indemnity*, saddling Garnett and writers Harry Ruskin and Niven Busch with a more difficult task, their work is nowhere near as effective as Chandler and Wilder's. Stars John Garfield and Lana Turner deserved better. Although Cain wrote *Double Indemnity* to cash in on the success of *Postman*, the film adaptations give the reverse impression. Nevertheless, *Postman* was by far the most commercially successful noir of the classical period. *Released on 2 May 1946*

The Big Sleep (1946)

Black and White – 114 mins

A Howard Hawks Production
A Warner Bros.–First National Picture
The Big Sleep
Screenplay by William Faulkner, Leigh Brackett and Jules Furthman
From the novel by Raymond Chandler
Director of Photography: Sid Hickox, ASC
Film Editor: Christian Nyby
Special Effects by E Roy Davidson and Warren E Lynch, ASC
Art Director: Carl Jules Weyl
Sound by Robert B Lee
Set Decorations by Fred M MacLean
Wardrobe by Leah Rhodes
Make-up Artist: Perc Westmore
Musical Director: Leo F Forbstein
Music by Max Steiner
Directed by Howard Hawks

FILM NOIR The Big Sleep

CAST: Humphrey Bogart (*Philip Marlowe*), Lauren Bacall (*Vivian Rutledge*) with John Ridgely (*Eddie Mars*), Martha Vickers (*Carmen Sternwood*), Dorothy Malone (*Bookshop Owner*), Peggy Knudsen (*Mona Mars*), Regis Toomey (*Bernie Ohls*), Charles Waldron (*General Sternwood*), Charles D Brown (*Norris*), Bob Steele (*Canino*), Elisha Cook Jr (*Harry Jones*), Louis Jean Heydt (*Joe Brody*)

SUMMARY: Philip Marlowe is hired by wealthy General Sternwood to investigate a man named Geiger, who claims that Sternwood's daughter Carmen owes on gambling debts. The General believes that the debts are not real, and that this is a cover for blackmail. The other daughter, Vivian, thinks that Marlowe has been hired to look for Sean Regan, a man who worked for the General but disappeared suddenly. Vivian discourages Marlowe from the case. Marlowe goes to a bookstore owned by Geiger and tails the man to a house, where he finds Carmen's car parked outside and waits for one of them to emerge. Instead, he hears a shot and a man escaping the house. Marlowe enters to find Carmen intoxicated in a chair and Geiger dead at her feet. Marlowe takes Carmen home, then hears that the family's chauffeur Owen Taylor has drowned. The next morning Carmen is blackmailed by someone who has a photo of her at the murder scene. Marlowe meets gangster Eddie Mars, who owns Geiger's house. The new blackmail attempt is the work of Joe Brody, but he is killed by Carol Lundgren, who worked for Geiger and thinks Brody did the murder. However, Marlowe realises that Taylor killed Geiger and Brody stole the photo from him. Marlowe gets back the pictures of Carmen, and the Sternwoods consider the matter settled. However, Marlowe is intrigued by Regan. It is widely thought that Regan ran off with Mars's wife Mona, but Brody's girl Agnes knows where Mona Mars is. Agnes contacts Marlowe via her friend Harry Jones; Mars sends his henchman Canino to kill Jones and Marlowe has to get the information direct from Agnes. He drives out of town and finds the garage where Mona Mars is, but Canino is also inside and knocks Marlowe out. While Canino is away at a telephone asking Eddie Mars how to proceed, Vivian appears and frees Marlowe. Marlowe kills Canino and then heads for Geiger's house with Vivian. It transpires that Carmen killed Regan, and Vivian asked for Mars's help in concealing this by making it look as if Regan had run away with Mona. However, Mars intends to blackmail Vivian over this when she inherits her father's money. The reason he had the gambling debts sent to the General was to see whether the old man knew about Carmen, but, from his reaction, they realised that he didn't and so couldn't be blackmailed. Marlowe phones Mars and they agree to meet at Geiger's house, but Mars doesn't know that Marlowe is already there. When Marlowe fires off a shot inside the house, Mars's goons assume that Mars has been ambushed. Marlowe hounds Mars out of the door to be shot by his own men, who assume he is Marlowe.

DIRECTOR: Howard Hawks (1896–1977), a trained pilot and holder of a degree in mechanical engineering from Cornell University, gained experience at Famous Players-Lasky's props department during his summer breaks. After a spell designing and testing aircraft, he eventually returned to the company as a scriptwriter. As an irresponsible gambler and womaniser, but reliable filmmaker, he fitted into Hollywood easily. In the late 1920s he moved into directing, overseeing *A Girl in Every Port* (1928) and *The Criminal Code* (1930) before finding great success with *Scarface* (1932). He felt his greatest talent lay in screwball comedies, as *Bringing Up Baby* (1938) and *His Girl Friday* (1940) attest, although at the time of *The Big Sleep* he had just completed a Hemingway adaptation, *To Have and Have Not* (1944), which was part of a picture-by-picture contract with Warners. Having worked as an independent for much of the studio era, Hawks easily adjusted to the break-up of the system and continued to make hits. His films after *The Big Sleep* include *Red River* (1948), *I Was a Male War Bride* (1949), *Gentlemen Prefer Blondes* (1953), *Rio Bravo* (1959), *Hatari!* (1962), a huge hit in Japan, and *El Dorado* (1967). The Academy realised its oversight in never having nominated him for an Oscar, and presented him with an honorary award in 1975.

WRITER: Raymond Chandler's work on *Double Indemnity* and the success of *Murder, My Sweet* turned his career around; his novels were selling again and he signed a lucrative Paramount contract. He slipped back into alcoholism and had a hellish time writing the script for *The Blue Dahlia* (George Marshall, 1946); a doctor was on standby to give him glucose injections because he had forsaken food entirely for alcohol. Although his antipathy towards Hollywood deepened, he enjoyed consulting on *The Big Sleep*. He adapted his own work for the first and only time as *The Lady in the Lake* (Robert Montgomery, 1947). Between two further novels, *The Little Sister* (1948) and *The Long Goodbye* (1953), he adapted Patricia Highsmith's *Strangers on a Train* (1951), and referred to director Alfred Hitchcock as 'that fat bastard' within his earshot. *The Long Goodbye* was a critical and commercial success, but Chandler became depressed after the death of his wife in 1954 and completed only one further novel, *Playback* (1958), prior to his own alcohol-assisted death in 1959.

William Faulkner (1897–1962), born in Mississippi, was working as a journalist in New Orleans when he wrote his first novel, *Soldier's Pay*

(1926), and he became the most notable chronicler of the decline of the great families of the South. He aimed for and reached a mass audience with *Sanctuary* (1931), and started working at MGM in the early 1930s. Scripts that he drafted during this time include *Today We Live* (Howard Hawks, 1933), based on Faulkner's own story *Turn About*, *The Road to Glory* (Howard Hawks, 1936) and *Gunga Din* (George Stevens, 1939). In the 1940s all of his novels dropped out of print and in 1943 he was forced to beg Warner Bros. for a job on junior writer's pay ($300 per week). Jack Warner cared little for literary reputations but came to admire Faulkner's work, which included the adaptation of *To Have and Have Not*. Among the films to which he made uncredited contributions was *Mildred Pierce* (Michael Curtiz, 1945). His career eventually regained its impetus and he was awarded the Nobel Prize in 1949.

Leigh Brackett (1915–78), a prose writer, had only very recently started working in movies with *The Vampire's Ghost* (Lesley Selander, 1945), which led to a B-picture for Columbia, *Crime Doctor's Manhunt* (William Castle, 1946). The call from Hawks, on the strength of her hardboiled novel *No Good from a Corpse* (1944), came as a complete surprise. 'Hawks read the book and liked it,' Brackett later said. 'He didn't buy the book, for which I can't say I blame him, but he liked the dialogue and I was put under contract to him.' Hawks admired her work on the film. 'She wrote that like a man,' he said later, which appears to have been his highest form of praise. 'She writes good.' Brackett was engaged on Hawks's *Rio Bravo* and *El Dorado*, wrote extensively for television and returned to Marlowe by scripting *The Long Goodbye* (Robert Altman, 1973). She was also one of the first crop of pulp science-fiction authors, contributing to *Planet Stories* magazine (her awesome-sounding stories included *Queen of the Martian Catacombs* and *Black Amazon of Mars*) and publishing novels including *The Long Tomorrow* (1955) and *Alpha Centauri – Or Die!* (1963). This led to her final assignment, the first draft of *The Empire Strikes Back* (Irvin Kershner, 1980).

Jules Furthman (1888–1966) had thirty years' screenwriting experience. He began as a journalist, sold his first scenarios in 1915 and soon moved up to writing scripts. In the early 1920s he directed three films, but was most valued as a screenwriter with credits such as *Mutiny on the Bounty* (Frank Lloyd, 1935). He worked for Josef von Sternberg eight times (including 1930's *Morocco* and 1932's *Shanghai Express*), and *The Big Sleep* was his fifth script for Hawks, who regarded him as 'damned good' and on a par with Faulkner and Hemingway. His other Hawks movies were *Come and Get It* (1936), *Only Angels Have Wings* (1939), *The Outlaw* (1943) and *To Have and Have Not*, and there was one more to follow – *Rio Bravo*.

DEVELOPMENT: In the autumn of 1944 Howard Hawks's intention had been to film a version of the play *Dark Eyes*, but Warner Bros. had other ideas. Following a preview of *To Have and Have Not*, Jack Warner told Hawks that he was impressed with the audience response to the Bogart–Bacall pairing. 'We ought to have another picture with those two,' Warner said. Hawks agreed, and Warner asked if he knew of any suitable material (there was no obvious part in *Dark Eyes* for Bacall). 'Yes,' replied Hawks. 'A little like *The Maltese Falcon*.' Warner asked, 'Will you make it?' Hawks agreed. (This, at any rate, is Hawks's version of the story. Other sources suggest that he was reluctant to make the film but it was in his interest to do as he was told, as his contract with Warners was all that prevented the IRS from repossessing his house.) Hawks later claimed that he purchased the screen rights to *The Big Sleep* 'the next day', but he had been negotiating over these rights for some time; there is also a story that he told Jack Warner he would need $50,000 to buy the rights, then made a deal with Chandler for $5,000 and kept the other $45,000 for himself. Other, more likely, sources state that Chandler received $10,000 for the rights.

Hawks engaged Faulkner and Brackett to work on the script in September 1944. Brackett was alarmed when she was told who she'd be writing alongside. 'I had been writing pulp stories for about three years, and here is William Faulkner, who was one of the great literary lights of the day, and how am I going to work with him? What have I got to offer, as it were?' In the event it was simple. Faulkner simply told her, 'I have worked out what we're going to do. We will do alternate sections. I will do these chapters and you will do those chapters.' Hawks had already stressed that the process did not need to be complicated. 'Don't monkey around with the book – just make a script out of it. The writing is too good.' The shooting draft was completed in eight days. 'I never saw what [Faulkner] did and he never saw what I did,' noted Brackett. 'We just turned our stuff in to Hawks.' Hawks liked to keep the script evolving via feedback from the cast and crew. 'He went into production with a "temporary",' said Brackett. 'He liked to get a scene going and let it run. He eventually wound up with far [more] story left than he had time to do on film.' Faulkner and Brackett remained on-set throughout to keep track of a script which gradually swelled into a dog-eared stack of annotated and overwritten pages. As the production became delayed after Christmas the team took the opportunity to trim it back, with Faulkner making cuts and smoothing over the cracks, Brackett rewriting Faulkner's scenes and then passing them to Hawks.

In December Faulkner had to return home to Mississippi, and mailed his final redrafted and additional scenes from the train (a sarcastic covering note pointed out that he was technically not being paid for these). Jules Furthman was brought on board in his place. With three-quarters of the film already shot, Hawks tried to write a final cut-down draft with Brackett and Furthman, and in frustration slashed twelve pages from the script. 'It was the sort of thing Howard would do, like a spoiled child,' his secretary Meta Wilde later commented. 'A sort of gut reaction: "To hell with it. Here goes. Twelve pages. That what you want? Okay!" ' Furthman constructed a workable ending from what was left. Shortening and cutting made the plot increasingly difficult to follow. 'I think everybody got confused,' noted Brackett. 'It's a confusing book if you sit down and tear it apart. When you read it from page to page, it moves so beautifully that you don't care.' One day Bogart asked her whether Owen Taylor, the chauffeur, was supposed to have been murdered or killed himself – the question arising because, if he *was* murdered, it wasn't clear who the killer was. She didn't know, so she asked Faulkner, who gave the same response. An equally stumped Hawks posed the question to Chandler via a telegram. 'Dammit, I didn't know either,' Chandler said later. When Jack Warner heard of this, he criticised Hawks for spending 75 cents on the telegram.

Remarkably the film remained quite faithful to Chandler's novel, which Brackett stressed was their 'bible': indeed, some parts towards the end are closer to the novel than the shooting script, as though constructed directly from the text. Vivian's presence was increased and she became Marlowe's love interest, which she is not in the novel, and some Marlowe/Vivian scenes are entirely new, although often serving the same function as scenes from the book. Although this was considered necessary in order to sell the film on the Bogart–Bacall pairing, it also performs a useful plot function by giving Marlowe a confidante to whom he can express aspects of the case which, in the novel, he keeps to himself. Regan is no longer Vivian's ex-husband, but an employee of General Sternwood. The ending is very different: in the novel Marlowe gets proof of Carmen's guilt when she tries to kill him too. He tells Vivian to get her out of the city, and says that he will 'deal' with Mars, although there is no suggestion that this will be a violent resolution. The film's version is more conclusive, but makes Marlowe more callous. There were also censorship cuts (see **ASPECTS OF NOIR**).

CASTING: Humphrey Bogart's career hit its stride with *The Maltese Falcon*. His next picture, *All Through the Night* (Vincent Sherman, 1942) was upgraded from B-movie to A-feature. Soon afterwards he was cast in *Casablanca* (Michael Curtiz, 1942), which gave Bogart his first Oscar nomination and installed him as Warners' biggest star. He was cast in *To Have and Have Not* alongside Hawks's new discovery from New York, Lauren Bacall (born Betty Joan Perske, 1924). Bacall came from a middle-class Jewish family; when her parents divorced she adopted her mother's name, Bacal. She studied at the American Academy of Dramatic Arts and found work as a model, adding the second 'l' to her name. Nancy Gross 'Slim' Hawks saw Bacall on the cover of *Harper's Bazaar* and recommended her to Howard; Bacall subsequently based her screen persona on Nancy. Bacall's chemistry with Bogart was plainly evident in *To Have and Have Not*: hence, *The Big Sleep*.

By the time the film was released, Bogart and Bacall were married. However, Bacall's career had stuttered (see **PRODUCTION**) and would never quite recover. She and Bogart cameoed as themselves in *Two Guys from Milwaukee* (David Butler, 1946), but their next vehicle *Dark Passage* (Delmar Daves, 1947) was poorly received, and although their final film together, *Key Largo* (John Huston, 1948), performed better, it did little for Bacall's career. Mired in disagreements with Warners over her roles, she took time out to have children. She fared better in the 1950s with *How to Marry a Millionaire* (Jean Negulesco, 1953) and *Written on the Wind* (Douglas Sirk, 1956) among others. However, she was often occupied by caring for her ailing husband.

Bogart's stardom remained solid in spite of his anti-HUAC stance. He made further noirs, *Conflict* (Curtis Bernhardt, 1945), *Dead Reckoning* (John Cromwell, 1947), *In a Lonely Place* (Nicholas Ray, 1950) and *The Enforcer* (Bretaigne Windust, 1951), as well as the acclaimed *The Treasure of the Sierra Madre* (John Huston, 1948), *The Caine Mutiny* (Edward Dmytryk, 1954) and *Sabrina* (Billy Wilder, 1954). He finally won an Oscar for *The African Queen* (John Huston, 1951). His last two films were *The Desperate Hours* (William Wyler, 1955) and *The Harder They Fall* (Mark Robson, 1956) before his death from cancer of the oesophagus in 1957. Bacall had been due to star alongside Bogart again, but instead scaled back her career, mixing occasional pictures with stage acting. Notable roles included *The Shootist* (Don Siegel, 1976) and *The Fan* (Edward Bianchi, 1981); she later made two movies alongside Nicole Kidman, *Dogville* (Lars Von Trier, 2003) and *Birth* (Jonathan Glazer, 2004).

Elisha Cook Jr had previously worked with Bogart on *The Maltese Falcon*. He always remained a supporting player, albeit one of the most recognisable in Hollywood, and few actors can rival his noir CV. He was in another of the earliest noirs, *I Wake Up Screaming* (Bruce Humberstone, 1941) and two key B noirs, *Phantom Lady* (Robert Siodmak, 1944) and *Dillinger* (Max Nosseck, 1945). Others include *Dark Waters* (André de Toth, 1944), *Blonde Alibi* (Will Jason, 1946), *Two Smart People* (Jules Dassin, 1946) and *The Killing*, under the entry for which this list continues.

PRODUCTION: *The Big Sleep* began shooting on 10 October 1944 with the scene of Marlowe entering the Sternwood mansion. In accordance with Hawks's desire to let a film develop organically, he shot his scenes as close as possible to chronological order. This was the first time Bacall had seen Bogart in weeks; the relationship they had begun during *To Have and Have Not* was put on hold while Bogart attempted to save his marriage to actor Mayo Methot. 'I said I'd respect his decision,' said Bacall later, 'but I didn't have to like it.' A week later, Warners formally announced Bogart's separation from Methot; less than two weeks after that, the couple got back together. *The Big Sleep* hastened the demise of their marriage, as Mayo was well aware of her husband's affection for his co-star; in turn, the breakdown of their marriage had an adverse effect on *The Big Sleep*.

Initially production went well. Bogart's domestic problems and drinking did not impact on the set, and he would arrive on time at nine o'clock fully prepared. Observers noted that he seemed to have the ability to learn his lines very quickly. 'On a Hawks film nobody gets their pages until five minutes before they're going to shoot,' said Brackett, recalling that Bogart would spend a few minutes in a corner studying his pages, then, when it came to shooting, 'he'd have it right down, every bit of timing, and he'd go through about fourteen takes waiting for the other people to catch up to him.' Hawks could afford to work loosely as he had kept the budget low. 'I had a deal with Warners whereby the cheaper I made it, the more money I was going to make.' He spoke to the head of the production department and told him, 'Look, I want to make some money. Anything you say goes.' They saved on apartment sets by shooting in an office building; location work scheduled for San Pedro was carried out in a tank at the studio. Accordingly, the budget came in well below that of *To Have and Have Not*.

Shortly before the film's release in 1946, Chandler wrote to his British publisher, 'The girl who played the nymphy sister was so good she shattered Miss Bacall completely. So they cut the picture in such a way that all her best scenes were left out except one.' Certainly a number of Vickers's scenes didn't make the finished film, although in some cases this may have been for reasons of decency more than anything else; during one scene she had been instructed by Hawks to simulate an orgasm. The innocent and virginal Vickers had no idea what he meant, and Hawks had no idea how to explain it. Regis Toomey volunteered to speak to her. 'Do you know what an orgasm is?' he asked. 'Mr Hawks wants you to be having an orgasm here.' Vickers replied that she didn't know. Toomey explained it, and Vickers returned to do the scene. 'She got the idea all right,' said Toomey. 'Howard liked the scene very much. "Reg," he said, 'if I ever have to explain an orgasm again, I'll have you come and do it." ' What is certainly true is that Hawks had too much footage and Vickers was a lower priority than Bacall, so her scenes may have been first to go.

As production entered November it was already slightly behind. A flu virus put Hawks and actor John Ridgely out of action for days. (Warners had staff director Peter Godfrey on standby if Hawks did not recover in time.) Bacall came down with laryngitis. The backlot sets were soaked with rain and needed time to dry. Finally, on 24 November Bogart arrived on the set over an hour late; unit manager Eric Stacey noted in his daily report that the actor had 'overslept'. In fact, Bogart's domestic problems were making him stressed and tired, and his drinking *was* now affecting his work. A little over a week later it was announced that Bogart and Methot were separated for good, but Bogart remained depressed and continued to arrive late for work. On 20 December Stacey made a note that 'It was necessary for Mr Hawks to speak to Mr Bogart for a half hour and straighten him out relative to the "Bacall" situation, which is affecting their performances in the picture.' The next day Hawks stopped shooting to perform some editing work and speak to his stars; he felt Bogart was losing focus, while Bacall's newfound stardom caused her to seek more influence. Meanwhile, Jack Warner put pressure on Hawks to finish the movie.

Shooting closed down for Christmas on 23 December, and Bogart spent the whole of Christmas Day (his birthday) alone in a hotel room drinking heavily. He didn't turn up for work on 26 December. Stacey found him at Methot's house, in no state to work. Hawks, trying to work without Bogart on a script in which every scene featured Marlowe, eventually sent everybody home. On 27 December no work was done on the film at all, 'account illness of Mr Bogart', according to Stacey's report. Warner was furious, and had the studio's accountants start adding up the losses in case he decided to charge them to Bogart. However, production manager Tenny Wright came to Bogart's defence, noting how professional he had been in the past and pointing out that other factors had hampered the film's progress far more seriously. Bogart confirmed this by returning on 28 December and continuing to work to his previous high standard. Hawks had been able to use the time to work on the script (see **DEVELOPMENT**), and shooting finally wrapped on 12 January 1945, 34 days behind schedule. On the last day Bogart shot a special trailer, in which he entered a library and said, 'I'm looking for a mystery yarn – something off the beaten track.' Due to the inexperience of first-time director Arthur Silver (who had previously only *written* trailers), the actor ended up directing this himself.

However, Warners then decided that, rather than playing on Bacall's existing image, as *The Big Sleep* did, it would be best to showcase her 'serious' acting skills first, and so the Graham Greene adaptation *Confidential Agent* (Herman Shumlin, 1945) took *The Big Sleep*'s slot in the schedule (a memo from Warner claimed that 'Bacall [is] about a hundred times better in *Confidential* than she is in *Big Sleep*'). The manoeuvre was a disaster, as *Confidential Agent* bore the brunt of a Bacall backlash. *The Big Sleep* played a few test screenings in 1945, and had been screened for GIs overseas (it was screened in the Philippines on VJ day); this print still exists, but is not the version as released.

A reluctant Hawks, who had broken his ties with Warners and whose working relationship with the leads had deteriorated, was brought back to oversee some reshoots when Warner waved $10,000 under his nose. Bacall's reputation needed to be restored, and Hawks's partner Charlie Feldman suggested to Warner that the film needed 'three or four additional scenes with Bogart of the insolent and provocative nature that she had in *To Have and Have Not*'. Philip Epstein (who was not credited) rewrote some scenes to emphasise the interaction between Marlowe and Vivian, and scripted some new two-hander scenes. (Hawks also did some work on these: 'It was during the racing season at Santa Anita and I had some horses out there, so I made them talk about riding a horse.') The scenes were completed over a six-day shoot starting on 2 January 1946, and the role of Mona Mars in one of these was recast from Pat Clark to Peggy Knudsen. Some scenes were cut to make way for the new material, principally a long and ponderous segment in which Marlowe visited the cops and explained to them who killed who and why; although this made the plot much clearer, it was felt to obstruct the narrative flow.

RECEPTION: The film was premièred on 23 August 1946 and released on 31 August. *Variety*'s reviewer felt that 'Miss Bacall comes through strongly' and showed less concern for narrative coherence than most critics in a review dated 14 August 1946. 'Hawks has given the story a staccato pace in the development, using long stretches of dialogless action and then whipping in fast talk between characters.' In addition, 'Low-key lighting and lensing by Sid Hickox help to further the mood, and other production appurtenances have been well used by Hawks,' and ultimately it was thought to possess 'plenty of boxoffice potential'. This last was borne out when the film grossed around $3 million domestically.

'If somebody had only told us – the scriptwriters, preferably – just what it is that happens in . . . *The Big Sleep*, we might be able to give you a more explicit and favorable report,' wrote Bosley Crowther in the *New York Times* on 24 August 1946. 'But with only the foggiest notion of who does what to whom – and we watched it with closest attention – we must be frankly disappointing about it.' Crowther considered that, 'if you haven't read the original, as we haven't, you are stuck', and he considered this chaotic lack of clarity to be 'a frequent failing in films made from Raymond Chandler's books'. Marlowe was thought to be 'continuously making shrewd deductions which he stubbornly keeps to himself', but, on the plus side, 'Much of the terseness and toughness of Mr. Chandler's style has been caught in the movement and dialogue.' The Bacall backlash continued, however. 'Miss Bacall is a dangerous looking female, but she still hasn't learned to act' – and overall the picture was thought 'likely to leave you confused and dissatisfied'.

Manny Farber, writing in the *New Republic* of 23 September 1946, was dissatisfied for other reasons. '*The Big Sleep* would have been a more effective study of nightmarish existence had the detective been more complicated and had more curiosity been shown about his sweetheart's relation to the crime,' he wrote. 'Though Bogart turns in another jolting performance as well as some good comedy, his detective is a limited dull person, who seems to have little sympathy with the sub-rosa world with which he [is] associated.' However, Farber did effectively identify where the film's noirishness lay. 'There is a fantastic quality to all this excitement due to the apparent lack of integration between crimes, the sudden appearance of bizarre underworld figures and their more sudden startling disappearances into the murky environment.'

The British reviews were broadly positive. 'Film titles become increasingly strange,' noted the *Evening Standard* on 29 September 1946. 'In the old days, the cinema-goer, when confronted with ... *The Private Lives of Henry VIII*, knew exactly where he was.' Not so here, claimed the waggish reviewer. 'Before seeing *The Big Sleep*, I had a feeling that it might tell of the legendary Rip Van Winkle's protracted slumber in the Catskill Mountains. On second thoughts I dismissed the idea.' However, the verdict was favourable. 'If you are not squeamish, and like your loving "tough", here is an exhilarating thriller where action triumphs totally over plot.' *The Times*, meanwhile, considered the film 'intelligent' and reserved particular praise for the performances. 'Miss Lauren Bacall gives an excellent account of this spoilt, arrogant, but not stupid girl,' noted the review in the 30 September 1946 edition, while it enthused, 'Mr Humphrey Bogart is all that could be wished, the general level of performance is high, and one small piece of acting has distinction – that of Mr Elisha Cook as a terrified little hanger-on of mere brutes.'

One man who very much liked it was Raymond Chandler. 'You will realize what can be done with this sort of story by a director with the gift of atmosphere and the requisite touch of hidden sadism,' he excitedly wrote to a friend when he saw the film. He was particularly enthused by Bogart's performance, stating that he 'is so much better than any tough-guy actor that he makes bums of the Ladds and the Powells. As we say here, Bogart can be tough without a gun.' However, the film was too tough for some; it was more violent than the novel (notably, Marlowe's beating was added) and this drew some criticism. James Agee described the film as 'brutal', 'sinister' and 'a new high in viciousness'.

Similar concerns troubled the press in Britain. A review in the 11 October edition of the *Spectator* noted that the gangster films of the 1930s 'could claim to, in addition to the thrills and horrors, a definite moral purpose: the organised hooliganism of the gangster was shown in conflict with the organised order of the community'. The review goes on to identify what may be the chief distinction between such films and the noir movement. 'The second cycle, which was presumably signalled by *The Maltese Falcon*, has developed rapidly a glossy, violent and completely amoral outlook.' While *The Big Sleep* was thought to be 'brilliantly directed and photographed', it and films like it were cited as 'typical of our general malaise, and one begins to wonder whether their complete abandonment of standards would be as acceptable in 1939 as it is today'. The reviewer ended by stating, 'I have to admit that I enjoyed every minute of it, as will most people, I suppose. But that is not necessarily an excuse for its production.'

In 1949 John Houseman wrote an article in *Vogue* claiming that the Marlowe films were amoral, which finally irked Chandler into a response and suggested that there were some aspects of *The Big Sleep* with which he was dissatisfied. 'I'm all for your demand that pictures, even tough pictures, and especially tough pictures, have a moral content,' he wrote in a letter to Houseman, and, while he agreed that there was no such content in the film of *The Big Sleep*, 'I feel a little annoyed with you for not realising that the book had a high moral content.'

ASPECTS OF NOIR: Although *The Big Sleep* is probably the most famous of the films featured in this book, it is also probably the least noirish, certainly in visual terms. In an article discussing how Hawks's established style interacted with the established style of film noir, Michael Walker notes that 'visually, it displays none of the noir stylistic features . . . Even when Marlowe is at the heart of the noir world . . . the typical noir use of chiaroscuro and areas of blackness is conspicuously absent.' The lighting is low-key, but the cinematography does not strive to create striking patterns; it is just a bit dark. Hawks was perhaps the greatest practitioner of classical Hollywood's 'continuity' style, a smooth flow of shots and action in which the camera avoids drawing attention to itself. It is his approach to the narrative, and what had to be left out of it, which is most instrumental in creating a noir world for the film.

The Production Code was introduced in Hollywood in 1930 following pressure from the Legion of Decency, a largely Catholic organisation campaigning against perceived immorality in motion pictures. The major studios recognised that this kind of self-regulation was the only way to stave off the spectre of external regulation, and the Code was drawn up by Will Hays, president of Hollywood's trade association. This contained guidelines on depictions of sex, violence, crime, religion and so on, and films were expected to follow it; of central significance to film noir were its pronouncements against sympathetic portrayals of adultery and criminals, and its credo that crimes could not go unpunished. In 1934 an office was set up, the Production Code Administration, to pass scripts and clamp down on perceived immorality. It was headed by Joseph Breen, described by Andrew Spicer as 'a virulently anti-Semitic conservative who believed he had to defend traditional morality against the commercial greed of a Jewish-dominated mass entertainment industry'. Film noir scholars have cheerfully characterised Breen as an enemy whom film noir eventually overcame, with movies like *Double Indemnity* and *Scarlet Street* (Fritz Lang, 1945) setting precedents which led to the Code's demise. Undesirable as the Code was, however, it forced filmmakers to suggest rather than state and hence the meanings of movies were more likely to be left open to interpretation. This 'resulted in a particular kind of ambiguity and textual uncertainty in movies regulated by the Production Code', as Richard Maltby notes. Noir was already embracing ambiguity through Expressionist and Poetic Realist influences, and the Production Code inadvertently added to this.

In adapting *The Big Sleep*, Hawks and his writing team were faced with a number of details which could not be carried across to the film. In an effort to retain the novel's structure and integrity, however, the scenes in question were altered as little as possible, the censurable elements simply glossed over. In most cases this does not affect the events themselves, but it leaves gaps where motivation and explanation should be. The first example occurs at Geiger's bookstore, which in the novel is explicitly a front for a pornography library. In the film it seems clear that the store conceals something illegal, but the strongest indication of this is the man who shiftily walks past Marlowe and into the room at the back. More significantly, Carol Lundgren kills Brody out of revenge, assuming that Brody killed Geiger. In the film Geiger appears to be nothing more than his boss and Carol's motivation seems a little weak, whereas Chandler makes it clear (in rather disdainful terms) that Geiger was a 'fag' and Carol his lover. Walker suggests that Carol's possession of a key to Geiger's house clearly suggests that they are lovers, but in the accumulation of detail this is likely to be lost on the audience – and the house has already been visited by so many people that another makes little difference. Carol's decision to move Geiger's body to the bed appears similarly obscure.

Overall, there remains a sense that the house conceals some form of deviance, a sense which has existed since Marlowe's discovery of Carmen there (again, there is a peculiar ambiguity here by comparison with the novel, in which Carmen is naked and explicitly on drugs; the film avoids both, but Walker notes that 'the camera pointing at her . . . suggests unspecified depravities'). We never get to see the photo of Carmen, which in the novel depicts her naked; a publicity shot of the character with Geiger dead at her feet was circulated to the press as if it were the blackmail photo, but, as Walker points out, the camera flash was seen before the shot was heard, so Geiger must still have been alive when the photo was taken. Marlowe appears to understand this noir world, but declines to interpret it for us as the Marlowe of the novel does; he is in control and can keep it at arm's length.

The second half of the novel poses no major censorship problems, but Hawks's new ending does. In the final scene, Marlowe questions Mars about the death of Regan but repeatedly interrupts his answers, suggesting a solution but immediately discrediting it by noting that, if Carmen killed Regan and Mars helped her to cover it up, why did he not recognise her when they met at Geiger's house? There are two possible explanations for this: either they pretended not to know each other for Marlowe's benefit (in the novel, Marlowe notices that 'the fear went out of her face' upon seeing Mars) or, since the novel casts Vivian as the one who asked Mars for help (Marlowe's earlier question to Vivian, 'What's Eddie Mars got on you?' clearly follows this line), it is entirely possible that Carmen and Mars really have never met. The fact that Marlowe's rapid-fire dialogue is characteristic of Bogart, and builds tension in this climactic sequence, disguises its true purpose of throwing confusion on events. Marlowe is driving a man to his death so that he can frame him for a murder in which Vivian is implicated. By hurriedly suggesting at this late stage that Mars really was the murderer, even though this goes against the entire plot of the film (it makes nonsense of Geiger's original blackmail attempt, which was a way of seeing whether the General knew about Regan's murder), Hawks raises the suggestion that justice is being done here, and that all the film's crimes will be punished as the Code demands. The movie's final impression is one of deep uncertainty, with the audience likely to be unsure of what they have just witnessed, and it is this repression of detail, rather than any visual stylings, which creates the film's noir world. As Manny Farber noted, the lack of obvious motivation creates a sense of chaos and Hawks's great contribution is to apply his fluid style to make this ride thrilling and unpredictable, rather than frustrating (although some viewers evidently still regarded it as such).

AFTERLIFE: The film was remade in 1977 by Michael Winner under the same title. Made and set in Britain, it is mainly notable for its starry cast: Robert Mitchum plays Marlowe for the second time in the 1970s (see Murder, My Sweet) and support comes from Edward Fox, Joan Collins, John Mills, James Stewart, Oliver Reed and Richard Todd.

AVAILABILITY: The Region 1 DVD is far superior to the Region 2 (D065026) version, as it features both extant versions of the film – the standard release cut and the preview version, featuring eighteen minutes of different footage – and a short documentary highlighting the differences between the two. The Region 2 just has a trailer.

The Killers (1946)

Black and White – 105 mins

Universal-International
Mark Hellinger Productions, Inc. Presents
Ernest Hemingway's *The Killers*
Screenplay by Anthony Veiller
From the Story by Ernest Hemingway
Director of Photography: Woody Bredell, ASC
Assistant to the Producer: Jules Buck
Film Editor: Arthur Hilton
Art Direction: Jack Otterson, Martin Obzina
Set Direction: Russell A Gausman, ER Robinson
Special Photography by DS Horsley, ASC
Director of Sound: Bernard B Brown
Technician: William Hedgcock
Gown Supervision: Vera West
Hair Stylist: Carmen Dirigo
Director of Make-up: Jack P Pierce
Assistant Director: Melville Shyer
'The More I Know of Love', Lyrics: Jack Brooks, Music: Miklos Rozsa
Music: Miklos Rozsa
Produced by Mark Hellinger
Directed by Robert Siodmak

CAST: Burt Lancaster (*Ole 'Swede' Andersen*), Ava Gardner (*Kitty Collins*), Edmond O'Brien (*Jim Reardon*), Albert Dekker (*Big Jim Colfax*), Sam Levene (*Lt Sam Lubinsky*), Vince Barnett (*Charleston*), Virginia Christin (*Lilly Harmon*), Jack Lamber (*'Dum-Dum' Clarke*), Charles D Brown (*Packy Robinson*), Donald MacBride (*RS Kenyon*), Charles McGraw (*Al*), William Conrad (*Max*)

SUMMARY: Two hit-men arrive in the small town of Brentwood and kill a garage attendant known as Pete Lund, or 'Swede'. Insurance investigator Jim Reardon, intrigued by a green handkerchief carried by the Swede, looks into the case. The Swede's real name was Ole Andersen, a former boxer. When an injury to his right hand ended his career, he fell in with criminals in Philadelphia and was sentenced to three years in prison when he took a burglary rap on behalf of his girlfriend, Kitty Collins. Upon his release he was co-opted into a $250,000 payroll heist at a hat factory set up by Kitty's new beau, Jim Colfax, along with 'Dum-Dum' Clarke and Blinky Franklin. Newspaper reports mentioned that one of the gang disguised his face with a green handkerchief, and this is the connection Reardon has been trying to make, as his company had to compensate the factory for this robbery. The crooks' rendezvous point was altered after a fire at the intended meeting-place; Kitty was sent to tell the Swede but claimed to him that he was being double-crossed, causing him to double-cross the others and take the money. He and Kitty made plans to run away with the cash, but Kitty stole it and ran out on him. Reardon discovers that Kitty secretly brought the money back to Colfax, and the whole thing was a set-up to avoid having to share the loot with Blinky and Dum-Dum. When Colfax happened upon the Swede in Brentwood, he sent the killers to execute him, to make sure that Dum-Dum and Blinky didn't discover the truth. However, as Reardon pursues the matter, Dum-Dum kills Blinky and goes after Colfax. They kill each other in a shoot-out and Reardon's evidence convicts Kitty.

DIRECTOR: Robert Siodmak (1900–73) was born in Dresden, Germany, and educated at the University of Marburg. In the mid-1920s he began working for UFA, the German state-funded film company, in a variety of roles including translating intertitles on American silent movies. His first directorial work was *People on Sunday* (1929), co-directed with Edgar G Ulmer and Fred Zinnemann, and which was co-written by Billy Wilder and Siodmak's brother Curt. As UFA's ties to the Third Reich gradually strengthened, the Jewish Siodmak was forced to leave. Like many such filmmakers he first went to Paris, where he made notable proto-noirs including *Hatred* (1938) and *Snares* (1939), before leaving for America. He got a contract at Paramount on the recommendation of Preston Sturges, but was disappointed with his low-grade assignments. Curt had taken a screenwriting job at Universal in 1937 and convinced them to hire his brother. After a few successful B-pictures he made his first noir, *Phantom Lady* (1944).

Few directors belong to noir as much as Siodmak, because he made so many contributions to the movement yet so few Hollywood films outside it. His follow-up *Christmas Holiday* (1944) was another noir, while his next four were noirish melodramas: *The Suspect* (1944), *The Strange Affair of Uncle Harry* (1945), *The Spiral Staircase* (1945) and *The Dark Mirror* (1946). On the strength of *Phantom Lady*, Mark Hellinger hired him for *The Killers*. Siodmak went on to make the docu-noir *Cry of the City* (1948), then repeated elements of *The Killers'* formula in *Criss Cross* (1948). *The File on Thelma Jordan* (1949) was his final noir; after a bad experience making *The Crimson Pirate* (1952), he moved back to Europe. He successfully sued Sam Spiegel for failing to credit his early contributions to the script of *On the Waterfront* (Elia Kazan, 1954). His latterday European films include *The Rough and the Smooth* (1959), *Escape from East Berlin* (1962) and *Custer of the West* (1967).

WRITERS: Ernest Hemingway (1899–1961), the Illinois-born son of a doctor, started a career as a journalist in his teens, taking a break in 1918 to serve with an ambulance unit in Italy, where he was wounded. He returned to journalism, then moved to Paris in the early 1920s and published the collections *Three Stories and Ten Poems* (1923) and *In Our Time* (1925). His second novel *The Sun Also Rises* (1926), capturing post-war disillusionment, established his tough, straightforward style and made him a critical and commercial success. He went on to publish *A Farewell to Arms* (1929), *To Have and Have Not* (1937), *For Whom the Bell Tolls* (1940), the Pulitzer prize-winning *The Old Man and the Sea* (1952) and numerous short stories, including 'The Killers' in 1927. He worked as a war correspondent during W.W.II and won the Nobel prize for literature in 1954. Following illness, he committed suicide with a shotgun in 1961.

Anthony Veiller (1903–65) was born in New York to a writer/director father and an actor mother, and he worked in journalism and theatre before becoming a screenwriter for Paramount with *The Witching Hour* (Henry Hathaway, 1934), which he also produced. He continued to write for cinema to the end of the 1930s, and received an Oscar nomination for *Stage Door* (Gregory La Cava, 1937). In 1940 he turned his attention to producing before being interrupted by W.W.II. During the war he scripted all seven of the *Why We Fight* compilations of documentary footage, and directed the fourth – *The Battle of Britain*

(1943) – himself (usually the direction was by Frank Capra and/or Anatole Litvak). *The Killers* followed his work on *The Stranger* (Orson Welles, 1946); after this he returned to the producer's role, then finally settled into screenwriting in the early 1950s. According to Veiller, most of the script for *The Killers* was actually written by John Huston (see **The Maltese Falcon**).

DEVELOPMENT: *The Killers* was based on Hemingway's 1927 short story of the same name; a hugely influential piece, it is possibly the ultimate example of the minimal, hardboiled crime story. Hemingway had fielded many requests to adapt this story for the screen, and refused them all. In 1945 he received an offer from journalist Mark Hellinger (1903–47). In New York Hellinger had flitted between the worlds of showbusiness and organised crime, spending his days writing a sentimental column of Broadway stories for the *New York Mirror* and his nights drinking with gangsters. A generous and well-liked man, he had written scenarios for movies such as *Broadway Bill* (Frank Capra, 1934) and *The Roaring Twenties* (Raoul Walsh, 1939) and had produced some pictures for Warners, before Universal offered him the chance to operate as an independent producer. Hellinger and Hemingway were well acquainted and the writer agreed to sell him the rights for $36,700.

Hellinger already had ideas on how to expand this 3,000-word short story into a feature film, using it as the basis for an opening sequence and then investigating the events that led up to it. Many years earlier there had been a robbery in Brooklyn which he had considered turning into a movie scenario; even though the crime had been expertly planned and executed, not long afterwards 'fully half the gang had been kicked off and the money had slipped away from the rest of 'em'. The producer's acquaintance with mobsters informed the film – he drew upon tales of Dutch Schultz, who had let slip some sensitive information while rambling on his death-bed. These notes and the original short story were ultimately passed to John Huston, who asked to be uncredited as he was under contract to Warners. On 14 February 1946 Huston gave this to Anthony Veiller to polish, although Veiller later confirmed that the bulk of the shooting script was composed of Huston's material.

As far as the opening sequence goes, the script was possibly Hollywood's closest adaptation from a prose source to date, with much dialogue taken word-for-word from the short story. The material that runs under the title sequence is added, but this involves no extra dialogue. The story opens with the two hit-men entering the diner, and the first lines of dialogue are more or less the same. Language was modified for the film, removing instances of the word 'hell' and unpleasant references to Sam as 'the nigger'. The town's name was changed from Summit to Brentwood for the movie, and in the story the Swede is not going by an assumed name – he's known to everybody as Ole Anderson. Some tightening up has taken place, with a few dialogue exchanges cut (including a conversation in which Max tells George, 'You ought to go to the movies more. The movies are fine for a bright boy like you'), but almost nothing has been added. The film breaks with the story at the point Nick Adams leaves the Swede alone; the Swede's death is not recounted in the story and instead Nick is followed outside, where he encounters the landlady, and then back to the diner, where he has a short conversation with George.

In developing the plot further, the script makes use of what details are given about the Swede in the story. Hemingway's description of the character is limited to 'He had been a heavyweight prizefighter and he was too long for the bed.' The Swede's landlady notes that he's 'an awfully nice man . . . just as gentle', but it is clear that he has got mixed up in something bad; Nick wonders aloud to George what the Swede did and George replies, 'Double-crossed somebody. That's what they kill them for.' One notable difference is that the Swede is said to come from Chicago – in the film this is altered to Philadelphia – but on the whole *The Killers* actually contains more of Hemingway than some films ostensibly based on his novels (such as Howard Hawks's *To Have and Have Not*).

Aspects of the script clashed with the Production Code: the censors noted an 'overemphasis on violence and murder', but the main cause for concern was that there was no flaw in the criminals' plan and that it was shown in detail; theoretically, a viewer might perform a successful heist by following this plan. The criminals had only failed because of their attempts to double-cross each other. However, the script was passed without a great deal of toning down.

CASTING: Burt Lancaster (1913–94) began as a circus acrobat, and during W.W.II was attached to a special unit undertaking duties such as induction and demobilisation and the provision of recreational facilities such as sports and entertainment. Writing, compèring and performing in revues led him to seek acting work upon his return to New York, and it was while in *A Sound of Hunting* (1945) that he was signed by Hal Wallis (former Warners executive producer, then an independent at Paramount). In January 1946 he was given a supporting role in *Desert Fury* (Lewis Allen, 1947). However, the film was not set to shoot until August, and Wallis's assistant Martin Jurow (formerly an assistant to Hellinger at Warners) wanted to do Hellinger a favour – so, with Wallis's approval, Lancaster was loaned out for *The Killers*. This came as a relief to Hellinger, whose insistence on avoiding stars and keeping the film story driven left him in danger of not casting a lead in time. He had wanted to borrow Wayne Morris from Warners, but could not afford the $75,000 the studio demanded and negotiations progressed too slowly; the only alternative was a Universal contract player, Sonny Tufts. Lancaster's take on the situation was that 'I was the cheapest thing in town, so they hired me.' His salary for *The Killers* was $20,000.

The Killers made Lancaster an overnight star. He quickly went independent, becoming a model for actors setting up their own production companies. His other noirs include *Brute Force* (Jules Dassin, 1947), *I Walk Alone* (Byron Haskin, 1947), *Sorry, Wrong Number* (Anatole Litvak, 1948), *Kiss the Blood Off My Hands* (Norman Foster, 1948), *Rope of Sand* (William Dieterle, 1949) and *Sweet Smell of Success* (Alexander Mackendrick, 1957), as well as his reunion with Siodmak to make *Criss Cross*. He directed and starred in *The Kentuckian* (1955). He was Oscar-nominated for *From Here to Eternity* (Fred Zinnemann, 1954), *Birdman of Alcatraz* (John Frankenheimer, 1962) and *Atlantic City* (Louis Malle, 1981) and won for *Elmer Gantry* (Richard Brooks, 1960). He was a notable liberal dissident and in the 1960s made offbeat films such as *The Swimmer* (Frank Perry, 1968). His final film was *Field of Dreams* (Phil Alden Robinson, 1989).

Ava Gardner (1922–90) had no ambition to be an actor, but was signed by MGM in 1941 when a talent scout happened upon a picture of her. The studio paid for acting lessons and trained her to subdue her strong North Carolina accent, after which she was given mainly uncredited bit parts in B-movies. In 1942 she married Mickey Rooney, but they divorced a year later, and at the time of *The Killers* she was better known for this than for any of her film roles. An appearance in the noir *Whistle Stop* (Leonide Moguy, 1946) had brought her to Hellinger's attention and he convinced MGM to loan her out. She was paid $350 per week for *The Killers* and her good reviews prompted MGM to give her higher-profile roles, although not usually in such great films. Between 1951 and 1957 she was married to Frank Sinatra. After an Oscar nomination for *Mogambo* (John Ford, 1953), she was given roles in *The Barefoot Contessa* (Joseph L Mankewicz, 1954) and *The Sun Also Rises* (Henry King, 1957). With her MGM contract finally over in 1958, she made *On the Beach* (Stanley Kramer, 1959) and then moved away from Hollywood, spending much of the 1960s living it up in Europe.

Edmond O'Brien (1915–85), another native New Yorker, was a lead in B-pictures until this role moved him up to the As. An experienced actor who was known for reciting Shakespeare soliloquies as party pieces (on one occasion, at a party for Sam Peckinpah, he performed a scene with Keith Moon), his most notable roles prior to *The Killers* were in *The Hunchback of Notre Dame* (William Dieterle, 1939) and *Winged Victory* (George Cukor, 1944). He is best known for his extraordinary performance in the noir *D.O.A.* (Rudolph Maté, 1950), but also appeared in *The Web* (Michael Gordon, 1947), *A Double Life* (George Cukor, 1947), *White Heat* (Raoul Walsh, 1949), *711 Ocean Drive* (Joseph M Newman, 1950), *The Turning Point* (William Dieterle, 1951) and *The Hitch-Hiker* (Ida Lupino, 1953), and directed two noirs of his own, *Shield for Murder* (1954) and the straggler *Man-Trap* (1961). He later played Winston Smith in *1984* (Michael Anderson, 1955).

Experienced Broadway actor Sam Levene (1905–80, born Samuel Levine) had starred alongside Lancaster in *A Sound of Hunting* and advised him well when the offers came from Hollywood, which perhaps accounts for his appearance here. William Conrad (1920–94), whose first credited role was that of Max, would later become well known to TV audiences for *Cannon* (1971–76), in which he played the eponymous detective, and *Jake and the Fatman* (1987–92), in which he did not play Jake. He also worked as a producer, director and voice-over man (he performed the opening narration on *The Fugitive* and *Buck Rogers in the 25th Century*).

PRODUCTION: Shooting commenced on 30 April 1946, with Siodmak behind the cameras; Hellinger's first choice had been Don Siegel, but he was unable to convince Warners to loan him out (see **AFTERLIFE**). Contemporary interviews see Hellinger extolling the virtues of working as an independent. 'Under the usual studio system, a producer is often handed a story for which he has no personal enthusiasm. He turns it over to a director who grudgingly agrees to "do his best with it".' By contrast, he believed that, 'when the independent field functions correctly, a very happy state exists'.

Hellinger's background in journalism led him to desire a sense of reportage and realism from *The Killers*, and much of the film was shot on location. The payroll heist sequence, achieved in a single take with eighteen camera stops and around sixty changes of focus, was designed to have a 'newsreel' quality, with its inflectionless voice-over. One of the most impressively staged scenes was that of the Swede's last fight, which was staged in front of a 2,000-strong crowd and saw Lancaster play out the scene opposite a real boxer (no doubles were used). Lancaster had spent much time beforehand being coached in his movements by a boxing champion. Gardner was also encouraged to appear more naturalistic; MGM characteristically caked its stars in make-up, but Siodmak instructed that she be made up more lightly for this role, and, unlike any of her MGM appearances, the singing sequence was not overdubbed by somebody else.

Siodmak and Bredell strived to create a 'non-pretty' camera style, which involved discarding close-ups and soft-focus 'glamour' shots of the actors. An article in *American Cinematographer* on this film was one of the first to examine the chiaroscuro lighting effects which partly define film noir. Bredell was asked about his approach, 'a style which he calls out-of-balance lighting, which is characterised by a sharp contrast between crystal white and velvet black. Purposely discarding fill illumination he managed to avoid wishy-washy grey halftones.' Bredell commented, 'The lighting set-ups were kept quite simple. It is a temptation for a cameraman to become spoiled because he is given too much equipment . . . and he feels that he must use all of it.' Hellinger had doubts about some of the more extreme effects, such as the morgue sequence where Reardon and Nick are swamped by the lights in front of them, making it almost impossible to see their faces. (Bredell's aim was to create the impression of a butcher's shop window.) Bredell and Siodmak both stood by the decision and Hellinger relented. Certain members of the cast were also unsure – complaints such as 'The audience can't see my eyes there' and 'One side of my face is dark' were heard when the dailies were run – but they came around to the style eventually. An example of its effectiveness is in the plotting scene, which was lit from high up and no fill was used, meaning that all the light was coming straight down on the actors. The hollows of their eyes were left dark, creating the impression of masks.

Bredell saw his camerawork as an extension of Hellinger's original plans for the film, as it was not driven by stars or spectacle, but by story. 'We had no elaborate sets with which to achieve unusual effects,' he commented. This meant that the crew 'had to get our interesting visual patterns with light and shadow. We tried to use *story* photography rather than stereotyped motion picture or star photography.' One can see what he meant by story driven during the scene of the Swede in jail; in one of the few soft-lit scenes in the film, the lighting does not flatter the actors, but creates a churchlike ambience to suggest the Swede's innocence. 'I hope that not too many people noticed the photography in *The Killers*,' added Bredell, 'because motion picture camerawork is only good when it goes unnoticed.' Siodmak agreed that it was best to keep things simple. 'In modern production it is a temptation to overdo the use of unusual techniques . . . rather than use unmotivated camera movement, we employed a relatively static camera and let our players work toward it.' He was also keen to involve some strongly visual storytelling, noting, 'I am happy if, out of an entire feature, I can place on film 500 feet of pure cinema.'

Lancaster, whose self-assured manner had helped him to win the part, later claimed that he had spent the entire shoot shaking with nerves and was amazed that none of this was visible in the finished film. 'I didn't have to be ostentatious or theatrical, just simple because I was playing this dumb guy,' he later said. 'I was lucky to be given the break in a role that didn't require any histrionics.' Siodmak was forced to shoot up to fifteen takes of some scenes due to Lancaster's hesitance, much to the actor's apologetic embarrassment. Lancaster remembered Siodmak as 'a charming man whose strength was in film noir because of his inventive use of the camera . . . If it went wrong, we just did it again. He didn't make any fuss.' Upon shooting the first scene in which he had to kiss Gardner, Lancaster found himself so 'deeply stirred' that he was unable to continue until Siodmak had cleared the set except for the two actors, the director and the cameraman.

In an unusual move, and one indicative of his confidence in the picture, Hellinger previewed scenes and sequences to the press before the film was completed. Although Hellinger was a relentless self-publicist, it seems clear that he was happy with how the film had turned out. 'We had a good association of creative personalities there – with everyone working together for the good of the picture.'

RECEPTION: There was a degree of concern that Hemingway would be displeased by the extensive reworking of his original story; an internal memo at Universal suggested, 'It might be a very good idea to have Mr Hemingway bumped off before releasing the picture.' The author was given a private screening at his retreat in Sun Valley, Idaho, to which he invited the entire population of the town (around fifty people). To Hellinger's relief, the author wrote back that it was 'the best screen adaptation ever made of any of my work'. The movie was previewed in July to Hellinger's journalist colleagues, who were relieved that they didn't have to pretend to like it; he also held a screening for his gangster friends or 'technical advisors', who were among the most enthusiastic viewers. It was released on 28 August 1946.

For New York Times critic Bosley Crowther, The Killers 'does not enhance the literary distinction of Hemingway's classic bit', as he wrote on 29 August 1946. 'But, as mere movie melodrama, pieced out as a mystery which is patiently unfolded by a sleuthing insurance man, it makes a diverting picture', even if the additional plot 'may not be precisely what Hemingway had in mind'. There was restrained praise for the cast and for Siodmak's direction. 'The tempo is slow and metronomic, which makes for less excitement than suspense.' Variety had been more impressed, feeling that the complex plot was 'all pieced together neatly for sustained drive and mood, finishing with exposé of a colossal double-cross. Every character has its moment to shine and does.' This 7 August 1946 review also noted, 'Performances without exception are top quality even though names have not assured boxoffice. It's a hand-picked cast that troupes to the hilt to make it all believable.'

'Hollywood has so frequently botched a good short story in extending it that this one instance of preserving the quality of the original is most cheering,' declared John McNulty in *The New Yorker* of 7 September 1946. 'From this tense bit Mark Hellinger and Tony Veiller, as producer and screenwriter, have contrived to build a full-length movie which is surely one of the best of the current crop of gangster films.' Similarly, 'Though there is a cheapness about *The Killers* that reminds you of five-and-ten jewelry, its scenes of sadism and menacing action are filled with a vitality all too rare in current movies,' commented Manny Farber in the *New Republic* on 30 September 1946. 'Besides its brutality, it has the noise, the jagged tormenting movement of keyed-up, tough flashy humanity that you get from a walk through Times Square.'

The British reaction was less rapturous. 'This is undoubtedly exciting,' wrote Patrick Kirwan in the *Evening Standard* on 18 November 1946, 'but the flashback manner of the plot's unfolding, and some unintelligibility in the dialogue, do not exactly make for clearness.' Although Kirwan thought that the individual scenes were good, he made the rather startling demand that 'Hollywood should now begin to pay some attention to British requirements. If the dialogue is to be slipshod, ill-delivered . . . then I foresee English captions for Hollywood films in the very near future.'

The American release had caused some controversy, with an article in *PM* magazine by Max Lerner using it as the starting point for a discussion of the harmful effects of screen violence. Campbell Dixon picked up on this debate in his *Daily Telegraph* review. 'Does it mean anything?' he asked of *The Killers* in the 18 November 1946 edition. 'Is it, as Mr Lerner complains, without a lesson? Morally, perhaps, yes. Actually, no.' Dixon's contention was that, while the film had failed to condemn crime, it had effectively warned of the perils of such activities. In other respects, the review was tepid. 'If I am not quite as enthusiastic as the producer about the "sensational discovery", Burt Lancaster, that is not unusual. At least he looks real.' There were a few good notices, however: the 15 November 1946 edition of the *Daily Herald* declared it to be 'played with a grim intensity all round, and . . . a first-class specimen of its kind', although it also warned, 'Don't, on any account, let the children see it. I'm not sure it is suitable for grandma, either.'

With the public, *The Killers* was a huge success. New York's 1,300-capacity Winter Garden Theater sold more than 120,000 tickets in the first two weeks, and ran the movie 24 hours a day to meet the demand. It was Universal-International's second most successful picture of the year. 'Whoever went to the movies with any regularity during

1946 was caught in the midst of Hollywood's profound postwar affection for morbid drama,' noted D Marshman in an article for *Life* the following year. 'Apparently delighted to pay good money for having their pants scared off, moviegoers flocked in record numbers to these spectacles.' Marshman identified the best examples as *The Killers, The Dark Mirror* and *The Spiral Staircase*, and declared Siodmak the master of such stories. *The Killers* was nominated for four Academy Awards – Best Director, Editing, Original Screenplay and Score – but won nothing.

ASPECTS OF NOIR: *The Killers* arguably demonstrates more noir elements than any other film, partly because of the collaboration between Siodmak and Hellinger. Siodmak's run of noirish melodramas leading up to *The Killers* often display Gothic stylings; he said of *The Sprial Staircase* that he and his crew 'tried to create a sort of surrealist film which put the audience into a trance, a state of hypnosis, so that they would accept the unfolding of events without asking themselves questions'. Although the visuals of *The Killers* are less overtly Gothic the influence of his earlier work is still there, for example the Swede's refusal to rise from the darkness in his room when Nick warns him of the killers' arrival. To an extent the Swede is caught in a paranoid nightmare, having been elaborately double-crossed, and his fatalistic attitude reflects his lack of control over events; above all *The Killers* is about fear of the past, an overriding Gothic motif. Hellinger, meanwhile, took a journalistic approach to filmmaking, drawing upon details of real crimes and employing Huston, a former boxer, to write a film about a former boxer. Although this was Hellinger's first film as an independent producer and there were only a few to follow, his work was highly influential (see **Force of Evil**). Several scenes in *The Killers* achieve a verisimilitude unusual in films of the period, particularly the boxing match and the heist sequence. Paradoxically, noir saw a movement towards both greater expressionism and greater realism, and films like *The Killers* demonstrate both simultaneously.

However, what really makes the film so rich in noir elements is the structure. Flashback narratives regularly figure in checklists of key noir elements, and half of the films covered in this book feature non-linear storytelling. *Stranger on the Third Floor* uses flashback in the most conventional way, inserting a few short scenes to supply pertinent information while the rest of the plot progresses chronologically. More specifically noirish is the device used in *Double Indemnity, Murder, My Sweet* and others, where the film begins with the story virtually over and the hero proceeds to tell it from the beginning. Such films do not possess the disorientating effect of the genuinely fragmented narrative, as the plot is generally arranged chronologically from this point on. In films like *Double Indemnity* the effect is to create a sense of fatalism, giving away part or all of the ending so that the film can concentrate on how and why things turned out this way. By contrast, *Murder, My Sweet* has a framing sequence which makes Marlowe appear more threatened than he really is; at the start it appears that he is blind and about to be tried for two murders, but at the end it is revealed that the blindness is temporary and Ann has corroborated his story. However, the flashback is not merely a trick to create tension, but a way of handing control of the narrative to Marlowe, giving him a voice-over akin to the first-person narration of the novel. Critics have labelled this the 'confessional' mode of flashback.

The Killers is arranged in a more complex fashion, labelled the 'investigative' mode. As noted by practically everybody who has seen both this film and *Citizen Kane*, the structures of the two films are similar in that the main character dies very early on, then another character speaks to people who knew him. Their reminiscences take the form of flashbacks. Even though both films gradually settle into a broadly chronological pattern after the first half-hour or so, they both use fragmented narrative to their advantage. In *Kane* these pieces of a life are disordered to emphasise the futility of trying to construct a complete picture: the past is dead. In *The Killers*, however, the past will not die – the Swede cannot escape it, nor can Kitty or Colfax – but the fragments of it need to be located and reordered from this chaotic state into something that makes sense. As the film's seeker-hero, Reardon takes this role and gives the narrative in the present its own momentum (note that after the final flashback, initiated by Kitty, the camera moves from a position behind Reardon to one in front of him – he has all the facts and can finally move forwards). The flashbacks cast Swede as a victim-hero; we know how his story ends before it begins, and the film shows us his decline. Siodmak's *Phantom Lady* also contains the two character-types, but its linear narrative means that victim-hero Scott is central to the first half-hour, then seeker-heroine Carol takes over for the rest of the film. Non-linear narrative allows *The Killers* to balance its threads more effectively, and encourages parallels to be drawn between them. Reardon's descent into the noir world often sees him follow in the Swede's footsteps, even back to the room where he was shot, and the handkerchief which symbolised Swede's love for Kitty comes to symbolise Reardon's obsession with the case.

The use of a variety of narrators might lead the viewer to suspect an element of unreliability to creep in (critics have suggested that this may be the case in some noirs with a single narrator, such as *Detour*). However, in accordance with classical Hollywood style, the camera never lies, not even when the characters do. Although heavily influenced by Expressionism, which is fundamentally about relating subjective experience, noirs are not in the business of showing things which did not happen. The most famous example of 'lying flashback' occurs in a film sometimes cited as a noir, *Stage Fright* (Alfred Hitchcock, 1950); the murderer, Johnny, narrates a version of events in which he is shown to be innocent. As critic Seymour Chatman puts it, 'the camera has conspired with Johnny to deceive us,' and this was not popular with audiences who expected the camera to be independent of the characters and operate with no motive other than telling the story. Films such as *The Usual Suspects* (Bryan Singer, 1995) and *Fight Club* (David Fincher, 1999) have demonstrated that the 'lying flashback' has since become an accepted cinematic device, but it is not entirely surprising that audiences should assume a flashback to be reliable. It contains much more information than a purely verbal account and hence we do not assume it to be *generated* purely by a verbal account.

This is particularly true in the case of Blinky's dying ramblings in *The Killers*; although the audience gets the full story, Reardon was presumably only able to extract a few crucial facts. Although we understand this flashback to be initiated by a character's verbal account, what the camera shows us must either be an objective depiction of the event produced for our benefit, or a glimpse inside the character's memory/imagination. The contemporary reaction to *Stage Fright* suggests that a 1940s audience would have assumed the former, while a contemporary audience probably assumes the latter. Walker suggests that the presentation of Colfax within the flashbacks of *The Killers* draws attention to the peculiar status of the device: 'although Nick can describe Colfax, he cannot name him, but the organiser of the heist in Charleston's flashback – who Charleston is *refusing* to name – is the same man.' *The Killers* notably denies any flashbacks from Colfax, who lies throughout his conversation with Reardon. Because the viewer knows more than Reardon, they are flattered into believing that their status as spectator is privileged. The 'lying flashback' takes away this privilege, arguably not only in the films where it is used but in every subsequent film the viewer sees.

Although *The Killers* does not subvert the flashback device, it nevertheless uses it to generate confusion. The viewer is not given the necessary information to comprehend the full significance of the first two flashbacks, and must understand them in retrospect; they are therefore less likely to realise that there is still some information missing, even after the final flashback is completed, because the scenes have to be fitted together mentally in a way that they have not been in the film. Even when all has been explained by Reardon, the sense of paranoia engendered by the film's twists remains powerful (the Swede died without fully understanding his situation). *The Killers* therefore contains all three of Walker's noir narrative types (see **Stranger on the Third Floor**): Reardon provides the detective story; Swede is the man destroyed by a femme fatale and the arrangement of the two strands in a fragmented flashback structure creates a paranoid nightmare. Walker describes it as one of the most 'complete' films noirs; it is also one of the best.

AFTERLIFE: The film sometimes ran on television under the title *A Man Alone*. In 1958 Andrei Tarkovsky, a film student in the Soviet Union, adapted the Hemingway story as his first short film, *Ubijtsi*. Tarkovsky went on to make *Ivan's Children* (1962) and *Solaris* (1972). In 1964 *The Killers* was remade for television by director-producer Don Siegel, Hellinger's first choice for directing the original. It starred John Cassavetes, Lee Marvin, Angie Dickinson and notably Ronald Reagan (playing the Colfax role, his first and only bad-guy performance in what turned out to be his final film). The completed film was judged too violent for TV and ended up being given a theatrical release to reasonable acclaim.

The theme developed by Miklos Rozsa for whenever the killers appear was used as the basis for the theme of the TV series *Dragnet* (1951–59, 1967–70, 2002–03).

AVAILABILITY: The VHS has been deleted and there is no Region 2 DVD, but the Region 1 DVD (I366515) is excellent: a two-disc set featuring a new transfer of the movie, a 1949 radio version (in which Lancaster reprised his role), a reading of Hemingway's original short story, an essay by Jonathan Lethem, Paul Schrader's 'Notes on Film Noir', Tarkovsky's student film version – and, on the second disc, the 1964 remake with further extras relating to that version.

The Locket (1946)

This minor noir from minor-noir director John Brahm is chiefly notable for giving Robert Mitchum his first noir role, but also for its audacious flashback structure, perhaps the most extreme example of flashback in all of film noir. It goes like this: Dr Harry Blair comes to see John Willis on his wedding day and warns him off Nancy Blair, the woman he is about to marry. To explain, Blair initiates a flashback which shows that he was once married to Nancy, but her first husband Norman Clyde (Mitchum) approached him and warned him away too. Clyde initiates his own flashback, explaining that they were very happy together until he discovered that Nancy was a kleptomaniac. Clyde asks her why this is, and she explains that it all goes back to when she was a child . . . This too is shown in flashback, bringing us to the point of a flashback within a flashback within a flashback. Ludicrous? Maybe, but it certainly enlivens what is otherwise a standard melodrama founded on the kind of dodgy psychoanalysis fairly common in 1940s movies. Like many RKO noirs, it was lensed by Nicholas Musuraca, which helps. *Released on 20 December 1946*

The Lady in the Lake (1947)

Although not considered the worst of the four Philip Marlowe movies of the 1940s – *The Brasher Doubloon* (John Brahm, 1947), based upon *The High Window* (1942), holds that dubious distinction – *The Lady in the Lake* is nevertheless a long way behind *Murder, My Sweet* and *The Big Sleep*, despite being the only film of Chandler's work that he adapted himself. (He was bored by the assignment, invented several new scenes and eventually removed his name from the script in protest over Steve Fisher's relatively minor revisions.) The film, directed by and starring Robert Montgomery, is almost universally considered to be a failed experiment on account of its 'subjective' camera style; with the exception of a few scenes in which Marlowe, alone in his office, speaks directly to camera, the film is constructed from point-of-view shots which place the spectator in Marlowe's position. Montgomery had the camera mounted on an attachment which rested on his stomach and kept the camera at his eyeline. The idea was to visually replicate Chandler's first-person narration, but the device was too literal, lacking an equivalent for the internal monologue and ultimately alienating the audience from Marlowe by denying them an actor to engage with (except for the aforementioned narration sequences, and some superbly staged mirror shots). However – and here commences the defence of the film – Chandler's Marlowe stories are not just about the detective, but also the characters he meets as his investigation progresses, and *The Lady in the Lake* emphasises this more than any other Marlowe film. The long takes, with actors having to play directly to the camera, allow the audience to observe the characters' changing reactions to Marlowe in minute detail – Audrey Totter in particular gives an excellent performance. It is also worth noting that the film arguably works better on a small screen than a large one; in a cinema the figures would appear to bear down on the viewer. On a television screen the relative scale of the viewers and characters is more equal, and the experience consequently more comfortable. *Released on 23 January 1947*

Out of the Past (1947)

A.K.A. *Build My Gallows High*

Black and White – 96 mins

An RKO Radio Picture
Out of the Past
Executive Producer: Robert Sparks
Screenplay by Geoffrey Homes
Based on his Novel *Build My Gallows High*
Director of Photography: Nicholas Musuraca, ASC
Art Directors: Albert S D'Agostino and Jack Okey
Special Effects by Russell A Cully, ASC
Set Decorator: Darrell Silvera
Make-up Supervisor: Gordon Bau
Music by Roy Webb
Musical Director: C Bakaleinikoff
Film Editor: Samuel E Beetley
Sound by Francis M Sarver and Clem Portman
Gowns by Edward Stevenson
Assistant Director: Harry Mancke
Produced by Warren Duff
Directed by Jacques Tourneur

CAST: Robert Mitchum (*Jeff*), Jane Greer (*Kathie*), Kirk Douglas (*Whit*), Rhonda Fleming (*Meta Carson*), Richard Webb (*Jim*), Steve Brodie (*Fisher*), Virginia Huston (*Ann*), Paul Valentine (*Joe*), Dickie Moore (*The Kid*), Ken Niles (*Eels*)

SUMMARY: A man named Joe arrives in the small town of Bridgeport and contacts Jeff Bailey, the proprietor of a gas station. Jeff realises that this means trouble for him, and explains his past to his girlfriend, Ann. Jeff's real name is Markham, and he used to work as a private detective in New York. A criminal named Whit hired him to find Kathie, a woman who stole $40,000 from him. Jeff traced Kathie to Acapulco, but fell for her and never reported back to Whit. She claimed she didn't steal the money. Jeff eventually told Whit he hadn't found her, then he and Kathie left for San Francisco, where they successfully hid out – until Whit hired Jeff's partner, Fisher, to find them. Kathie shot Fisher dead and disappeared, leaving Jeff to discover that she did indeed steal Whit's $40,000. Jeff went to Bridgeport to live in anonymity. Joe works for Whit and brings Jeff to see him. Jeff discovers that Kathie is back with

Whit. Whit hires Jeff to steal some incriminating papers from a lawyer named Eels, who is threatening to expose Whit's tax evasion to the IRS. Jeff goes along with it but his suspicions of a frame-up are correct; Eels is killed and Whit possesses an affidavit which will incriminate Jeff for the murder. Jeff puts Kathie on the spot and she admits the frame-up, giving Jeff the information he needs to find the papers. Jeff is now wanted for the murders of Eels and Fisher, but offers Whit the papers in exchange for the affidavit. Joe tries to kill Jeff but Jeff is saved by the deaf boy who works at his gas station. Whit agrees to a deal but, before the exchange can be made, Kathie kills Whit and convinces Jeff to run away with her. However, Jeff tips off the police and their exit from the town is blocked. Kathie shoots Jeff and she is shot by the police. After the inquest, Ann asks the deaf boy if Jeff really intended to go away with Kathie; the boy releases her from the situation by saying yes.

DIRECTOR: Jacques Tourneur (1904–77) was born in Paris, but moved to America in 1914 when his father Maurice, a noted silent director, started to work in Hollywood. In 1924 he took an office job at MGM and went on to work for his father as a script supervisor and editor. He continued to do so after Maurice returned to the French film industry, and it was in Paris that Tourneur directed his first film, *Un Vieux garcon* (1931). After four more films he moved back to Hollywood in 1935, doing B-pictures and second-unit work. In 1939 he directed *Nick Carter, Master Detective* for MGM. In the early 1940s he was assigned to Val Lewton's B-picture unit at RKO, where the studio was attempting to rival Universal's horror movies, and directed Lewton's first three features, *Cat People* (1942), *I Walked With a Zombie* (1943) and *The Leopard Man* (1943). As a result of these and the propaganda piece *Days of Glory* (1944), he graduated to A-pictures at RKO with *Experiment Perilous* (1944) and *Canyon Passage* (1946) before being assigned *Out of the Past*. Although the film is regarded as one of the essential noirs, he made few others: *Berlin Express* (1948) and *Nightfall* (1957) are generally regarded as such. His other great triumph was the British horror movie *Night of the Demon* (1957). In the 1950s he made a number of historical romances and westerns before moving into television, with work on *Northwest Passage*, *Bonanza* and a 1964 episode of *The Twilight Zone* ('Night Call') in addition to occasional films. He retired in the late 1960s.

WRITER: Geoffrey Homes was a pseudonym for Daniel Mainwaring (1902–77): 'Geoffrey' and 'Homes' were his middle names. A mystery writer, he had produced one novel under his given name, *One Against the Earth* (1933), but found greater success when he changed his name for *The Man Who Murdered Himself* (1936). His first Hollywood work in 1935 was in the capacity of publicist. After his seventh novel *No Hands on the Clock* (1939) was filmed by Frank McDonald in 1941 he was able to move into screenwriting. His first screenplay was *Secrets of the Underground* (William Morgan, 1942) and he went on to become a staff writer at Pine-Thomas Productions, which sold support features on to Paramount. 'I wrote six pictures in one year,' he recalled in 1973, 'all of which I'd just as soon forget except *Big Town* [William Thomas, 1947].' Initially Mainwaring had been able to produce novels alongside his screenwriting, but the demands of Pine-Thomas made this impossible and he was starting to feel frustrated. 'At the end of the year I fled to the hills and wrote *Build My Gallows High* [1946]. Bill Dozier, head of RKO, bought it and me with it.' The rights to the novel cost $20,000.

Build My Gallows High turned out to be Mainwaring's final novel, as he was subsequently kept busy by his screenwriting work, although he departed RKO in 1949. 'Howard Hughes dropped my option when I refused to work on *I Married a Communist* [Robert Stevenson, 1949]. He used that project to get rid of a lot of writers, directors and actors.' Unsurprisingly he wrote many more noir scripts, working on *The Big Steal* (Don Siegel, 1949), which reunited Mitchum and Greer, *The Lawless* (Joseph Losey, 1950), based on his own short story 'The Voice of Stephen Wilder', *The Tall Target* (Anthony Mann, 1951), *Roadblock* (Harold Daniels, 1951), *This Woman Is Dangerous* (Felix Feist, 1952), *The Hitch-Hiker* (Ida Lupino, 1953), *A Bullet for Joey* (Lewis Allen, 1955), *The Phenix City Story* (Phil Karlson, 1955) and *Baby Face Nelson* (Don Siegel, 1957). His most famous film, however, is probably *Invasion of the Body Snatchers* (Don Siegel, 1956) – by which time he had started writing under his real name again. From the late 1950s onwards, he combined further film work with scripts for television, before retiring in the late 1960s.

DEVELOPMENT: *Build My Gallows High* had been a departure for Mainwaring. 'I wanted to get away from straight mystery novels. Those detective stories are a bore to write. You've got to figure out "whodunit".' This new novel was focused more around exploring the characters, and Mainwaring acknowledged *The Maltese Falcon* as a strong influence. Given Mainwaring's previous experience, Bill Dozier was happy for him to adapt his own work for the screen and assigned the project to William Duff. However, Dozier then left RKO for Universal and Duff was less confident in the writer's abilities. After Mainwaring completed a first draft, James M Cain (see **Double Indemnity**) was assigned to rework it. 'That's the way things work,' said Mainwaring. 'You'd turn around and spit and some other writer would be on your project.' Mainwaring was unimpressed with Cain's draft, claiming, 'Jim Cain threw away my script and wrote a completely new one. It had nothing to do with the novel or anything.' This is not entirely accurate. Cain did work from Mainwaring's original draft but changed it substantially, including the characters' names (one change was thankfully retained in the finished film: Kathie's original name was Mumsie McGonigle). Cain also simplified the structure, blending Jeff's flashbacks (which in Mainwaring's script were spread over the whole film) into one long section near the beginning. A narrative device which Mainwaring had attempted in his first draft was dropped by Cain. 'Originally we used a trick,' Mainwaring said. 'The first script had the deaf and dumb boy as the narrator . . . it flashed back twice, and it just didn't work.'

Duff took the Cain and Mainwaring drafts, consulted Tourneur (to whom he intended to allocate the project) and passed both scripts on to RKO contract writer Frank Fenton, asking him to combine them into a finished draft. Fenton worked mainly from Mainwaring's script but took on board Cain's structural modifications and revised much of the dialogue. Mainwaring returned to do a final draft, which by this stage was fairly close to his book; he later described it as 'basically . . . the same, although there were more characters in the novel'. Scenes which had taken place in New York in the novel were moved to San Francisco, 'because we wanted to shoot there'. Further to this, the ending went through two changes. 'At the end of the novel Bailey is killed by Whit's men, not by Kathie and the police.' However, the bleakness of the ending still worried the studio. 'The front office said, Jesus you can't end it with them dead there. You've got to put something on it.' The film was rounded off with a more hopeful coda for Ann.

CASTING: Initially, Duff and Mainwaring hoped to entice Humphrey Bogart (see **The Maltese Falcon** and **The Big Sleep**), then one of Warner Bros.' biggest contract stars, to come to RKO and make *Build My Gallows High*. Mainwaring, who had partly modelled his novel on *The Maltese Falcon* and had always envisaged Bogart playing the lead role, made the approach personally. 'When I finished the script I took it down to Newport where Bogart was living. He was going to do it, but Warners wouldn't let him. So then we took Mitchum.'

Robert Mitchum (1917–97) was not the next choice after Bogart. Early trade advertising listed Dick Powell as the star (see **Murder, My Sweet**; connected with this was a plan to have Edward Dmytryk direct instead of Tourneur). However, Mitchum's profile had risen sharply with his Oscar nomination for *The Story of G.I. Joe* (William A Weldman, 1945), and *Build My Gallows High* was ideal for him. Born in Connecticut, he had an ill-disciplined childhood, was arrested for vagrancy at the age of fourteen, and did time on a Georgia chain gang. He did a variety of jobs (including ghostwriting an astrology column) and got into acting via an amateur theatre group in California. He won his first film roles in 1943; in that year alone he appeared in nineteen films, usually flag-waving pieces about America's soldiers or *Hopalong Cassidy* movies. After the success of *G.I. Joe*, RKO cast him in *Till the End of Time* (Edward Dmytryk, 1946) and the noir *The Locket* (John Brahm, 1946). His fee for *Build My Gallows High* was $10,400, and he was given his own dressing room on the RKO lot for the first time. 'Gosh, I must be getting to be somebody,' he reportedly said when he saw it, 'this room even has a phone.'

Jane Greer (1924–2001, born Bettejane Greer) often said that she had learned her acting skills after suffering palsy, which partially paralysed her face and required her to relearn how to move it. 'I was learning to direct my as-yet expressionless feelings, as well as gaining an ability to express emotion by a very conscious manipulation of my muscles.' A beauty queen and model in her teens, she modelled army uniforms on the cover of *Life* magazine in 1942. Media tycoon Howard Hughes saw the cover and tracked her down, then signed her to a personal contract – although it started to appear that this was rather more personal than she had anticipated, as she did little work for him and he kept her a virtual prisoner. Eventually he sub-contracted her to RKO, where she appeared in *Dick Tracy* (William Berke, 1945) and the noirs *Two O'Clock Courage* (Anthony Mann, 1946) and *They Won't Believe Me* (Irving Pichel, 1947). 'It was a great, great part,' she said of *Out of the Past*. 'Anybody would die for a part like that. The way they build her up before you even see her.' She appeared alongside Mitchum again in *The Big Steal* (Don Siegel, 1949) but then an erratic Hughes, still holding her under contract, refused to let her work. She was freed in 1951 and went on to make *The Prisoner of Zenda* (Richard Thorpe, 1952) and *Run for the Sun* (Roy Boulting, 1956), but shortly after this her career wound down. She made occasional pictures and worked in television from the 1960s onwards, and in 1990 guested in three episodes of *Twin Peaks*.

Kirk Douglas (born Issur Danielovitch Demsky, 1916) came from a poor Russian-Jewish immigrant family in New York, and he won an acting scholarship and worked on Broadway before service in W.W.II. In the meantime, one of his old classmates, Lauren Bacall, had made good. She convinced Hal Wallis to screen-test Douglas on his return, and Wallis cast him in the noir *The Strange Love of Martha Ivers* (Lewis Milestone, 1946), which led to his role in *Out of the Past*. His career gathered pace with *I Walk Alone* (Byron Haskin, 1948), which was the first of several films with Burt Lancaster, and the boxing noir *Champion* (Mark Robson, 1949), for which he was Oscar-nominated. His roles over the next decade included the noirs *Ace in the Hole* (Billy Wilder, 1951) and *Detective Story* (William Wyler, 1951), *The Bad and the Beautiful* (Vincente Minnelli, 1952), *20,000 Leagues under the Sea* (Richard Fleischer, 1954), *Paths of Glory* (Stanley Kubrick, 1957) and *Spartacus* (Stanley Kubrick, 1960). Subsequently, he made numerous war films and westerns, and directed two films of his own: *Scalawag* (1973) and *Posse* (1975).

PRODUCTION: *Build My Gallows High* was a fairly large production for RKO, with a shoot lasting 64 working days at several locations. Most work was undertaken in the area of Lake Tahoe and the Pathé lot in Culver City, with studio work taking place on the RKO sound stages, but there was also a second unit shooting material in San Francisco, New York and Acapulco. Tourneur travelled to Bridgeport, California, on Saturday, 19 October 1946, and the rest of the crew and most of the cast arrived on Monday. As Mitchum was not due to arrive until Thursday, work began with the very first and very last scenes, in which he did not appear. The star came in by private plane, but the plane's brakes failed and upon landing it crashed through a fence, hopped over a ditch and destroyed an outhouse before finally coming to a stop. Mitchum hopped out and hitched a ride to the set, arriving to find the company deeply concerned as to his whereabouts and welfare. 'He walked in on us,' said co-star Paul Valentine. 'Everybody looked up. And the first words out of his mouth were "Anybody here got any gage?" ' 'Gage' was slang for marijuana, which goes some way towards explaining Mitchum's languid delivery and heavy eyelids. 'He smoked marijuana all the time on the set,' according to Mainwaring. Mitchum was also wearing his hair 'long' (by 1940s standards), having come straight from the noirish western *Pursued* (Raoul Walsh, 1947), and was told by Tourneur to find a barber. Bridgeport didn't have one, and ultimately Mitchum drove two hours and 78 miles before he found one.

The mountain shoot took three weeks, prolonged by bad weather. On account of snow, shooting had to be stopped on the afternoon of 26 October and the company was completely unable to work on 29 October. RKO sent up a projector and some films to watch, but this did little to alleviate everybody's frustration. 'We all went a little stir-crazy very fast,' commented Valentine. One symptom of this appeared when RKO's on-set publicist convinced the local Shoshone tribe of Native Americans to pose for a series of photographs initiating Mitchum into the tribe. He wore a feathered headdress and gave Chief Owanahea the secret handshake. The company also took the opportunity for some drinking sessions, one of which ended with RKO being presented with a bill for $135 for damage done by Mitchum to his cabin.

Although the tortuous script frequently baffled its cast ('I think we lost a few pages in the mimeo department,' joked Mitchum at a read-through), the director smoothed the way. 'Jacques Tourneur's direction was very simple to understand,' said Jane Greer, recalling that he had said to her, 'Zzjjane, do you know what *ahm-pahs-eeve* mean?' She responded that, yes, she did know what 'impassive' meant. 'No "big eyes",' Tourneur continued. 'No expressive. In the beginning you act like a nice girl. But then, after you kill the man you meet in the little house, you become a bad girl. Yes? First half, good girl. Second half, bad girl.' Tourneur's notion was that the actors should be like musical instruments, all tuned to the same key; as the film was based around Mitchum's character, the other cast members adopted his pace and tone. Tourneur also told Greer, 'At first you wear light colours. After you kill the man, darker colours. At the end, black.' She later noted that 'it would have worked had they not screwed up the production schedule and made us do some later scenes early and the clothes weren't all ready, so you wore whatever fit.'

The film reunited Tourneur with cinematographer Nicholas Musuraca (see **Stranger on the Third Floor**), with whom he had previously worked on *Cat People*. Although Musuraca is best known for his studio-based efforts, this film saw him apply his low-key approach to location shooting. He operated a system of using as few lights as possible, correcting problems by repositioning lights rather than adding extra lights to compensate. 'Any time I find myself using a more than ordinary number of lights for a scene,' he said, 'I'll find I've slipped up somewhere, and the extra lights are really unnecessary.' Greer certainly noticed the difference from her previous work. 'It was so dark on set, you didn't know who else was there half the time.'

There was a degree of rivalry between Mitchum and Douglas, partly on account of their differing acting styles. 'It was a hoot to watch them going at it,' said Greer. 'They were two such different types. Kirk was something of a method actor. And Bob was Bob. You weren't going to catch him *acting*. But they both tried to get the advantage.' It may also have been a factor that Douglas was paid more than Mitchum for the film and did much less work, getting $25,000 for two-and-a-half weeks while Mitchum, who was on contract, received his standard $1,000 per week for a little over ten weeks' work. Greer noted that Mitchum's lack of interest in the acting process was partly an affectation. 'He would arrive for work in the morning and say, "What are the lyrics?" That's what he called his lines, his dialogue. He hadn't got around to looking at the script yet, he'd say.' Believing that this was the secret to Mitchum's offhand, naturalistic delivery, Greer tried it herself one day, attempting to learn her lines during make-up. It didn't work. 'I was stumbling over my first line. And he knew the script backward and forward. It was part of his act.'

Production wrapped on 9 January 1947. Unusually Tourneur worked on the edit with Samuel Beetley, who described him as 'one of the finest directors I ever worked with. He was artistic and he knew what the editor needed.' Beetley also noted that a sense of instability was brought to the film by Tourneur's insistence 'upon never returning to the same camera angles when intercutting scenes'. One scene which was shot but discarded was the demise of Whit, which was left out so that the audience discovered his death along with Jeff. The gap between production of a final cut and the film's eventual release was fairly lengthy, which can be attributed to Bill Dozier's departure from RKO. His replacement, Dore Schary, 'didn't like *Out of the Past* because it had been bought before he came', noted Mainwaring. 'He didn't like anything that was in progress at the studio before he got there. He tried to get rid of all of them. He just threw them out without any decent publicity.' One final change to the film came with a report produced by Dr Gallup's Audience Research Inc, which stated that audiences would find the novel's original title morbid. Hence, shortly before release it became the rather more evocative *Out of the Past* – although the subsequent British release retained *Build My Gallows High*.

RECEPTION: The film was released on 13 November 1947. 'There have been double- and triple-crosses in many of these tough detective films,' noted Bosley Crowther in the next day's *New York Times*. 'But the sum of deceitful complications that occur in *Out of the Past* must be reckoned by logarithmic tables, so numerous and involved do they become.' Crowther therefore felt that *Out of the Past* was 'likely to leave the napping or unmathematical customer far behind'. Up to a point he found it 'intensely fascinating', praising its 'smooth realistic style . . . fast dialogue, and genuine settings in California and Mexican locales'. It was purely the complexity which prevented the film from being enjoyable, as 'it's very snappy and quite intriguingly played . . . Mitchum is magnificently cheeky and self-assured as the tangled "private eye", consuming an astronomical number of cigarettes in displaying his nonchalance.' Although defeated, Crowther declared, 'the challenge is worth a try.'

Variety was reasonably impressed, judging the film 'sturdy film fodder for twin bill situations' and describing it as 'a hard boiled melodrama strong on characterisation' on 19 November 1947. 'Considerable production polish, effective direction and compelling mood slot it for

attention of ticket buyers who go for violence and help overcome a
tendency towards choppiness in story unfoldment.' Mitchum was
thought to give 'a very strong account of himself', while overall the film
was technically impressive. 'Tourneur pays close attention to mood
development; achieving realistic flavor that is further emphasized by real
life settings and topnotch lensing by Nicholas Musuraca.' Grouchy as
ever, James Agee belatedly contributed his two cents on 24 April 1948.
'Conventional private-eye melodrama,' he wrote in *The Nation*. 'More
good work by Musuraca, largely wasted.' He applied the same
judgement to the film's use of Kirk Douglas. 'Bob Mitchum is so very
sleepily self-confident with the women that when he slopes into clinches
you expect him to snore into their faces.'

'I rather liked this,' noted an early British review in the *Daily Herald*
on 4 December 1947. 'Old-time gangster stuff, unashamed and fully
charged with peril.' Other critics were less impressed, largely because
they couldn't follow it. 'I couldn't make head or tail of *Build My
Gallows High*. Make my movies clear, is my plea,' said the *Daily
Graphic*'s reviewer on 19 December 1947. 'Mr Robert Mitchum is
woodenly trying to explain to Miss Virginia Huston . . . why he came to
fall for Miss Greer, a bad woman. One glance at Miss Greer made any
explanation superfluous.' In this case, the film's disorienting atmosphere
merely resulted in a loss of interest. 'By the end of the picture everybody
(except Miss Huston) had been bumped off. They could have included
her too, for all I cared.'

'Several critics have expressed their failure to gather any meaning from
Build My Gallows High,' noted Richard Winnington in the *Chronicle* on
20 December 1947. 'Perhaps a simple synopsis would help everybody.'
Winnington provided one, and went on to derive a great deal of meaning
from the film. 'Is there not in this sort of American Activity . . . to be
detected the neurosis lurking behind the Coca-Cola bar?' Hang on, he's
on to something there – keep going. 'Is this not an outcrop of the
national masochism induced by a quite aimless and mechanised society
proceeding rapidly on its way to nowhere?'

ASPECTS OF NOIR: In its variety of locations, *Out of the Past*
underlines a number of things about noir's sense of place. The most
immediately noticeable aspect is that it opens not in the city, but in a
small town in the countryside; this is rare for film noir, which generally
takes place in an urban milieu. The most common themes and subjects of
noir – organised crime, alienation, corruption, greed, permissiveness –
are all suited to such a setting. The Expressionist sensibility also works
better in the city because the city is itself artificial; it is more difficult to
shoot the countryside in such a way that it looks stylised and inauthentic.

Above all these films deal with fear of the modern world, so it makes sense that they are set at the heart of it (and so often in Los Angeles, that most modern and unrealistic of cites; see **Force of Evil** and **Kiss Me Deadly**). Yet the modern is also enticing, promising wealth and excitement, and this is how film noir's heroes are drawn in. The private detective is supposed to be able to move within the city more effectively than anybody, so it is particularly striking in *Out of the Past* to find such a figure trying to make a life away from it.

In common with *The Killers*, the small town is a hiding place for a doomed hero with a dark past, and is immediately intruded upon by an urban figure who has come in search of the hero. In both cases the hero turns out to be working at a gas station. While the Swede in *The Killers* managed to exist peacefully until he was found (although he was clearly quite detached from the community), there is a sense in *Out of the Past* that Bridgeport is trying to reject Jeff: Ann is warned that he is a poor choice of husband. This dramatically reduces the options of the urban noir hero, who struggles to survive in the city but cannot leave it. Jeff's transient nature reflects Spicer's description of the noir city as 'symbolically homeless, its denziens act[ing] out their lives in public spaces: in diners, bars, nightclubs, automobiles, streets, alleyways, impersonal luxurious hotel suites or cheerless, uncomfortable apartments'.

The noir style and the urban environment generally go hand in hand for obvious reasons: high-contrast lighting suits enclosed spaces with flat walls and artificial light sources. This is underlined in *Out of the Past*, as Leighton Grist notes, 'Bridgeport and its environs are generally shot in Hollywood's typical high-key style,' and indeed these scenes look rather like footage that has been accidentally cut in from a different film – a slick MGM romance, perhaps. Meanwhile, the 'exotic' setting of Acapulco and particularly Jeff's trip to San Francisco after being hired/set up by Whit make use of familiar low-key noir photography. 'The elements of each style graphically reflect the qualities stereotypically associated with the setting,' says Grist, 'the country is traditionally linked with openness, honesty and clean living, the city with oppression, dishonesty and corruption.' Because *Out of the Past* visually dramatises this conflict in a way that most noirs only imply, it underlines the trapped nature of the urban noir hero. It also plays some clever games with the Bridgeport setting. 'Whit's house at Tahoe,' Grist points out, 'is the setting of both high-key and low-key scenes. The house is in the country, but is fundamentally of the city.' This alerts the viewer that the house is not a safe space for Jeff, or indeed for Whit: the chaos of the noir city can reach them both here. As Jeff leaves Bridgeport for the last time, it is as if he decides that if he cannot live there he cannot live at all.

The use of Acapulco is also interesting. In spite of its multinational influences and creative personnel, film noir is a distinctively American form, bound up with (whether supporting or opposing) American values. The majority of these films take place in the USA itself, but there are examples to the contrary and these are usually set in central or South America. The reasons for this are fairly straightforward, since filmmakers are more likely to take what is close to them as subject matter and it is more economical to do so. However, because films noirs tend to be based around crime and lust, this has implications for how other countries are represented. Observing Bart and Laurie's plan to escape to Mexico in *Gun Crazy*, Jim Kitses notes 'the reactionary ethnic coding that runs through film noir', in which 'Mexico, Rio and other Latin locations are invariably the sites of abandon and treachery'. In the case of *Gun Crazy* Bart and Laurie's destination is motivated by prosaic convenience – it is the closest country to which they can escape – but analysis of a film such as *Gilda* (Charles Vidor, 1946) underlines Kitses's point more forcefully. Buenos Aires is characterised as 'a libidinal space in which the normal rules do not apply' in Spicer's terms, and indeed it is a site of treachery in which all three protagonists are from other countries. This would matter less were it not for the tacked-on 'happy' ending, in which Gilda and Johnny look forward to the possibility of a more stable life in America. 'The cultural coding of noir as social myth enshrines the paranoia of its alienated white hero in an insistent stereotyping of racial and ethnic minorities as signifiers of the dark shadow-world,' concludes Kitses. 'In these terms, film noir – black cinema – is inescapably racist, the marginalisation of "other" cultures embedded in its dramatic and visual language.'

However, it is worth pointing out that racial and ethnic minorities are nowhere near the most prominent signifiers of the noir world (it has often been noted how infrequently the films portray non-whites in any capacity). The blanket tag of racism appears too strong, and xenophobia is perhaps more appropriate. A film such as *The Clay Pigeon* (Richard Fleischer, 1949) is highly instructive: the villain is a former officer in a Japanese POW camp who victimised the hero during the war, and the hero stumbles upon his criminal plot to launder stocks of dollars which the Japanese would have used had they succeeded in occupying America. Despite this the film goes out of its way to avoid a racist message, contriving a scene in which the hero hides in the apartment of an Asian-American woman whose husband (also Asian-American) died heroically in the war. The scene has no plot relevance and seems to be there solely to emphasise that any racial connection between the villain and the war widow is insignificant; at the same time, however, by constructing its 'good' Asians as American the film reinforces national boundaries. Even so, there is a contrary example in *Out of the Past* itself: Jeff and Kathie's relationship appears somehow sustainable when they remain in Acapulco and the betrayal only occurs when they return to America.

In film noir, as in many Hollywood films, villains are often played as foreign or by foreign actors; most threatening of all is the person of indeterminate nationality, like *The Maltese Falcon*'s Cairo, *Gilda*'s Mundson or *The Lady from Shanghai*'s Elsa. The fact that the critique of American values exists within film noir as well is part of the noir protagonist's dilemma, in as much as they struggle within America but refuse to go anywhere else; those who try, like Jeff, are ultimately drawn back to the modern urban space which destroys them. Film noir had gradually shifted its focus from the claustrophobia of the dense inner city in the 1940s to urban sprawls and suburbs in the 1950s (as identified in a study by Edward Dimendberg); it seems that by the 1980s the noir aesthetic had spread to the pastoral spaces of America, which in the 'classical' period offered some hope. This was quashed by neo-noirs such as *Blood Simple* (Joel Coen, 1984) and *Blue Velvet* (David Lynch, 1986).

AFTERLIFE: In 1984 the film was remade by Taylor Hackford as *Against All Odds*, starring Jeff Bridges, Rachel Ward and James Woods; in this version, the 'detective' is not a professional but an unemployed football player who is hired to find a missing wife. The most notable thing about this is that Jane Greer is in it, playing the mother of the Kathie character.

The 14 November 1987 edition of *Saturday Night Live* celebrated the 40th anniversary of *Out of the Past* by bringing Mitchum in to guest host the show, and reuniting him with Greer for a sketch spoof of the film.

AVAILABILITY: There's no Region 2 DVD, and the Region 1 includes no extras (the *Saturday Night Live* sketch would be a wonderful addition). The VHS has been deleted.

The Lady from Shanghai (1948)

Black and White – 87 mins

Columbia Pictures Presents
The Lady From Shanghai
Director of Photography: Charles Lawton Jr, ASC

Associate Producers: Richard Wilson and William Castle
Musical Score by Heinz Roemheld
Musical Director: MW Stoloff
Story based on a Novel by Sherwood King
Film Editor: Viola Lawrence
Art Directors: Stephen Goosson and Sturges Carne
Set Decorators: Wilbur Menefree and Herman Schoenbrun
Gowns: Jean Louis
Assistant Director: Sam Nelson
Sound Recording: Lodge Cunningham
Song 'Please Don't Kiss Me' by Allan Roberts and
Doris Fisher
Screen Play and Production: Orson Welles

CAST: Rita Hayworth (*Elsa Bannister*), Orson Welles (*Michael O'Hara*) with Everett Sloane (*Arthur Bannister*), Glenn Anders (*George Grisby*), Ted de Corsia (*Sidney Broome*), Erskine Sandford (*Judge*), Gus Schilling ('*Goldie' Goldfish*), Carl Frank (*Galloway*), Louis Merrill (*Jake*), Evelyn Ellis (*Bessie*), Harry Shannon (*Cab Driver*)

SUMMARY: Wandering sailor Michael O'Hara rescues the beautiful and wealthy Elsa Bannister from a gang of ruffians in a New York park. Her husband, crippled criminal lawyer Arthur Bannister, is about to sail his yacht home to San Francisco via Acapulco, and hires O'Hara for his crew. Along the way O'Hara becomes infatuated with Elsa. Upon arrival in San Francisco Bannister's partner Grisby offers O'Hara $5,000 to help Grisby stage his own death, so he can walk out on his responsibilities. O'Hara is to confess to having murdered Grisby; Grisby will be declared legally dead, but without a body O'Hara cannot be convicted. O'Hara accepts. However, Grisby's real plan is to frame O'Hara for Bannister's murder and collect the insurance payout which their partnership will receive. Bannister's divorce detective Broome discovers the plot, so unbeknown to O'Hara Grisby kills him. O'Hara stages Grisby's murder, but shortly afterwards Grisby turns up dead. Bannister unsuccessfully defends O'Hara at the resulting trial, but O'Hara escapes from the courtroom before the jury can return its verdict. Meeting Elsa, he tells her that he knows that she killed Grisby; they were plotting together to collect the insurance, but when Grisby killed Broome she realised Grisby had become unreliable. Elsa plans to kill O'Hara too, but Bannister finds them in a funhouse hall of mirrors and a shootout ensues. O'Hara is the only one to walk out alive, and a letter left by Bannister clears his name.

DIRECTOR: Orson Welles (1915–85, born George Orson Welles), a prodigy as a child, was directing theatre productions by the age of twenty, including a version of *Macbeth* with an all-black company in Harlem. As an actor he also worked in radio, playing comic-book hero *The Shadow*. In 1937 he founded the Mercury Theater with John Houseman, which ran several successful productions and broadcast plays on CBS radio, including an adaptation of HG Wells's *The War of the Worlds*, which reworked the story as a news broadcast and which many listeners took as genuine. The controversy attracted the attention of RKO, and in July 1939 Welles struck a deal to write, produce, direct and act in two films, with his choice of cast and crew and control over all footage until delivery of the final cut. RKO only held approval over the storyline and the ability to cap the budget. By any standard this was a remarkable deal; considering Welles was 24 years old and had never made a film before, it was incredible; and in the Hollywood of 1939 it was astonishing. Welles brought the Mercury company to RKO and made *Citizen Kane* (1941), a film which has lost none of its power even after every one of its visual, technical and narrative tricks has been plundered by subsequent filmmakers, and which has topped every *Sight and Sound* all-time-greatest film poll since 1962.

Kane was not a box-office success, however, and, because Welles had taken longer than expected to shoot it, he waived his RKO deal in favour of a more standard agreement for two further films; he gave them *The Magnificent Ambersons* (1942), the bleak tale of a wealthy family's decline, then vanished to Rio to work on a vague idea for a portmanteau film called *It's All True*, leaving *Ambersons* in the hands of his editor Robert Wise (who would direct 1959's *Odds Against Tomorrow*). Unfortunately, RKO had the right to final cut, and after very mixed previews *Ambersons* was cut to two-thirds its original length. Meanwhile, Welles frittered away the studio's money in Rio and was cut off. He never finished *It's All True* or worked for RKO again. He made a mediocre noir, *The Stranger* (1946), for independent producer Sam Spiegel 'to prove to the industry', Welles said, 'that I could direct a standard Hollywood picture, on time and on budget, just like anyone else'. He then returned to the theatre to work on a musical version of Jules Verne's *Around the World in 80 Days* (1873). (See **Touch of Evil** for more Welles.)

WRITER: Sherwood King (1904–81) was a crime writer whose novels include *Between Murders* and *Death Carries a Cane*. *If I Die Before I Wake* (1938) was the only one of his novels to spawn a film adaptation. Other writers said to have worked on the script were Charles Lederer (1911–76), who worked on pictures with Howard Hawks such as *His*

Girl Friday (1940) and *I Was a Male War Bride* (1949), and Fletcher Markle (1921–91), who later became a television director.

DEVELOPMENT: In April 1946 financial backing for Welles's *Around the World in 80 Days* fell through at a late stage, leading him to ask some old Hollywood contacts for more money so that he could collect the costumes he'd ordered. Welles's version of the story was that he was in Boston, where the play was having a trial run before moving to New York. He called Harry Cohn of Columbia on the telephone in the theatre's box office (other versions of the story cite the lobby of his hotel) and stated that, if Cohn forwarded the money, Welles would direct a movie for him based upon this terrific novel he'd been reading, called (and here Welles grabbed the closest novel to hand, a book belonging to the girl behind the desk) *If I Die Before I Wake*.

Whatever happened (and, where Welles is concerned, the best policy is often to plump for whichever version of events seems most entertaining), on 26 April, the day before the play opened, Cohn did indeed lend Welles $25,000 against the profits of *If I Die Before I Wake* or, in the event of the property being unavailable, an alternative film agreed by both parties. The reason why Cohn agreed to forward Welles the money where others had refused may have been because in 1943 Welles had married Columbia's top box-office star, Rita Hayworth (see **CASTING**). Although they had a daughter together, the marriage had fared poorly: Welles was unfocused, juggling numerous projects and frequently absent. By 1946 the couple had grown apart, but Hayworth believed a reconciliation was possible if their working lives could be brought together for a while. She asked Cohn to let Welles direct a movie with her as the star. Cohn, lacking confidence in Welles's reliability, contacted Sam Spiegel. Spiegel confirmed that his work with Welles on *The Stranger* had gone smoothly, and there was no reason to believe that hiring Welles was a risk.

In spite of boasting songs by Cole Porter, *Around the World in 80 Days* was not a hit and closed after 75 performances, leaving Welles to fulfil his obligation to Cohn. Welles had already secured the film rights during May, while the play was still running, and sold them on to Columbia for a nominal fee. Bizarrely, it transpired that Columbia had previously owned the rights – William Castle (1914–77), a B-movie director who eventually racked up dozens of credits in myriad genres, had bought them for $500 in 1938 and sold them to Columbia on the understanding that he would be involved in any production. Although the option had presumably lapsed, Welles knew Castle and had talked about working with him before, and was happy to honour the deal. Castle worked on a treatment, and possibly a first draft of the script; he remained attached as associate producer.

Welles spent a brief period on Catalina Island, where he wrote his own draft of the script extremely quickly – it is unclear whether this emerged from impatience to fulfil his commitment to Columbia or a desire to impress with his efficiency. With Hayworth confirmed to star, the picture was given a large hike in budget: Cohn had originally figured on $350,000 but increased this to $2 million. Accordingly, Welles was to broaden the story's scope, which in the novel had all been set on Long Island. The film would take in a sea voyage from New York to San Francisco via the Panama Canal. Further, uncredited work on the script was performed by Fletcher Markle and Charles Lederer, and it went through a number of working titles: *Black Irish* and *Take This Woman* gave way to *The Girl from Shanghai* and eventually *The Lady from Shanghai*.

CASTING: Rita Hayworth (1918–87, born Margarita Carmen Cansino) was the daughter of Spanish dancer Eduardo Cansino. While performing in her father's act at the age of fifteen she was signed by Twentieth Century-Fox, where she played bit parts as Rita Cansino. Following a move to Columbia, Harry Cohn moulded her into a leading actress; she changed her name to Hayworth, had electrolysis to raise her low hairline and her hair was dyed auburn. *Only Angels Have Wings* (Howard Hawks, 1939) and a loan-out to Warner Bros. for *The Strawberry Blonde* (Raoul Walsh, 1941) raised her profile, and she employed her dancing skills alongside Fred Astaire in *You'll Never Get Rich* (Sidney Lanfield, 1941) to become Columbia's top star. Her greatest success was the noir *Gilda* (Charles Vidor, 1946), to which *The Lady from Shanghai* would be the follow-up.

Welles would later deny that the casting of Hayworth had been his decision, and claim that it had been forced upon him by Cohn. However, a letter sent by Welles to Castle in the very early stages of development notes, 'I could play the lead and Rita Hayworth could play the girl.' Welles infuriated Cohn by having Hayworth's distinctive hair cut short and dyed blonde. The couple did move back in together during production, but the move did not save their marriage; they divorced in 1948 and she married the playboy Prince Aly Khan, before stepping back from movies to concentrate on her family life. This marriage also failed, and Hayworth's career had lost its impetus. A few good roles came her way – *Miss Sadie Thompson* (Curtis Bernhardt, 1953) and *They Came to Cordura* (Robert Rossen, 1959) – but in the 1960s she suffered ill health (diagnosed in 1980 as early Alzheimer's disease) and retired in the early 1970s. 'I was lucky to have her,' Welles later said when reflecting on *Shanghai*. 'Rita's awfully good in it, don't you think?'

Actors from Welles's Mercury repertory filled other roles in the *Shanghai* cast. Everett Sloane (1909–65) had played Bernstein in *Citizen*

Kane, as well as appearing in *Journey into Fear* (1942), a film written by Welles and Joseph Cotten for RKO. At the time of *Shanghai* Sloane was still working largely in radio and Welles believed that he did not move particularly well when acting; this was why Welles instructed him to adopt the physical handicap he displays in the film, whereby he walks with a cane firmly aligned to each hip. ('Of course he loved it,' Welles later said, 'all actors love to play cripples.') He was later highly successful in television, appearing in guest roles on dozens of popular dramas and doing voice work on *The Famous Adventures of Mister Magoo* (1964), but overdosed on barbiturates in 1965 (an apparent suicide, as he feared that he was going blind). Small roles went to other actors who had made their screen debuts in *Kane*: Gus Schilling, Harry Shannon and Erskine Sandford. By contrast, Glenn Anders (1889–1981) was an actor whom Welles had met recently, while working in radio in New York. Despite having worked on highly successful Broadway productions such as *Hell Bent for Heaven* (1924) and *Strange Interlude* (1928), he was having trouble finding work. Welles telephoned him out of the blue, offering him a $1,250-per-week contract if he could be on location in a matter of days. Upon arrival he was instructed to play Grisby's corpse, as Welles had not yet defined what the character would be like. Also making his film debut was Ted de Corsia (1903–73), later to appear in *The Big Combo*.

Welles himself took the male lead. Cohn later told him that he would never again hire the same person to direct and play a lead role in a film. 'Why?' asked Welles. 'Because I can't fire anybody,' replied Cohn. 'What's the use of owning my own studio? I might as well be janitor.'

PRODUCTION: Production commenced in October 1946 with location work in San Francisco, including the waterfront at Sausalito, Chinatown, Golden Gate Park's Steinhart Aquarium and the Valhalla Bar and Café. The exterior shots of the funhouse were shot at Whitney's Playland, but the inside would all be constructed back at Columbia once the Acapulco sequences were completed. While scouting locations in Acapulco, Welles had noticed that Errol Flynn's yacht *Zaca* was moored there and suggested to the matinee idol that part of *The Lady from Shanghai* could be filmed on it. Flynn agreed to a deal whereby he would be paid $1,500 per day to skipper the yacht and arrange the crew's lunches. This was perhaps not the wisest move given that Flynn's parties on board the *Zaca* were frequent and legendary, but shooting began there in mid-October regardless.

Flynn did not take the shoot very seriously. He drank heavily, steered the boat haphazardly and generally discouraged attempts to get any work done. On the first day of filming one of the camera assistants suffered a fatal heart attack, and Flynn ordered that the man be buried at sea in a duffel bag (eventually the corpse was dropped off in Mexico as quietly as possible). Hayworth attempted to make Welles jealous by flirting with Flynn during breaks. The locations selected by Welles were hazardous and not always suitable for filming: river sequences were shot amid crocodiles, and tropical insects were attracted to the lights, obstructing them. One such insect bit Welles, causing his eye to swell to three times its normal size and forcing the crew to take a break while Welles writhed in his cabin, loudly proclaiming that he was convinced he was going to die. Hayworth collapsed from heat exhaustion, and found her performance hampered by sinus problems. (Her illness later caused production to be shut down for a month.) Whole scenes had to be reshot because the light meter couldn't gauge the reflection being thrown up by the water, causing the film to be overexposed. Meanwhile, Welles, who seemed to relish working in chaos (upon hearing John Ford's comment that the best things in films happen by accident, Welles said, 'Yes . . . you could even say that a director is a man who presides over accidents'), continued to rewrite the script as he went. The Acapulco shoot took 35 days in all, substantially over schedule, and the company was recalled to California in spite of Welles's protests that they only needed three more days to get the rest of the footage they needed. The missing shots were performed in front of process screens, which was more expensive and time-consuming than the extra location work would have been.

Back at Columbia, Welles made use of the largest sound stage the studio had and constructed the funhouse set for the final shoot-out sequence. This was to be based on *The Cabinet of Dr Caligari* (Robert Weine, 1919); Welles ordered a print for reference, but nobody could find one in Hollywood. New York's Museum of Modern Art obligingly sent its copy for Welles's use. The set included a 125-foot slide which reached the ceiling and a hall of mirrors which contained a total of 2,912 square feet of glass (24 two-way mirrors behind which Welles could place his camera, plus eighty ordinary mirrors). Much of the set and many of the props were personally painted by Welles, working through the night. As the production ran over schedule, other cameramen came in to replace the credited Charles Lawton, in the form of Rudolph Maté and Joseph Walker.

Meanwhile, the opening sequence in Central Park was the longest crane shot any Hollywood movie had ever attempted, as the camera followed Elsa's carriage for three-quarters of a mile. Needless to say, these sequences were not cheap, and Cohn became concerned. He bugged Welles's office, but the tactic rebounded when it was discovered by the director; it is characteristic of Welles that, rather than speaking with greater restraint when in the bugged room, he started making things up, cheerfully relating on-set disasters that hadn't actually happened and waiting for Cohn's furious reaction. On other days he would preface meetings in his office by putting on his radio-announcer's voice: 'Good morning! This is the Mercury Office. We welcome you to another day of fascinating good listening.' At the end of the meeting he would sign off with music. (Welles's filmmaking career might have been rather more successful had he not possessed this strange urge to antagonise moguls for no particular purpose.) The production wrapped in March 1947, three months late and $400,000 over budget.

It seems that Welles may have learned from one of his past mistakes; rather than skipping out on the editing process, as he had with *The Magnificent Ambersons*, he remained on-hand throughout – not that it did much good. He assembled a rough cut lasting 155 minutes, but Cohn had retained the right to final cut and only allowed Welles to make suggestions to Columbia's chief editor, Viola Lawrence. As Lawrence worked to bring the film down to a reasonable length, Cohn became aware that there were not enough close-ups of Hayworth; Welles reluctantly went back and shot more footage. At some point between the rough cut and the final version Welles personally previewed the film in Santa Barbara, for which he constructed a temporary soundtrack from the Columbia library, and intended that this be used as a blueprint for the final version, with new music that matched the tone of the temporary soundtrack. Ultimately, however, the score ended up being heavily influenced by *Gilda*; Cohn decided that a song was an essential ingredient of any Hayworth movie (even though her vocals in *Gilda* had been dubbed by Anita Ellis) and ordered one added to *The Lady from Shanghai*. This was 'Please Don't Kiss Me', and Welles shot a scene of Hayworth singing it at a further cost of $60,000. The song became a refrain throughout the movie, informing all parts of the score, and Welles disliked this intensely. He dismissed Heinz Roemheld's music as 'Disney' in a memo to Cohn. Regarding the scene of Elsa diving from the rocks, he wrote that 'the dive is treated as though it were a major climax or some antic movement in a Silly Symphony, a pratfall by Pluto the Pup or a wild jump into space by Donald Duck.' He also felt that more use should have been made of 'realistic' sound effects, such as wind and water on the yacht sequences, and that the gunshots and breaking glass in the closing sequence should have been allowed to stand without music. Although disappointed by the loss of some good Acapulco material and much of the funhouse sequence (which he was proud of), his main complaints were directed towards the soundtrack. 'If the lab had scratched initials and phone numbers all over the negative, I couldn't be unhappier with the results,' Welles concluded.

Cohn viewed the final version (now running at just 87 minutes) and declared that, if anybody could explain the story to him, he would give them a thousand dollars. Welles believed that he could still make a great movie out of it if he was allowed to produce his own edit, but Cohn refused.

RECEPTION: Although the film was ready for release in the spring of 1947, Cohn was so disappointed by it that he feared it would damage Hayworth's star status. He needed a strong follow-up to *Gilda* and so Hayworth's next release was the Technicolor musical *Down to Earth* (Alexander Hall, 1947). *The Lady from Shanghai* was held back in the USA for over a year, receiving its first screenings in France on 24 December 1947. By the time of its American release on 9 June 1948 (on the lower half of a double bill), it had already been seen in Finland (released 13 February 1948), Britain (7 March), Australia (11 March) and Sweden (15 March). To say that the film was buried in the USA is to put it mildly.

The British reviews classed it as an interesting curio. 'Even a minor work by Mr Orson Welles is never without its interest,' stated *The Times* on 8 March 1948, 'and, while *The Lady from Shanghai* is definitely minor, it is rich in its undertones, its felicitous and imaginative passages of direction.' The review was willing to forgive the vagueness of the plotting, recognising that 'Mr Welles is more interested in the motives than the mechanics of murder': also, 'more important than the obscure moves by which the passengers in a luxury yacht approach their deaths is Mr Welles' ability to disturb the blandly tidy surface the screen normally presents by the ruffles of cross-purposes, of conflicting sounds, of bizarre contrasts.'

Welles often found greater appreciation in Europe, most notably France – but it is clear that he had his British fans as well. 'Orson Welles has stated publicly that the powers in Hollywood would not tolerate another *Citizen Kane*,' noted Richard Winnington in the *Chronicle*, also on 8 March 1948. 'In lieu of expressing a real idea (and he has them) Welles has been allowed to flourish as the Boy Wizard of the screen.' Again, *Shanghai* was characterised as skilled knockabout entertainment. 'In one scene you may locate Welles the observer, commentator, satirist and original – the trial scene. Otherwise it is Welles the Bogey Man dedicating his Magic to every facet of the Hayworth personality and body.'

The trial scene was similarly praised in *Time and Tide*: 'For all his airs I suspect that Mr Welles may be just a Big Boy at heart,' noted its reviewer on 13 March 1948. 'I have to grant him one first-rate bit of film craft, a court-scene which is original and bitterly incisive.' This review was more critical of the plotting. 'Orson Welles' films always seem rather like a bad dream to me. They have the same intermittent fascination, the same power to horrify, the same total failure to add up to sense.' His performance was given greater credit, with a surprising lack of criticism for the absurd Irish accent. 'Welles and Everett Sloane, as the cripple, act impressively, whatever their parts may mean; Miss Hayworth looks only partly exhumed or embalmed.'

Bosley Crowther had an entirely different view of the trial, suggesting in the *New York Times* of 10 June 1948, 'Tension is recklessly permitted to drain off' during this sequence 'which has little save a few visual stunts'. He further expressed his disappointment that the film 'could have been a terrific piece of melodramatic romance. For the idea, at least, is a corker and the Wellesian ability to direct a good cast against fascinating backgrounds has never been better displayed.' Again, the writing was cited as the principal culprit, suggesting that, as the film's producer, 'Mr Welles might better have fired himself – as author, that is – and hired somebody else to give Mr Welles, as director, a better script.'

Variety rated the film as 'okay boxoffice' on 14 April 1948. 'It's exploitable and has Rita Hayworth's name for the marquees. Entertainment value suffered from the striving for effect that features Orson Welles' production, direction and scripting.' The script was thought to be the main problem, being 'wordy and full of holes which need the plug of taut story telling and more forthright action'. Welles's 'rambling style' was said to have 'occasional flashes of imagination, particularly in the tricky backgrounds he uses to unfold the yarn, but effects, while good on their own, are distracting to the murder plot'. Its lack of usefulness as a vehicle to advance its star's career was also confirmed. 'Miss Hayworth isn't called on to do much more than look beautiful. Best break for players goes to Sloane.' In the *Motion Picture Herald* of 17 April, George H Spiers stressed that 'Columbia's *The Lady from Shanghai* is a picture dominated by the writing, acting and production of Orson Welles,' and that Welles had 'emerged with a picture that is interesting and artistic, but one which requires the constant attention of the audience'. However, like *Variety*'s reviewer, Spiers assumed that 'exhibitors should have little trouble selling the picture for there are the star names to decorate the marquee and attract patrons, and once inside those who appreciate fine production values should find this enjoyable.' Both reviews were incorrect: the film's final gross from the domestic market was just under $1.5 million.

ASPECTS OF NOIR: As we have already seen, *The Lady from Shanghai* is one of many noirs which drew criticisms of incomprehensibility (see **The Big Sleep** and **Out of the Past**). In the case of *Shanghai* it is difficult to know whether the plot became confused during the editing process or whether it was always like that, but Welles did not seem to think that any important story points had been lost when his film had been hacked down to programmer-length. Regardless, the film we have is a useful example of noir's relationship with the Gothic, which goes far beyond the already discussed influence of Universal horror films. In his book *The Literature of Terror*, David Punter discusses the late eighteenth-century Gothic novelists Anne Radcliffe and Matthew Lewis, noting that these writers were not relating 'behavioural histories of individuals, but fables about those points of vision and obsession where individuals blur into their own fantasies.' Films noirs frequently revolve around an obsession with a mystery or a woman (or both) and a similar distortion of narrative occurs as a result. 'Once I'd seen her,' says O'Hara in the opening narration of *Shanghai*, 'I was not in my right mind for quite some time.' Rather than opening up the possibility for the supernatural, the noir hero becomes susceptible to the noir world. Perhaps more pertinently, the critic Fred Botting describes the themes and devices introduced into Gothic by Edgar Allan Poe, including 'doubles, mirrors and the concern with modes of representation . . . the play of internal and external narrations, of uncertain psychological states and uncanny events; and the location of mysteries in a criminal world'. Poe created a reasoning hero to operate in this world: the detective, a role which many noir heroes (including O'Hara) must play to see out the narrative.

In *Shanghai* the eventual explanation of what occurred is not watertight. Grisby's ploy to have himself 'murdered' is cunningly worked out, but apparently merely a front for his and Elsa's plan to frame O'Hara for the murder of Bannister. However, how they planned to frame O'Hara is not made entirely clear, and he is far more readily framed for the murder of Grisby as he has positioned himself to take the blame for this crime. O'Hara retrospectively expresses astonishment at his own stupidity, but he is seen as desperately desiring the money as a way of securing Elsa's affections. The explanation is less important than the presence of a twist which the hero cannot comprehend and must attempt to deal with. The twist is another favoured device of the Gothic novel; writing on Matthew Lewis's *The Monk* (1796), Punter notes that the author 'delights in complications of narrative' (also that 'The reader is made to move through a series of stories, and stories within stories' – reflecting the flashback narratives of *The Killers* et al). The complexity does not merely generate tension through its unpredictability, but reflects the disintegration of the hero's psyche as the narrative itself appears to disintegrate.

Similarly, the source of the animosity between Bannister, Grisby and Elsa is never identified, although Bannister draws attention to it: 'If you think George's story is interesting, you oughta hear the one about how Elsa got to be my wife!' Elsa's response: 'You want to tell him what you've got on me, Arthur?' The matter is never returned to, and instead O'Hara relates his story about the sharks. This does suggest that the characters are motivated by something in addition to money: Elsa worries about being cut off from Bannister 'without a cent', but was clearly induced to marry him through blackmail. Grisby, meanwhile, speaks of his fear of nuclear war and while his plan to 'disappear' is an invention this does not mean that his fear isn't genuine. Both characters therefore feel trapped, Elsa in her marriage and Grisby in the urban environment which he believes will soon be destroyed, and Bannister possesses a hold over them both which exploits their fear of the past. Again, the definition of 'a fearful sense of inheritance in time with a claustrophobic sense of enclosure in space' (see **Stranger on the Third Floor**) would seem to apply.

The imprisoned woman is a typical Gothic device, although in the Gothic romance she will usually be a far more sympathetic character whose male adversary persecutes her and/or keeps a secret from her. There is a strand of melodrama based on this model that runs parallel with film noir and often crosses into it, as many were directed by notable noir directors. Edgar G Ulmer's *Bluebeard* (1944) was a reworking of the folk tale which prefigures this entire genre; other examples are *My Name Is Julia Ross* (Joseph H Lewis, 1945), *The Spiral Staircase* (Robert Siodmak, 1945) and *Secret Beyond the Door* (Fritz Lang, 1948). It has often been suggested that these Gothic melodramas express women's fears about men in the way that film noir expresses male fears about women, and while this is obviously a simplistic view it can often be usefully applied; in a sense the persecuted wife and the married femme fatale are two sides of the same coin, viewed from different extremes. In an essay on *The Lady from Shanghai*, Andrew Britton argues that Welles's film sits at one end of that spectrum. He claims that Hayworth's character in *Gilda* 'combines elements of both the femme fatale and the trapped wife': men are attracted by her 'charismatic sexuality', but simultaneously need to overpower it and nullify its threat to them. The character of Gilda was in keeping with Hayworth's established screen persona: sensual, smart and fluid of movement. By contrast, *Shanghai*'s Elsa is highly stiff and artificial, her sexuality a mask which enables her to manipulate men for her own ends, and Britton argues that, because the film never problematises this view of women, there is a core of misogyny to it.

However, Elsa's artificial nature is also interesting in the context of Gothic, especially when the film arrives at the climactic shoot-out in the hall of mirrors; as Catherine Spooner notes, 'Gothic texts do not necessarily privilege surface but rather consistently foreground it in order to interrogate the surface-depth relationship.' The assumption that the depth is more authentic than the surface is frequently called into question. The film arguably plays upon Hayworth's established image here, as a means of suggesting the presence of another, more 'natural' self which Elsa systematically represses; a Gothic reading would identify that this other self is only another performance, a different but no more authentic Rita Hayworth. Once her duplicity is revealed, we are invited to consider the surface-depth relationship by the endless duplication of identical images of her, and the way that Bannister shoots at the various Elsas indiscriminately suggests that the distinction is irrelevant. Notably we never see any of these shots hit their targets, thereby denying us a moment when we can identify which are the real Elsa and Bannister. (There is, additionally, an obvious visual pun on the characters' duplicitous nature.)

When this type of narrative is treated with the Expressionist devices favoured by Welles, it takes on a dreamlike quality which again can be found in many Gothic novels. Horace Walpole's *The Castle of Otranto* (1765) was inspired by one of its author's dreams, and accordingly it operates upon a dreamlike logic where the plot has momentum but makes little overall sense. Andrew Spicer notes numerous references to dreams in Sherwood King's novel (its title, *If I Die Before I Wake*, suggests potential danger in dreaming), a theme which is less apparent in the film's dialogue, but is picked up in its unbalanced mise-en-scène. Like a dream, the plot appears to make sense on a scene-to-scene basis but is less coherent as a whole, mainly due to the apparent absence of motivation on the part of Bannister, Grisby and Elsa. Whether by accident or design, the film remains unresolved, contrary to classical Hollywood style. 'The narrative seems not so much to progress towards a resolution,' says Spicer, 'as compulsively double back; its present retelling is just one more effort to extract the meaning of the story.' Coupled with O'Hara's identity as a sailor, under this reading he emerges as a version of Coleridge's Ancient Mariner, cursed to retell his story. One can criticise some noirs, especially Welles's, for allowing style to overcome substance, but, in the light of Gothic scholarship, this does not make them necessarily lesser works.

AVAILABILITY: The Region 2 DVD (CDR 17896) contains background material from Welles's friend and acolyte Peter Bogdanovich, in the form of a twenty-minute featurette and a full-length commentary. The original trailer is included, as is that for *Gilda*, and there's a gallery of posters and lobby cards. It is also available as a Region 1 (IMP4859DVD) with the same features. The earlier PAL VHS has been deleted.

Force of Evil (1948)

Black and White – 80 mins

The Roberts Production of
Force of Evil
Screenplay by Abraham Polonsky and Ira Wolfert
Based upon the Novel *Turner's People* by Ira Wolfert
Music by David Raksin
Director of Photography: George Barnes, ASC
Operative Cameraman: Jack Warren
Art Director: Richard Day
Editorial Supervision: Walter Thompson
Film Editor: Arthur Seid
Executive Production Manager: Joseph C Gilpin
Assistant Director: Robert Aldrich
Musical Director: Rudolph Polk
Casting Director: Jack Baur
Set Decoration: Edward G Boyle
Head Grip: Carl Gibson
Make-up Supervision: Gus Norin
Hair Stylist: Lillian Lashin
Wardrobe Supervision: Louise Wilson
Hats by Kenneth Hopkins
Dialogue Director: Don Weis
Sound Engineer: Frank Webster
Assistant Film Editor: Howard Lee Paul
Produced by Bob Roberts
Directed by Abraham Polonsky

CAST: John Garfield (*Joe Morse*) with Thomas Gomez (*Leo Morse*), Marie Windsor (*Edna Tucker*), Howland Chamberlin (*Freddie Bauer*), Roy Roberts (*Ben Tucker*), Paul Fix (*Bill Ficco*), Stanley Prager (*Wally*), Barry Kelley (*Detective Egan*), Paul McVey (*Hobe Wheelock*) and introducing Beatrice Pearson (*Doris Lowry*)

SUMMARY: In New York, the 'numbers racket' is big business: people bet their small change on what lucky number will come up in the newspaper each day. In spite of the presence of numerous numbers 'banks' around the city, the practice is also illegal. Gangster/businessman Ben Tucker plans to take over the racket, by fixing the number on 4 July to come up as 776. An abnormally high number of people bet 776 on that date, and this will clear out the banks. Tucker will be poised to pay off these banks' debts and take them over, consolidating the racket into a single 'combination' owned by him. Wall Street lawyer Joe Morse is helping to legalise the racket, but he has another interest: his older brother Leo runs a small numbers bank and will be ruined by the operation. Joe is not allowed to tell Leo about the fix, but still tries to convince his brother to sell out to Tucker on 3 July and save his bank. Leo won't agree, so Joe puts his bank out of action by having the cops raid him. As Tucker takes over, Joe installs a reticent Leo as head of the thirteen banks in the combination. Leo's old bookkeeper Bauer has also kept his role, but finds the business now rife with gangsters. Bauer wants to quit, but is told that he will be killed; he is also approached by a member of Bill Ficco's mob. Ficco used to be Tucker's partner and wants in on the combination. Bauer calls the cops, and Leo and his staff are arrested again. Leo tells Joe that he wants out and Joe agrees to become head banker. However, Ficco's men kidnap Leo; Bauer, who leads them to Leo, is killed. Tucker makes peace with Ficco, accepting his mob into the combination as enforcers, and tells Ficco to release Leo. However, Leo has already been killed. A furious Joe surreptitiously leaves his tapped telephone off the hook and lets the cops hear everything about the combination and the murder of Leo. When Tucker becomes aware of this, a gunfight ensues which leaves Tucker and Ficco dead. Joe descends to the bank of the river and finds his brother's body, and resolves to help the law to close the racket down.

DIRECTOR: Abraham Polonsky (1910–99) was born in New York and graduated from the law school at Columbia University, but was quickly bored by working at a law firm. He met writer and broadcaster Molly Goldberg, who asked for his help on some points of law in a story she was writing, and with her support Polonsky began a radio writing career while teaching literature. He involved himself with left-wing causes, encouraging local workers to unionise. He published two novels, *The Goose Is Cooked* (1942) and *The Enemy Sea* (1943), the latter of which prompted Paramount to offer him a screenwriting contract. 'However appalled I was by the industry and its product,' he later said, 'the medium overwhelmed me with a language I had been trying to speak all my life.' Polonsky was determined to be involved in the war effort and joined the OSS, with Paramount agreeing to keep the job open pending his return. His OSS duties included the 'Black Radio' project, broadcasting misinformation into Germany, and interrogating captured German officers (including Rudolf Hess), but he resigned rather than take part in a counter-revolutionary operation in China. On returning to Paramount, he was dissatisfied with the work and requested a loan-out to the independent Enterprise Studios to write *Body and Soul* (Robert Rossen, 1947). *Force of Evil* was his directorial debut.

Subsequently Polonsky went to Twentieth Century-Fox and adapted *I Can Get it for You Wholesale* (Michael Gordon, 1951) from the novel by Jerome Weidman – which led to another offer to direct. Although Polonsky was happy living in France and working on a novel, *The World Above* (1951), he returned because HUAC was gearing up for more hearings and he wanted to take a stand against them. At his hearing in April 1951 he was ludicrously labelled 'the most dangerous man in America' and blacklisted. After writing his novel *A Season of Fear* (1956), he returned to New York and wrote for film and television under pseudonyms, collaborating on the script for *Odds Against Tomorrow* (Robert Wise, 1959). Later in the 1960s he started writing under his own name again, and became a successful script doctor. He directed two more films, *Tell Them Willie Boy Is Here* (1969) and *Romance of a Horsethief* (1970), but retired following a heart attack. He taught at the University of Southern California and wrote another novel, *Zenia's Way* (1980), and a play, *Piece de Resistance* (1981).

WRITER: Ira Wolfert (1908–97) was also a New Yorker. In his capacity as a war correspondent in the Pacific Theatre he won a Pulitzer Prize. *Tucker's People* was published in 1943 and his later novel *American Guerilla in the Philippines* (1945) was also adapted for the screen, under its original title (Fritz Lang, 1950). That his work was never adapted for the screen again is perhaps best explained by the fact that in the early 1950s he was declared by HUAC to be a Communist by association, on the grounds that he had sponsored the Scientific and Cultural Conference for World Peace (which was an anti-antiCommunist gathering, rather than a Communist one) and was supposedly 'affiliated with from five to ten Communist-front organizations' as well as being 'supported by Soviet Agencies, press or radio'. Certainly Wolfert had spoken out against the persecution of Communists by HUAC.

DEVELOPMENT: '*Body and Soul* made money,' Polonsky commented. 'It was a hit. When it was a hit, I was a hit. I had never directed anything. But I figured I could do it.' Enterprise's co-founder Bob Roberts liked Polonsky and made him aware that he could direct, if he wanted to. Polonsky returned to Roberts and said, 'I'd like to direct Garfield's next one for you even though I don't have any directing experience.' Roberts replied, 'Okay, go ahead. But make it a melo.' By this Roberts meant that he was looking for a melodrama; noirs, with their heightened sense of reality, were often referred to in Hollywood as melodramas.

(As an aside, the term 'melodrama' has since acquired pejorative associations and been transferred to the 'women's film'. This is a typical example of the manner in which entertainment with a predominantly female audience has been denigrated. 'Melodrama was a term of product classification used within the industry, and its trade meaning seems to have been almost diametrically opposed to that which criticism has put it,' says Richard Maltby. 'As far as the industry was concerned, James Cagney, not Joan Crawford, made melodramas . . . and it clearly expected these pictures to appeal predominantly to the men in the audience.' It is worth remembering that in the 1940s Hollywood expected its audience to be mostly female, and the bigger-budget films tended to be aimed at a female audience. Noirs, which were expected to appeal to men, were smaller productions and less commercially successful. While not denying that the noir movement is a hugely interesting aspect of film history, there is a hint of sexism in the way that the bigger-budget films of the 1940s are often characterised as artless and hackneyed by comparison.)

Working at an independent company, Polonsky was given a great deal of freedom to make the film he wanted. 'I knew that was where the fun was. The director spends the money. And it's harder to replace him . . . it 's a very expensive hobby. Getting rid of the writer is cheaper.' As material, Polonsky suggested *Tucker's People*. 'It had an allegory, true then and even more bitterly apt today; a milieu and characters familiar as my own habits; a hint of the language of the unconscious I could use as dialogue.' Furthermore, it would work as a melodrama. 'The book had a clear parallel to Fascism. I mean, that's an ordinary metaphor you find in all economic writing . . . gangsterism is capitalism, or the other way around. I don't know if that's true, but anyhow it's a metaphor when you're desperate.' He was aware that he was briefly in an enviable position. 'The great thing about success in Hollywood is that everything you say is considered potentially profitable. So, even though this was a potentially arty subject . . . I proposed it and they accepted it.'

Polonsky got in touch with Wolfert, who accepted the offer to write the first draft of the adaptation. 'What he wrote was good,' said Polonsky, 'but it was clearly Ira Wolfert writing a screenplay from one of his own novels. It's very difficult for a novelist to escape his own work.' Polonsky extensively rewrote Wolfert's draft, although the two men participated in lengthy discussions throughout this process. 'I no longer remember anything except the days Wolfert and I spent endlessly talking along the beaches. Under the windy sun we didn't reason so much as proclaim discoveries.' Polonsky stated, 'We eliminated the discursive power of the book and substituted for it so to speak centers of suggestion . . . Then it became obvious that some characters would play larger roles and others would disappear.' Tucker had been a central figure in the novel, but in the switch to a visual medium the two writers felt that he would possess more power if largely unseen. 'It was necessary for what I was trying to do,' said Polonsky. 'The more shadowy Tucker is, the more omnipresent the feeling of what he represents.' In spite of these changes, the novel's integrity had to remain. 'Adapting a book to film is fundamentally a moral crisis,' Polonsky said.

Studies of the film have often claimed that the script is written in blank verse. 'No,' was Polonsky's response when questioned about this. 'But the babble of the subconscious, yes, as much as I could, granted the premise that I was committed to a representational film.' He tried to 'use the succession of visual images, the appearance of human personality in the actors, and the rhythm of words in unison or counterpoint. I varied the speed, intensity, convergence and conflict for design, emotion and goal.' Commenting on the end of the film, which suggests that Joe learns from this experience, Polonsky stressed that the film was 'not a parable', or at least was not intended as such. 'It was a mixture of cop-out . . . and significance. It was a gangster film, and in those days, censorship was much stronger.' The ending was designed to appease the censor, suggesting hope in a collaboration between Joe and the forces of law and order. 'But that was *completely* on the surface. I didn't mean it at all. What I really meant were all those words at the end and all those images: "Down, down, down." '

CASTING: John Garfield (1913–52, born Jacob Julius Garfinkle; friends called him 'Julie') was from a Jewish Lower East Side family in New York and often found himself caught between the police and local gangs. At a school for 'problem' children he started acting and boxing, before eventually enrolling in the Ouspenskaya Drama School. In 1932 he joined the Civic Repertory Theater, where he made his Broadway debut as Jules Garfield, before moving to the left-wing Group Theater and winning acclaim in Clifford Odets's *Awake and Sing!* (1935). In 1938 he signed a contract with Warner Bros. (where he became John Garfield) and was Oscar-nominated for his debut, *Four Daughters* (Michael Curtiz, 1938). His first noir was *The Fallen Sparrow* (Richard Wallace, 1943); others include *The Postman Always Rings Twice* (Tay Garnett, 1946 – made on loan to MGM) and *Nobody Lives Forever* (Jean Negulesco, 1946). When his Warners contract came to an end in 1946 Garfield became one of the first actors to set up his own production company, Enterprise, and starred in *Body and Soul*, for which he received another Oscar nomination.

Garfield's career was cut short when the suspicions of HUAC fell on him. He had never been a communist (Polonsky claimed that Garfield

was not really a political man) but became a target due to his association
with the Group Theater and the liberal commitment of much of his work
(as well as *Force of Evil* he took a supporting role in *Gentleman's
Agreement* (Elia Kazan, 1947) in solidarity with its condemnation of
anti-Semitism). Although there were some other great roles – *The
Breaking Point* (Michael Curtiz, 1950) and the noir *He Ran All the Way*
(John Berry, 1951) – HUAC had him blacklisted in 1951 for refusing to
'name names'. The stress of this experience contributed to his death from
a heart attack in 1952. 'He defended his streetboy's honour,' said
Polonsky, 'and they killed him for it.'

First choice for the role of Leo Morse was Lee J Cobb, but he insisted
on wearing a hairpiece because he was thinking of reinventing himself as
a leading man. The resulting disagreement saw the role recast with
Thomas Gomez (1905–71, born Sabino Tomas Gomez), who had drifted
into acting after high school and ended up on Broadway after experience
with Luntz & Fontaine's touring theatre company. Universal signed him
in 1942, first casting him in the B-picture *Sherlock Holmes and the Voice
of Terror* (John Rawlins, 1942). A role in *Phantom Lady* (Robert
Siodmak, 1944) helped him move up to the likes of *Ride the Pink Horse*
(Robert Montgomery, 1947), for which he was Oscar-nominated. He
also appeared in the noirs *Johnny O'Clock* (Robert Rossen, 1947) and *I
Married a Communist* (Robert Stevenson, 1949) and took a role in *Key
Largo* (John Huston, 1948), and, although he remained very much a
supporting actor in Hollywood he was a distinguished lead on
Broadway. Also politically committed, he was a director of the Screen
Actors Guild for many years.

This was the film debut of Beatrice Pearson (born 1920). 'She was
brought to my attention by Martin Jurow, now a considerable producer
himself,' said Polonsky. 'He worked for our company at that time.'
Pearson's previous experience came from the stage, and it was to the
stage that she returned after making just one other film – the racial
drama *Lost Boundaries* (Alfred Werker, 1949) – and retiring from
movies. 'They didn't know how to use her,' said Polonsky, possibly
being tactful (see **PRODUCTION**). *Force of Evil* also provided the most
substantial role yet for one-time Miss Utah, Marie Windsor (1919–2000,
born Emily Marie Bertelsen), who had previously laboured in bit parts;
she was to become an icon of low-budget films during the 1950s (see **The
Killing**).

PRODUCTION: 'We had that big Hollywood machine which the
success of *Body and Soul* had delivered into our hands,' said Polonsky,
'and we didn't mind seeing what we could do with all that horse-power.'
He was given an excellent crew, including Robert Aldrich (see **Kiss Me**

Deadly) as assistant director and George Barnes (1892–1953), who Polonsky rated as 'probably one of the best cameramen we ever had in this town. He had deep-focus long before other people used it, before Welles and Tolland hit it.' Polonsky was presumably referring to Barnes's celebrated work on *Rebecca* (Alfred Hitchcock, 1940); his subsequent credits include *The File on Thelma Jordan* (Robert Siodmak, 1949). Barnes and Polonsky did a few days of test shooting, the results of which the director described as 'beautiful and vague. That is to say, the standard romantic photography that he'd been doing, which was absolutely against everything I intended to do on this picture.' The director 'tried to tell George what I was looking for, but I couldn't quite describe that to a cameraman, because I didn't know what to say'. In the end he went out and bought a book of Edward Hopper's Third Avenue paintings. 'Even when people are there, you don't see them; somehow the environments dominate the people.' *Office at Night* (1940), depicting a man and a woman working late, seems a particular influence on *Force of Evil*. 'I went to Barnes and I said, "This is kind of what I want." "Oh, that!" He knew right away what "that" was, and we had it all the way through the film.'

The interiors were shot on the Enterprise lot in Los Angeles over the summer of 1948, but the shoot also took in location work in Manhattan. Polonsky was keen to place his characters alongside the city's impressive architecture, including Trinity Church, the Treasury Building, Wall Street and the George Washington Bridge. 'Of course,' he added, 'you die at the foot of the bridge, but that happens all the time – we fall off our monuments. We spend our lives falling off our monuments.' This sense of grandeur was replicated in the studio sets, with their classical décor. 'The audience immediately accommodates that as being recognizable, significant, weighty – suggesting power and authority.' The effect was that, 'when you come to portray this story, which is actually a destructive analysis of the system, the décor gives you the tension that's necessary to disrupt the given situation.' A good example was the long take of the staircase which Tucker and Joe walk down near the beginning. 'They're on their way to hell, you see. But in the beginning, it looks like they're coming down a grand staircase. It's only later that you find out where they're really going.' Polonsky further noted of this scene, 'the voices are right on mike but the people are a mile away. I did that all the time. It was the style of the film,' in as much as 'I used the rhythmic line of the dialogue sometimes with the images, and sometimes against the images.'

Garfield struggled with the character of Joe Morse. 'Abe, I just don't understand this guy,' he told the director early on. 'I mean, what is he?' Polonsky told him, 'Just think of him as the same character you played in

Body and Soul, only with a college degree.' The next day, Garfield attached a Phi Beta Kappa fraternity key on a watch chain to the suit he wore as Joe. After this, he never lost his handle on the character. A rather less successful piece of casting was that of Pearson who, according to Windsor, continually made unreasonable demands on the crew to the point where they were half-seriously discussing dropping a sandbag on her head. Pearson and Gomez hated each other so much that Polonsky took to filming their scenes separately and editing the conversations together later, so that Pearson and Gomez didn't have to be in the same room together.

As *Force of Evil* was in post-production, Enterprise went bust after taking huge losses on its $5 million war film *Arch of Triumph* (Lewis Milestone, 1948). 'There was nobody upstairs to tell them "No",' said Polonsky. 'Nobody to stop over-spending or keep an eye on the budget.' Enterprise sold the distribution rights to *Force of Evil* to MGM, despite the fact that it is possibly the least MGM-esque film to have been made in America in the whole of the 1940s. The completed film was handed to MGM; this originally ran at almost ninety minutes, but some footage was cut late in the day. The main casualty of the cutting was a framing sequence of Joe testifying about the racket in court. It is unclear whether this change was made by Polonsky, MGM or the censors, but, as it would have had the effect of establishing Joe's eventual change of heart from the very beginning, it seems likely that Polonsky cut it. An eight-year-old Beau Bridges ended up on the cutting-room floor, having played Tucker's son Frankie in some scenes, and Sheldon Leonard's role as the head of a rival numbers bank went. The director also noted, 'I originally had a scene with the law, but I eliminated it. After all, who cares about *them*?'

Polonsky later expressed his satisfaction with the film (although he disliked the score), and his disappointment that he was unable to develop his use of film language. The collapse of Enterprise was partly responsible, but also 'the blacklist took the machine away from us,' as the director said. 'While we had possession . . . we couldn't wait to waken in the morning, knowing that each day would surprise us. We had the right feelings. Only our plane never flew.'

RECEPTION: MGM did not promote its acquisition widely. 'It got lost in the general dissolution of Enterprise Studios,' said Polonsky. 'Had we stayed in business we could have rescued it and made some money.' The film was released, entirely inappropriately, on 25 December 1948. 'It may be said that *Force of Evil*, which opened at Loew's State on Christmas Day, is not the sort of picture that one would choose for Yuletide cheer,' wrote Bosley Crowther in the *New York Times* on 27 December 1948. 'But for all its unpleasant nature, it must be said that this film is a dynamic crime-and-punishment drama, brilliantly and broadly realised.' Crowther praised the film's 'eloquent tatters of on-the-wing dialogue' and tried, in vain, to alert the public to 'a real new talent in the medium, as well as a sizzling piece of work'. The 'new talent', incidentally, was not Beatrice Pearson. 'New to the business of directing, Mr Polonsky here establishes himself as a man of imagination and unquestioned craftsmanship.'

Variety was a great deal less enthusiastic. '*Force of Evil* fails to develop the excitement hinted at in the title,' declared its review on 29 December 1948, describing the film as 'a missout for solid melodramatic entertainment, and will have to depend upon exceptionally strong exploitation and the value of the John Garfield name for the box office'. If anything, however, the review was optimistic about its commercial potential, noting its MGM backing. 'That distribution and the assured playdates mean that some coin will be returned, but the film lacks the essentials necessary to swing it through all situations at a profit.' The problem with the film was that 'A poetic, almost allegorical, interpretation keeps intruding on the tougher elements of the plot. This factor adds no distinction and only makes the going tougher.'

In Britain the film was released as part of a double bill with the noir *Act of Violence* (Fred Zinemann, 1948) and was not widely reviewed. Following on from her *Act of Violence* review in *The Sunday Times* of 24 April 1949, Dilys Powell noted, 'I find the second, less-advertised film in the programme superior; in fact, despite a theme . . . which I do not profess to understand, *Force of Evil* never for a moment lets the spectator escape its grip.' Whereas *Act of Violence* was thought to use 'conventional one-syllable cinema dialogue . . . *Force of Evil* credits the audience with intelligence in its ears as well as its eyes.' Furthermore, 'The passages of fast action are brilliantly done, and the kidnapping, with the death of the informer, take us back to the best days of the gangster cycle in the thirties.' Unfortunately, the *National Chronicle*'s review of 28 April 1949 was more typical and can be quoted here in its entirety: 'An efficiently made and in its way quite ruthless exposé of the New York "numbers racket".' Not negative, but it was hardly going to cause a stampede to the box office. (And it didn't.)

ASPECTS OF NOIR: *Force of Evil* is not a typical example of the late 1940s semi-documentary branch of film noir – but since there is a question mark over whether such films constitute noir anyway, and *Force of Evil* is most definitely a noir, this seems a good place to discuss the subject.

An increase in location work in Hollywood had begun during the war as a response to the restriction on new materials for set-building. As equipment became lighter and more portable, location work started to become actively desirable to a number of filmmakers (although some studio heads were initially resistant, as it made their productions more difficult to monitor). After the war American critics and filmmakers were inspired by the Italian neo-realist movement, exemplified by such films as *Rome, Open City* (Roberto Rossellini, 1945) and *The Bicycle Thief* (Vittorio de Sica, 1948). Many such films were shot on location with small budgets, naturalistic lighting and non-professional actors. Similar approaches had existed in Hollywood as far back as Alfred Hitchcock's noir *Shadow of a Doubt* (1943), which had made much use of its Santa Rosa location. Rather than populate scenes with extras, Hitchcock let passers-by wander through the shots to create a sense of realism. Subsequently Twentieth Century-Fox head Darryl Zanuck was keen for producer Louis de Rochemont to move the studio's lower-budget productions out of the studio, to free up space for big-budget, studio-bound projects such as costume dramas. The result of this was *The House on 92nd Street* (Henry Hathaway, 1945), a very literal movement towards greater realism based on the true story of how the FBI had prevented Nazi spies from seizing the formula for the atomic bomb. De Rochement had previously been responsible for the successful *March of Time* newsreel series and used elements of their style to add verisimilitude, including an omniscient voice-over narration, and its use of real FBI agents and the genuine locations where events had taken place was used as a selling point. It worked, and the film was a substantial hit.

Fox went on to adopt this as a house style for its crime films, although it was imitated by other studios, most notably Universal-International. Mark Hellinger's work as an independent producer through Universal resulted in a small number of highly influential films with elements of semi-documentary style, the first of which was *The Killers*. Hellinger's career was cut short by a fatal heart attack in 1947 but one of the last films he set up, *The Naked City* (Jules Dassin, 1948), was arguably the ultimate expression of his approach and took much of the credit for developing the semi-documentary style. A police thriller shot on the streets of New York, its journalistic, investigative tone is summed up in its title as well as the closing line, 'There are eight million stories in the naked city . . . this has been one of them.' Its subsequent prominence over *The House on 92nd Street* probably reflects that the earlier film was very much of its time, a sensational celebration of America's victory in the war, while *The Naked City*'s effort to tell a quite ordinary murder story in detail, and make it interesting, has been more influential and comes closer to what we think of as 'realism' than an espionage drama. In addition, it clearly influenced *He Walked by Night* (Alfred Werker,

1948) which in turn spawned the TV series *Dragnet* (1951–59, 1967–70, 2002–03), so its status in popular culture looms large.

These films' status as noir is debatable because, although they embrace the toughness and clipped dialogue of noir, their ideology is frequently more conservative. The use of real cases from the files of the police, the FBI and the US Treasury often resulted in films which placed those institutions in a highly positive light, and critics such as Michael Walker have asserted, 'Ideologically, they are the polar opposite to films noirs: they celebrate the efficacy of the American crime-fighting institutions that film noir views with such suspicion.' However, not all critics agree. Andrew Spicer contends that 'their politics were more ambivalent than is usually recognised,' and Walker does go on to note a number of films which contain both noir and semi-documentary elements: Hathaway's later pictures *Kiss of Death* (1947) and *Call Northside 777* (1948) have a bleaker side, and *T-Men* (Anthony Mann, 1948) has a more noir visual style which undercuts the 'realism' of the piece.

A good example is *Cry of the City* (1948), made at Fox by Robert Siodmak shortly after *The Killers*. Shot mainly in New York, the noir photography of his earlier films is replaced with a naturalistic grey look (the Expressionist style of earlier noirs had flourished in the controlled studio environment, but was less common outdoors). Its tale of cop Lt Candella (Victor Mature) and criminal Martin Rome (Richard Conte) who grew up in the same neighbourhood invites parallels, but no excuses are made for Rome: he just turned bad. The cop's obsessive pursuit of the case has a noirish edge to it, particularly under Walker's homosexual reading ('If we take it that all along Candella has been harbouring an unrequited love for Rome, everything falls into place') but there remains an emphasis on police procedure, as all of the people who have helped Rome along the way are punished and the film encourages the viewer to see this as selfishness on Rome's part. However, docu-noirs do not always side against the criminal: Sterling Hayden portrays more sympathetic criminals in *The Asphalt Jungle* (John Huston, 1950) and *The Killing*, both of which include documentary elements (the latter making use of the omniscient narrator).

Among all this, *Force of Evil* is an unusual film, as its script and dialogue are quite stylised. The fact that much of it is filmed on location in New York does not necessarily make it a docu-noir: other films of this period such as *Out of the Past* and *Gun Crazy* feature a similar level of location work. The New York setting is worth pointing out, as noirs are more likely to be set in California than anywhere else (most of the films featured in this book are set largely in California, and no less than three tell the story of a journey which starts in New York and ends in tragedy in California). This may simply indicate laziness or frugality on the part of Hollywood, unwilling to move outside its back yard, but many of the key noir fiction writers wrote about California, despite not being from the state: Chandler was drawn to Los Angeles, Hammett to San Francisco. James M Cain struggled for a voice until 'I moved to California and heard the Western roughneck: the boy who is just as elemental inside as his Eastern colleague, but has been to high school, completes his sentences, and uses reasonably good grammar.' By contrast, semi-documentaries tend to be set in New York, as though it is a more 'realistic' place than Los Angeles, with its Hollywood 'dream factory'.

This is one of the aspects that pushes *Force of Evil* into docu-noir territory. It does not take place in the chaotic noir world inhabited by Philip Marlowe; there is none of the random fatalism seen in *Detour*; nor is there the 'mad love' which drives the characters in *Double Indemnity* and *Out of the Past*. The world of *Force of Evil* is orderly and detailed, explained to us in full by Joe or one of the other characters, and there are no unexpected events. In many other semi-documentaries, at least some of this attention to detail would be devoted to showing us the mechanisms of the justice system, but this is not the case here. The focus is entirely on the criminal organisation, with the law no more than a background presence which is frequently corrupt. It often seems there is no hope: the criminal organisation is a relentless force (of evil, natch) which leans on people until they acquiesce and disposes of those who won't. Although this film has gangsters in it, it is unlike the majority of gangster films due to its lack of action (even the climactic shoot-out happens in near-total darkness). The examination of this world, and what it does to its characters, is made so compelling as to make action unnecessary.

The film has a clear sense of political purpose. Seizing upon a situation that existed in the 1940s, as gangsters sought to become legitimate businessmen, *Force of Evil* demonstrates how easily corporate techniques of takeover and merger apply to criminal operations. The film heavily implies that the gangsters embody the values of right-wing America, and equates anybody who holds such values with criminals. The film has very little sympathy for anybody involved in the racket: Doris emerges with the most credit for realising that working for the bank makes her a criminal. Leo, who has clung to the belief that he has been running his own criminal operation fairly, finally realises that he too is a crook and wants out, making no excuses for himself (his comment that he gave up his future so that Joe could be a lawyer is more a criticism of Joe than a defence of his own choices). Polonsky characterises Leo as 'even worse' than Joe; 'he felt he had an ethical basis. It is even true in American society today. Small businessmen feel ethically superior to trusts, and our laws reflect it.' While the semi-documentary has often been characterised as right-wing moralising, *Force of Evil* amounts to left-wing moralising.

While the film does not attempt the kind of didactic authority of the newsreel-style semi-documentaries, it does have the air of an exposé. Director Martin Scorsese, who grew up in New York in the 1940s, stated, 'The numbers racket . . . was going on around us all the time and here was a film which dealt with it honestly and openly and had a crooked lawyer with whom we could identify.' Scorsese also cited *Force of Evil* as 'a great influence on me', and although it largely went unnoticed at the time it is arguably the noir most reminiscent of 1970s New Hollywood cinema – which, in turn, was hugely influential on the cinema which came after it. Meanwhile, the 'realistic' police stories seen in the likes of *The Naked City* spawned numerous variations on film and particularly on television, suggesting that, while docu-noir may not be the best-loved branch of film noir, it is perhaps the most influential.

AFTERLIFE: The film sometimes ran under the alternative titles of *The Numbers Racket* and *The Story of Tucker's People*. The 1977 TV movie *Force of Evil* has nothing to do with this production.

AVAILABILITY: In the UK *Force of Evil* is only available on VHS (2ND1010). It has been released as a Region 1 DVD with no special features.

Gun Crazy (1949)
A.K.A. *Deadly is the Female*

Black and White – 87 mins

United Artists Presents
Gun Crazy
A King Bros. Production
Screenplay by MacKinlay Kantor and Millard Kaufman
From the *Saturday Evening Post* story by MacKinlay Kantor
Music by Victor Young
Assistant to the Producers: Arthur Garner
Director of Photography: Russell Harlan, ASC
Film Editor: Harry Gerstad
Sound Engineer: Tom Lambert
Production Designed by Gordon Wiles

Music Editor: Stuart Frye
Orchestrations by Leo Shuken and Sidney Cutner
Song 'Mad About You', Music by Victor Young, Lyrics by
Ned Washington
Assistant Director: Frank S Heath
Production Manager: Allen K Wood
Set Decorator: Raymond Boltz Jr
Dialogue Coach: Madeleine Robinson
Script Continuity by Jack Herzberg
Technical Adviser: Herman King
Miss Cummins's Wardrobe by Norma
Produced by Maurice King and Frank King
Directed by Joseph H Lewis

CAST: Peggy Cummins (*Annie Laurie Starr*), John Dall (*Bart Tare*) with
Berry Kroeger (*Packett*), Morris Carnovsky (*Judge Willoughby*), Anabel
Shaw (*Ruby Tare*), Harry Lewis (*Clyde Boston*), Nedrick Young (*Dave
Allister*), Rusty Tamblyn (*Bart Tare, age fourteen*)

SUMMARY: After being caught stealing a gun, teenager Bart Tare is
sentenced to a reform school in spite of pleas by his sister (also his legal
guardian) and his two best friends, Clyde Boston and Dave Allister. After
leaving school and serving some years in the army Bart returns to his
hometown, where Clyde is sheriff and Dave a newspaper reporter. They
celebrate by going to a carnival, where Bart out-shoots the resident
trick-shooter, Annie Laurie Starr, and is given a job. Boss Packett
becomes jealous of Bart and Laurie's obvious attraction to each other
and they are fired. The pair marry and live happily on the road until they
lose all their money in Vegas. At Laurie's suggestion they start to hold up
cash registers, then move on to robbing banks. However, Bart is
reluctant to kill and so Laurie suggests one last job which they can retire
on: a payroll heist. They succeed, but Laurie kills two people and the
money is traced and seized at their hotel. A penniless Bart and Laurie
escape and hide out at his sister's house. Clyde and Dave find them and
offer them the chance to give themselves up. Bart and Laurie continue to
run, but, when cornered by Clyde, Dave and several policemen, Bart
shoots Laurie to prevent her killing his old friends. The other policemen
fire, killing Bart also.

DIRECTOR: Joseph H Lewis (1907–2000) was born in New York. His
brother Ben was an editor in silent-era Hollywood and helped Lewis get
an office job at MGM in the early 1930s. Lewis moved up to camera
assistant at MGM before becoming an editor at low-budget Mascot

FILM NOIR Gun Crazy

Pictures (which subsequently became Republic). On moving to Universal, as a director of B westerns he was nicknamed 'Wagon Wheel Joe' for his habit of framing shots through the spokes of a wheel. He directed the first three East Side Kids comedies for Monogram (starting with 1940's *Boys of the City*), before tackling horror (1941's *The Invisible Ghost*), crime thrillers (1942's *Secrets of a Co-Ed*), and an entry in the Falcon series (1945's *The Falcon in San Francisco*). His first film for Columbia, the noir B-movie *My Name Is Julia Ross* (1945), is a cult classic, and the follow-up, *So Dark the Night* (1946), was also a noir. Later that year Lewis directed the musical numbers on *The Jolson Story* (1946), which helped him move up to A-pictures. After three more films for Columbia, including the docu-noir *Undercover Man* (1949), Lewis sought work elsewhere. (See **The Big Combo** for more Lewis.)

WRITER: MacKinlay Kantor (1904–77, born Benjamin McKinlay Kantor) added the extra 'a' to his name because he felt it sounded more Scottish. His mother was editor of the *Webster City Daily News* and he published his first efforts at journalism while at high school. He started writing fiction around the same time, publishing his first story (*Purple*) in 1922 and his first novel (*Diversey*, about gangsters) in 1928. Although mainly noted for his historical fiction, Kantor's crime writing has been suggested as an influence on Cornell Woolrich, often displaying a nightmarish aspect as apparently inexplicable events unfold. His work for the pulps includes *The Second Challenge* (1929) and *The Light at Three O'Clock* (1930); he produced early examples of the police-procedural narrative for *Detective Fiction Weekly*, including *The Trail of the Brown Sedan* (1933). 'Gun Crazy' was a short piece published in the *Saturday Evening Post* in 1940. His work was adapted for the screen several times, including the 1945 story 'Glory for Me' which became *The Best Years of Our Lives* (William Wyler, 1946). In 1955 Kantor published *Andersonville*, a novel about the American Civil War, for which he won the Pulitzer Prize.

Millard Kaufman was a noted Hollywood screenwriter, but he did not write this; he merely allowed his name to be used as a front for Dalton Trumbo (1905–76). Born in Colorado, Trumbo worked as a newspaper reporter and editor, turning his hand to novel-writing with the pacifist *Johnny Got His Gun* (1939). In 1935 he became a screenwriter, penning *Road Gang* (Louis King, 1936) for First National; he later moved to RKO, and wrote the Oscar-winning *Kitty Foyle* (Sam Wood, 1940). The 1940s saw Trumbo become Hollywood's best-paid screenwriter but this came to an end in 1947, when he was blacklisted for his hard left-wing views and refusal to co-operate with HUAC. *Gun Crazy* was his first post-blacklist screenplay. Subsequently Trumbo moved to Mexico to continue writing for Hollywood throughout the 1950s under a variety of fronts and pseudonyms, during which time his original story for *Roman Holiday* (William Wyler, 1953) and script for *The Brave One* (Irving Rapper, 1956) both won Oscars. On the first occasion, Trumbo let fellow writer Ian McLellan Hunter take the credit and collect the award; on the second, confusion reigned as the credited writer 'Robert Rich' failed to appear. Trumbo eventually revealed that he was Rich in January 1959, safe in the knowledge that Kirk Douglas had promised to break the blacklist and give him an on-screen credit for *Spartacus* (Stanley Kubrick, 1960). He returned to work in Hollywood on films such as *Papillon* (Franklin Schaffer, 1973) and in 1971 directed his own adaptation of *Johnny Got His Gun*.

DEVELOPMENT: The King brothers – Maurice, Frank and Herman, whose original family name was Kozinski – had been left fatherless at an early age and turned to bootlegging liquor during Prohibition as a means of supporting themselves and their mother. They subsequently founded a slot-machine company, made substantial profits and moved into movie production, with Maurice developing scripts, Frank in charge of production and Herman overseeing distribution. Their criminal background and unwillingness to toe Hollywood lines made them perpetually disreputable, but they were confident in their instincts. 'We know what'll be good subjects,' Maurice King once said. 'We like action and movement and psychological mysteries – close to life, though.' They started out cheaply in the 1930s, making B-features for PRC, then moved up to Monogram, where they made one of the most celebrated 'poverty row' movies, *Dillinger* (Max Nosseck, 1945), which was Oscar-nominated for its script. Their follow-up *The Gangster* (Gordon Wiles, 1947) flopped and they intended their next movie to be a higher-quality project through United Artists. Seeing that Kantor had fallen out with the majors during a disagreement with Sam Goldwyn about *The Best Years of Our Lives*, they spoke to him about scripting a slice-of-life drama called *Passport in Purple*. Kantor pitched them *Gun Crazy* instead, suggesting that it could be shot on location in his hometown of Webster City, Iowa, and the Kings commissioned this idea.

Kantor's first draft, dated 24 March 1947, had central characters called Nelly and Toni and was around 180 pages long (Lewis's later claims that it was an unfilmable 375 pages have been discredited). The extra material mostly came at the beginning and made the film more overtly autobiographical, relating the formative years of Nelly (later to become Bart) in greater detail. Kantor had also been a gun enthusiast as a child; he had the same upsetting experience of shooting a small bird (in his case a sparrow); and he grew up with no father in the home. Accordingly, these elements were given far greater emphasis in the script. Kantor suggested that the opening credits should run over a montage of different guns being fired, ranging from small ones to large. The first scene would have depicted Nelly's father, Jay Coulter, being shot down by a posse; Jay, a W.W.I veteran, had come to imagine himself a latter-day Jesse James and gone on a crime spree. The ending was also different, with Laurie going through with her plan of kidnapping the baby and suffering a literally harrowing death, run over and mauled by a disc harrow belonging to a farmer whom she had shot.

Lewis noted that Kantor 'has never forgiven me' for his treatment of *Gun Crazy*'s script. 'Maybe I took out some of the things that he liked . . . he's the only one I ever spoke to who said he thought the picture was horrible.' On the day that Dalton Trumbo returned home from the Washington HUAC hearings of October 1947, the Kings contacted him about *Gun Crazy*. The hearings had seen him issued with a citation for contempt of court, for which he was due to serve a year's prison sentence commencing in June 1950. He had incurred legal costs and MGM had suspended his lucrative contract; he was about to embark upon a further legal battle to force MGM to pay it off, but needed money in the meantime. No major studio would employ Trumbo, but the Kings had different priorities. 'Politics didn't enter into it at all,' commented Frank King. 'I guess he spoke his mind before Congress, and that was all right with us. But we never discussed that at all. We were just interested in making pictures.' They offered him $3,750 over eighteen months for his work on the script. Trumbo later stressed that he did not feel exploited. 'A lot of independents never paid more than that. When I and others plummeted in value, we naturally found ourselves in this new market, and naturally these independent producers availed themselves of our services.' The money he'd been offered was as much as the Kings could reasonably spend. 'There was no big deal to it,' said Frank King. 'We just had a short budget to make a picture and saw this as an opportunity to get a fine writer whom we could not otherwise afford.'

The Production Code office had made extensive comments on Kantor's version, which Trumbo was obliged to incorporate. The censors had called Kantor's script 'a very worrisome story . . . which, by its very nature, must inspire sympathy throughout, not only for the criminal, but for his *criminal acts* as well.' The eroticisation of gun crime was less of a concern, or perhaps simply didn't occur to them, but the repetition of violence and lack of any 'voice for morality' were heavily questioned. The censor insisted upon the central couple marrying, but also suggested 'a greater recognition on the part of [Nelly], himself, for the career of crime into which Toni has led him'. Thus, as Trumbo rewrote the characters as Bart and Laurie, he made Bart express more reticence while Laurie became more of a villain.

Trumbo submitted a draft of 146 pages on 17 November 1948. His main alteration was to introduce the young Bart's trial as a device for running through some key childhood moments in flashback. The parallel between the scene of young Bart out shooting with his friends, and their reunion when Bart leaves the army, helped bridge the lengthy gap in the narrative. This was an impressively elegant way of shortening the beginning, bringing Laurie's appearance forwards and getting to the action more quickly; it was probably also the alteration which most displeased Kantor, to whom this material meant a great deal, but Trumbo's surgery was justified. The ending also changed to something more akin to the filmed version. The final shooting draft, dated 5 April 1949, was shorter still – just 116 pages. The use of Kaufman's name as a front on the credits set a precedent that was much used by blacklist writers in the 1950s. Not only was it useful for the Kings to avoid being seen to break the blacklist, but also Trumbo needed it to appear that he had not broken the terms of his MGM contract if he was to force the studio to pay it off – and this included not working for other studios.

CASTING: Peggy Cummins (born 1925) was originally from Wales and acted on the British stage and screen from an early age, making her debut in *Dr O'Dowd* (Herbert Mason, 1940). She became known as an exciting young actress and was brought across to Hollywood to star in *Forever Amber* (Otto Preminger, 1947) for Twentieth Century-Fox. However, production was halted after three weeks so that the script could be revised, and it was decided that Cummins was unsuitable for the part. (Her scenes were reshot with Linda Darnell.) This damaged Cummins's Hollywood career, as she found only lower-profile roles. Lewis felt that she was a perfectly good actress who had been made a scapegoat on *Forever Amber* and not only did she deserve a second chance, but also she – like Trumbo – would be willing to take a step down in salary and prestige for the sake of a good job. The character of Laurie changed from Canadian to British to accommodate her casting. However, the commercial failure of *Gun Crazy* meant that it was her last American film. Other notable work in Britain includes *Meet Mr Lucifer* (Anthony Pelissier, 1953), Ealing comedy *The Love Lottery* (Charles Crichton, 1954) and *Carry On Admiral* (Val Guest, 1957 – which is not one of the *Carry On* series), although in the early 1960s she gave up film work and returned to the theatre. However, *Gun Crazy* and the horror *Night of the Demon* (Jacques Tourneur, 1957) ensured that she became a cult figure in cinema.

The film career of John Dall (1918–71, born John Dall Thompson) surprisingly never quite took off, even though he was Oscar-nominated for his movie debut, *The Corn Is Green* (Irving Rapper, 1945), a Hollywood movie rather bizarrely set in Wales. He followed this with the Civil War drama *Another Part of the Forest* (Michael Gordon, 1948) and a compelling performance in Alfred Hitchcock's real-time film *Rope* (1948). His next film was *Gun Crazy*, for which he lobbied hard and only won when the Kings failed to secure Gregory Peck or Dana Andrews in the role. 'I wanted to have a boy who would portray weakness; and the girl great strength,' noted Lewis. However, he 'didn't want the boy to act this . . . I wanted a boy who already had it, it was there inside.' Of those whom he considered for the role, two stood out, 'and only for one reason, because I honestly believed they belonged to the gay set.' Whether it came via prejudice or otherwise, Lewis got the effect he wanted from Dall. 'He played himself in that regard; and he did a magnificent job, without acting as a weakling. I never told him at any time that he was the weaker of the two.' After this, Dall made only the noir *The Man Who Cheated Himself* (Felix Feist, 1950) before spending the rest of the 1950s doing TV and stage work. Following a substantial role in *Spartacus* (Stanley Kubrick, 1960), his final film was *Atlantis, the Lost Continent* (George Pal, 1961).

PRODUCTION: Lewis would later recall *Gun Crazy* as 'just a brilliantly executed film from every angle, from every department, all the way through. And it took extreme courage and guts on the producers' part to allow me to shoot a film like that.' The film was budgeted at $450,000 and allotted a thirty-day shoot, largely on location as Kantor had originally suggested but not in Webster City. The Kings claimed that bad weather was to blame for the shift, but it was probably more to do with convenience and cost. An irritated Kantor broke with the production. The locations used were all on the west coast: the towns of Montrose and Reseda in California were used for the bank jobs; the Armour Plant in the final robbery was actually on East Olympic Boulevard, Hollywood; and the fictional San Lorenzo Mountains were represented by Baldwin Lake Estates and Topanga Canyon. In accordance with the low budget, the leads mostly wore their own clothes, and Laurie's beret, which evoked Bonnie Parker, was Cummins's idea.

The Production Code continued to influence production, insisting that Lewis could not linger on any shots of the guns and advising him to shoot extra coverage of some sequences to allow for later editing. An earlier version of the script saw Bart shooting out light fittings during the second robbery, causing glass to rain down on terrified employees flattened on the floor and thus discouraging any heroics. The censor raised concerns over this, stating that it would be wise to shoot 'some protection shots, merely showing them leaving'. Although the script had changed substantially by the time it went into production, it seems that Lewis did use this approach. A still from the Rangers & Growers heist shows action which did not make it into the film, strongly suggesting that this sequence was cut for violence. Lewis believed that the Code's approach was often misjudged, noting that he was also not permitted to linger on any death scene and the result was that the deaths lacked impact and felt unreal. 'So when she shoots the guard and he drops, that was done so quickly that it's really an illusion.'

The most celebrated sequence in *Gun Crazy* is the bank hold-up which was achieved in a single take. The original script outlined this in a seventeen-page sequence in which Bart and Laurie drove into town, entered the bank, told all the customers to lie down, went inside the vault, took the money and drove away with cops in pursuit – a standard-issue bank robbery scene. Lewis became convinced there was an opportunity to do something much more interesting. 'I didn't know what it was,' he later said, 'but I knew it wasn't that, and I said, "Jesus Christ, Joe, you can't make films like this – this is junk. Now think, goddammit, think!" ' Lewis drove out to Montrose, where the exteriors were to be shot, and scouted it. Then he returned, bringing with him two extras (a man and a woman) and his own 16mm camera. He sat them in the front seats and told them to drive into town and to the bank, talking to each other as they went. Lewis sat on the back seat and shot this with his 16mm. 'Now, when we see the bank through the windshield and all,' he told the man, 'you get out, walk into the bank, then turn right around. Count to ten or something.' The man did so, and after a while Lewis told the woman, 'Now you get out of the car; count to three and by that time he'll come running out.' The three of them drove away, Lewis still filming.

Everybody else was still planning the bank hold-up on the assumption that the inside of the bank would have to be created in the studio. 'They were going to build sets, everything – everything. I came back to my producers and told them I had an idea how I wanted to shoot this thing in one setup.' The Kings were intrigued, but a production manager stated flatly that it was impossible. Lewis announced, 'Gentlemen, I want to show you something.' He led them into a projection room and screened his 16mm dummy run. The sequence would no longer involve going inside the bank; instead, it would thrive on the tension of not knowing what was happening inside. It was agreed that, if Lewis could pull it off, this would mark *Gun Crazy* as a remarkable picture.

The car used was a stretch version of the Cadillac used in the rest of the film, which appeared identical at the front but accommodated extra seats in the back. The seats were removed to make room for the crew and equipment. The most difficult part would be when the camera had to track forwards to keep Peggy Cummins in shot when she stepped out of the car; this was achieved by mounting a saddle on a flat board, then placing this on top of another board with a layer of grease in between. It was then possible for the cameraman to sit in the saddle, and the crew could slide him back and forth as required. The shot was partly made possible by brand new portable equipment, which Lewis was given the first opportunity to use, the sound-recording equipment could be stored in the back and button microphones could be placed under the sunshades at the top of the windscreen, picking up all of Cummins and Dall's dialogue inside the car. For the dialogue that took place outside the car, two sound men were secured to the luggage rack with parachute straps, picking up the sound with boom microphones. Lighting was provided by 'two little fill lights, working off batteries'.

Finally, Lewis prepared his actors. 'Now look, you know the intent of this scene. I have no dialogue for it because none can be written,' he told Cummins and Dall. The only part which he could provide was Laurie's conversation with the policeman; everything else would be subject to what actually happened on the road in front of them. 'The dialogue you will supply is what you see. You're coming into a strange town, if there are people in the way, you'll refer to that.' The first take was a complete success; there was no need for a remount. 'It turned out to be just a magnificent shot,' Lewis said later. 'And rather than four or five days, it took about three hours of shooting in the morning. In those days you'd get about three to four pages a day.'

Lewis claimed that the use of a swamp in the final sequence was his own idea. 'Dramatically I wanted to use a swamp from the first . . . it's great because you can dictate the tones, the qualities . . . a splash in the water can create hysteria if there's silence all around you.' This doesn't address the unlikelihood of finding a swamp in the middle of the mountains, but never mind. Lewis's copy of the script contained a note next to the final scene: 'Shoot ending (alt.) of Laurie killing Bart who stands in front pleading not to shoot at Dave and Clyde. Both endings.' It is unknown whether he did shoot this, but he ultimately made the decision to go with Trumbo's ending. The censors were particularly concerned with whether the film ended on an appropriate moral tone, and judged whether there was sympathy for the criminal protagonists at their demise. 'Yes and no,' they concluded. 'Some sympathy generated for John Dall, none for Peggy Cummins.' This was considered acceptable and a Production Code Seal for the film was eventually granted on 9 September 1949, somewhat grudgingly. It was 'Issued upon the understanding that in all release prints . . . the scene of Cummins and Dall kissing on the bed will be the one in which you blur and fade out.'

Even after it had been passed by the censors, the film was still trimmed by local boards in Maryland, Massachusetts, Ohio and Pennsylvania.

Distribution remained an issue. 'Just after we made the film,' commented Lewis, 'Metro [MGM] offered a million dollars for it. Of course, the film cost considerably less than that.' However, MGM stipulated that the Kings' production credit would be removed, ostensibly to reduce prejudice about the Kings' product. The Kings refused and went with their original plan of distributing through United Artists. When UA viewed *Gun Crazy*, they realised that it could be presented as more than just another lurid thriller, and decided upon a change of title. Lewis happened to be in the office of UA's Eddie Small, discussing his next project, when the company heads in New York called and instructed Small to find a 'classier' title. 'You cannot give it another title,' was Lewis's response when Small told him of UA's intent. 'The title it has is most provocative.' Small agreed, but had to follow his superiors' instructions and called upon the UA staff to come up with a new title – all suggestions would be considered, and the winner would get $50. One of Lewis's friends, Arthur Gardner, was the winner. 'We often laugh about it,' said Lewis. 'He came up with *Deadly Is the Female*, and I wanted to vomit. But he won fifty bucks.'

RECEPTION: The film was released on 1 December 1949. *Variety* got an early look and drew attention to the title change. '*Gun Crazy*,' read its review on 2 November 1949, referring to Kantor's original story, 'comes to the screen under the odd title of *Deadly Is the Female*. Hiding behind that ordinary tag is a shoot-'em-up story of desperate love and crime.' The verdict was reasonably positive, declaring that the film's 'chances in the general market are fair and b.o. will be moderate, depending upon the type of selling used to get it over'. According to Lewis, however, the type chosen by United Artists was none. 'The film was not sold, because there was no sales organisation behind it. United Artists' distribution had become nil. And mostly the film just laid there on the shelf. It never played anywhere, really.' UA had expected it to gross around $8 million. It made closer to $8.

United Artists effectively admitted its mistake by reissuing the film as *Gun Crazy* on 24 August 1950, only to be quite reasonably rejected by exhibitors who didn't want to touch a failed movie under a different name. It was decisions such as this which led to UA running into financial problems. Some sources continue to list the film as *Deadly Is the Female*, this being its title on initial release, but, in accordance with (a) the filmmakers' intentions, (b) recent commercial releases and television screenings and (c) aesthetic considerations, it is listed here as *Gun Crazy*. It was reviewed more upon its second run, although not terribly well. 'Even with some adroit camouflaging,' wrote Howard Thompson in the *New York Times* of 25 August 1950, 'the Palace's new picture . . . is pretty cheap stuff. *Gun Crazy* just about covers it.' Many aspects of the film were praised: 'the actual script . . . is a fairly literate business' was followed by 'The dialogue is quite good and the photography is first rate. In fact, director Joseph H Lewis has kept the whole thing zipping along at a colorful tempo which deserves a much better outlet.' It was the subject matter which Thompson found difficult to get to grips with: 'this spurious concoction is basically on a par with the most humdrum pulp fiction.'

The British reviews were similar, adding a small amount of umbrage towards Cummins for having the temerity to leave Britain and make pictures like this. 'Not five years out of London,' complained the *Observer* on 23 July 1950, 'and Hollywood has . . . cast her as a hard, homicidal, middle-western fairground trick shooter who can knock the iris out of a bank-teller's eye at fifty yards and spend the cash on mink in fifty minutes.' Oddly, she was thought to be sporting 'a pathetic little apology for an American accent', although the character is explicitly British. Of Laurie's claims that 'I'm yours, and I'm real,' the reviewer considered, 'the former is unsupportable and the latter unbelievable.' Others found praise for Lewis, particularly Dilys Powell. 'One could dismiss the piece with no more ado were it not in parts uncommonly well directed,' she wrote in *The Sunday Times* on 23 July 1950. 'The American cinema rarely fails with a hold-up or a chase; but here the approach to the scene of a robbery . . . and the tension of waiting are handled with more than the usual skill.' Ultimately, however, she too came to the conclusion that 'It is a pity that Mr Lewis was not given material less uneven and less crude.'

Lewis, who often rated *Gun Crazy* as the best of his own films, was dismally disappointed. 'The only success that picture had was the Bel Air circuit and the studios – every studio ran it.' The chief fascination for other filmmakers was the single-take hold-up sequence. One afternoon at his tennis club, Lewis took a telephone call from Billy Wilder. 'I'm here at the studio with a bunch of guys and we just ran your film – it's great,' said Wilder. 'How'd you do that shot in the car?' Lewis replied, 'Billy, I promised I wouldn't tell.' Wilder responded, 'No, we had an argument at the studio yesterday. I say you used at least three to four background-projection machines – and somebody said you might have shot it real. I say it's impossible.' Lewis just said, 'Billy, I'm sorry. It's real, all right.'

ASPECTS OF NOIR: After Bart and Laurie have lost all their money, but before they turn to crime, Bart comments, 'Well, we've still got a full tank of gas': a sentiment which embodies the spirit of the road movie, and it is interesting to consider *Gun Crazy* as an example of this genre. The early road movie was chiefly an offshoot of comedy: examples include *It Happened One Night* (Frank Capra, 1934), *Sullivan's Travels* (Preston Sturges, 1941) and most obviously the Bob Hope/Bing Crosby/Dorothy Lamour series which began with *Road to Singapore* (Victor Schertzinger, 1940). A notable exception was *You Only Live Once* (Fritz Lang, 1937) which depicted a framed crook's attempt to escape with his wife to Canada and dodge a murder rap. The film drew upon elements of the true story of Bonnie and Clyde, but made its lead character a man unjustly accused of a crime, as did another fugitive-couple noir released the previous year to *Gun Crazy*, Nicholas Ray's *They Live by Night*. Such films have much in common with the 'wrong man' thriller, several examples of which were made by Alfred Hitchcock (1935's *The 39 Steps*, 1937's *Young and Innocent*, 1942's *Saboteur*), in that they permit the audience to enjoy a character's transgressive behaviour in an 'innocent' way. Richard Maltby asserts, 'It is through the false appearance of the hero or heroine's guilt that the forbidden desires that the viewer has on their behalf are enacted, but . . . the hero and heroine never imagined those forbidden desires.'

As has been seen, the heroes of film noir do imagine the forbidden desires of crime, sex and violence, and enact them; the fact that such characters are often punished with death at the end is not all that relevant, as the viewer still spends the intervening time engaging with them. An essay by Ian Leong, Mike Sell and Kelly Thomas notes, 'The thrill of the genre . . . is its ability to suspend, at least briefly, the conservative narrative structure which always destroys the bad couple.' The most resonant road movies which followed the noir era – *Easy Rider* (Dennis Hopper, 1969), for example, or *Vanishing Point* (Richard C Sarafian, 1971) – position their heroes as not just outsiders, but also outlaws, and many more use the model of the fugitive couple – *Bonnie and Clyde* (Arthur Penn, 1967), *Badlands* (Terrence Malick, 1973), *Thelma and Louise* (Ridley Scott, 1991) – as seen in *Gun Crazy*. This type of road movie is therefore based upon a film-noir model. As Alain Silver and James Ursini note, 'Unlike other fugitive couples, who flee to save themselves from unjust accusations, Bart and Laurie choose to become criminals.'

Early on, Bart is warned that Laurie 'ain't the type that makes a happy home'. Although the very first thing that the couple does upon breaking free of the carnival is to get married, this has little to do with conforming to conventional expectations of the family unit: its main effect is to give the impression that Bart and Laurie are embarking on an endless honeymoon, where the realities of life do not apply. Certainly Laurie never intends to adopt a conventional lifestyle and dismisses any notions Bart might have about this: later, her lack of respect for the domestic lifestyle is hilariously demonstrated in her suggestion that they kidnap one of Ruby's children. While they make plans to abandon the criminal lifestyle and go into hiding once they have enough money, and Laurie talks of wanting 'things', the money they steal is given little focus and they are rarely seen enjoying its benefits (the exception is the mink which Laurie buys with the money from the payroll heist, a detail which seems included largely so that Laurie can symbolically lose it as they run from the FBI).

It seems as though the real, unspoken point of the crimes is to bind Bart and Laurie together. *Detour* shows a hero whose accidental crimes condemned him to a life on the road, but Bart and Laurie seem to actively desire such a fate. Their crimes fund this while preventing them from ever going home again – or at least preventing Bart from going home (when we meet Laurie she is already nomadic). 'Didn't it ever occur to you,' asks Bart, 'that, once we started, we could never ask anybody for help . . . for the rest of our lives? We're all alone, and always will be.' The outlaw couples of *Bonnie and Clyde* and *Badlands* act in a similar way, and, although the protagonists of *Thelma and Louise* do not set out with the intention of committing crime, their subsequent separation from the rest of society is liberating. This pattern even extends to films without outlaw couples: *Vanishing Point* features a hero who enjoys the solitude of the road and condemns himself to remain there. The figure of the obsessive who is isolated from society as a result of their obsession is a noir archetype, as it covers every femme fatale's victim as well as the seeker-heroes who continue to investigate long after it stops being sensible to do so. Bart and Laurie are both obsessed with guns, and with each other. (As is often the case, guns represent the sex which cannot be shown and the fetishism of guns by both characters creates gender ambiguity; Laurie's first appearance sees her playfully shoot a blank at the camera, from Bart's point of view.)

When Laurie attempts to reassure a disorientated Bart that she is real, he replies, 'You're the only thing that is, Laurie. The rest is a nightmare.' Leong, Sell and Thomas perceptively note that 'the action sequences are distinguished by their stylistically different use of film stock, lighting, and editing'; the famous long take of the bank robbery naturally occurs in real time, and the payroll heist is depicted in similar detail. Although Lewis's visual techniques in *Gun Crazy* are not noticeably noirish, he does use 'documentary' crime-film techniques to make these sequences more tense than the rest of the film, giving the viewer some idea of the excitement which Bart and Laurie get from their activities. Again, this raises the notion that the activity of being a criminal couple is more important than the financial reward, and the notion is confirmed when Bart and Laurie, having agreed to split up after the payroll heist, realise that they cannot bear to be apart even though staying together results in a greater chance of them being captured. The climax, which recalls *High Sierra* (Raoul Walsh, 1941) as the lovers hide out on the mountain, sets the pattern for many road-movie heroes: to stop moving or to return home is, ultimately, to die.

AFTERLIFE: *Gun Crazy* has been cited as an influence on *Bonnie and Clyde*, but director Arthur Penn claimed never to have seen it. The film later inspired *Guncrazy* (Tamra Davis, 1992), which isn't a remake but uses the premise of a young criminal couple on the road. It also derives some elements of its plot from *They Live By Night*.

AVAILABILITY: There is no Region 2 DVD or UK VHS, but there is a Region 1 DVD that includes just the trailer.

D.O.A. (1950)

This has one of the best gimmicks in all of film noir, opening with accountant Frank Bigelow (Edmond O'Brien – see *The Killers*) walking into a police station to report his own murder. In flashback we see Bigelow fall victim to deliberate iridium poisoning, following which he is told that he has less than 48 hours to live and searches desperately for his killer. In the end, although he inadvertently allowed the iridium to enter the country he was not its intended target. Directed by Rudolph Maté (more usually a cinematographer) after Robert Siodmak's Weimar film *The Man Who Searched for His Own Murderer* (1931), it is the archetypal fatalistic, paranoid noir. It cleverly mixes the roles of victim-hero and seeker-hero – in spite of Bigelow's determination, he is dying and so cannot shake off the mantle of victim – to create a pointless yet compelling narrative in which Bigelow wastes his last couple of days on Earth seeking revenge, gripped by an existential obsession with solving this mystery and dispensing justice, when he would be better off enjoying the life which he has only just come to appreciate. O'Brien's performance marks him out as one of noir's unsung heroes. *Released on 30 April 1950*

In a Lonely Place (1950)

Probably the best of director Nicholas Ray's noirs, which also include *They Live by Night* (1948), *On Dangerous Ground* (1951) and *Macao* (1952), *In a Lonely Place* is a characteristically brooding, psychological Columbia noir (although it was made by Santana, Humphrey Bogart's production company). Screenwriter and war veteran Dixon Steele (Bogart) is suspected of murdering a coat-check girl, but the testimony of starlet Laurel Gray (Gloria Grahame) keeps the police from investigating him. However, Dixon's alibi is not completely watertight, and, as Laurel falls in love with him and the police continue to investigate, Dixon's violent nature becomes apparent. Eventually the true murderer is found, but not before Laurel has realised that, whether Dixon killed the girl or not, he was capable of doing so, and she leaves him. It is said that aspects of the film mirrored the relationship between Ray and Grahame, who were married at the time (it is notable that her character's name seems like a corruption of her own, although the character was named before her casting). The effects of this film are further discussed under *Sunset Boulevard*. Released on 17 May 1950

Sunset Boulevard (1950)

Black and White – 110 mins

A Paramount Picture
Sunset Boulevard
Written by Charles Brackett, Billy Wilder and
DM Marshman Jr
Director of Photography: John F Seitz, ASC
Art Direction: Hans Dreier and John Meehan
Special Photographic Effects: Gordon Jennings, ASC
Process Photography: Farciot Edouart, ASC
Set Direction: Sam Comer and Ray Moyer
Editorial Supervision: Doane Harrison
Costumes: Edith Head
Edited by Arthur Schmidt
Make-up Supervision: Wally Westmore
Sound Recording by Harry Lindgren and John Cope
Assistant Director: CC Coleman Jr
Music Score by Franz Waxman
Produced by Charles Brackett
Directed by Billy Wilder

CAST: William Holden (*Joe Gillis*), Gloria Swanson (*Norma Desmond*), Erich Von Stroheim (*Max von Mayerling*) with Nancy Olson (*Betty Schaefer*), Fred Clark (*Sheldrake*), Lloyd Gough (*Morino*), Jack Webb (*Artie Green*) and Cecil B DeMille (*Himself*), Hedda Hopper (*Herself*), Buster Keaton (*Himself*), Anna Q Nilsson (*Herself*), HB Warner (*Himself*), Franklyn Farnum (*Undertaker*), Ray Evans (*Himself*), Jay Livingston (*Himself*), Larry Blake (*1st Finance Man*), Charles Dayton (*2nd Finance Man*)

SUMMARY: The body of screenwriter Joe Gillis lies in a swimming pool in front of a mansion on Sunset Boulevard. As the film flashes back a few months, Joe is seen broke and desperate to sell a script in order to prevent his car from being repossessed. While driving on Sunset Boulevard, he spots the repo men and hides in the garage of what he thinks is an abandoned mansion; however, the house belongs to Norma Desmond, a former star of silent movies. She hires Joe to help her with the script for her comeback and insists that he move into the mansion. Norma is deluded, believing that she is still a star but her fan letters are fakes written by her butler, Max (who, it is later revealed, was her first husband and director of several of her early pictures). Joe is never paid for his work, but he is expensively kept by Norma. Joe leaves her on New Year's Eve but returns when she attempts suicide. She admits that she is in love with him. Joe stays, but is gradually tempted away by Paramount scriptreader Betty Schaefer's offer to collaborate on a script. He stays with Norma during the day but works with Betty at night. Betty falls for Joe as well, despite being engaged to his friend Artie Green, an assistant director. Norma discovers that Joe is writing with Betty and becomes jealous. Joe tells Betty to go back to Artie, then leaves Norma for good, intending to go home to Ohio. Norma shoots him as he walks down the driveway and he falls into the pool.

DIRECTOR: Billy Wilder's follow-up to *Double Indemnity* was *The Lost Weekend* (1945), which saw him team up again with writer/producer Charles Brackett and won the Oscars for Best Picture, Best Director, Best Screenplay and Best Actor (Ray Milland). Afterwards he was given the special commission of colonel in the US Army so that he could go to Germany and assist with the rebuilding of the country's film industry. Upon his return he made a musical comedy, *The Emperor Waltz* (1948), before tackling a piece about the occupation, *A Foreign Affair* (1948). After *Sunset Boulevard*, Wilder continued to make a variety of notable and often excellent films, including *Ace in the Hole* (1951), *Sabrina* (1954), *The Seven Year Itch* (1955), *The Spirit of St Louis* (1957), *Love in the Afternoon* (1957), *Some Like It Hot* (1959),

The Apartment (1960 – which again won him the Oscars for Best
Picture, Director and Screenplay), *Irma la Douche* (1963), *The Private
Life of Sherlock Holmes* (1970) and *The Front Page* (1974). His final
film, released in 1981, was *Buddy Buddy*. In later life he took up
sculpture. He died in 2002.

WRITER: Charles Brackett (1892–1969) studied law at Harvard. By the
time he graduated in 1920 (his progress had been delayed by service in
W.W.I), he had already published his first novel, *The Council of the
Ungodly* (1920), and although he moved into practising law he
continued to write short stories and articles for magazines, eventually
producing a second novel, *Weekend* (1925). In 1926 he was offered the
post of drama critic on *The New Yorker*, and gave up legal work to
pursue this. His stories began to sell in Hollywood and in 1932
Paramount contracted him as a staff writer. His work was initially
unspectacular, but the studio's decision to partner him with Wilder
turned out to be inspired. Once Wilder had completed his first directorial
assignment, Brackett was allowed to produce their next film, *Five Graves
to Cairo* (1943), and although they briefly split for *Double Indemnity*
they made four further films as a writer-director-producer team, of which
Sunset Boulevard was the last. After amicably splitting from Wilder,
Brackett continued to do acclaimed work as a writer and producer for a
further decade, receiving his third screenplay Oscar for *Titanic* (Jean
Negulesco, 1953), which he also produced. His other credits as
writer-producer include *Niagara* (Henry Hathaway, 1953) and *Journey
to the Center of the Earth* (Henry Levin, 1959), and he also produced
The King and I (Walter Lang, 1956). He retired in the early 1960s.

This was DM Marshman's first screenwriting credit. There were only
two others: *Taxi* (Gregory Ratoff, 1952) and *Second Chance* (Rudolph
Maté, 1953).

DEVELOPMENT: Billy Wilder's friend Armand Deutsch claimed that
Wilder had scribbled the words, 'Silent picture star commits murder.
When they arrest her she sees the newsreel cameras and thinks she is
back in the movies,' on a scrap of paper in the early 1940s. 'We kept
going back to *Sunset Boulevard* for years,' Wilder said. 'Brackett and I
had thought of [the idea] long before we tackled it . . . We would work
on it, then put it in a drawer while we worked on another picture.' There
was a need for the concept to find its moment. 'What made it work
would not work in pictures today,' said Wilder in 1993. '*Sunset
Boulevard* was made in 1950 and back then you could still dramatise –
and still have a very valid background – about the demise of silent
pictures.'

'*Sunset Boulevard* came about,' said Brackett, 'because Wilder, Marshman and I were acutely conscious of the fact that we lived in a town which had been swept by a social change', which he compared to that 'brought about in the old south by the civil war'. It is difficult to exaggerate how much sound altered cinema, making it arguably a different medium – as radio is a different medium from television. It also required a very different acting style and 'Over-night, the coming of sound had brushed gods and goddesses into obscurity.' (It is notable that women seemed to suffer more than men.) Wilder stated that to do a modern equivalent, 'with some star who's simply out of the spotlight – it's not as good as having someone who was one of the biggest stars here, but suddenly there are no parts for her.' The writers' concept of her changed as the scripting went on. 'At first we saw her as a kind of horror woman – an embodiment of vanity and selfishness,' said Brackett, however, 'as we went along, our sympathies became deeply involved with the woman who had been given the brush by thirty million fans.' Wilder also drew upon his own career – the script which Joe and Betty write together, about a couple who work incompatible hours and so hardly see each other, draws upon one of Wilder's final scripts from his Berlin period, *Das Blaue vom Himmel* (Victor Janson, 1934). 'The night shot where Holden and Nancy Olson walk on the lot,' Wilder said, 'she tells how she grew up there, at Paramount . . . That's my wife's background we used. Audrey's mother worked in wardrobe.'

Although Brackett was clearly involved, he received no screenwriting fee for the film – only his producer's salary – indicating that the bulk of the work was performed by Wilder and Marshman. The first 61 pages were submitted on 21 December 1948, with the covering note, 'This is the first act of *Sunset Boulevard*. Due to the peculiar nature of the project, we ask all our co-workers to regard it as top secret.' The protracted development process continued through to the end of production. Wilder usually worked from a completed script, but on this occasion he and Brackett developed it as they went along. When Gloria Swanson (see **CASTING**) arrived for her screen test, she was given a few pages of script to study. 'I thought it might be all they had,' she later said. The ideas were still not nailed down, and all they knew of the ending was that there was to be a murder. 'Am I murdered or do I do the murdering?' asked Swanson. 'We don't know yet,' replied Wilder. However, there was no lack of confidence in the production. 'Each day, we would receive more script,' Swanson said. 'It was clear to all of us, it was brilliant. All of us believed we were making a wonderful film.'

CASTING: Wilder's original notion was to cast Mae West as the faded star, but director George Cukor knew West and told Wilder that she was too much like Norma Desmond. 'Mae, for example, lived with a man who, unknown to her, not only answered her fan mail for her, but also wrote the letters.' Wilder and Brackett considered Pola Negri, the Polish silent-cinema star, and approached Mary Pickford, the star of the 1910s who co-founded United Artists (she felt it was at odds with her image, apparently believing she still had an image).

Then, Cukor suggested Gloria Swanson (1897–1983, born Gloria May Josephine Svensson). As a teenager Swanson had worked as an extra in Chicago and married actor Wallace Beery, with whom she went to Hollywood. After a few films she was spotted by Cecil B DeMille, who cast her in *Don't Change Your Husband* (1919) and *Male and Female* (1919). Her work with DeMille made her one of Paramount's leading stars. She became an independent producer through United Artists and, although *Sadie Thompson* (Raoul Walsh, 1928) brought an Oscar nomination, the follow-up *Queen Kelly* was a disaster (see **PRODUCTION**). Swanson's initial talkies brought success, with another Oscar nomination for *The Trespasser* (Edmund Goulding, 1929), but her career then went into swift decline. Her final film of the 1930s was *Music in the Air* (Joe May, 1934), which Wilder had written for Twentieth Century-Fox shortly after arriving in Hollywood. Her only film between this and *Sunset Boulevard* was an unsuccessful comeback for RKO, *Father Takes a Wife* (Jack Hively, 1941), in which she also played a famous actress.

'I knew she wanted to get back to movies,' said Cukor. 'When they asked Gloria to take a screen test, she almost threw it all away. But she called me, and I told her it's worth it.' Swanson remembered his precise words as 'If they ask you to do ten screen tests, do them, or I'll personally shoot you . . . These are the people who did *Lost Weekend*, and I suggested you to them.' Swanson's real reason for avoiding the test was that she felt she wasn't very good at them. 'If my career had depended on a few minutes of a screen test, I probably would have been selling ribbons somewhere.' Brackett reassured her that it was a formality. Her fee for the film was $150,000: 'one of the great bargains in film history,' commented Wilder. However, it irritated her that she was perceived as old. 'She was fifty years old, that's all,' Wilder said. 'But for some reason, there was this abyss between the silent pictures and talkies, and some people thought she was seventy or eighty years old.'

Montgomery Clift signed up to play Joe Gillis but then backed out two weeks before shooting began (he was having an affair with an older woman, and found the subject matter uncomfortably close to home). Wilder asked Fred MacMurray, but he was booked. Barbara Stanwyck recommended William Holden (1918–81), whom she had once saved from being fired by Harry Cohn two weeks into production of *Golden*

Boy (Rouben Mamoulian, 1939) – which eventually made Holden an overnight star. Although Wilder noted that 'she wasn't exactly objective about him,' he sent Holden what he had of the script. 'It took Bill Holden two hours to read it, drive to my house, and say yes,' said Wilder. Holden's fee was $39,000 less than Clift's.

Columbia and Paramount, who shared his contract, had placed Holden in largely unremarkable films during the 1940s. 'Bill was very much underestimated as an actor,' noted Wilder, who had been pleasantly surprised by the actor's intelligence. 'He was such a natural leading man, people didn't notice how good an actor he was.' *The Dark Past* (Rudolph Maté, 1948) and *Born Yesterday* (George Cukor, 1950) were superior roles, but his Oscar nomination for *Sunset Boulevard* failed to alter the studios' perception of him. After Wilder cast him in *Stalag 17* (1953), for which he won an Oscar, and *Sabrina* (1954), his career shifted towards more sophisticated roles. He negotiated part-ownership of *The Bridge on the River Kwai* (David Lean, 1957), which made him financially secure for life. He made fewer notable films: an exception was *The Wild Bunch* (Sam Peckinpah, 1969). He was Oscar-nominated again for *Network* (Sidney Lumet, 1976). His final film, *S.O.B.* (Blake Edwards, 1981), was a satire on Hollywood. Plagued by alcoholism for much of his life, he died after falling and cutting his head on a table.

Erich von Stroheim (1885–1957) was an acclaimed director in the silent era, with credits including *Blind Husbands* (1919), *Foolish Wives* (1922), *Greed* (1924), *The Merry Widow* (1925) and *The Wedding March* (1928). Stroheim also had scores of acting credits and had worked with Wilder on *Five Graves to Cairo*. Stroheim made a huge contribution to fleshing out Max, suggesting that he used to be Norma's director and husband. 'That was beautiful, a wonderful idea,' said Wilder. 'Stroheim didn't mind playing a butler so long as the character had once been somebody important.'

Nancy Olson (born 1928) had only two previous screen credits when she was cast in *Sunset Boulevard*. Paramount was impressed by her chemistry with Holden and cast them together in *Union Station* (Rudolph Maté, 1950), *Force of Arms* (Michael Curtiz, 1951) and *Submarine Command* (John Farrow, 1951), but she put her career on hold in the mid-1950s to concentrate on her family. Following her divorce in 1957 she returned to acting, but the roles were no longer there for her. She appeared in *The Absent-Minded Professor* (Robert Stevenson, 1961) and its sequel *Son of Flubber* (Robert Stevenson, 1963). After this she mainly turned her attention to theatre. Also worthy of note is Jack Webb (1920–82), who appeared in the docu-noir *He Walked by Night* (Alfred Werker, 1948), which was part-inspiration for

bove The Maltese Falcon: Spade (Humphrey Bogart) roughs up Cairo (Peter Lorre)

elow Double Indemnity: Neff (Fred MacMurray) and Phyllis (Barbara Stanwyck) try to

*ss away a murder

Above **Murder, My Sweet:** Marlowe (Dick Powell) lights a rather suggestive cigarette for Helen (Claire Trevor)

Right **Detour:** Al (Tom Neal) and Vera (Ann Savage) plot a con to steal more money than this film cost to make

MONEY LOANED

bove The Big Sleep:
[M]arlowe (Humphrey
[B]ogart) rescues Vivian
[L]auren Bacall) in the
[m]ean streets

[r]ight The Killers:
[p]erpetual loser the
[S]wede (Burt Lancaster)
[in] the middle of his last-
[ev]er fight

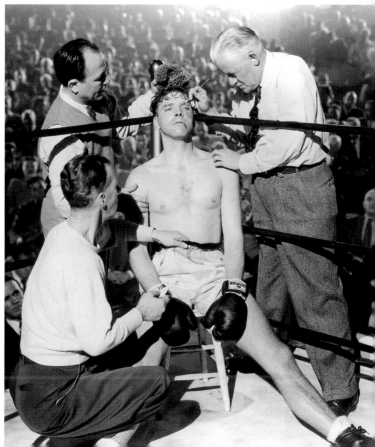

Above The Lady from Shanghai: Elsa (Rita Hayworth) and Bannister (Everett Sloane) reflect on each other's actions

Left Force of Evil: 'I die almost every day,' says Leo (Thomas Gomez), but this time isn't metaphorical

Above Gun Crazy: Bart
(John Dall) trick-shoots
his way into the
affections of Laurie
(Peggy Cummins),
against the wishes of
Packett (Berry Kroeger)

Right Sunset Boulevard:
Faded actress Norma
(Gloria Swanson) about
to become famous again
– for the wrong reasons

Left The Big Heat:
Gloria Grahame,
possibly losing patience
with the incessant
demands of director
Fritz Lang

Below The Big Combo:
Mr Brown (Richard
Conte), the apparent
source of all New York's
crime, taunts Diamond
(Cornel Wilde)

Left Kiss Me Deadly:
Taking the money isn't
an option, so Carver
(Gaby Rodgers) opens
the box

*Right The Night of
the Hunter:* Powell
(Robert Mitchum)
idiosyncratically enacts
the battle between good
and evil

Left The Killing: Elisha Cook gears up for yet another bleak film noir death sequence

Below Touch of Evil: Vargas (Charlton Heston, looking as Mexican as can be expected) queries the evidence 'discovered' by Quinlan (Orson Welles)

his *Dragnet* radio series (1949–56), TV series (1951–59, 1967–70) and movie (1954, also directed by him).

Cecil B DeMille (1881–1959) was a founder of Lasky's, the company which became Paramount; he was one of the chief exponents of the feature film over the short. He produced and directed more than seventy films, but remained closely identified with Swanson. Hedda Hopper (1885–1966, born Elda Furry) started as an actress in 1916, but in 1938 began a career as a gossip columnist and soon quit acting altogether. An anti-Communist and friend of J Edgar Hoover, she enthusiastically assisted the HUAC witch-hunts, and was instrumental in the campaign to undermine *Citizen Kane* (Orson Welles, 1941). Wilder also wanted to cast Hopper's arch-rival Louella Parsons, 'but Louella knew quite well she would lose that duel because Hedda was a former actress, and she would wipe the floor with her.' Norma's bridge club comprises Buster Keaton (1895–1966, born Joseph Frank Keaton VI), second in popularity only to Charlie Chaplin among the comedians of the silent era; Swedish-born Anna Q Nilsson (1888–1974), reckoned to be one of the very first movie stars after her prolific work in the 1910s and 1920s, although she spent much of the 1930s and 1940s taking bit-parts; and British actor HB Warner (1875–1958), also a silent star, who had fared better in talkies and was often cast by Frank Capra. At the piano during Artie's New Year's Eve party are Ray Evans (born 1915) and Jay Livingston (1915–2001), who had composed songs for numerous 1940s films and found even greater success after *Sunset Boulevard*, co-writing the popular tunes 'Que Sera Sera' and 'Silver Bells'.

PRODUCTION: *Sunset Boulevard* went into production under the title *A Can of Beans*, allegedly because Wilder and Brackett were nervous that others in Hollywood would not appreciate their portrait of the film business. However, Wilder later claimed, 'I was never worried that Paramount would regard *Sunset Boulevard* as an anti-Hollywood picture. The first question was: would this be a successful picture?' He also believed that one of his cameos provided insurance. 'It's a pro-Hollywood picture for no reason other than that the most powerful man on the Paramount lot back then, Cecil B DeMille, is in the picture . . . and he behaves in the most humane way.' The budget was $1,572,000.

Production commenced on 26 March 1949 with exteriors and establishing shots, the first of which was the Los Angeles County Morgue – a shot which would ultimately go unused. Shooting proper began on 18 April 1949, with Wilder again working alongside *Double Indemnity*'s cinematographer, John Seitz. 'Johnny, keep it out of focus,' Wilder told him, 'I want to win the foreign picture award.' Olson was fond of Seitz. 'I remember he came over and turned my head,' she said. 'I wondered if I had done something wrong. He was very nice and kind, and explained so that I would understand, "I wanted your profile because you have a very good nose." ' The first scenes tackled were in Joe's apartment, a specially constructed set, before moving on to exteriors of Norma's mansion. This key location wasn't really on Sunset Boulevard: it was located on Wilshire and Irving Boulevards, and had been built in 1924 at an approximate cost of $250,000. Its second owner was J Paul Getty, who bought it for his wife Mary. She kept it as part of the divorce settlement, and allowed *Sunset Boulevard* to use it in exchange for building her a swimming pool – the one in which Joe dies. Shooting continued here for two weeks, including the bridge game on 3 May.

Wilder was pleasantly surprised by Swanson's attitude. 'She was so right for the part, I was willing to put up with anything . . . remember, here was a star who used to ride in a sedan chair from her dressing room to the set.' Wilder braced himself for diva-like demands during *Sunset Boulevard*, but found instead that 'she worked like a horse, a very professional horse, a Lipizzaner'. Stroheim informed Wilder that he and Swanson had co-produced a silent movie, *Queen Kelly*, for United Artists in 1929, but the market's rapid shift towards talkies created pressure and Swanson had fired Stroheim as director because, she said, 'he was crazy'. The film was never properly finished. In 1931 extra footage was shot to cover the numerous gaps, but Stroheim was able to veto any US screenings (it received a European release). Stroheim suggested that, if Wilder could get hold of the footage, extracts could be used for a scene in which Norma Desmond watched one of her old films, supposedly directed by Max. Paramount purchased 122 feet of the film for $1,000. 'It was a brilliant idea because almost no-one had ever seen *Kelly*,' said Swanson. 'Erich and I even decided that it had weathered the years very well, glowed like a classic, and might actually be rereleased.' (It eventually played in America in 1966.) Scenes in other rooms of Norma's mansion were completed later, on two large studio sets.

On 16 May the company shot a scene in which the Hollywood columnist Sidney Skolsky – playing himself – asks Gillis if he has any good news. 'Just sold an original for a hundred grand to the King brothers,' replies Gillis. '*The Life of the Warner Brothers*. Starring the Ritz brothers. Playing opposite the Andrews sisters. But don't get me wrong – I love Hollywood.' This scene was eventually dropped. The Cecil DeMille scene was shot on 23 May on the same sound stage on which he had made *Samson and Delilah* (1949), the sets for which were brought out from storage. The director was nervous about performing in front of the cameras, but Swanson reassured him – 'Mr DeMille, if you're just yourself, you'll be wonderful.' He was paid $10,000 for his appearance. Work on the Paramount lot continued with the scenes of Gillis and Betty writing their script, which were shot between the hours of 7.30 p.m. and 4.30 a.m. Production wrapped with a few retakes on 23 June, including the final close-up on Norma. The shoot had taken 'about sixty days', according to Wilder. 'If only every picture could have gone so smoothly!' However, he ended up restarting production several times during the editing process, including retakes of Norma's suicide attempt (7 July) and the first meeting of Gillis and Norma (9 July), plus location work on 20 October and, in the new year, a whole new opening sequence.

Like *Double Indemnity*, a large section of *Sunset Boulevard* was dropped after previews. The company had filmed a prologue on location in the LA County Morgue, which began with a corpse being wheeled in. 'There are about six other corpses under the sheets,' Wilder explained. 'Then we sort of see through the sheets to the faces, and the people are telling each other the events leading to their deaths.' The others were all very short – 'a kid who drowned, and . . . a guy who came from the Midwest and bought himself a little avocado ranch in the San Fernando Valley who had a heart attack' – but the final corpse, Joe Gillis, told a longer story, and the film proper began. Wilder thought the sequence pleasingly odd and felt it 'was very well shot', and he attended a preview in Evanston, Illinois. 'The picture starts, and they bring the corpse in on the slab, and they put the name tag on the toe of Holden, and it was the biggest laugh I ever heard in my life.' It was the wrong kind of laughter. The audience just couldn't take it seriously and it coloured their reaction to the entire film. Wilder walked out and sat dejectedly on the stairs. A woman stepped out of the theatre and walked past him. 'She looked right at me and said, "Have you ever seen shit like this before in your life?" And that was before you were accustomed to hearing that kind of talk from women.' Another preview on Long Island yielded the same result, and Wilder decided to drop the sequence.

Release had to be delayed six months while Wilder, Brackett and Marshman came up with a new opening. This would be shorter and more straightforward, and Holden's narration became more abstract – audiences were less likely to laugh at him if they couldn't see him. To compensate for his disappointment at losing the original sequence, Wilder came up with the showpiece shot of Holden floating in the pool. When this was filmed, distortion from the water prevented them from getting a clear shot under water – so a large mirror was placed at the bottom of the pool, reflecting an image of Holden up to the camera. 'We tested it with a rubber duck and it worked,' said Wilder, although there was still the problem of Holden having to play dead in the water, eyes and mouth open. 'And the water was cold,' said Wilder. 'But Bill was a great athlete, and he did it better than the rubber duck.' The film finally wrapped on 5 January 1950.

RECEPTION: *'Sunset Boulevard* was the talk of the entire studio,' Nancy Olson remembered. 'You know, in those days, they'd show rushes from everything that was filmed all at once, all in a block. Who would sit there through all that?' However, she found that people started making the effort to go, just to catch scenes from the film. Not everybody was favourably disposed: it is said that, after the Hollywood première, MGM's Louis B Mayer told Wilder, 'You have disgraced the industry that made you and fed you. You should be tarred and feathered and run out of Hollywood.'

The trade press was favourable. 'For audiences who remember [Swanson] with nostalgia she will be terrific,' wrote James D Ivers in the *Motion Picture Herald* of 22 April 1950, 'and those who never saw her can now see for themselves what the movies had before they added sound.' Rating the film 'Excellent', Ivers noted, 'The theme and its treatment make the picture definitely adult.' On 19 April 1950, *Variety* wrote, 'Because it is tied in with a pseudo-exposé of Hollywood, the peek behind the scenes undoubtedly will fascinate a considerable slice of the theatre-going public,' predicting fruitful box-office returns. 'On this count they rate a nod for daring, as well as credit for an all-round film-making job that, disregarding the unpleasant subject matter, is a stand-out.' Wilder and Brackett 'have made their story extremely "trade-y"' and the film industry family circle will appreciate the exposure of studio foibles'.

The film was released on 4 August 1950. *'Sunset Boulevard* is by no means a rounded story of Hollywood, past or present,' wrote Thomas M Pryor in the *New York Times* of 11 August 1950. 'But it is such a clever compound of truth and legend – and is so richly redolent of the past, yet so contemporaneous – that it seemingly speaks with great authority.' He praised all departments: Swanson 'dominates the picture'; Holden's work was 'the finest acting of his career'; Olson's role 'beautifully portrayed'; Wilder and Brackett 'have kept an essentially tawdry romance from becoming distasteful and embarrassing'. In fact, the only flaw cited by Pryor was the one which had so delayed the film's release: 'the authors permit Joe Gillis to take us into the story of his life after his bullet-ridden body is lifted out of Norma Desmond's swimming pool . . . a device completely unworthy of Brackett and Wilder.' One wonders what he would have made of the morgue scene.

Writing in *The New Yorker* on 19 August 1950, Philip Hornburger similarly expressed dislike for the device – but also for the film generally, which he described as 'a pretentious slice of Roquefort' of which 'Not the least unfortunate aspect . . . is the fact that the narrator is a corpse. He is one of the more remarkable corpses in cinema history.' His review went on to note, 'Since *Sunset Boulevard* contains the germ of a good idea, it's a pity it was not better written,' and believed that the filmmakers had 'substituted snappy photography and dialogue for what could have been a genuinely moving tragedy. It seems . . . that the authors never quite made up their minds whether they were with Miss Desmond or against her.' Hornburger did have some praise for the acting, but 'even their combined highly skilled efforts cannot make up for the essential hollowness of the enterprise'.

The British reaction was also mixed. '*Sunset Boulevard* is the most intelligent film to come out of Hollywood for years,' wrote Dilys Powell in *The Sunday Times* on 20 August 1950, 'lest the idea of intelligence in the cinema should lack allure, let me also say that it is one of the most exciting.' She did admit that 'To what degree it will excite people who don't know what films were like twenty-five years ago is, perhaps, open to question,' but ultimately, 'a certain detachment in the manner of the piece cannot destroy its claim to be regarded as an exceptionally distinguished piece of work.'

William Whitebait set out to be more critical, but one can almost see him change his mind as the review goes on. 'In a cynically adoring fashion Hollywood has always been fond of bringing out its dead,' he wrote in the *New Statesman* of 26 August 1950. 'In turning its arc-lights on a forgotten star *Sunset Boulevard* makes no very original claim. But to play the part of this once-fetching favourite a real star from the silent days has been chosen.' Halfway through, Whitebait notes, 'The more one writes about *Sunset Boulevard* – admirable title, by the way – the better it seems.' He went on to state, 'The film seems and is overlong, but for so much of the time it so brilliantly comes near hitting every mark that we may wonder why in our enjoyment there should be this core of dissatisfaction,' and concluded, 'There is "more in" *Sunset Boulevard* than in the earlier triumphs of Billy Wilder, *Double Indemnity* and *Lost Weekend*, though I can't help feeling they were far better films.'

The film was nominated for ten Oscars (acting nods for Swanson, Holden, von Stroheim and Olson, plus Picture, Script, Director, Cinematography, Music, Editing). In the end it just won Best Script and Best Music.

ASPECTS OF NOIR: Hollywood has always told stories about itself, based on the not unreasonable assumption that if people are interested in movies then they will also be interested in movies about movies. This tradition reaches from *What Price Hollywood?* (George Cukor, 1932) and its better-known remake *A Star Is Born* (William A Wellman, 1937) through *Singin' in the Rain* (Gene Kelly, Stanley Donen, 1952) and *The Last Tycoon* (Elia Kazan, 1976) to *Barton Fink* (Joel Coen, 1991) and *The Player* (Robert Altman, 1992). *Sunset Boulevard*'s ambivalent view of the industry which produced it was nothing new; the key dramatic point of *A Star Is Born* regards the 'price of fame'.

What *Sunset Boulevard* does is apply film-noir logic to a Hollywood setting. By consciously mixing the 'past and present, the real and imaginary' the film creates Hollywood as an ambiguous space where fictions are constantly being created: not just the fiction films which are its stock in trade, but also the fictions about Hollywood in interviews and gossip columns which sell those films. Even if there was a 'true' Hollywood, the movies themselves are incapable of depicting it. The existential ramifications of existing in such a place define the film's noir world, with Gillis trapped in a fiction like those which he himself is employed to produce (note how he deliberately speaks to Betty in clichéd love-scene dialogue). Richard Maltby identifies an unwritten rule that 'the history of Hollywood must conform to the conventions of its own narratives', this being 'the means by which public attention was diverted away from the routine, mechanical, standardized aspects of the industry's central operations toward its more attractive, glamorous periphery.'

In accordance with this, *Sunset Boulevard* recycles the structure of Wilder's earlier *Double Indemnity*, casting Norma as the femme fatale from whom Gillis cannot escape. However, because this is a Hollywood story all actions feed back into Hollywood itself, so Gillis is not goaded into conspiring with Norma to commit a crime – instead, he 'conspires' with her on a script. Later, when Gillis starts working on another script with Betty, this is interpreted by Norma as infidelity. Crime is replaced by writing, and sex is also replaced by writing: writing is ironically made into an illicit activity. Additionally, the fear of the past so common in noir applies to Gillis (and it is rarely so vividly realised as here, in Norma's vividly Gothic decaying house, inside which she projects her own films like ghosts of her younger self), yet it is not his own past that fatally ensnares him but the past of Hollywood. The town is not only host to its present myths but its previous ones, and in *Sunset Boulevard* the silent era represented by Norma is a past which cannot quite be repressed but which seems to bear down upon the industry's creatives. In the light of Gillis's failure to sell a script, it is possible to read *Sunset Boulevard* as an expression of the pressure he feels to live up to the great achievements of Hollywood's past, which eventually destroys him.

Although Wilder was never a political filmmaker it is interesting to consider Gillis's identity as a screenwriter in the light of the then-recent

HUAC hearings. The activities of HUAC had a particular impact upon film noir because many of the movement's filmmakers were left-wingers who either fell under suspicion because of their views (even though a large number of them were not, and had never been, Communists) or refused to identify colleagues who were Communist party members. HUAC also had a tendency to point the finger at foreign nationals who had emigrated to America to work in Hollywood, which caused problems for the likes of Fritz Lang. Writers were the worst affected by the blacklisting: of the 'Unfriendly Nineteen' who refused to co-operate with HUAC's 1947 hearings, thirteen were principally known for their writing work. It is notable that, so soon after this, *Sunset Boulevard* presents us with a screenwriter victim-hero.

A good companion piece is *In a Lonely Place* (Nicholas Ray, 1950), released less than three months earlier. Again the central character is a screenwriter, Dixon Steele (Humphrey Bogart, who had a great affinity with writers and was one of the few actors to be welcome at the Warners writers' table), but, unlike victim-hero Joe Gillis, Steele is more of an 'homme fatal', a source of excitement but also of menace for starlet girlfriend Laurel Gray (Gloria Grahame). When a girl turns up dead whom Steele was the last known person to see alive, suspicion falls upon him but he treats the matter lightly (asking if the police are going to arrest him 'for lack of emotion'). The fact is, the plot reads like something out of one of Steele's scripts and he treats it just the same, as a mildly diverting story. Familiarity with the heightened narratives of Hollywood cinema has numbed Steele to the significant difference between these and reality, and *In a Lonely Place* plays further games with the audience by presenting this notion in the context of a movie. Steele is hounded for the appearance of guilt until it ruins his relationship with Laurel, perhaps a reflection of HUAC, but the potential for violence still exists within him, resulting in an ambivalent message. By making Steele a war veteran, the film further underlines that at that time the average able-bodied American male would probably have seen, and perhaps even done, more gruesome things than the cinema could show (see **The Big Heat**).

As a final point of comparison between *Sunset Boulevard* and *In a Lonely Place*, it is noticeable that likeable loser Joe Gillis dies a failure, while the script written by the cold and violent Dixon Steele is hailed as brilliant – a comment on the nature of creative personalities?

AFTERLIFE: Swanson was irritated by the legacy of *Sunset Boulevard*: far from resurrecting her career, it resulted in her being repeatedly offered identical roles. 'I'd had a very successful career for years but one film dominated,' she said. 'Sometimes I wasn't glad I did the film . . .

When I die, I want to be remembered as Gloria Swanson, not as Norma Desmond.' Stroheim later professed to loathe the film, referring to it as 'that damned butler role'. Holden and Wilder revisited the subject matter in *Fedora* (1978), which concerns a strangely ageless star coming out of retirement.

The film was mounted as a stage musical by Andrew Lloyd Webber and was hugely successful; however, because Wilder had made it while under contract to Paramount, he did not own the property and so made no money from it.

AVAILABILITY: *Sunset Boulevard* is available on Region 2 (PHE8066) and Region 1 DVD with extras including a making-of featurette, the script for the original morgue sequence, a commentary from critic Ed Sikov, a map of the Hollywood locations, featurettes on the costumes and music, a trailer and photo galleries.

The Narrow Margin (1952)

Another RKO effort, *The Narrow Margin* concerns an LA cop (Charles McGraw, who was one of the killers in *The Killers*) escorting the wife of a crime boss (Marie Windsor – see *Force of Evil* and *The Killing*) on a train from Chicago. It is one of the most celebrated B-movies of the era, demonstrating substantial creativity on limited resources; most of the film takes place on the small train set, with cabins and corridors redressed to stand in for each other, and director Richard Fleischer eliminated the time-consuming process of moving the walls to make way for the camera by using a hand-held for most of these scenes, rocking it to simulate the train movement. As a consequence it is highly dynamic, featuring some nice tracking shots and an impressive fight sequence which places the spectator right in the middle. This suits the taut nature of the script, which features more plot twists and reversals in its 71 minutes than most films manage inside two hours. *Released on 3 May 1952*

Angel Face (1952)

One of Robert Mitchum's later RKO noirs, *Angel Face* casts him as Frank Jessup, a former racing driver who now drives ambulances, and follows his involvement with Diane Tremayne (Jean Simmons), a twenty-year-old who lives with her father and wealthy stepmother. The plot bears similarities with *The*

Postman Always Rings Twice, turning on a murder which the central couple are tried for and acquitted of, only to suffer from subsequent guilt. However, *Angel Face*'s Frank is entirely innocent, feels no guilt and although intrigued by Diane he is wary of her and always remains at a distance (although, as it turns out, he is still too close for his own good). Diane is an interesting figure among femmes fatales, as her awareness of her own sexuality is limited: she is childlike (indicated by the fact that she does not smoke or drink) and resentful of her stepmother. Director Otto Preminger (previously responsible for one of 1944's major noirs, *Laura*) uses relatively balanced photography, but the film has distinct noir elements – principally Simmons, who plays the character as being quietly insane and therefore unpredictable. The impression of a world lacking in any certainties is compounded when Diane tries to confess to her lawyer, who tells her that truth is not what she says, but whatever the jury decides. The film also has one of the most abrupt down endings ever seen – the noir equivalent of dropping a ten-ton weight on a cartoon character. *Released on 11 December 1952*

The Big Heat (1953)

Black and White – 90 mins

Columbia Pictures Corporation Presents
The Big Heat
Screenplay by Sydney Boehm
Based upon the *Saturday Evening Post* serial by William P McGivern
Gowns by Jean Louis
Director of Photography: Charles Lang, ASC
Art Director: Robert Peterson
Film Editor: Charles Nelson, ACE
Set Decorator: William Kiernan
Assistant Director: Milton Feldman
Make-up by Clay Campbell
Hair Styles by Helen Hunt
Sound Engineer: George Cooper
Musical Director: Mischa Bakaleinikoff
Produced by Robert Arthur
Directed by Fritz Lang

CAST: Glenn Ford (*Dave Bannion*), Gloria Grahame (*Debby Marsh*), Jocelyn Brando (*Katie Bannion*) with Alexander Scourby (*Mike Lagana*),

Lee Marvin (*Vince Stone*), Jeanette Nolan (*Bertha Duncan*), Peter Whitney (*Tierney*), Willis Bouchey (*Lt Wilkes*), Robert Burton (*Gus Burke*), Adam Williams (*Larry Gordon*), Howard Wendell (*Commissioner Higgins*)

SUMMARY: Policeman Tom Duncan commits suicide. His wife telephones gangster Mike Lagana and he tells her to call the police. The case is investigated by Detective Sergeant Dave Bannion, who wonders why there was no suicide note. The police are contacted by Lucy Chapman, who was having an affair with Duncan and says that it wasn't suicide. Soon afterwards Lucy turns up dead, and Bannion becomes suspicious – but is warned off by a threatening phone call. Bannion confronts Lagana, leading one of Lagana's minions to booby-trap Bannion's car with dynamite. However, Bannion's wife Katie is first to use the car and she is killed instead. A desolate Bannion realises that the corruption extends into the police and quits. He establishes that a man named Larry was responsible for the bomb and starts tracking him down, but first encounters violent mobster Vince Stone and his girlfriend Debby Marsh at a bar. Bannion threatens Stone, who leaves without Debby; instead she leaves with Bannion, but plays dumb when he asks about Stone's activities. Stone knows that Debby left with Bannion and when she returns home he throws boiling coffee in her face. A scarred and frightened Debby tells Bannion where to find Larry Gordon. At gunpoint, Larry tells Bannion that Duncan was sick of his corrupt life and told all about Lagana's operation in his suicide note. His wife kept the note secret and gets regular pay-offs from Lagana; additionally, if she dies, the information will go to the papers. Bannion comes close to killing Duncan's wife himself, but when he tells Debby this she does the job for him. She also gets revenge on Stone, throwing boiling coffee in his face, but he shoots her dead. Bannion arrives and Stone is arrested. The crime syndicate is exposed and Bannion returns to work.

DIRECTOR: Fritz Lang (1890–1976), born in Vienna, wrote his first scripts in 1916 while convalescing after suffering serious injury during his service in the Austrian Army. He graduated to directing in Germany and is recognised as a chief exponent of Expressionist cinema for his films *Metropolis* (1926), *M* (1931) and *The Testament of Dr Mabuse* (1933, a sequel to his own 1922 film *Dr Mabuse the Gambler*). The last of those was banned in Germany for its subversion of Nazi party slogans. Joseph Goebbels offered to compensate Lang with a job at UFA, the state-supported studio which was increasingly being used for propaganda; when Lang pointed out that his mother was Jewish, Goebbels replied, 'We'll decide who's Jewish.' Lang left the country the same night, leaving most of his personal possessions behind. He subsequently arrived in Hollywood.

Lang's Hollywood career has often been overshadowed by his hugely influential German period, but it produced several significant works. It was he who fused the Expressionist style with Hollywood thrillers and melodramas; his acclaimed 'wrong man' dramas *Fury* (1936) and *You Only Live Once* (1937) were key influences on the noir movement. In 1943 he directed *Hangmen Also Die!* (1943), depicting the Nazis' revenge on the Czechs for assassinating Heydrich. *The Woman in the Window* (1944) was the first of several noirs, including *Scarlet Street* (1945), reckoned to be the first Hollywood movie in which a crime went unpunished; *Secret beyond the Door* (1948); *House by the River* (1950), for Republic Pictures; two with cinematographer Nicholas Musuraca, *Clash by Night* (1952) and *The Blue Gardenia* (1953); and *The Big Heat*. He went on to make further noirs, *Human Desire* (1954 – a remake of Jean Renoir's 1938 *La Bete Humaine*), *While the City Sleeps* (1956) and *Beyond a Reasonable Doubt* (1956), which turned out to be his last Hollywood film. He returned to Germany to make a two-part melodrama, *The Tiger of Eschnapur/The Indian Tomb* (1959) and a belated third *Dr Mabuse* film, *The Thousand Eyes of Dr Mabuse* (1960), before retiring.

WRITER: William P McGivern (1918–82) was a former police reporter from Illinois who had become a crime writer in the early 1950s. His fiction is characterised by corrupt figures and a strong moral stance. *The Big Heat* was the first film to be based on his work, and subsequently his novels *Shield for Murder* (1951), *Rogue Cop* (1954), *The Darkest Hour* (1955) and *Odds Against Tomorrow* (1957) spawned adaptations. He later worked in television, including credits on *The Virginian* (1962–63) and *Kojak* (1974–76, one of his episodes was entitled *A Shield for Murder*). His novel *Killer on the Turnpike* (1961) was adapted for television as *Nightmare in Chicago* (1964), which was directed by Robert Altman and helped Altman break into movies. McGivern's original scripts include *I Saw What You Did* (William Castle, 1965), *The Wrecking Crew* (Phil Karlson, 1969) and *Brannigan* (Douglas Hickox, 1975).

Sydney Boehm (1908–90) was a good match for McGivern, having also been a police reporter. After fourteen years at the *New York Evening Journal*, he took a job in Hollywood in the mid-1940s and became a hardboiled specialist, with credits on *The High Wall* (Curtis Berhardt, 1947), *Undercover Man* (Joseph H Lewis, 1949) and *Union Station* (Rudolph Maté, 1950). He would later adapt two more McGivern novels, *Rogue Cop* (Roy Rowland, 1954) and *Hell on Frisco*

Bay (Frank Tuttle, 1955 – from *The Darkest Hour*), and in the late 1950s became a producer, before retiring in the late 1960s.

DEVELOPMENT: McGivern's novel was originally published in seven parts, between December 1952 and February 1953, in the *Saturday Evening Post*. Midway through this run, the story was purchased by Columbia and quickly developed into a script, with a first draft being ready on 20 January 1953. Boehm remained largely faithful to the novel, although he made Bannion less of an intellectual (in the novel he is prone to quoting philosophers) and more of an everyman, and reduced the level of police-procedural detail. Some of the build-up to Katie's death was cut, as this occurs around halfway through the book (in the film it is more like a third of the way through). The book makes it clear that Bannion is attracted to Debby (whose surname there is Ward) but is disgusted with himself regarding these feelings. 'I wouldn't touch anything of Stone's with a ten foot pole,' he tells her. The film does not address this directly (and Ford does not play Bannion as being attracted to Debby), but darkens Bannion's character in other ways: in the novel he stops himself from killing Mrs Deery (the character who became Bertha Duncan in the film), but in Boehm's version he is halted by the intervention of the cops. In the novel the denouement occurs differently, with Lagana dying from a heart attack and Stone being shot in the street while running from the cops. Debby is already dead by this stage, having killed herself after shooting Mrs Deery, and so does not get her revenge on Stone. However, the scene of Bannion telling her about Katie originates from the novel.

On 8 January 1953 Fritz Lang arrived at Columbia on a one-year contract, having recently been cleared by HUAC. For his first month he was briefly assigned to a different movie, but producer Jerry Wald put him on the new crime picture instead. '*The Big Heat*, which deals with crime in a big city, takes me back to my earliest beginnings in the movies,' Lang told the *Columbia News Service* on 1 February. 'During World War I, when I was convalescing from wounds in an army hospital, I wrote my first film script. It was a crime story, too.' The director joined Boehm for around a month to oversee the redrafting process, although he was not permitted to make any vast contribution. It is interesting that there is a significant black character in McGivern's *The Big Heat* who was ultimately excised from the script, given that Lang had previously attempted to use black actors in two of his films and been barred from doing so – a lynch-mob victim in *Fury* and the maid in *House by the River* were the roles which eventually went to white actors. The plot function of the character in *The Big Heat* was taken by the old lady who gives Bannion the lead regarding the car bomb.

Aside from this, Lang was reasonably happy not to interfere with the script. 'Lang said he had liked all the characters in the book,' McGivern later wrote, 'and although this wasn't essential to him in making a film, it gave him something special to work with.' The writer also said that Lang had admitted identifying with Bannion, and that the film came to represent his experience with the Nazis: the lead character 'appealed powerfully to Lang's own sense of frustration and humiliation at being forced to leave Germany. In a sense, Lang said, he had stood up to Goebbels and Hitler, but did so by running away.'

CASTING: Glenn Ford (born Gwyllyn Samuel Newton Ford, 1916) was born in Canada but moved to California at an early age and pursued an acting career, signing with Columbia in 1939. He played small roles at the studio during the early 1940s, then joined the marines in W.W.II. Upon his return, Bette Davis secured him a loan-out to Warners for *A Stolen Life* (Curtis Bernhardt, 1946), but his real breakthrough was the noir *Gilda* (Charles Vidor, 1946) opposite Rita Hayworth (see **The Lady from Shanghai**; they appeared together in six films). This positioned him as Columbia's solid, dependable lead, which turned out to be a mixed blessing as he was cast in a succession of decent but anonymous programme pictures. Exceptions include *The Man from Colorado* (Henry Levin, 1948) and the noir *Undercover Man* (Joseph H Lewis, 1949). His casting is a good indication of how Columbia regarded *The Big Heat*: not as prestigious as Lang's early Hollywood work, but a superior genre picture. Ford worked with Lang again on *Human Desire*. His fortunes improved with *Blackboard Jungle* (Richard Brooks, 1955), which gave him a superior choice of roles and in 1958 he was voted the number-one box-office attraction. He starred in the TV series *Cade's County* (1971–72) and played Pa Kent in *Superman* (Richard Donner, 1978). He is perhaps best known for his western roles, in which he always felt comfortable, and was quicker on the draw than any other actor in Hollywood (he could draw and shoot in 0.4 seconds). He retired from features after *Border Shootout* (CT McIntyre, 1990).

Gloria Grahame (1923–81, born Gloria Hallward) was a descendant of King Edward III of England. Born in Los Angeles and tutored at her mother's stage school, Gloria signed an MGM contract in 1943 but was rarely used and got her first prominent role on loan to Columbia for *It's a Wonderful Life* (Frank Capra, 1946). On moving to RKO she appeared in her first noirs, *Crossfire* (Edward Dmytryk, 1947) and *A Woman's Secret* (Nicholas Ray, 1949 – between 1948 and 1952 she was married to Ray), but again her studio struggled to cast her and again she found success on loan to Columbia, with *In a Lonely Place* (Nicholas Ray, 1950). After a couple more RKO noirs, *Macao* (Josef von

Sternberg, Nicholas Ray, 1952) and *Sudden Fear* (David Miller, 1952), a breakthrough came with a Best Supporting Actress Oscar for *The Bad and the Beautiful* (Vincente Minnelli, 1952) at MGM. The award came just as she started work on *The Big Heat*. This opened up a fruitful period in Grahame's career (although she acquired a reputation for being difficult), including *Human Desire, Naked Alibi* (Jerry Hopper, 1954), *Oklahoma!* (Fred Zinnemann, 1955) and *The Man Who Never Was* (Ronald Neame, 1956). She also appeared in *Odds Against Tomorrow* (Robert Wise, 1959). Her marriage in 1960 to former stepson Anthony Ray caused a scandal and helped kill her film career for a while.

Lee Marvin (1924–87) became an actor in his native New York after finding a career as a plumber unsatisfactory. In the early 1950s he appeared in his first films, and *The Big Heat* was the first to bring him recognition. Subsequently he often played military, western or police roles, although his next was a biker in *The Wild One* (Lazlo Benedek, 1954). After three years in the lead of the TV series *M Squad* (1957–60) he appeared in *The Man Who Shot Liberty Valance* (John Ford, 1962), *The Killers* (Don Siegel, 1964), the early neo-noir *Point Blank* (John Boorman, 1967), *The Dirty Dozen* (Robert Aldrich, 1967) and *The Big Red One* (Samuel Fuller, 1980).

PRODUCTION: Shooting started on 11 March 1953. By this stage in his career Lang had acquired a poor reputation in Hollywood: his temperamental nature, his dislike of producers and (probably) his habit of wearing a monocle which was widely suspected to be an affectation made him monumentally unpopular with colleagues (as it had in Germany). This partly accounts for the declining prestige of his Hollywood work, as he had gone from directing 'message' films to quickie crime pictures. Columbia offered the promise of a fresh start, and by the time he signed for the studio he had altered his image from that of a technical virtuoso who delivered groundbreaking work to that of a technical virtuoso who could deliver a slick programmer quickly without screwing it up or spending too much money. 'The more the audience is absorbed in the story and the more they forget the camera angles, the little sly tricks of direction, and the director's "touch", the better the picture is,' he claimed in publicity shortly before *The Big Heat*. He was also fond of characterising himself as good at handling difficult actresses, so it is interesting to note that both his leading ladies on this film later claimed that they had been treated very badly.

In spite of his new public image, Lang remained the perfectionist he had always been. He liked to run through scenes over and over again, and on *The Big Heat* this included instructing Jocelyn Brando (sister of Marlon), on her first day in her first-ever film, to go through the motion of cutting the large steak in the dinner scene 25 times, failing to specify why he found each take unsatisfactory. By the end of the day she was ready to quit, and it was only due to a supportive chat with Ford that she remained on the film. Later, in one of the first scenes involving Bannion's daughter, the little girl playing the role couldn't pronounce 'roof' in the way Lang wanted. He repeated the word back to her over and over again until the girl was on the verge of tears. Unsurprisingly he reacted very badly to Gloria Grahame, whose playful acting style meant that she never did any take the same way twice. Lang later claimed that she had asked him to change the script so that her character was the daughter of a wealthy industrialist rather than a street kid who had got lucky. He claimed to have dealt with her by threatening to 'show your back all the time and get a parrot to say your dialogue!' if she didn't stop complaining. (Although many of Lang's stories are known to be inaccurate, casting doubt on them all.)

It is true that Grahame was frustrated with a lack of good dialogue in the film, and later claimed that her husband Cy Howard contributed her two best lines: 'We're sisters – under the mink' to Bertha Duncan, and her comment on the décor, 'I like it – early nothing.' Evidence for this is that a story about the couple in a December 1952 issue of the *Herald Examiner* quotes Howard as having made the latter witticism, before *The Big Heat* was scripted. However, Grahame professed satisfaction with the part in contemporary publicity. 'I dote on death scenes which linger in an audience's memory,' she told *Silver Screen*. 'I don't want to be typed as a woman with a face nice enough to look at, but I am interested in roles that sometimes turn a cinema-goer away in horror.' (It certainly did that – see **RECEPTION**.) 'I didn't mind having my face horribly scarred because my gangster boyfriend threw a pot of boiling coffee over me. Being glamorous in movie roles all the time is not only artificial but horribly monotonous.'

Shortly before production, Jerry Wald considered this crucial sequence and on 27 February sent a letter to Lang and Robert Arthur stating, 'You should underline the extent to which Debby is anxious to preserve her beauty and the extent to which her face is important to her before the incident with the coffee.' His contention was that if 'her beauty [is] the principal object of her vanity, the burning of her face becomes that much more tragic for her'. This resulted in the placement of a number of prominent mirrors on the set of Stone's apartment, which Grahame took the opportunity to look into at various moments. 'The coffee business was in the book,' said Lang, stating that Debby would not have been badly burned 'unless the coffee was a hundred degrees. So while the gang is playing poker in one room – it is one of those damned touches of mine – I showed that the coffee on the stove is steaming.' After seeing the picture, McGivern observed that the camera had gone to Stone rather than Debby, and, thus, 'It is not the spectacle of scalded, ruined beauty, but the evil of Marvin's face and lips, glistening and quivering in Lang's close-up of him, that gives realistic horror to the scene.'

Ultimately the film took less than four weeks to shoot, one of Lang's quickest. However, a memo from Arthur suggests that the opening had to be reshot, as it is dated 10 April and so would have been written and carried out after production closed. In this, Arthur noted that the original opening, which showed the suicide of Duncan in full view, had been rejected by the censors as unacceptably violent. Arthur's alternative suggestion was basically identical to the opening shot as released.

RECEPTION: The film was released on 14 October 1953. *Variety* liked it: 'Columbia has a taut, exciting crime melodrama in this well-made presentation,' it wrote on 23 September. 'It is cut considerably above the average cops-and-robbers feature in the writing, directing and playing, and should hit a prosperous boxoffice level in release.' The reviewer considered that 'Ford's portrayal of the homicide sergeant is honest and packs much wallop. Lang's direction builds taut suspense, throwing unexpected, and believable, thrills at the audience as the scenes unfold.'

'Say this for Fritz Lang, who directed, and Sydney Boehm, who wrote the script: They haven't insulted their players by putting them in a game of tiddlywinks,' wrote Bosley Crowther in the *New York Times* of 15 October 1953. 'No matter about the implications of shady cops and political goons. The script is so vague in this department that no specific allusions may be found.' Lang and Boehm's 'only concern ... is a tense and eventful crime show, and this they deliver in a fashion that keeps you tingling like a frequently struck gong.' Crowther stressed, 'It isn't a pretty picture. But for those who like violence, it's fun.' A more ambivalent *Time* review claimed that '*The Big Heat*, like many another movie thriller, gets off to a fast start and then slows to a walk,' on 2 November. 'Since all the characters are merely carbon copies from previous cops-and-robbers films, Gloria Grahame runs away with the picture by giving some complexity to her role of a female lush on the make for mink coats.'

In Britain the film was not widely reviewed, perhaps on account of the 'X' certificate it received. 'Fritz Lang's gangster film at the Rialto, *The Big Heat*,' wrote Dilys Powell in *The Sunday Times* of 9 May 1954 'is well worth looking at for those with the stomach for violence.' She found it 'exciting, made with cold, savage skill, played for all it is worth by Glenn Ford and Gloria Grahame'. *Monthly Film Bulletin* agreed that Grahame was 'showily effective' but was less impressed, stating in April 1954, that 'In its stereotypical way, the story of crime and administrative corruption is slickly written and directed, although Fritz Lang seems to have lost most of his old power to sustain dramatic tension.' The brutality of the film was not felt to be justified, as while 'a sequence such as the murder of Bannion's wife generates a certain authentic shock effect, the main impression left by the film is one of violence employed arbitrarily, mechanically and in the long run pointlessly.'

ASPECTS OF NOIR: While *The Big Heat* was being shot in April 1953, the *New York Times* ran a report on the level of complaints the State Department had been receiving about violence in Hollywood films. The strongest complaints had come from Sweden, but Australia, Britain, India and Indonesia had also expressed concerns. This appears to have had little or no impact on *The Big Heat* itself, which *Halliwell*'s notes was 'Considered at the time to reach a new low in violence', but over the next few years an increasing number of noirs would face opposition for their violence (*The Big Combo*, *Kiss Me Deadly*) where their predecessors had drawn concern only for a lack of morality and identification with criminals.

The rise in film violence can be seen as partly an offshoot of the slackening of attitudes towards the depiction of crime and the need for clearly stated morals in Hollywood films. However, W.W.II also seems to have been a significant factor. A number of films noirs dealt with the moral ambivalence that followed the end of the war – *Gilda* is a good example – and initially it would often be a repressed presence, with a number of films being based around characters who are called to, or cannot, account for a 'missing' period in their lives (such as *Out of the Past*). There would often be a greater brutality in those films which did acknowledge the war, such as *Cornered* (Edward Dmytryk, 1945), about a veteran whose wife was murdered by collaborators. This brutality was generally considered permissible in films about the war: as Andrew Spicer notes, 'audiences had been shown Nazis or the Japanese represented as sexually twisted psychopathic killers in patriotic war films.' Generic hybrids such as *Cornered* set a precedent for post-war thrillers to continue this portrayal, and it became difficult for the censors to argue that any character who was positioned as an undesirable criminal could not be seen to commit similar acts of violence. This can be seen in *The Big Heat*, in which Bannion's 'traditional' two-fisted heroic violence contrasts with the sadistic, casual violence of Stone.

However, this does not excuse Bannion's violence altogether, and the point of the film is really that a traumatic experience can turn a good man brutal. Again, the then-recent war clearly informs this notion. The scale of the war made it more difficult for Americans to deny the existence of brutality not only in others but also in themselves, as many veterans struggled to come to terms with what they had seen and done. As *In a Lonely Place* (Nicholas Ray, 1950) demonstrates, these experiences were more extreme than anything Hollywood movies had depicted (see **Sunset Boulevard**). The tacit acknowledgement that such things existed probably helped to make them more acceptable on-screen, although it is difficult to produce evidence of this. What does seem likely was that filmmakers thought it necessary for violence to be portrayed more realistically, not sanitised or glorified. This certainly seems the case with *Kiss Me Deadly*, for example. Lang spoke of the importance of showing 'the result of violence', and *The Big Heat* focuses on an action which has permanent ramifications for Debby. 'In one way, that's the danger of things,' noted Lang of the reaction to the film, suggesting that, if something was too convincing, 'people believe it. I wonder how many wives have thrown hot coffee in their husbands' faces and were very disappointed with the result, and said, "Lang is a lousy director." '

Ultimately, however, one must also recognise that violence could be included in these films at least partly for its own sake. Hollywood's perceived audience went through a significant change in the 1950s gradually moving from concentrating on women in their twenties and thirties to aiming films at teenaged males. Maltby identifies this change as having started around 1955, the year of *The Big Combo*, which was an early attempt to combine an A-picture with elements of the emerging 'exploitation' flick, and what marks it out as 'exploitation' is the way that its approach to sex and violence borders on the unacceptable, appealing to teenagers' desire for transgression (and presenting things that were prohibited on television). As Aldrich noted, the violence in *Kiss Me Deadly* was necessary in order to please the core Spillane audience for whom he was ostensibly making the film: he could depict that violence as distasteful, but he could not leave it out altogether. If we like a film, there is often a temptation to demonstrate that it is morally justified, but we shouldn't assume that such a justification exists.

AFTERLIFE: The Hong Kong police thriller *Cheng shi te jing* (Andrew Kam, Johnny To, 1988) was released in America as *The Big Heat*, but is not a remake of the earlier film.

AVAILABILITY: *The Big Heat* is only available on DVD as a Region 1 (06532) with no extras. The VHS edition is still available.

The Big Combo (1955)

Black and White – 88 mins

Allied Artists Pictures Corporation Presents
The Big Combo **by Philip Yordan**
Piano Soloist: Jacob Gimpel
Jean Wallace's Wardrobe Designed by Don Loper
Production Manager: Rudi Feld
Film Editor: Robert Eisen
Music Editor: Robert Tracy
Assistant Editors: Mack Wright and Robert Justman
Set Decorator: Jack McConaghy
Hair Stylist: Carla Hadley
Make-up: Larry Butterworth
Set Continuity by Mary Chaffee
Lighting: Harry Sundby
Sound: Earl Snyder
Special Photographic Effects: Jack Rabin and Louis DeWitt
Director of Photography: John Alton
Music by David Raskin
Produced by Sidney Harmon
Directed by Joseph Lewis
A Security-Theodora Production

CAST: Cornel Wilde (*Leonard Diamond*), Richard Conte (*Mr Brown*), Brian Donlevy (*Joe McClure*), Jean Wallace (*Susan Lowell*), Robert Middleton (*Police Capt. Peterson*), Lee Van Cleef (*Fante*), Earl Holliman (*Mingo*), Helen Walker (*Alicia Brown*), Jay Adler (*Sam Hill*), John Hoyt (*Nils Dreyer*), Ted de Corsia (*Bettini*), Helene Stanton (*Rita*), Roy Gordon (*Audubon*), Whit Bissel (*Doctor*), Steve Mitchell (*Bennie Smith*), Baynes Barron (*Young Detective*), James McCallion (*Lab Technician*), Tony Michaels (*Photo Technician*), Brian O'Hara (*Mr Malloy*), Rita Gould (*Nurse*), Bruce Sharpe (*Detective*), Michael Mark (*Fred*), Philip Van Sandt (*Mr Jones*), Donna Drew (*Miss Hartleby*)

SUMMARY: New York Police Lieutenant Leonard Diamond is obsessed with cracking a crime syndicate run by Mr Brown. When Brown's girlfriend Susan attempts suicide, she mutters 'Alicia' while delirious and Diamond follows the lead. He arrests Brown's known associates and asks them about Alicia, but fails to pick up a man named Bettini. His superior Captain Peterson tells him to drop the case. Diamond is picked up and interrogated by Brown, who asks him why he is investigating Alicia. The action convinces Peterson that Diamond was indeed on the right track, and the case is reopened. Diamond tracks down Bettini, who tells him that Brown killed somebody on a Trans-Atlantic boat trip. The captain, Nils Dreyer, is now an antiques dealer; he refuses to tell Diamond anything, and is promptly murdered. However, Diamond discovers that Dreyer held a photograph of Brown with Alicia and Grazzi, the previous head of the syndicate who has retired to Sicily. Diamond believes that Alicia was murdered, and tells Susan this. Brown responds by giving Susan a recent photograph of Alicia, supposedly proving that she too is in Sicily. Brown orders a hit on Diamond, but his goons Fante and Mingo accidentally kill Rita, a show-girl who is keen on Diamond. Susan leaves Brown and gives Diamond the photo. Diamond realises that the photo was not taken in Sicily at all and that the murder victim was not Alicia, but Grazzi. He traces Alicia to a rest home and Diamond convinces her to give evidence, but when she sees Brown again she becomes paralysed by fear. Brown has his right-hand man Joe killed, then covers up the murders by planting a bomb on Fante and Mingo; however, Mingo survives and makes a statement against Brown. Brown kidnaps Susan and attempts a getaway, but Diamond tracks him to a private airfield and arrests him.

DIRECTOR: This was one of three films to be credited to Joseph Lewis, better known as Joseph H Lewis, director of *Gun Crazy* and many others. Since that film Lewis had gone to MGM to direct the noir *A Lady without Passport* (1950), but then encountered a fallow period of four years in which he made only three films. These included a further noir, *Cry of the Hunted* (1953), before he landed the assignment of making *The Big Combo*. Afterwards Lewis wound down his film career with a few more westerns, and his experience in the genre made him a valuable commodity when western series came to dominate television in the late 1950s. Lewis was a major director on the half-hour series *The Rifleman*, directing 51 episodes between 1958 and 1963. He also did one episode of *Bonanza* (1963), two of *Gunsmoke* (both 1965) and the pilot episode of *Branded* (1965). The cash from reruns of these series enabled him to retire comfortably to his yacht for three decades. He died in 2000.

WRITER: Philip Yordan (1914–2003), the son of Illinois-based Polish immigrants, started writing in the early 1940s with three Broadway plays including *Anna Lacusta* (1945). In 1942 he began a lengthy screenwriting career. He supplied the story for *Dillinger* (Max Nosseck, 1945) and claimed to have received a call from Louis B Mayer asking him to block its production because, 'In the '40s the studios, all the

majors, had signed a consent agreement not to make gangster pictures.'
As a King Bros. production *Dillinger* was not subject to this and Yordan
refused. Yordan had part-ownership of the film, which turned out to be
one of the most successful 'poverty row' productions ever and earned
him a lot of money as well as an Oscar nomination. His other noir work
includes *Whistle Stop* (Leonide Moguy, 1946), *The Chase* (Arthur
Ripley, 1947), *House of Strangers* (Joseph L Mankiewicz, 1949), *Edge
of Doom* (Mark Robson, 1951), *Detective Story* (William Wyler, 1951)
and *The Harder They Fall* (Mark Robson, 1956). He was
Oscar-nominated again for *Detective Story* and won for *Broken Lance*
(Edward Dmytryk, 1954). In the 1950s he lived in Paris and often
allowed his name to be used as a front for blacklisted writers, some of
whom also used his house as a writing space. In the 1960s he worked
increasingly as a producer, but continued to write well into the 1990s.

DEVELOPMENT: Allied Artists was the new name for Monogram, one
of the old 'poverty row' studios which spent the 1950s trying to adjust to
the new climate as the studio system broke up. The solid foundation of
the system had made Monogram one of the more successful
independents, but the company no longer enjoyed a guaranteed market
for its largely B-movie product and in 1953 it reinvented itself as a
financier of projects by big-name directors and stars, resembling the
United Artists of the 1930s (hence the none-too-imaginative name,
although admittedly Allied Artists had been the title of one of
Monogram's subsidiaries). Although it made deals with John Huston,
Billy Wilder, Humphrey Bogart and William Wyler, the cost of
producing prestige A-pictures was too high for AA to bear. It therefore
attempted to splice this approach with the burgeoning 'exploitation'
market: low-budget films which attracted a youthful audience via
controversial subject matter.

   As noted by critic Chris Hugo, *The Big Combo* was designed to
include 'exploitation' elements (criminal violence, sexual suggestiveness,
a low budget disguised by the noir aesthetic) with 'prestige' elements
(big-name stars and a genuine attempt to explore social problems). With
this combination in mind, it seems highly likely that Lewis was hired to
direct precisely because he combined technical proficiency with a
reputation for handling low-budget productions. Yordan rarely spoke of
the film afterwards and professed a lack of fondness for it, noting that he
disliked stories that did not have heroes. As far as he was concerned, *The
Big Combo* appears to have been hackwork.

CASTING: In the lead male and female roles, Allied and Lewis cast
husband and wife Cornel Wilde (1915–89) and Jean Wallace (1923–90,

born Jean Walasek). Wilde's family came from Hungary. He turned down a place in the Olympic fencing team in order to pursue acting ambitions, and it was while he was coaching Laurence Olivier in the sport that he secured a contract with Warner Bros. An early appearance came in the noir *High Sierra* (Raoul Walsh, 1941). He went to Twentieth Century-Fox and became a leading man with an Oscar-nominated performance as Frederic Chopin on loan to Columbia in *A Song to Remember* (Charles Vidor, 1944). His other noir roles include *Leave Her to Heaven* (John M Stahl, 1945), *Road House* (Jean Negulesco, 1948) and *Shockproof* (Douglas Sirk, 1949); he also made a number of swashbucklers and was best known for his role as the trapeze artist in *The Greatest Show on Earth* (Cecil B DeMille, 1952).

In 1951 Wilde married Wallace. She had also been acting since the 1940s, although with less success; she had previously been married to Franchot Tone and her first big roles had been alongside him, in a noir dealing with race issues, *Jigsaw* (Fletcher Markle, 1949), and a supporting part in *The Man on the Eiffel Tower* (Burgess Meredith, 1949). However, she and Tone were divorced by the time these films came out and Wallace attempted suicide for the second time (the first had been in 1946). *The Big Combo* became her second film with Wilde, following *Star of India* (Arthur Lubin, 1953). After this Wilde set up his own production company and directed eight features. Wallace appeared in only six more films, all directed by Wilde; they played the title roles in his *Lancelot and Guinevere* (1963). Of the two Wilde-directed films in which she did not appear, *The Naked Prey* (1966) is considered to be his best overall. The couple divorced in 1981.

The casting of Mr Brown was more problematic. 'We had cast Jack Palance in the part,' commented Lewis later, 'and he was very flighty and wanted to do things in a manner I didn't understand; nor did the producers.' The day before shooting started, he was dropped from the movie. Lewis suggested Richard Conte (1910–75) as a last-minute replacement. 'We wanted somebody who had a little suaveness, you know, a little dignity.' Conte was playing tennis at Lewis's club, and was fortunately available. 'He read the script that afternoon, said he'd like to do the part, and the next morning he went to work.' Conte's Italian roots made him a popular choice for gangster roles, doubtless compounded by a diminutive stature which recalled Edward G Robinson (the two had been cast as father and son in Yordan's *House of Strangers*). His other noir roles were numerous: *The Spider* (Robert D Webb, 1945), *Somewhere in the Night* (Joseph L Mankiewicz, 1946), *Call Northside 777* (Henry Hathaway, 1948), *Cry of the City* (Robert Siodmak, 1948), *Thieves' Highway* (Jules Dassin, 1949), *Whirlpool* (Otto Preminger, 1949), *The Sleeping City* (George Sherman, 1950),

Under the Gun (Ted Tetzlaff, 1950), *Hollywood Story* (William Castle, 1951), *The Raging Tide* (George Sherman, 1951), *The Blue Gardenia* (Fritz Lang, 1953), *Highway Dragnet* (Nathan Juran, 1954), *New York Confidential* (Russell Rouse, 1955) and *The Brothers Rico* (Phil Karlson, 1957). He played more supporting roles in the 1960s and, after appearing in *The Godfather* (Francis Ford Coppola, 1972), he spent his last few years working in Italian cinema.

Former accountant Lee Van Cleef (1925–89), best known for the western roles which commenced with his cinema debut in *High Noon* (Fred Zinnemann, 1952), also appeared in a number of later films noirs such as *Kansas City Confidential* (Phil Karlson, 1952), *The Naked Street* (Maxwell Shane, 1955) and *Accused of Murder* (Joseph Kane, 1956). However, westerns dominated his career, from traditional efforts like *Gunfight at the OK Corral* (John Sturges, 1957) and *The Man Who Shot Liberty Valance* (John Ford, 1962) to popular TV incarnations like *Rawhide* and *Branded* to spaghetti westerns like *For a Few Dollars More* (Sergio Leone, 1965) and *The Good, the Bad and the Ugly* (Sergio Leone, 1966).

Ted de Corsia, previously in *The Lady from Shanghai*, had a number of noir supporting roles including *The Naked City* (Jules Dassin, 1948), *The Enforcer* (Bretaigne Windust, 1951), *A Place in the Sun* (George Stevens, 1951), *The Turning Point* (William Dieterle, 1952), *Man in the Dark* (Lew Landers, 1953), *Crime Wave* (André De Toth, 1954) and *The Killing*.

PRODUCTION: In creating *The Big Combo*'s distinctive noir lighting effects on the film's tight schedule, Lewis was indebted to cinematographer John Alton (1901–96). 'This man was, unfortunately for him really, so good,' said Lewis, 'he was too good for the studio he was at, and he frightened all other photographers . . . He frightened the executives who hired the photographers. And what was the result? They kicked him out.' Alton had been the one to lend a noir sensibility to Anthony Mann's *T-Men* (1947) and *Raw Deal* (1948), and would later oversee the colour noir *Slightly Scarlet* (Allan Dawn, 1956). Lewis noted that he could describe a shot to Alton off the top of his head, anything he wanted. 'He'd say, "Fine." And I'd go and sit down for a few minutes, and suddenly he'd say, "Ready." ' By lighting a scene simply, with just a few lights, Alton could achieve set-ups which seemed impossibly quick. 'He had them all buffaloed with his technique,' said Lewis. 'Me, too. It was magic. He'd put a light there, a backlight there, and a front light kicker here, and say, "Ready." '

Although the film would later become notorious for its violence, during production most of the controversy centred around a different issue. Lewis spoke to Jean Wallace about the motivation of her character, asking why this nice girl would have fallen for a gangster in the first place. Wallace responded that she didn't know. 'Then how do you expect to make this film?' asked Lewis. 'Well, we'll just go according to the script,' Wallace replied. 'No, Jean,' said Lewis, 'you must have an approach. If you are to give a good performance, you must have an approach – you must know what you're about.' Naturally, Lewis had given the matter some thought himself. 'This is what attracts you,' he said, 'no respectable man from Nob Hill is going to love you the way this gangster's going to love you.' Wallace asked him to elaborate. 'Jean, when this man takes you in his arms, he doesn't stop at kissing you on the lips . . . he covers you *all*.' She was furious. 'How *dare* you?' she demanded. 'Why, even Cornel doesn't talk to me that way!' Lewis stressed that he was inferring nothing about her – he was talking about her character – and, when Wallace had got over the shock, she understood the significance of this for the dynamic between Mr Brown and Susan.

Lewis explained how he wanted this to work in one particular scene between the two characters. 'I know what you mean,' said Wallace, 'you don't have to say any more. But the day we have to shoot this sequence, will you get Cornel off the set? Because I can't face him.' Lewis arranged for Wilde to be viewing some rushes at the time and set up the scene, but Wallace was still tense. 'I think she was afraid to betray herself for fear Cornel would raise hell with her,' said Lewis later, 'but at that precise moment I had envisioned [as Richard Conte disappears from shot], I went "uh-uh-uh" off-scene, and that was recorded.' Lewis was pleased with the result, but 'Cornel never forgave me for it'. When Wilde saw the scene he demanded, 'How dare you shoot a scene like this with my wife. How *dare* you?' The director adopted the line which he would always defend the scene with: 'What did I do? Show me, what have I done?' Lewis contended that anybody who was capable of reading the scene as a depiction of oral sex should not be shocked by it, and those who were not capable of making this connection would not be shocked anyway. He faced the same reaction when called before the Production Code committee, one of whom flatly commented, 'This filth of showing a guy going down on a woman is not for the American audience.' Lewis responded, 'This wasn't my intention at all – I left it to your imagination. If you want to imagine this, that's up to you. But you never saw him kiss that girl below her neck.' The censor asked where Conte was supposed to have gone. 'How the hell do I know?' replied Lewis. 'What does an actor do when you move in on a close up of someone else? Go sit down somewhere, I guess.' Lewis was also asked what his intention had been in constructing the shot this way, but he would not be drawn. 'You supply me with the emotion: that's why I left it to the audience. But don't tell me I'm filthy, or a filthy director.'

The film's much-praised airstrip scenes also owed much to Alton. 'They wanted us to go out to the airport and fog it in for the final scene,' said Lewis. Alton went to the sound-stage and made a suggestion. 'Look, let's put black velvet around there,' he said, 'and one light up there, and that's it.' All this material was shot on the stage, making a substantial budgetary saving and creating the disquieting atmosphere that contributes to the ending's uncertain tone. Lewis also deflected credit for the notion of shooting Joe's death subjectively, with the hearing-aid pulled out. 'One of the grips came to me with that, and I accepted it.'

Upon finishing *The Big Combo*, Lewis took a break from filmmaking. The stress of being a 'quickie' director, working long hours with limited resources, had told upon him. 'I had a heart attack when I was forty-six years of age,' he said. 'It knocked me for a loop and for one year I didn't work, I just rested.'

RECEPTION: The film was released on 13 February 1955. 'This is another saga of the honest cop who lets nothing sway him from the self-appointed task of smashing a crime syndicate and its leader,' noted an ambivalent *Variety* on 16 February. The film featured 'grim melodramatics that are hard-hitting despite a rambling, not too credible plot, and is cut to order for the meller fan who likes his action rough and raw. In that market it should do okay.' The author, however, did not apparently identify with said market. 'In this stress on the seamier side of gangland and its denizens, the [film] gets too realistic. One torture scene in particular will shock the sensibilities and cause near-nausea.' How times change: today the scene appears relatively mild (see **AFTERLIFE**). 'The moronic fringe of sadists will enjoy this, and all the little kiddies will be sick to their stomachs.'

Aside from the violence, Howard Thompson in the *New York Times* thought the film dated. '*The Big Combo* isn't very big or very good,' he wrote on 26 March 1955. 'Even with the combo of a capable cast . . . and the kernel of a provocative plot, the result is a shrill, clumsy and rather old-fashioned crime melodrama with all hands pulling in opposite directions.' Interestingly the violence was felt to work against any sense of fidelity to real life: 'the entire picture, for all the frenzied attempts at realism, is carefully and expansively rigged with brutality and violence (six corpses, for the record)' and the film was declared 'a sputtering, misguided antique'. Allied Artists' attempt to appeal to the 'moronic fringe' described by *Variety*, as well as those interested in its critique of corporate American values, was not a successful one, as the violence tended to overshadow its intelligence in the eyes of most contemporary critics.

The film encountered censorship problems upon its British release and was reduced to a running time of just 81 minutes. 'Although some cuts have obviously been made,' noted *Monthly Film Bulletin* in February 1956, 'this remains a gangster thriller of an unusually violent and ugly kind,' again drawing attention to the torture scene which had 'unpleasant implications, although mercifully the details (in the version distributed here, at any rate) are left to the imagination'. However, the production was not altogether dismissed; it was described as 'a crisp, professional job; the acting is never less than competent and some of the details are adroitly drawn'.

ASPECTS OF NOIR: 'Paranoia' is a word that crops up repeatedly in studies of film noir, and the present study is no exception. It is often employed to describe something about the films which is difficult to grasp, an indiscriminate sense of fear. The disorientating and fatalistic nature of such films is a key part of this, as when the hero believes he is doomed he is likely to interpret inexplicable events as inevitable elements of his downfall. However, 'paranoia' properly refers to delusions of persecution or self-importance. Its more common contemporary usage, to describe sensations of intense fear or suspicion, is informal and is probably what most people mean when they talk about the 'paranoia' of film noir. As Jonathan Buchsbaum notes in his essay 'Tame Wolves and Phoney Claims: Paranoia and Film Noir', it is possible to more rigorously apply the term as it is used in psychoanalysis.

Buchsbaum looks at a study of 1950s American political paranoia, noting that it comprised a simplified worldview which assumes everything to be part of an overarching conspiracy, a large accumulation of evidence which nevertheless does not prove the thesis and requires a substantial deductive leap, a dismissal of domestic problems as merely symptoms of the conspiracy, and the positioning of America as destined to defend freedom. Buchsbaum links this with Sigmund Freud's suggestion that male paranoia is related to a suppression of homosexual feelings. The paranoiac, encouraged by society to regard homosexuality as weak, overcompensates by postulating the existence of an enemy which must be resisted at all times, thereby giving him a reason for a constant display of strength. He is always in need of fresh evidence and so rather than ignore anything which does not support his thesis he will search for a way to make it fit. (It should be noted that Freud's ideas have often been appropriated by those who regard homosexuality as a psychological problem, but Freud noted that the subject is generally a homophobic hetereosexual who cannot accept feelings of homosexual desire and therefore homophobia is the problem.)

Buchsbaum applies this to *Double Indemnity* and *Murder, My Sweet*. In the former case Neff's belief that Keyes is on to him is paranoid, as seen in the way that Neff is confident with Phyllis before the crime but loses this confidence when she becomes available. Unable to confront his failure to satisfy her, he compensates by developing a paranoid thesis against Keyes. This further ties into Freud's notion that an object of the paranoiac's homosexual desire may become the imagined persecutor, as a consequence of denying all positive feelings towards that person. The example of *Double Indemnity* works particularly well because Neff's paranoia is unwarranted, whereas many noirs show the hero's paranoia to be justified. However, Buchsbaum notes that this is another function of the flashback narrative in the likes of *Murder, My Sweet*: the subjective recollection privileges details which directly affect the narrator, making everything seem like a plot against him. This is reinforced by the way that the police racketeers from Chandler's novel, an impersonal gang of 'businessmen', are dropped from the film, leaving just the Grayle family plot which has mostly been staged so that Marlowe will not discover that Helen is really Velma. This personalisation of the case is typical of the noir private-eye narrative: 'The private eye continues investigations that the police cannot solve for solution of the crime is not a personal obsession with them.'

Notably the study does not relate this to the Woolrich-style noir, the narrative type generally labelled as 'paranoid'; Buchsbaum's examples come directly from Chandler and Cain, the other two narrative types. An examination of a Woolrich noir such as *Phantom Lady* (Robert Siodmak, 1944 – see **Phantom Lady boxout**) reveals this as a missed opportunity. In *Phantom Lady* the conspiracy is genuine, but we can still read it as an externalisation of the hero's state of mind. The result might be described as a paranoid fantasy, in which the paranoiac is vindicated and the conspiracy overcome in a psychologically satisfactory way. Scott is unhappily married and about to leave his wife when she is murdered. He then perceives a conspiracy which makes him seem culpable and therefore implies some vast aversion to her. Although Scott does not know it, the man behind this conspiracy was having an affair with his wife, satisfying her when Scott no longer could and therefore threatening his heterosexuality. Scott is unable to overcome the conspiracy himself but it is uncovered and eliminated by Carol, to whom he proposes at the end. The conspiracy therefore represents Scott's fear that his failed marriage is a signal of homosexual desires, while Carol's resolution of it dispels that fear and indicates that she is 'right' for him in a way that his wife was not.

By the time of *The Big Combo*, Buchsbaum claims that paranoia had assumed 'a more metaphorical meaning, as institutions and bureaucracies assume a more prominent place in the plots and cannot be assimilated to the more purely subjective construction of the protagonist'. However, *The Big Combo* suggests that a paranoid reading is still possible when Diamond states, 'Mr Brown isn't a man, he's an organisation.' This simplification of organised crime to the work of a single man conforms to the earlier definition of paranoia, as does Diamond's linking of Brown to the murder of a gas-station attendant by four youths who have nothing to do with Brown's combination. The tenuous connection does not ignore the crime, but creates a chain which links it into, and exaggerates the importance of, the conspiracy. Just as the political paranoiac believes that domestic problems are best dealt with by fighting the conspiracy, so Diamond pours all his resources into pursuing Brown.

As a consequence of the film's limited means, little indication is given of how big Brown's organisation really is, since he works with a handful of henchmen throughout. It is eventually revealed that his control partly stems from an illusion which he orchestrates: the illusion that Grazzi is still alive and approves Brown's status. Brown encourages the paranoid worldview which keeps him successful. 'Who runs the world?' he asks Bennie in his first scene and claims that hate has put him where he is, but it is really his self-assurance that keeps him in control. He does not necessarily need to be running everything because it is enough that people *believe* that he does, to the extent that the criminal world fears him and the police believe that it is futile to try and catch him. Diamond's fellow officers never query his claims about Brown (he is 'a very influential citizen', according to Captain Peterson) yet they do not share his obsession with the case, suggesting that Diamond feels a greater need to show strength than others.

Diamond takes the case personally, while Brown treats Diamond as an insignificance, confidently goading him. 'Don't you see, Joe?' Brown says with light sarcasm. 'He's a righteous man. Personal feelings mean nothing to him.' The implication is the opposite, that Diamond's personal feelings about Brown have exceeded his sense of righteousness. Brown is methodical, destroying evidence as he goes and torturing Diamond without marking him, while Diamond is haphazard, desperately trying to link scraps of information together and making things fit more by luck than by judgement. When Diamond is taken off the case and spends the evening with Rita, she goes home unfulfilled, even though it was Diamond who confidently initiated the contact. Rita ascribes this to his being hung up on Susan, but his scenes with Susan suggest little warmth. As Diamond's paranoia is centred on Brown, a psychoanalytic reading suggests suppressed homosexual desire. This also suggests why Susan is with Brown, because he is assured in his heterosexuality while Diamond is sexually repressed: note that she leaves him immediately after the attempt to kill Diamond, which could be described as Brown's first paranoid act (it contrasts with the killing of Dreyer, which was against his instructions). The film has often been read as a patriarchal tug-of-war between Diamond and Brown over Susan, but this also fits into the paranoid reading; another critic, Eve Kosofsky Sedgwick, notes that 'in any erotic rivalry, the bond that links the two rivals is as intense and potent as the bond that links either of the rivals to the beloved.' This she describes as 'the routing through women of male homosocial desire', and Susan is an obvious example. Additionally, the presence of homosexual characters who threaten the hero in some way is often an indicator of suppressed desire, and the hit is carried out by Mingo and Fante, probably the most obviously homosexual characters in film noir (they sleep in the same room).

The abrupt end of the film denies us the opportunity to see whether Diamond's suggestion – that removing Brown will remove the source of a vast amount of crime – ever comes to pass. Most critics agree that the film strives for a downbeat tone which suggests that the battle is never over. 'The end of *The Big Combo*,' writes Chris Hugo, 'offers only the slim chance of an interlude in what seems to be an ongoing nightmare.' He further suggests, 'There is no evidence that the set-up which Brown represents is in a state of dissolution just because his particular section is undone,' but this involves discrediting Diamond's original assessment. The notion of Diamond as a paranoiac, simplifying the world in order to make his own position within it clearer, is a highly effective way of doing this and constructs Mr Brown as a fantasy figure, a catch-all focus for the paranoid Diamond, held up for the audience to see through to the greater complexity of the real world.

AFTERLIFE: *Reservoir Dogs* (Quentin Tarantino, 1991) also features a torture sequence involving a radio, an ear and a cop tied to a chair; the actor playing the cop also bears a certain resemblance to Cornel Wilde. In its day, the scene was as controversial as *The Big Combo*'s had been.

AVAILABILITY: *The Big Combo* is available on Region 2 (IMP1462DVD) and Region 1 DVDs, both vanilla editions. At the time of writing, however, the film is not available in its original aspect ratio of 1:1.85.

Kiss Me Deadly (1955)

Black and White – 105 mins

Victor Saville Presents
Mickey Spillane's *Kiss Me Deadly*
Photographed by Ernest Laszlo, ASC
Production Supervisor: Jack R Berne
Art Director: William Glasgow
Set Decorator: Howard Bristol
Film Editor: Michael Luciano, ACE
Assistant Director: Robert Justman
Assistant to the Producer: Robert Sherman
Sound: Jack Soloman
Casting Supervisor: Jack Murton
Make-up: Bob Schiffer
'Rather Have the Blues' sung by Nat 'King' Cole and
Kitty White
Orchestrations by Albert Harris
Radio Announcers: Sam Balter and Joe Hernandez
Photographic Effects and Title: Compete Film Services
Music Composed and Conducted by Frank Devol
Screenplay by Al Bezzerides
Produced and Directed by Robert Aldrich

CAST: Ralph Meeker (*Mike Hammer*), Albert Dekker (*Dr Soberin*), Paul Stewart (*Carl Evello*), Juano Hernandez (*Eddie Yeager*), Wesley Addy (*Lt Pat Murphy*), Marion Carr (*Friday*), Marjorie Bennett (*Manager*), Fortunio Bonanova (*Carmen Trivago*), Madi Comfort (*Nightclub Singer*), Robert Cornthwaite (*FBI Agent*), Nick Dennis (*Nick*), Jack Elam (*Charlie Max*), Jesslyn Fax (*Horace's Wife*), Percy Helton (*Doc Kennedy*), Jack Lambert (*Sugar Smallhouse*), Mort Marshall (*Ray Diker*), Strother Martin (*Harvey Wallace*), James McCallion (*Horace*), Silvio Minciotti (*Mover*), Ben Morris (*Radio Announcer*), Paul Richards (*Attacker*), James Seay (*FBI Agent*), Leigh Snowden (*Cheesecake*), Jerry Zinneman (*Sammy*) and introducing Maxine Cooper (*Velda*), Cloris Leachman (*Christina*), Gaby Rodgers (*Carver*)

SUMMARY: Private detective Mike Hammer picks up a woman named Christina in the desert outside Los Angeles after she runs in front of his car. She and Hammer are accosted by thugs; she is interrogated and they are left to die, but Hammer survives. He is questioned by federal agents and realises that the incident must be linked with something bigger. Cop Pat Murphy warns him off, revoking his PI and gun licences. A scientist named Ray Diker directs Hammer towards Christina's old apartment and he finds her roommate Lily Carver. Hammer is given a new car as a bribe, but he realises that it is booby-trapped and gets his mechanic, Nick, to find out who rigged it. Diker names some people who knew Christina and Hammer starts with Lee Kawolsky, an ex-boxer who was killed. Kawolsky's manager says that he was threatened by two thugs in the employ of Carl Evello, who also warns Hammer away. Hammer's secretary Velda is getting information about a man named Dr Soberin, who, according to Diker, is also involved. Carver tells Hammer that 'they' came for her and he lets her hide at his apartment. Hammer discovers that Nick has been murdered. Velda is kidnapped; Hammer is taken to a beach house and told that Velda will be set free if he tells them what Christina knew. Hammer escapes and realises that Christina had swallowed something important before she died. He goes to the morgue and finds a key, which opens a sports club locker, which contains a box filled with intense light and heat. Hammer returns to his apartment but Carver has gone. Murphy tells Hammer that Carver has been dead for a week. Dr Soberin and the woman who has been impersonating Carver (her real name is Gabrielle) are at the beach house with the box, preparing to leave town. Soberin refuses to split the contents with Gabrielle and she kills him. Hammer arrives too late to stop Gabrielle opening the box. As she and the house are consumed in nuclear fire, Hammer rescues Velda.

DIRECTOR: Robert Aldrich (1918–83) came from a wealthy Rhode Island family, and had family ties to the Rockefellers. He became interested in film at university and used family connections to get a production assistant job at RKO in 1941. From there he moved to become an assistant director; producer Sam Spiegel rated him the best assistant in Hollywood and he soon went freelance, working with the likes of Chaplin, Renoir and Zinnemann as well as supporting Polonsky on *Force of Evil*. Also working as a production manager, he gained a reputation for efficiency. In the early 1950s, having failed to chair a feature-film project of his own, he earned his first director's credits in television; these were enough to get him a gig directing *Big Leaguer* (1953), a B-movie for MGM. A second, *World for Ransom* (1954), reworked the TV series he had directed, *The Affairs of China Smith* (1952–53), although he was not credited. Two westerns followed – *Apache* and *Vera Cruz* (both 1954) – which were highly profitable and led him to be offered *Kiss Me Deadly*. After this he was able to form his own production company, Associates and Aldrich, which made nearly all of his subsequent 25 films. These included *The Big Knife* (1955), *The Last Sunset* (1961), *Whatever Happened to Baby Jane?* (1962), *The Dirty Dozen* (1967), *Ulzana's Raid* (1972) and *Twilight's Last Gleaming* (1977). He was one of the first of the post-studio system independents. Always firmly on the left of the industry, he was President of the Directors Guild of America (DGA) from 1975 to 1979, doing much to win more control for directors over their films: he claimed that the studios never forgave him. His last film was . . . *All the Marbles* (1981).

WRITER: As a youth in Brooklyn, Mickey Spillane (born Frank Morrison Spillane, 1918) enjoyed the heroic fiction of Anthony Hope and Alexandre Dumas as well as America's emerging comic-book culture. In the mid-1930s he started writing stories for pulp magazines and diversified into radio and comic books, writing for freelance studio Funnies, Incorporated. During W.W.II he worked as a flying instructor in the US Air Force, before returning to Funnies to discover his work taken over by younger writers and women, who had unionised. He broke the union by working for sub-union wages, then upped his fees once he had re-established himself. He went on to write for *Captain America*, *The Human Torch* and *Sub-Mariner*, and created a detective called Mike Danger. In 1946, needing $1,000 to buy a plot of land for a new house, he rattled off a novel called *I, The Jury* (1947) in three weeks, reusing his Mike Danger character under the name Mike Hammer. His publisher, Dutton, was unconvinced as to its literary merit and alarmed by its violence, but they thought it would sell and published it anyway. To date it has sold over eight million copies. *Kiss Me, Deadly* (1952) was the fifth Hammer novel and Spillane's seventh overall, after which he took a break to concentrate on work for the Jehovah's Witnesses. Dissatisfied with the casting in the first four Mike Hammer films, he played the role himself in *The Girl Hunters* (Roy Rowland, 1963). Around the same time he returned to novel writing. He has sold around two hundred million copies of his books.

AI Bezzerides (born 1908) started out as a crime novelist but diversified into screenplays when he adapted his own *Long Haul* (1938) as *They Drive by Night* (Raoul Walsh, 1940). He worked on a variety of film projects but specialised in crime, with credits including *Desert Fury* (Lewis Allen, 1947), an adaptation of his own novel *Thieves' Market* (1949) under the title *Thieves' Highway* (Jules Dassin, 1949), *Sirocco* (Curtis Berhardt, 1951), *On Dangerous Ground* (Nicholas Ray, 1952) and *A Bullet for Joey* (Lewis Allen, 1955). After *Kiss Me Deadly* he largely moved into television, scripting episodes of the western series *Rawhide*, *Bonanza* and *The Virginian* before co-creating *The Big Valley* (1965–69).

DEVELOPMENT: 'I regret having accepted the job of making *Kiss Me Deadly*,' Aldrich told Francois Truffaut in 1956. 'Two horrible films had already been made of the Spillane series, and I should have refused.' The hugely successful Mike Hammer books had been turned into films by Parklane Productions: *I, The Jury* (Harry Essex, 1953) and *The Long Wait* (Victor Saville, 1954) were released through United Artists. Aldrich's two successful westerns had also come out through UA, and Parklane offered him the job of *Kiss Me Deadly* – at that time the most recent Hammer book. Like Saville, Aldrich hated Spillane's novels, but he took the job anyway, 'provided [Saville] would let me make the kind of movie I wanted and provided I could produce it', knowing that it was a good career step. 'You lessen the enemy [when you produce your own films]. Then you only have the distributor to fight.'

Bezzerides was similarly unimpressed with the material. '[Aldrich] gave me the Mickey Spillane book . . . I said, "This is lousy. Let me see what I can do." You give me a piece of junk, I can't write it. I have to write something else.' Aldrich would later claim that 'The original book . . . had nothing. We just took the title and threw the book away,' but this is not an accurate reflection. The level of similarity has often been understated, as many of the film's scenes and plot details come from the novel. These are as follows: Christina (called Berga in the novel), wearing nothing but a trenchcoat, flagging down Hammer's car; his lie to get them through the roadblock; the interrogation of Christina and the attempt to kill both her and Hammer; Velda and Pat coming to see Hammer in hospital; Hammer being questioned by the FBI; Pat taking Hammer's PI licence and gun; Hammer beating up a man who was shadowing him; the encounter with Christina's former landlord and landlady; Hammer going to Carver's new apartment, and elements of their first meeting; Hammer being given the booby-trapped car and asking his mechanic (Bob in the novel) to trace it for him; Hammer speaking to the driver who killed Kawolsky in a 'traffic accident'; the characters Carl Evello, Sugar Smallhouse, Charlie Max and Evello's half-sister, Friday (although this is her surname in the novel); Carver's claim that 'they' came for her and she hid in the basement (although in the novel she is already staying with Hammer when this happens); Velda trying to get close to William Mist, but eventually being kidnapped; the kidnapping of Hammer (although he is not given the truth serum in the novel) and his trick of getting the thugs to kill Evello for him; the key in Christina's stomach which opens a sports club locker with the merchandise inside; Hammer beating up the club's desk clerk; Carver turning out to be an impostor in the employ of Dr Soberin; and her non-fatal shooting of Hammer.

Yet, while Bezzerides's script is clearly rooted in Spillane's novel, the two are very different. All of the material from the book was completely rewritten, so barely a word of Spillane's dialogue remains, and Bezzerides added a number of quirky details in his efforts to 'make every scene, every character interesting': 'I'm a big car nut, so I put in all that stuff with the cars and the mechanic. I was an engineer so I gave the detective the first phone answering machine in that picture.' The addition of the Rossetti poem (which is misquoted, compressing the fifth, sixth and seventh lines with the eleventh and twelfth and substituting 'we' for 'I' in the twelfth line – but never mind) and the refashioning of William Mist from a hood to a dealer in abstract art seem like snide comments on the 'lowbrow' perception of Spillane's novels. (Asked about the art references, Aldrich stated, 'That's all Bezzerides.') The emphasis of each scene is also very different, with the result that the film has an entirely different meaning from the book (see **ASPECTS OF NOIR**).

Crucially, Bezzerides changed the nature of the 'macguffin', which in the novel is a shipment of drugs stolen from the Mafia; the change was motivated by censorship requirements, which (until the 1956 release of Otto Preminger's *The Man with the Golden Arm*) prohibited the depiction of drugs. Bezzerides elected to completely remove the Mafia and Aldrich gave him the credit for the film's most memorable aspect: 'That devilish box . . . I just put Bezzerides's wonderful idea on film.' In retrospect, when asked 'about the hidden meanings in the script, about the A-bomb, about McCarthyism, and so on', Bezzerides stated, 'I can only say that I didn't think about it when I wrote it. Those things were in the air at that time and I put them in.' This was partly due to the speed at which he was working: elements entered the script subconsciously because 'It was automatic writing.' The script was finished in 'About three weeks. I wrote it at home, day and night . . . I wrote it fast because I had contempt for it.'

Regarding the violence, Bezzerides said, 'Those characters fit those stories, that's all. I don't sympathise with their violence. But it is more interesting to write. Violence, traumatic events, these are the things that go deep.' This was one aspect of the novel which he retained. 'The character in the book is that way. I just heightened his natural violence. I tell you, Spillane didn't like what I did with his book. I ran into him in a restaurant and boy, he didn't like me.' It is worth noting that the title is not exactly the same as that of the novel, as the comma was removed: *Kiss Me, Deadly* rather cheesily suggests that the kisser (Hammer) is deadly, whereas in *Kiss Me Deadly* the word 'deadly' could describe the kiss itself. This draws the emphasis away from Hammer and on to the dangerous nature of his actions: the 'deadly kiss' might be the nuclear explosion at the end. (In this chapter, the book and film are distinguished by the presence or absence of this comma.)

CASTING: Although Aldrich was less than pleased to be filming a Spillane novel, he was delighted with the cast he was able to put together. Principally he was keen to cast Ralph Meeker (1920–88, born Ralph Rathgeber) in the lead role, and got him. 'I thought he was a very exciting actor,' said Aldrich, 'new and fresh. Plus, I didn't need a real star to get the money for the film. The name "Mickey Spillane" . . . was enough.' A stage actor in the 1940s, having replaced Marlon Brando on Broadway in *A Streetcar Named Desire*, Meeker made his film debut in *Teresa* (Fred Zinnemann, 1951). *Kiss Me Deadly* was one of a few leading roles he won in the 1950s, but he would come to be regarded as a supporting player. His lead roles would often be unconventional, such as in *Something Wild* (Jack Garfein, 1961). Aside from *Kiss Me Deadly*, his most praised work was a supporting role in *Paths of Glory* (Stanley Kubrick, 1957); he worked with Aldrich again on *The Dirty Dozen* (1967). His other films include *The St Valentine's Day Massacre* (Roger Corman, 1967) and *The Anderson Tapes* (Sidney Lumet, 1971), and he made numerous TV guest appearances in everything from *The Green Hornet* to *ChiPS*.

Aldrich also gave '. . . and introducing' film roles to three friends whom he felt deserved a break. Maxine Cooper had worked in television prior to *Kiss Me Deadly* and enjoyed a marked increase in work after the film, but her career never quite took off. Gaby Rodgers had in fact acted on film before, in *The Big Break* (Joseph Strick, 1953) but otherwise remained confined to television. *Kiss Me Deadly* was her only other film. Of the three, it was the one with the smallest role who went on to the greatest career: one-time Miss America runner-up Cloris Leachman (born 1926) had already worked extensively in television and would continue to do so, accruing credits in *Lassie* (1957–58), *The Twilight Zone* (1961), *Dr Kildare* (1964), *The Mary Tyler Moore Show* (1970–75), *The Facts of Life* (1986–88), *The Simpsons* (1991), *The Twilight Zone* again (2003 – playing the same character) and *Malcolm in the Middle* (2001–04). She is the only woman to have won Emmy awards in five different categories. She also made several other films, including *Butch Cassidy and the Sundance Kid* (George Roy Hill, 1969), *Young Frankenstein* (Mel Brooks, 1974) and *Crazy Mama* (Jonathan Demme, 1975), and won a Best Supporting Actress Oscar for *The Last Picture Show* (Peter Bogdanovich, 1971).

PRODUCTION: The film was allotted a relatively meagre budget of $425,000 and a brief production schedule of 22 days, commencing on 27 November 1954; Gaby Rodgers later described it as 'a quickie movie, a one-take kind of thing'. Aldrich did have ambitious plans for the visual style, however. 'On *Kiss Me Deadly* you had a chance to establish a very graphic, hard-hitting, short-cut, staccato kind of style for that movie,' he said. 'That wasn't brand new but it was new for that kind of film.' There were only two studio sets, which were Mike and Velda's respective apartments. 'I rented a tiny old disused studio in which we constructed the sets of the two flats,' said Aldrich – the studio in question was Sutherland Studios. 'All the rest was shot in real interiors, more or less fixed up for the occasion.' All location work was undertaken in Los Angeles, which was partly a budgetary decision (it saved money on sets) but also suited the pseudo-realistic style Aldrich was looking for.

Asked about the large number of long takes in the film (most notably Hammer's scenes at the boxing gym and at Trivago's apartment, both done in single takes), Aldrich noted, 'It has a direct relation to economy and personnel. Ernie Lazslo is a very good cameraman, but his trademark isn't speed. That was a problem.' With the tight schedule, 'If you elect to go with a cameraman that's not very, very fast, you have to, up front, make the decision that you are not going to get the kind of coverage you'd normally like.' This also put more pressure on the cast, as Aldrich had to 'hope that the performances are good enough, because they're cast in concrete'. There was no option to cover a badly delivered line by dropping in material from another take.

Aldrich also didn't give his actors much direction, trusting them to develop their own characterisations following a two-week rehearsal period. This produced some memorable results. 'Va-va-voom was Nick Dennis,' stated Aldrich. 'He asked me if he could use it. I'd love to be able to take credit for it because it's part of the language.' Rodgers asked him how he wanted her to play Lily, and he responded that he envisioned the character as a lesbian. (She also asked whether she had any scenes with other women and he said no; hence this element would never have to be made explicit, making it easy to get past the censors.) In accordance with this, Rodgers elected to cut her hair short and wear a tuxedo-like jacket for her later scenes. She also spoke to Spillane, which she found to be no help at all, and read the novel. Noting that Lily was a drug addict, she adopted a spaced-out manner (the only trace of the film's original macguffin). Rodgers asked what was supposed to be in the box. Aldrich's response was vague. It has often been assumed by critics to be an atomic bomb, and indeed the director described it to Rodgers as 'atomic', but its operation is nothing like that of a real atomic bomb and so there is room for interpretation. Notably, it seems alive when opened. 'We worked a long time to get the sound of it,' said Aldrich. 'We finally used the sound of an airplane exhaust overdubbed with the sound made by human vocal chords when someone breathes out noisily.'

The film wrapped on 23 December 1954. Rodgers's impression of Aldrich was 'a lovely man, jolly, easy-going. A Catholic', and the sadistic nature of the finished film therefore came as a surprise to her. However, Aldrich was careful to ensure that this was not gratuitous. While editing *Kiss Me Deadly* he wrote an article for the *Herald Tribune* in response to an attack from *New York Times* critic Bosley Crowther on the violence of *Vera Cruz*. To demonstrate how his depiction of violence operated, Alrdich described a scene he had recently put together – the torture of Christina. 'The camera focuses first on the helpless girl and her antagonists. The situation leading up to this moment of torture is well established and is a logical development of the plot.' From the point at which the villains laid their hands on Christina, 'suspense is maintained, the violence high-keyed and the horror spotlighted through the sound effects, focussing the camera on a series of close shots, on her feet, her hands, shadows on the wall and similar devices'. Because of this, Aldrich estimated that '60 per cent' of what the viewer saw in the scene 'will be the product of their own thinking'. This description bears little relation to anything in the film as released, suggesting that this sequence was heavily trimmed. Certainly United Artists insisted on some minor cuts. Prior to release, the film encountered a campaign by the Catholic Legion of Decency, who disagreed with Aldrich's claim that he had produced 'a movie of action, violence, and suspense in good taste' (cheekily, he also claimed that 'we kept faith with 60 million Mickey Spillane readers' in preserving the story's violence). An article in *America: The National Catholic Weekly Review* claimed that Aldrich's defence 'springs . . . from subhuman thinking. It defends depravity, tries to justify morbidity and totally misrepresents the record of human violence as portrayed, without being glamorized, in great literature.' However, the Production Code Administration passed the film with a 'B' rating, which Aldrich pointed out in his claim that the Legion was being unreasonable: 'there certainly could not be this wide divergence between the opinion of the Legion and that of the Code Administration. The Legion has even failed to recognize any voice of moral righteousness.' Worse condemnation of the film was to follow.

Regarding the opening credit roll (which famously runs from the top of the screen to the bottom), a memo from United Artists read, 'Mickey Spillane's name must be above the title and in the same type style as appears on the *Kiss Me Deadly* Signet Book Jacket.' Interestingly, there is no credit for Spillane's novel, as there is for Hemingway's story on *The Killers*: Spillane's credit confirms his ownership of the property, but acknowledges no creative contribution.

RECEPTION: *Kiss Me Deadly* was released on 18 May 1955. Aldrich's assessment was that 'most people in America put it down as a Spillane movie done with a little more energy, a little more compression . . . they didn't understand at all the political implications'. This is certainly reflected in *Variety*. 'The ingredients that sell Mickey Spillane's novels . . . are thoroughly worked over in this latest Parklane Pictures presentation,' read its review on 20 April 1955. 'The combo of blood, action and sex which has attracted exploitation b.o. in previous entries should repeat here for the situations that find this type of filmfare sells tickets.' The attempts to do something interesting with the material were characterised as minor flaws, with Meeker's performance judged 'acceptable, even if he seems to go soft in a few sequences. Aldrich's handling is acceptable, too, although he prolongs the footage to an unnecessary hour and 45 minutes by his deliberate pacing of many individual scenes.' The objective was described as 'some kind of fissionable material', or 'At least, that appears to be what all the shooting and shouting is about because the viewer isn't taken into guarded confidence until near the footage windup and even then the subject remains rather obscure.'

The film suffered from a lack of promotion. Some newspapers and television stations would not advertise it following the Legion of Decency's campaign and it was not reviewed in the *New York Times*, perhaps owing to the public feud between Aldrich and the paper's main reviewer Bosley Crowther. When the Kefauver Commission – a government body investigating the corruption of American youth – came to Hollywood, it viewed *Kiss Me Deadly* and declared it one of the greatest cultural menaces produced that year. In spite, or perhaps because, of the controversy, the film did manage to break even (it had been cheap to make). Spillane disliked the film, as he disliked all the films based on his work. 'I don't like any of them, because they don't read the books,' he later said. 'In *Kiss Me Deadly* my story is better than his story.'

The film did not run in the UK owing to concerns over violence, although *Monthly Film Bulletin* did run a review from what was clearly an edited print (it is cited as having a running time of 96 minutes): 'The censor has excised a few (presumably brutal) moments, making one scene almost incomprehensible.' On this showing, the film at least gained more recognition for its efforts. 'The latest Mike Hammer adventure is distinguished from its predecessors by an extraordinary arty style,' its reviewer noted in August 1955, 'bold, formalised low-key effects, tilted shots, extreme close-ups, complicated long takes, sometimes outré compositions.' The critic felt that the clash 'of "art" and pulp literature is, at the least, curious. One cannot say that Robert Aldrich's direction lends clarity . . . indeed, at times it further obscures [the narrative]; but it does create an atmosphere of its own.'

Fortunately for Aldrich, critics in France noted the same things and appreciated them far more. 'I had a career due to the European reaction to *Kiss Me Deadly*,' the director later acknowledged. Bezzerides commented, 'I couldn't believe what went on there. Truffaut, for Christ's sake, thought it was one of the best pictures made. I was awed.' Claude Chabrol, writing in *Cahiers du Cinema*, hailed it thus, 'Here it is, the crime film of tomorrow, liberated from everything and especially from itself, illuminating with its powerful sunlights the abysses of the infamous "thing".' Chabrol realised that the incongruous treatment of the novel signalled the filmmakers' lack of affinity for it. 'For its construction it chooses the worst, the most lamentable material that can be imagined, the most nauseous product of the genre fallen into putrefaction: a novel by Mickey Spillane.' Under this reading it is significant that Bezzerides did not merely throw the book away (see **ASPECTS OF NOIR**). The result only paid lip service to generic conventions, with the ostensible story 'treated off-screen and summed up for the simpletons quickly and quietly. For the subject of the film is more serious: images of Death, Fear, Love and Horror are passed quickly in review.'

Aldrich 'appreciated their enthusiasm', but was ambivalent over whether he agreed with it. He explained his feelings on the matter many times; with his having first appeared to disown the political commitment of the film, it was widely assumed that he disliked it. 'No, I like the picture very much,' he clarified. 'I just don't think it was as important a film as some people thought it was.' Giving Bezzerides a portion of the credit, he noted, 'It was a time in America when the McCarthy thing was in full bloom and that was the principal anti-Spillane attitude . . . an anti-Spillane picture about Spillane. It was anti-McCarthy and anti-Bomb in a minor way.' However, 'once you got outside the United States the whole importance of that disappeared, and the French and others read into it all sorts of terribly profound observations.'

ASPECTS OF NOIR: When people talk about a film being better if you've read the book, they usually mean that the book fills in details which the film did not manage to accommodate. In the case of *Kiss Me Deadly*, the film gains another level when you realise that it is more than just an adaptation of the novel: it is a reaction to it.

Aldrich had been closely associated with many of those cast out of Hollywood by the HUAC witch-hunts, but was too junior to be singled out. Accordingly, it is unsurprising that he was unimpressed with Mickey Spillane's work, its right-wing sensibility clearly signalled in the likes of *One Lonely Night*, in which he battles Communist conspiracies. Aldrich described Mike Hammer as 'anti-democratic' and was disappointed that his critique of Spillane's ideology went unnoticed by many: 'when I asked my American friends to tell me whether they felt my disgust for that whole mess,' he told Truffaut, 'they said that between the fights and the kissing scenes they hadn't noticed anything of the sort.' In an essay on the film, Edward Gallafent suggests – with justification – that this was because 'What they have done is to create a different model of the hero and then offer a critique of that figure, rather than treating Spillane's hero from an oppositional point of view.'

It is true that the Mike Hammer of this film is different from the one who appears in the novels. However, directly condemning Spillane's Hammer within the confines of an adaptation of *Kiss Me, Deadly* would be very difficult, since the world depicted in the novel is one which is designed to suit Hammer's methods and justify his actions. Hammer is driven by his hatred of 'the Mafia', depicted as a foreign monolithic entity which implies that criminality is 'unAmerican' and comes from without. Assuming that Aldrich and Bezzerides were loath to portray this worldview, this would have created a film in which Hammer was paranoid and deluded, and it would have been necessary to demonstrate where his assumptions were unfounded. (Other cautionary vigilante-revenge thrillers such as *The Big Heat* operate by contrasting the hero's behaviour with what he was like before he was driven to revenge and/or allowing him to pull up just short of crossing a significant line, neither of which would serve to criticise Hammer.) This would have lacked subtlety and probably resulted in a polemical and not terribly entertaining film. Instead, what we see in *Kiss Me Deadly* is a degradation of Hammer initiated by a bored screenwriter trying to amuse himself. Whether or not Bezzerides set out to undermine the character, one can argue that his dislike influenced his reworking, especially since he did not strive to create a version of Hammer he liked (probably as a result of his recognition that the character's violence, though distasteful, was dramatically valuable). Interestingly, both versions push the private-eye figure to different extremes and signal the end of the archetype's heyday.

The major difference is the nature of Hammer's work. The film's version specialises in divorce cases rather than solving crimes, and he prefers to construct evidence of infidelity rather than find it: either he or Velda seduce the client's spouse. (Even here one can draw similarities between book and film, as Velda uses her sexuality to obtain information in both.) He is a bottom-feeder profiting from the moral bankruptcy of others. It must be said that, if one isolates *Kiss Me, Deadly* from the other Hammer novels, this addition for the film is not so much a change, but the filling-in of a glaring hole at the centre of the novel: Hammer is not hired to investigate the death of the woman he picked up but makes

the case a personal crusade, for which he is not paid. The reader
presumes that this is a deviation from his usual behaviour, as Hammer's
work must typically provide an income, but the precise nature of this
work is not stated.

This generally goes unnoticed, as the reader is accustomed to the role
of private detective being a flexible one (*The Maltese Falcon* and
Murder, My Sweet both feature detectives being hired as temporary
bodyguards), but it demonstrates how Spillane pushes the private-eye
figure to one extreme. A common trait of the noir detective is that he
continues to pursue the case beyond the point where it is still necessary
(or even advisable) to do so, demonstrating that it has become a personal
obsession. Spillane discards this and makes the case personal from the
start, dropping in figures who repeatedly tell Hammer not to get
involved. The amount of actual detective work Hammer does is small, as
he relies heavily on outside sources for his information (more so than in
the film). Spillane therefore uses the conventions of the detective story to
engineer a sequence of confrontations in which Hammer can express his
moral opposition to various criminal figures and satisfy his desire for
revenge. Any relation to the reality of detective work is rendered
irrelevant, and Hammer comes to resemble one of the comic-book
superheroes for whom Spillane had also written. The task Hammer
undertakes in *Kiss Me, Deadly* is much greater than anything Marlowe
ever attempted, taking down as much of 'the Mafia' as he possibly can.
The news that Hammer is out to seek revenge is enough to strike fear
into criminal hearts and his victory is not so much a consequence of
greater strength, technique or resources than of the moral superiority
that Spillane bestows upon him. (However, Hammer conspicuously
lacks the ethical code of most comic-book heroes: Superman, for
example, never kills.)

Bezzerides's elaboration on the nature of Hammer's work, while
derogatory to Hammer, does not directly change the plot. However, it
does take away his nobility, so his self-interested pursuit of 'the great
whatsit' feels more consistent with his character than the grand,
self-righteous altruism of the novel. Where the book's Hammer is a big
man, the film's is a pitifully small one and the two characters operate in
very different worlds, powerfully underlined by the change of locale. The
novel takes place in New York, a place of structures and hierarchies
where organised crime is *very* organised. The film takes place in a
version of Los Angeles which is 'the city of the future', as Andrew Spicer
describes it, 'a postmodern centrifugal sprawl with no centre, its
inhabitants lost by the sides of the endless freeways'. This is a world
without moral absolutes, a world that implicitly has no place for
Spillane's Hammer. Having begun with Spade and Marlowe and their

artificial yet necessary codes of justice and progressed through Jeff Bailey's doomed romanticism, we end with a Mike Hammer who wanders through the noir world in search of a prize, the nature of which is obscure even to him, and who relishes the violence which results.

This is arguably the film's greatest criticism of the book, that its central character has different aims but acts in the same way – a point which could not have been made except by drawing scenes from the book, such as Hammer's beating up of the innocent desk clerk. Admittedly in the novel the clerk is ruder, and admittedly the scene where he traps the morgue attendant's hand in the drawer is germane to the film, but the film does lack Hammer's brutal interior monologue; not only is the novel's interrogation scene more graphic, showing Hammer throttling Evello before leaving him just alive enough to die at the thugs' hands, but also Hammer considers the fatal confusion of identity a 'joke' that is 'too good to pass up'. The film's different outcome also results in the loss of another horrifying bit of violence from the novel: the duplicitous 'Carver' has recently had an alcohol rub when Hammer discovers her true identify, so he sets fire to her. There is a clear link between this and her self-inflicted death by fire in the film; it is through this process of drawing parallels while making contrasts that the film sets itself up in opposition to the novel, and, in reacting against one extreme concept of the private detective, the film creates another – the most extreme which film noir would produce.

AFTERLIFE: For many years *Kiss Me Deadly* was widely circulated in a truncated version. This print lost 81 seconds of material, and the upshot was that Hammer and Velda were not seen to escape from the beach house at the end: the house merely explodes in a fireball, presumably taking them with it. This untidy splice led to many critics praising the bravura of Aldrich and Bezzerides in producing such a stark and brutal ending. Led by erroneous research, some suggested that any material featuring the pair stumbling in the surf had been added into some prints by the studio against Aldrich's wishes and should not be present on 'correct' prints. However, when queried about the ending years after release, Aldrich noted, 'I have never seen a print without, repeat, without Hammer and Velda stumbling in the surf. That's the way it was shot, that's the way it was released.' His intent had been to show 'that Mike was left alive long enough to see what havoc he had caused, though certainly he and Velda were both seriously contaminated'. (In addition, Hammer presumably had to be left ostensibly alive for his next film outing, regardless of the extent to which this film contradicted the others.) This certainly has a powerful effect on the meaning of the ending: as Glenn Erikson notes, 'By dwelling on Hammer's powerlessness against the fiery evil he has released, the film's original final statement now firmly reinforces Bezzerides' condemnation of the whole Spillane ethos.'

The origin of the problem remains a mystery, as this was not a troublesome scene from a censorship point of view. Erikson suggests that it was an error in handling the original negative, after duplication work for the original release prints had been completed. Accidental damage to the negative might have been concealed by swift re-editing: the poor quality of the splicing, the ill-matched music and the cheap 'THE END' caption on the incomplete version suggest that it was not performed with access to full facilities. The basis for all current versions of *Kiss Me Deadly* is a print recovered in 1996 from the artefacts donated by Aldrich to the DGA after his death. Not only was this in better condition than most existing prints, but also it was complete. (It is possible that this problem never affected the UK; some British publications from before the discovery refer to the complete ending.)

Considered by many (including the present writer, and Paul Schrader) to be the finest film noir, *Kiss Me Deadly* has been referenced in a number of other films, most notably *Repo Man* (Alex Cox, 1984), which features a reversed credit roll and echoes the mysterious box early on, in the opening of a car boot. The suitcase in *Pulp Fiction* (Quentin Tarantino, 1994) also seems like a descendant of the 'mysterious whatsit'.

AVAILABILITY: The film is available on Region 2 (16847DVD) and Region 1 DVDs, both featuring the original trailer and presenting the film in its original 1:1.85 aspect ratio.

The Night of the Hunter (1955)

Black and White – 93 mins

Paul Gregory Productions Presents
The Night of the Hunter
From the Novel by Davis Grubb
Screenplay by James Agee
Music by Walter Schumann
Photography by Stanley Cortez, ASC
Art Direction by Hilyard Brown
Assistant Director: Milton Carter
Film Editor: Robert Golden, ACE

Production Manager: Ruby Rosenber
Set Decoration: Al Spencer
Wardrobe: Jerry Bos
Assisted by Evelyn Carruth
Make-up: Don Cash
Hair Stylist: Kay Shea
Sound: Stanford Naughton
Property Man: Joe La Bella
Special Photographic Effects: Jack Rabin and Louis DeWitt
Produced by Paul Gregory
Directed by Charles Laughton
Released Thru United Artists

CAST: Robert Mitchum (*Harry Powell*), Shelley Winters (*Willa Harper*), Lillian Gish (*Rachel Cooper*) with James Gleason (*Birdie Steptoe*), Evelyn Varden (*Icey Spoon*), Peter Graves (*Ben Harper*), Don Beddoe (*Walt Spoon*), Billy Chapin (*John Harper*), Sally Jane Bruce (*Pearl Harper*), Gloria Castilo (*Ruby*)

SUMMARY: Self-proclaimed preacher Harry Powell travels around West Virginia, marrying widows in small towns and killing them for their money. He tells himself that he is doing the Lord's work. Arrested for stealing an automobile, Powell finds himself sharing a cell with Ben Harper, who robbed a bank, killed two people and stole $10,000. The money has never been recovered, but Harper's son John knows where it is. Harper talks about the money in his sleep but doesn't reveal its location, and after he is executed Powell goes to see Harper's widow, Willa, and convinces her to marry him. Realising that John is the key to the money, Powell kills Willa and claims that she has run away, placing the children in his care. John and his sister Pearl take the money (hidden in Pearl's rag doll) and escape the house, taking a boat down-river. Powell follows. John and Pearl find refuge with Rachel Cooper, a middle-aged woman whose son has died and who looks after children whose unmarried mothers cannot support them. Powell finds them but Rachel calls in the state troopers, who by this time have discovered Willa's body. Powell is arrested and John, recalling his father's arrest, surrenders the money. The children are safe in Rachel's care.

DIRECTOR: Charles Laughton (1899–1962) was born in Scarborough and attended the Royal Academy of Dramatic Art in London after W.W.I, and graduated with the Gold Medal. In 1926 he won his first role on the West End stage, and in 1928 became the first actor to play Hercule Poirot, in *Alibi*. In the same year he did his first film work in silent comedies. In 1931 he went to America with the play *Payment Deferred*, which was produced for the screen by MGM (Lothar Mendes, 1932). Laughton retained his role and began his Hollywood career, although he also continued to work in Britain. His films include *The Island of Lost Souls* (Erle C Kenton, 1932), *The Private Life of Henry VIII* (Alexander Korda, 1933), for which he won the Best Actor Oscar, *Mutiny on the Bounty* (Frank Lloyd, 1935), *Les Miserables* (Richard Boleslawski, 1935), *The Hunchback of Notre Dame* (William Dieterle, 1939), *The Suspect* (Robert Siodmak, 1945), the noir *The Big Clock* (John Farrow, 1948) and *The Man on the Eiffel Tower* (Burgess Meredith, 1950), in which he played the French detective Maigret. He also worked twice with Alfred Hitchcock, on *Jamaica Inn* (1939) and *The Paradine Case* (1948). Although Laughton never directed another film, he continued to direct for the stage and made several further acting appearances, including *Witness for the Prosecution* (Billy Wilder, 1957) and *Spartacus* (Stanley Kubrick, 1960). He also continued his highly popular reading tours. His final film was *Advise and Consent* (Otto Preminger, 1962).

WRITERS: In the early 1950s Davis Grubb (1919–80) worked in advertising in West Virginia, but had a sideline writing short stories for *Collier's Magazine*. He expanded one of these, a piece called 'The Gentleman Friend' about a young widowed mother who is subject to the attentions of a travelling salesman, into a first novel: *The Night of the Hunter* (1953). The book had been written in six weeks, incorporating other experiences. 'I was drinking in the local taverns and I got into the habits of the night workers and the people who went around at night looking for whatever: loneliness, or drugs, or sex.' It was in one such bar that he saw a man who had the words LOVE and HATE tattooed across his knuckles. Grubb's other novels include *A Dream of Kings* (1955), *Watchmen* (1961), *Fools' Parade* (1969) and *Ancient Lights* (1980).

James Agee (1909–55) was a novelist and major film critic who had made a few ventures into screenwriting with his scripts for *The Quiet One* (Sydney Meyers, 1948) and *The African Queen* (John Huston, 1951), the latter of which was Oscar-nominated. He had also worked on sections of *Crin Blanc* (Albert Lamorisse, 1952) and *Face to Face* (John Brahm, Bretaigne Windust, 1952), in which he also acted. His novels – including *Permit Me Voyage* (1934), *Let Us Now Praise Famous Men* (1941) and *The Morning Watch* (1951) – did not gain recognition until after his death, when his uncompleted *A Death in the Family* was published and won the 1958 Pulitzer Prize for Fiction. A frequent theme of his film writing is that movies are not as good as they were back in the silent days, proving that there have always been people who complain that Hollywood movies are not what they used to be, even at the height of the so-called Golden Age.

DEVELOPMENT: Paul Gregory (born Jason Lenhart, 1920) and Laughton had recently formed a production company, putting on the first Broadway runs of *John Brown's Body* (1953) by Stephen Vincent Benet, *Don Juan in Hell* (1951) and *The Caine Mutiny Court-Martial* (1954). Laughton took a very active role, cutting and reworking the scripts as rehearsals progressed. While working on the last of these three, Gregory was informed that *The Night of the Hunter* – which had not yet been published – could be good film material. He passed the book on to Laughton, who had toyed with the idea of directing for the screen. Laughton's relationship to religion was highly complex and he felt that *Hunter* explored the issue in a particularly interesting way. 'Hollywood has been looking for forty years, Davis,' he wrote to the author, 'to find a story about the church, what it is and what it does, and you've found a way of doing it that we can put over.' Gregory commented that Laughton was 'absolutely anti-religious in the denominational sense and I think that it was a marvellous opportunity to show that God's glory was really in the little old farm woman, and not in the Bible totin' sonofabitch'.

Once the rights were secured and a distribution deal made with United Artists, Laughton and Gregory engaged the services of Agee to produce the screenplay – Laughton felt that he lacked the experience to write the script himself – and Agee was paid $30,000 for his work. However, Laughton was keen to involve Grubb as well, and engaged in correspondence with the writer. Grubb noted, 'I had been filming *The Night of the Hunter* in my head as I wrote it.' Upon discovering that Grubb had studied art at college, Laughton asked him for sketches of a number of scenes. 'My dear Dave,' Laughton wrote upon receipt of these, 'the pictures are a real success. People say Oh! Oh yes of course! There would have been all sorts of battles fought, preventing people from pushing it into a really good-looking film.'

According to Gregory, Agee's contribution was more fraught. The writer was drinking heavily and spent an initial fortnight at Gregory's guest home in Santa Monica flat out on the floor, before he was moved to the Chateau Marmont. 'Charles wouldn't come near him,' said Gregory, 'and because of that Jim drank even more.' However, as Laughton's biographer Simon Callow convincingly points out, Gregory had an agenda in criticising Laughton and a handful of correspondence from Laughton and Agee suggests a different story. Agee ultimately produced an overlong, 350-page script which was very detailed and adopted a highly realistic approach, using newsreel footage and expensive montage sequences to establish the locations. Gregory claimed that Laughton never looked at this; what is definite is that this script was at odds with what the director – who saw the novel as 'a fairy-story, really a nightmarish sort of Mother Goose tale' – had imagined. Agee was not rejected altogether, and was often present on-set during production. Laughton brought him to a private screening of every DW Griffith film at New York's Metropolitan Museum of Modern Art. 'I'm fascinated,' wrote Agee during development, 'and about 95% confident, in many of the things Charles learned and showed me out of the Griffith films we saw.' By drawing upon silent-era methods of visual storytelling, Agee believed that they could 'make the story-telling faster, and more genuinely "movie", than they've been in years'. Laughton's final draft lost no scenes or characters from the novel (and lifted much dialogue wholesale), but simply stripped it down without looking for any equivalent for the interior monologues which were a feature of the novel. Instead, he would attempt to reproduce its dreamlike rhythms visually.

In a letter to Gregory in January 1955, Agee noted, 'My feeling was, and is, that Charles had such an immense amount to do with the script, that it seems to me absurd to take solo credit, much as I'd like it.' He went as far as to state, 'At times, I've even felt that it should be given to him entirely; I can withdraw from that position only in realising that I was useful, as a sort of combination sounding-board and counterirritant.' Laughton didn't want to hog the credits and was happier for them to be divided as simply as possible. Gregory assured Agee, 'We do not feel, in any sense, that a change in the credit should be made where you are concerned. We feel that you made a great contribution to *The Night of the Hunter.*' He added that they would have gladly removed Agee's name to protect him 'if we thought the picture were bad . . . but since we think it is great, we feel that you will be happy and proud that you had something to do with it.' Sadly Agee died in May 1955.

CASTING: After *Out of the Past*, Robert Mitchum's bad-boy image had been cemented by his conviction for possession of marijuana. He had expected this to kill his career stone dead, but just prior to this he had been in the acclaimed noir *Crossfire* (Edward Dmytryk, 1947) and went on to make a string of pictures that, together with *The Locket* and *Out of the Past*, make a strong case for him as the definitive leading man of film noir: *Where Danger Lives* (John Farrow, 1950), *His Kind of Woman* (John Farrow, 1951), *The Racket* (John Cromwell, 1951), *Macao* (Nicholas Ray, Josef von Sternberg, 1952), *Angel Face* (Otto Preminger, 1952) and *Second Chance* (Rudolph Maté, 1953). In 1954 he left RKO, made two adventure films at Fox, then signed on for *The*

Night of the Hunter – widely regarded as his best film and best performance.

Mitchum made a further noir, *Thunder Road* (Arthur Ripley, 1958), for which he also generated the story; *Cape Fear* (J Lee Thompson, 1962) recalled his *Hunter* performance; and *Ryan's Daughter* (David Lean, 1970) saw him prove his versatility. However, the critics had mixed feelings towards him, partly because of his apparent disdain towards his profession. 'I got three expressions,' he once said, 'looking left, looking right and looking straight ahead.' This led some viewers to suspect that somewhere Mitchum was laughing at them for bothering to watch him. As someone who appeared to take acting less seriously than any other man alive, he found himself out of step with the Method generation. However, he received ringing endorsements from his directors. 'All the tough talk is blind,' commented Laughton. 'He's a literate, gracious, kind man and he speaks beautifully – when he wants to. Bob would make the best Macbeth of any actor living.' In the 1970s Mitchum played Philip Marlowe in *Farewell, My Lovely* (Dick Richards, 1975) and *The Big Sleep* (Michael Winner, 1977). In the 1980s and 1990s his output varied: one notable role was in the remake of *Cape Fear* (Martin Scorsese, 1990). He died in 1997.

Shelley Winters (born Shirley Schrift, 1920) spent most of the 1940s playing uncredited bit-parts, but got a break with *A Double Life* (George Cukor, 1947), which led to roles in the noirs *Cry of the City* (Robert Siodmak, 1948), *Johnny Stool Pigeon* (William Castle, 1949) and *He Ran All the Way* (John Berry, 1951). She was Oscar-nominated for *A Place in the Sun* (George Stevens, 1951) but sought to improve her skills further, and took acting classes with Laughton which led to her role in *Hunter*. Subsequently she appeared in the noirs *The Big Knife* (Robert Aldrich, 1955) and *Odds Against Tomorrow* (Robert Wise, 1959) as well as *Lolita* (Stanley Kubrick, 1962). She won Best Supporting Actress Oscars for *The Diary of Anne Frank* (George Stevens, 1959) and *A Patch of Blue* (Guy Green, 1965).

The casting of Lillian Gish (1893–1993, born Lillian Diana de Guiche) tied in with Laughton's enthusiasm for DW Griffith. One of the biggest stars of the silent era, she had worked regularly with Griffith, including on *The New York Hat* (1912), *The Battle of the Sexes* (1914), *The Birth of a Nation* (1915), *True Heart Susie* (1919), *Way Down East* (1920) and *Orphans of the Storm* (1921). As a young man Laughton had been obsessed with *Broken Blossoms* (1919) and on his death-bed said, 'I fell in love with Lillian Gish.' Her film work had been sporadic since the advent of sound; finding herself rejected by the studios, she returned to the stage. *Duel in the Sun* (King Vidor, 1946) brought her only Oscar nomination, but almost put her off movies permanently. However, she liked the moral dimension of *Hunter* and accepted the part.

Peter Graves (born 1926) had recently worked with John Ford on *The Long Gray Line* (1955) and would go on to become a TV legend for the lead role of Jim Phelps in *Mission: Impossible* (1967–73, 1988–90). He can also be seen in *Airplane!* (Jim Abrahams, David Zucker, Jerry Zucker, 1980). Neither of the two children, Billy Chapin and Sally Jane Bruce, went on to adult careers.

PRODUCTION: Laughton's spirit of close collaboration continued throughout the shoot. Composer Walter Schumann (who had worked with Laughton in theatre) remained on-set throughout, with Laughton taking him through the scenes where he felt the music was of particular importance and telling him, 'In these scenes, you are the right hand and I am the left.' Mindful of the difficulties of getting the rhythms of the music to match the rhythm of each scene, Laughton shot extra coverage of the music-heavy scenes to give Schumann options. Stanley Cortez, whose childhood ambition had been to conduct orchestras, also tended to think musically and (at Laughton's suggestion) explained to Schumann what music had influenced his lighting work. Along with assistant director Milt Carter, editor Robert Golden and art director Hilyard Brown, Schumann and Cortez were taken to dinner by Laughton every evening so that they could discuss the next day's work. The pre-production period had been quite short; instead, according to Cortez, 'It was designed from day to day in fullest detail, so that the details seemed fresh, fresher than if we had done the whole thing in advance.' In the middle of production, Laughton and Gregory decided that Brown, Carter, Cortez and Golden deserved percentage points on the film. Even so, Laughton was very much in charge. 'He was a sort of head of the family on set,' said Mitchum, 'which is as it should be.' Meanwhile, Gregory let his director have more or less free rein; in his own words, 'if that fat son of a bitch doesn't know what he's doing then I'm dead anyway.'

Mitchum adopted his characteristic attitude of insubordination on the set, registering his differences with Gregory by urinating into the radiator of his car. He also spent many of his filming breaks enjoying a drink with Shelley Winters (although he was unconvinced of her acting calibre). The objections of a Welfare Department employee tasked with looking after the children's interests were silenced by Mitchum when he discovered her covertly enjoying a beer. In fairness, young Billy Chapin was highly impressionable where Mitchum was concerned, coming to regard the star as his idol. (The boy could be encouraged to put in his best performance by taking Mitchum as his example.) Even so, Mitchum was quick to decide that Laughton was the best director he had ever worked with and never wavered from this opinion. 'I knew what Charles was thinking, he knew what I was thinking. We had no problems, ever. I just tried to please him, you know, I was showing off for him.' The cast held Laughton in almost universally high regard. Graves, recalling John Ford's refusal to accept suggestions from his cast, said, 'Moving from Ford to Charles was like walking from hell to heaven.' Concerned that the film might become too heavy and work against his 'fairy-tale' concept, Laughton encouraged Mitchum to introduce elements of slapstick into his performance (in particular the cellar scene, in which a shelf falls on his head, he trips on a jar and then pursues the children up the stairs with his arms outstretched like Wile E Coyote). This was the aspect with which Grubb found himself least satisfied.

The film's budget was $795,000, which at this time was not a great deal. Because of this, and because production fell behind, most of it was shot in the studio at Culver City, even the children's trip down the river: 'when I tell people that,' said Cortez in later years, 'they go white.' In addition the film was a period piece, set in 1930, and it was common to shoot anything historical in the studio (all the cars seen are 1923–30 models). Some location work was carried out by the second-unit directors, brothers Terry and Denis Sanders, in Ohio. ('Despite all efforts of West Virginia to look like West Virginia,' stated the press notes, 'it is a photogenic fact that Ohio, for filmic purposes, looks more like West Virginia than West Virginia.') Many of these were establishing shots of the river filmed from a helicopter, closely following sketches made by Laughton. Further location work was done with the full cast and crew at Lee's Ranch in Chatsworth, California, and the prison material was shot in Moundsville, West Virginia (there was an attempted prison break in process at the time, which forced the company to wait five days until things had calmed down). Only one of the location sequences was felt to be unsatisfactory: the one which was to be cut into the scene of John seeing Powell from the barn window. This, one of the most memorable shots in the film, was ultimately achieved with a perspective trick: that's not Mitchum on the skyline, nor is he riding a horse. It is actually a midget (Chapin's double) riding a donkey. This was one of a few shots to be played out on something akin to a stage set, with the actors in front of a deceptively simple backdrop. The scenes in Willa's bedroom took place on a basic frame with Mitchum and Winters playing out the action ten feet in front. (See **ASPECTS OF NOIR**.)

Laughton's notion was that John was the main viewpoint character, and the sets and camerawork were designed as such. A story which tells of the director finding himself stuck on how to end the scene of Powell calling the children inside as they hide the money is indicative of how attuned the team was to Laughton's concept of the film. Upon hitting this point and finding that no solution presented itself, Laughton shouted, 'Golden! What do I do now?' Golden – who, among the crew, was least enamoured of Laughton but still responded keenly to the film's challenges – suggested the point-of-view shot which confirms where the film's central conflict lies. 'The one thing Laughton couldn't do was wing it,' Golden said. 'He just didn't have the experience.' In spite of falling behind, the shoot was completed in just 36 days. Mitchum had to leave early to start work on *Not as a Stranger* (Stanley Kramer, 1955) and his final scenes, depicting his arrest outside Rachel's house, were shot on his Sundays off on two consecutive weeks. They still didn't quite get all the coverage they'd wanted and had to make do in the editing room. Golden found this a little frustrating, but not as much as Laughton's demands upon him regarding this sequence: the director had not permitted Golden to start cutting during production, so that Laughton would be able to supervise editing throughout post-production.

RECEPTION: The film was released on 29 September 1955, following very mixed previews. Gregory and Laughton felt that the best strategy would be to open the film in a small number of theatres at first and allow word-of-mouth to build, but United Artists followed the then increasing trend for a wide simultaneous release.

Many reviews drew unfavourable comparisons with the novel. 'The relentless terror of Davis Grubb's story got away from Paul Gregory and Charles Laughton in their translation of *The Night of the Hunter*,' wrote *Variety* on 20 July 1955, describing the film as 'rich in the promise of things to come' from the producer-director partnership, 'but the completed product, bewitching at times, loses sustained drama via too many offbeat touches that have a misty effect.' The stylisation which Laughton had thought crucial to the film's meaning was instead characterised as detrimental to it. 'So many scenes are productions of camera angles, symbolism, shadows and lighting effects to the extent that story points are rendered nebulous.' In commercial terms, 'Initial draw should be okay but the long-distance b.o. staying power looks dubious for the general market.'

Writing in the *New York Times*, Bosley Crowther displayed an appreciation of what the film was trying to achieve. 'The trenchant and troubling proposition they are obviously aiming to convey is that being a child in the midst of sordid adults is a terrible experience,' he wrote in the *New York Times* on 20 September 1955. However, 'This is a difficult thesis to render both forceful and profound in an hour and a half of tangled traffic with both melodramatic and allegorical forms.' There was praise for Mitchum and his role. 'There is more than malevolence and menace in his character. There is a strong sense of Freudian aberration, fanaticism and iniquity.' The fatal blow arrived in John McCurtew's *New Yorker* review of 8 October 1955, which characterised *The Night of the Hunter* as 'a fairly eclectic item that is alternately really artistic and dismally arty, with the latter characteristic, alas, predominating'. It was that sense of 'artiness' which ultimately damaged the buzz around the film. 'There is a solid melodramatic point in this situation, but in exploiting it Mr Laughton all too frequently becomes fearfully entangled with dreary allegory,' McCurtew continued, feeling that 'he lays on the contrast between the goodness of the lady [Gish] and the wickedness of the parson with a trowel.' Even so, the film 'has in its favor the fact that it doesn't go in for any of the usual movie banalities, and if it fails, as I think it does, it fails honorably'.

In the *Observer*, CA Lejeune also noted Laughton's ambition. 'His subject is nothing less than the fight between good and evil,' Lejeune wrote on 27 November 1955, calling the film 'a confusion of real and false film art; at moments startlingly original, at others desperately phoney. It might have done better with a different actor in the leading part.' This view was shared by most of the British critics, who did not respond favourably to Mitchum's performance. 'Mr Laughton's direction is fantastically mannered, and the whole film leaves a sourish flavour. But it is by no means the work of a fool.'

'I have not the space I would like for discussing *The Night of the Hunter*,' bemoaned Dilys Powell in *The Sunday Times* of 27 November. 'It is a curious and unusual piece, full of literary dialogue a good deal of which doesn't come off, full of visual symbolism a good deal of which does.' Interestingly, she was of the opinion that it would have been better had Laughton played Powell. 'All the same this murky film is neither boring nor risible.' The *Sunday Dispatch*'s Harris Deans did not appreciate the film's other qualities. 'Robert Mitchum can't carry this story of a mad parson who alternates hymns with homicide,' he wrote, also on 27 November. 'It should have been a sinister film, but mainly it was grin-ister.' Ho ho, Mr Deans.

Upon seeing the reviews, UA decided to prioritise Mitchum's *Not as a Stranger* instead and did little to promote *The Night of the Hunter*. Laughton attempted to assist the campaign by recording a talking-book version of the novel for RCA, but the film was not a success and Laughton took it very personally. He adapted a draft screenplay from Norman Mailer's novel *The Naked and the Dead*, which he and Gregory had selected as their next project, but was so disillusioned that he never directed it, or anything else for the cinema. (The Sanders brothers finished the script and the Raoul Walsh-directed result was successful when released in 1958, although Mailer hated it.)

ASPECTS OF NOIR: *The Night of the Hunter* is one of those films which calls into question our definition of film noir, as it is quite unlike any other film in the cycle (indeed, it is quite unlike any other film). So what qualifies it as noir? It initially seems facile to suggest that it is principally because the film was made in black and white, but the production team behind *The Night of the Hunter* did consider using colour film – which would have almost certainly diminished the film's noirish aesthetic.

We strongly associate film noir with black-and-white, although there were several colour films which might be dubbed noirs and almost certainly would be had they been made in black-and-white, such as *Niagara* (Henry Hathaway, 1953), *Slightly Scarlet* (Allan Dwan, 1956) and *Vertigo* (Alfred Hitchcock, 1958). It is notable that the point which is generally considered the cut-off for classical Hollywood and film noir – the end of the 1950s – was also when colour started to become the norm (the unwieldy and expensive Technicolor system, which simultaneously ran three separate negatives of red, blue and green, had been replaced in the 1950s by Eastmancolor, which used a single colour negative). 'For the best part of two decades until well into the 1950s,' notes Richard Maltby, 'color was promoted as a spectacular production value in its own right.'

The difference between monochrome and colour photography is clearly more than just one of production values, even though it has often been seen as such. Discussing the different effects of black-and-white and colour comic books, Scott McCloud states, 'Colors objectify their subjects. We become more aware of the physical form of objects than in black and white.' Although in cinema the movement of the subject makes us more aware of their physical form than in a still image, the use of colour has a similar impact nevertheless. This is particularly true of films where the graphic qualities of the image are emphasised, as in a great many noirs; without the distinguishing effect of colour it is easier to appreciate the composition of an image, particularly in terms of light and shade.

When colour first appeared in Hollywood in the mid-1930s, it was promoted as adding 'enhanced realism' to motion pictures. Natalie Kalmus, chief consultant for Technicolor, said in 1938 that colour 'enables us to portray life and nature as it really is'. Although she acknowledged that dramatic construction still had the largest part to play ('It is not enough that we put a perfect record on the screen. That record must be molded according to the basic principles of art'), the message was that colour gave Hollywood's fictions a greater degree of verisimilitude and this was seen as an automatically good thing. This did not become true straight away, however; as Maltby notes, 'In the 1940s, a color movie was most likely to be a musical; Hollywood represented itself in color, while the rest of the world was in black-and-white.' His explanation was that, because colour was only used on a few big-budget films, it clashed with the established language of most other Hollywood cinema which had itself become accepted as a brand of realism. The very nature of colour suggests another reason. Because the form of objects becomes more apparent in colour, we become more aware of their true natures and, while this makes an image of a real object appear more realistic, it also has the effect of making 'fake' objects – for example, a painted backdrop – appear *less* realistic. In black-and-white the audience does not notice so much that a painted backdrop is flat because black-and-white images have that quality anyway, but in colour this flatness sharply contrasts with the three-dimensional objects in the foreground. In addition, colour tends to make it obvious when artificial light is being used to stand in for natural light. In studio-system Hollywood, where studio-bound films were the norm, colour showed up their artificiality in a way that black-and-white never had. Its application to the inherently artificial world of the musical was therefore its most appropriate usage.

Although Cortez had originally envisaged that the film would be shot in colour, it is obvious why Laughton wanted it to be in black-and-white. Imagine *The Night of the Hunter* in colour and it becomes a very different film. Consider the trip down the river: some of the crew (Gregory, for one) felt that it would have been better shot on location, and until production slipped behind that remained an option. However, this would have lost much, if not all, of the fairy-tale effect which was central to Laughton's concept of the film. Cortez later remarked, 'When [Laughton] saw the rushes, he said, "My god, how did you do that?" and I said, "because you used the word fairy-tale." ' The association is with pictures in story-books, which the more two-dimensional nature of black-and-white film suits perfectly: at the same time, black-and-white discourages the viewer from judging the scene by standards of realism. In colour the sequence would have lost subtlety, becoming too obviously false. The story-book appearance would have been overemphasised by the gaudiness of an artificial light trying to appear natural, and the scene would have run the risk of tipping over into sentimentality. The alternative would have been to shoot on location in colour, which would probably have looked fine but not as visually startling as the film which ultimately emerged.

In the case of Powell riding across the skyline as John watches from the barn, a version was shot on location which was felt to be uninteresting. In the version that was used, the horse's feet appear to be planted directly on the horizon itself: the likelihood of such a sight occurring in reality is remote, involving the existence of a small and perfectly flat ridge which blocks from sight everything behind it. Yet the more you look at this shot, the more you realise that it is like a child's drawing, with the ground represented by a straight line and the object placed on the ground. This ties in with the notion of the film being seen from the child's point of view, and again the association with a two-dimensional image is made more rational by the use of black-and-white. There is quite simply no way the shot could be recreated in colour or on location. In colour the sky would have been an obvious backcloth, the dawn light a dull lamp glow; on location, the silhouette would not be feasible and the figure on horseback would have to be picked out from the background some other way.

The Night of the Hunter was a late example of Expressionist cinema's influence on Hollywood, an influence which largely manifested itself in film noir. This approach had become less apparent in noir since the late 1940s, and this decline is linked to the increasing prominence of the semi-documentary and the use of location shooting. There were clear advantages to shooting on location and in many cases the films look better than if they had been shot in a studio, but daytime location shooting discouraged visual stylisation and even where night shooting was concerned it was still easier to shoot for realism. It was by no means impossible to adopt an Expressionist style on location, as *Touch of Evil* demonstrates (indeed, the opening tracking shot sees Welles take advantage of working in the larger space), but the kind of stylised settings seen in *The Night of the Hunter* would not be found outside the studio. It had to be shot there and it had to be shot in black-and-white, or it would not have achieved its remarkable effects.

Thus, *The Night of the Hunter* calls our definition of film noir into question in a more fundamental way. As noted, within noir there were developments towards a new kind of realism (night-for-night shooting, single-source lighting, less flattering portrayal of actors, mix of happy and sad endings) and greater stylisation (fragmented narrative, extreme angles, emphasis on the graphic qualities of the image, deliberate disorientation of the viewer). The question is, is one of those developments more fundamental to film noir than the other? Are they both necessary, or can a film be noir by displaying just one of them? The realist side of film noir, as discussed under **Force of Evil**, eventually became something which we would not think of as noir, and the more realistic it became, the more straightforward and less noirish it tended to be. By contrast, *The Night of the Hunter* arguably marks the point at which the Expressionist approach was no longer acceptable as part of a mainstream Hollywood product, but was seen as something 'arty' which was not of interest to a mass audience. However, this aspect of film noir is the core of its appeal for many contemporary critics, including the present writer.

Hollywood's abandonment of black-and-white film, as colour began to produce a more 'realistic' effect on location, is closely related to the discontinuation of this spirit of stylisation. Film noir was the optimum artistic use of the studio-centric, black-and-white mode of operation which characterised studio-system Hollywood: a system which was set up to produce commercial product but which surprisingly created the ideal conditions for producing stylised images in the context of a narrative film. This was recognised by filmmakers who deliberately chose noir as a way of indulging their experiments while producing a saleable product. Andrew Spicer notes that some later examples such as Kubrick's *Killer's Kiss* (1955) use noir 'to graft avant-garde techniques onto mainstream film-making', but 'the art house film circuit was insufficiently developed at this point to sustain noir as an avant-garde mode'. As colour trickled down to even the lowest-budget productions, a stigma of 'artiness' began to attach itself to new black-and-white films. The mixed reaction to Laughton's extensive stylisation of *The Night of the Hunter* can be seen as a portent of this, and signals the imminent end of 'classical' film noir – although later filmmakers would revive the style with the aid of filters and superior colour film stock, creating what has been rather unflatteringly described as 'noir lite'.

AFTERLIFE: A 1991 TV movie remake, *Night of the Hunter*, was directed by David Greene and starred Richard Chamberlain in the Mitchum role. It has been widely dismissed as utterly rubbish.

AVAILABILITY: The film is available on Region 2 (21231DVD) and Region 1 DVDs, with an original trailer included.

The Killing (1956)

Black and White – 83 mins

Harris-Kubrick Presents
The Killing
Associate Producer: Alexander Singer
Camera Operator: Dick Tower
Gaffer: Bobby Jones
Head Grip: Carl Gibson
Script Supervisor: Mary Gibsone

Sound: Earl Singer
Best Boy: Lou Cortese
2nd Assistant Cameraman: Robert Hosler
Construction Supervisor: Bud Pine
Chief Carpenter: Christopher Ebsen
Chief Painter: Robert L Stephen
Make-up: Robert Littlefield
Wardrobe: Jack Masters
Special Effects: Dave Koehler
Set Decorator: Harry Reif
Assistant Set Decorator: Carl Brainard
Music Editor: Gilbert Marchant
Sound Effects Editor: Rex Lipton, MPSE
Assistant Director: Milton Carter
2nd Assistant Directors: Paul Feiner and Howard Joslin
Production Assistant: Marguerite Olson
Prop-man: Ray Zambel
Transportation: Dave Lesser
Women's Wardrobe: Rudy Harrington
Hairdresser: Lillian Shore
Process Cameraman: Paul Eagler
Director's Assistant: Joyce Hartman
Miss Windsor's Costumes by Beaumelle
Photographic Effects: Jack Rabin and Louis DeWitt
Director of Photography: Lucien Ballard, ASC
Art Director: Ruth Sobotka
Film Editor: Betty Steinberg
Music Composed and Conducted by Gerald Fried
Screenplay by Stanley Kubrick
Dialogue by Jim Thompson
Based on the novel *Clean Break* by Lionel White
Produced by James B Harris
Directed by Stanley Kubrick

CAST: Sterling Hayden (*Johnny Clay*), Coleen Gray (*Fay*), Vince Edwards (*Val Cannon*), Jay C Flippen (*Marvin Unger*), Ted de Corsia (*Randy Kennan*), Marie Windsor (*Sherry Peatty*), Elisha Cook (*George Peatty*), Joe Sawyer (*Mike O'Reilly*), James Edwards (*Track Parking Attendant*), Timothy Carey (*Nikki Arcane*), Kola Kwariani (*Maurice Oboukhoff*), Jay Adler (*Leo the Loanshark*), Tito Vuolo (*Joe*), Dorothy Adams (*Ruthie O'Reilly*), Herbert Ellis (*Guard*), James Griffith (*Mr Grimes*), Cecil Elliott (*Lady with Small Dog*), Joseph Turkell (*Tiny*), Steve Mitchell (*Ron, Airline Clerk*), Mary Carroll (*Woman asking*

Kennan for Help), William Benedict (*First Airline Clerk*), Charles R
Cane (*Plainclothesman at Airport*), Robert B Williams (*Plainclothesman
at Airport*)

SUMMARY: Fresh out of prison, Johnny Clay has made meticulous
plans for a $2 million racetrack heist which he tells Fay, his girlfriend,
will be the 'big one' – the last job he ever needs to do. He has assembled a
gang of non-criminals in crucial positions: two track employees, cashier
George Peatty and bartender Mike O'Reilly, plus Randy Kenman, a
policeman who can patrol the track on the day of the robbery. In addition
he engages two men to cause diversions: Maurice Oboukhoff, a wrestler
who will start a fight in the bar, and Nikki Arcane, a skilled rifleman who
is to shoot the winning racehorse during the seventh race of the day.
While confusion reigns George will let Johnny into the staff area, where
Johnny will pick up a gun which Mike will have left in his locker. Johnny
will then put on a mask and steal the takings, drop the sack of money to
Randy, who will be waiting outside the window at a pre-arranged time to
take the money to a drop-off point. Johnny will then leave the track
inconspicuously and pick up the money, and they will all rendezvous later
that evening. The plan comes off, although Nikki is shot dead trying to
escape. Unfortunately, George has told his wife Sherry about the plan and
her lover Val Cannon tries to step in and take the money at the
rendezvous point. Johnny has not yet arrived with the cash and a nervous
shoot-out ensues, killing everybody in the room. Johnny realises that
something is amiss and heads straight for the airport, meeting Fay there.
However, the suitcase containing the money is too large to go on as hand
luggage and must be checked in. On its way to the plane it falls from the
baggage cart and its cheap lock springs open, scattering the money across
the airfield. Johnny resigns himself to his arrest.

DIRECTOR: Stanley Kubrick (1928–99) was born in New York, the
son of a doctor. He was a photographer for *Look* magazine at seventeen,
and in 1950 he made a documentary short, *Day of the Fight*, which he
sold to RKO. The studio commissioned a second from him, *The Flying
Padre* (1951). After a couple of promotional shorts he made his debut
feature, *Fear and Desire* (1953); like *Day of the Fight* this was financed
by family and friends (the bulk of the cash coming from Kubrick's
wealthy Uncle Martin). Subsequently he shot the noir *Killer's Kiss*
(1955) in New York thanks to a large investment from a family friend;
this was purchased by United Artists and led to *The Killing*. Kubrick
then made the acclaimed war movie *Paths of Glory* (1957) and appeared
to have broken into the ranks of major Hollywood directors upon
replacing Anthony Mann on *Spartacus* (1960). However, Kubrick then

moved himself and his family to Hertfordshire (largely out of fear of nuclear conflict and satisfaction with the conditions for making movies in Britain), and never left. Thereafter, his output was idiosyncratic and sporadic, but always interesting; a notorious perfectionist, he insisted upon a lot of control and often produced his own work as well as directing. His British period comprised *Lolita* (1962), *Dr Strangelove; or, How I Learned to Stop Worrying and Love the Bomb* (1963), *2001: A Space Odyssey* (1968), *A Clockwork Orange* (1971), *Barry Lyndon* (1975), *The Shining* (1980), *Full Metal Jacket* (1987) and *Eyes Wide Shut* (1999), the last of which he completed shortly before he died. His work is marked by a certain coldness and distance, using framing and focus in such a way that the viewer is not aligned with the characters, and often by the use of natural light. His common subject is that of the individual caught inexorably in a system beyond their control.

WRITERS: Lionel White (1905–85) was a popular paperback novelist who was known for his crime capers including *The Big Caper* (1955), *Hostage for a Hood* (1957), *Death Takes the Bus* (1957) and *Steal Big* (1960). His debut *Clean Break* (1955) is characteristic of his work, featuring a meticulously detailed robbery which is thwarted by the team's failure to operate effectively together. (There's a *Killing* in-joke in *Steal Big*, when something called 'Kubric Novelty Company' turns out to be a front for black-market arms dealers.) Other films based on White's work include *Pierrot le Fou* (Jean-Luc Godard, 1965), based on *Obsession* (1962), *The Money Trap* (Burt Kennedy, 1965), based on his 1963 novel, and *The Night of the Following Day* (Hubert Cornfield, 1968), based on *The Snatchers* (1953).

Jim Thompson (1906–77) was known as one of the toughest hardboiled novelists and was much admired by Kubrick for such works as *The Killer Inside Me* (1952), *A Hell of a Woman* (1954) and *After Dark, My Sweet* (1955). He subsequently worked on the script for Harris-Kubrick's *Paths of Glory* (apparently to placate him after the credits fiasco on *The Killing* – see **DEVELOPMENT**). His later novels include *The Kill-Off* (1957), *The Getaway* (1959), *The Grifters* (1963), *Ironside* (1967), *The Undefeated* (1969), *King Blood* (1973) and *This World, Then the Fireworks* (1983, published posthumously). An abrupt resurgence of Hollywood interest in Thompson's novels began in the late 1980s with an adaptation of *The Kill-Off* (Maggie Greenwald, 1989), followed by *The Grifters* (Stephen Frears, 1990), *After Dark, My Sweet* (James Foley, 1990), *The Getaway* (Roger Donaldson, 1994) and *This World, Then the Fireworks* (Michael Oblowitz, 1997). The absence of any adaptations during his own lifetime is partly a reflection on the often brutal nature of his work.

DEVELOPMENT: James B Harris was one of a number of producers and aspiring producers invited to a screening of *Killer's Kiss*, as Kubrick was looking for contacts in the industry – and help in selling his film to TV. The two hit it off, and formed Harris-Kubrick Pictures. Harris started looking for material for the company's first film, and looked for another crime story to follow *Killer's Kiss* (Kubrick was unimpressed by the noir movement generally, but he was a fan of hardboiled fiction and was aware that crime movies were suitable for New York shooting and relatively easy to sell). Harris bought a copy of *Clean Break* because the cover blurb sounded good, took it home and read it in one sitting. He phoned Kubrick and told him how much he'd enjoyed it; Kubrick also read it in one sitting. Both were impressed by the elaborate nature of the robbery at its centre, and also by its non-linear narrative. The partnership sought the rights and discovered that United Artists, the studio which had just distributed *Killer's Kiss*, had already been contacted by Frank Sinatra about his plans to buy the book and film it for the studio. However, all concerned were becoming impatient with Sinatra's indecision and Harris-Kubrick took advantage; Harris offered an immediate $10,000 of his own money for the rights and told United Artists that he and Kubrick were going to do the movie. Unfortunately, UA had been interested in the property principally as a Sinatra vehicle and its interest cooled. Having already invested in the novel, Harris and Kubrick began to work on a screenplay that they could shop around.

In need of a writer who could work in the hardboiled vernacular of the novel, they hired Jim Thompson (whose *The Killer Inside Me* Kubrick had also considered as source material). Thompson, who had never written for the cinema before, brokered a deal which gave him a $1,000 advance for working on the screenplay of *The Killing*, plus the rights to a novella called *Lunatic at Large* which Thompson had written with adaptation in mind. He moved into a Manhattan hotel room and went for regular meetings with Kubrick, which the director found an uncomfortable experience. As a hardboiled writer, Thompson was the genuine article, turning up for work in a scruffy raincoat with a bottle of booze in a paper bag. (He would offer the bottle to Kubrick, and the intimidated director would decline.) Sticking with the basic structure of the novel, Kubrick outlined which scenes he wanted to include and discussed with Thompson how he wanted each one to work. Thompson then went back to his room and wrote the scenes, applying his skills to dialogue (Maurice's speech regarding gangsters and artists is all Thompson's work) and character interaction (he fleshed out George and Sherry's relationship) and also giving Mike motivation in the form of his ill wife. Thompson's alcoholism meant that he could be erratic, but he delivered the script that Harris and Kubrick were looking for.

When he saw the film, Thompson was greatly displeased by the way he had been credited: 'Screenplay by Stanley Kubrick, Dialogue by Jim Thompson'. He considered legal action, which Harris thought ridiculous. 'We hired Thompson *because* of his dialogue. The structure of the story was already pretty much there, and we all contributed changes.' Nevertheless, Thompson's anger is understandable; if, as Harris said, everybody contributed changes to the screenplay, why did Kubrick take the overall credit? Kubrick did give fairly precise instructions from which Thompson worked, but his credit strongly implies a more physical writing contribution. Contemporary reviews demonstrate that Thompson's work went largely unnoticed as a result.

At various stages the film was to be titled *Clean Break*, *Day of Violence* and the somewhat absurd *Bed of Fear*, before *The Killing* was settled upon.

CASTING: Harris-Kubrick distributed the script for *The Killing* far and wide; one copy arrived in the hands of Sterling Hayden (1916–86, born Sterling Relyea Walter). Hayden had run away to sea at the age of seventeen and commanded his first ship at nineteen. Working as a model and actor to subsidise his naval exploits, in the 1940s he was contracted to Paramount. He joined the marines during the war and his duties included gun-running to the Yugoslav Communist resistance. This led him to briefly become a Communist himself – 'I wonder whether there has ever before been a man who bought a schooner and joined the Communist Party all on the same day,' he reflected – but he left after six months. After seeing out his Paramount contract, then making *The Asphalt Jungle* (John Huston, 1950) for MGM, Hayden fell foul of HUAC. Aware that he was in a very precarious position, he agreed to 'name names' but found himself unpopular in Hollywood and deeply regretted his actions. 'I don't think you have the foggiest notion of the contempt I have had for myself since the day I did that thing,' he said later. His aim had been to save his acting career, yet he often noted that he disliked acting. In re-establishing himself he became far more prolific and his films included the noirs *Crime Wave* (André de Toth, 1954) and *Suddenly* (Lewis Allen, 1954). Harris and Kubrick were thrilled when he signed on to make *The Killing*; the book and film of *The Asphalt Jungle* had influenced *Clean Break* and they were confident that this replication of a winning formula would sell the movie to United Artists. However, UA was less impressed with Hayden, and would only back the project to a total of $200,000. Kubrick would cast Hayden again in *Dr Strangelove*, and in the 1970s he appeared in *The Godfather* (Francis Ford Coppola, 1972) and *The Long Goodbye* (Robert Altman, 1973). Other interesting facts about Hayden are that he married and divorced the same woman (Betty Ann de Noon) three times; that he was cast in *Jaws* (Steven Spielberg, 1975) but had to pull out due to tax problems; and that in 1976 he published an acclaimed novel, *Voyage*.

Coleen Gray (born Doris Bernice Jensen, 1922) had her earliest credited roles in films noirs – *Kiss of Death* (Henry Hathaway, 1947) and *Nightmare Alley* (Edmund Golding, 1947) – before a notable role in the western *Red River* (Howard Hawks, 1948). In the 1950s she made numerous appearances on TV and in minor genre movies, including the noirs *The Sleeping City* (George Sherman, 1950) and *Kansas City Confidential* (Phil Karlson, 1952), and several horror and science-fiction films. Another mainstay of low-budget movies, Marie Windsor, had previously appeared in *Force of Evil*. Since then she had appeared in numerous westerns but her great triumph had been the highly regarded B-movie *The Narrow Margin* (Richard Fleischer, 1952). Other noir roles include *The Sniper* (Edward Dmytryk, 1952), *City that Never Sleeps* (John H Auer, 1953), *Hell's Half Acre* (John H Auer, 1954), *No Man's Woman* (Frank Adreon, 1955) and *The Girl in Black Stockings* (Howard W Koch, 1957). From the 1960s onwards she divided her time between film and television, including the mini-series *Salem's Lot* (1979), and served a 25-year stint as a director of the Screen Actors Guild.

Two actors already encountered more than once in this book are mentioned here for the last time. Elisha Cook Jr had other noir roles following *The Big Sleep*, including *Fall Guy* (Reginald LeBorg, 1947), *Born to Kill* (Robert Wise, 1947), *The Long Night* (Anatole Litvak, 1947), *The Gangster* (Gordon Wiles, 1947), *Flaxy Martin* (Richard Bare, 1949), *Don't Bother to Knock* (Roy Baker, 1952), *I, The Jury* (Harry Essex, 1953), *Accused of Murder* (Joseph Kane, 1956), *Chicago Confidential* (Sidney Salkow, 1957), *Plunder Road* (Hubert Cornfield, 1957) and *Baby Face Nelson* (Don Siegel, 1957). Having also appeared in *Stranger on the Third Floor* and *The Maltese Falcon*, Cook is arguably noir's most consistent presence in front of the cameras boasting an impressive array of violent deaths. He remained prolific in both television and cinema (a notable role was in *Hammett* (Wim Wenders, 1982)) and his career only slowed down in the mid-1980s. Loss of speech following a stroke in 1990 halted his career, and he died in 1995.

Ted de Corsia also pops up again here, having previously had roles in *The Lady from Shanghai* and *The Big Combo*. Since the latter film, he had appeared in *Slightly Scarlet* (Allan Dwan, 1956) and *The Steel Jungle* (Walter Dongier, 1956); after *The Killing* he had two further noir roles in *The Midnight Story* (Joseph Pevney, 1957) and *Baby Face Nelson*. By the late 1950s he had become a much-employed television actor and remained so until his death in 1973.

PRODUCTION: Having secured backing of $200,000 from United Artists, Kubrick and Harris ran into their first problem: no racetracks on the east coast would permit them to film *The Killing* on their premises (it is unclear whether this was a general policy or a reaction to the subject matter). The partnership relocated to California, and upon budgeting the movie were alarmed to discover that they would need $330,000 to cover the costs. Having been instructed that under no circumstances would UA supply additional funding, Harris raided his own savings for $80,000 and borrowed a further $50,000 from his father. They then set to work, planning a 24-day shoot.

Kubrick's previous films had seen him do his own cinematography, but as *The Killing* was being made in Los Angeles with studio money the director reluctantly conformed to union regulations and hired an experienced ASC member in the form of Lucien Ballard. Kubrick's youth (he was 27 at the time of shooting) and self-confidence led to much on-set tension. 'There was an air of resentment all around us,' recalled Harris. 'Stanley had his own ideas how things were to go and people resented his encroaching on their contributions.' This was most evident in his working relationship with Ballard. In later years Kubrick would become famous for his use of wide-angle lenses (see **ASPECTS OF NOIR**), and insisted that much of *The Killing* be shot with a 25mm lens, which was one of the widest lenses then available, including on the innovative 'through-the-walls' tracking shot. He left Ballard to set up the shot, which was to be achieved with a dolly on tracks running parallel with the edge of the set. Ballard reasoned that the shot would be easier to light if the camera was set up further away, with a 50mm lens that would magnify the subject and give an image size that was basically identical to what Kubrick had asked for. Kubrick returned and Ballard explained all this to him: Kubrick's response was to tell Ballard that he was fired unless he set up the shot again with a 25mm. It is a testament to Ballard's professionalism that, despite Kubrick's youth, he recognised that the director was ultimately in charge and followed Kubrick's instructions.

Kubrick also sent Ballard to shoot documentary-style footage of the racetrack for the title sequence, but was deeply unimpressed with the results. Associate producer Alexander Singer (who had worked with Kubrick on *Day of the Fight* and introduced him to Harris) went back for another try, shooting with a clockwork Eyemo camera at the Golden Gate racetrack in San Francisco, and produced results so much better that Kubrick used his footage throughout the film, not just in the title sequence.

Relations with the cast could also be awkward. 'I kept waiting for him to direct, and nothing happened,' said Coleen Gray, 'which made me insecure . . . Maybe the fact that I felt insecure was fine for the part – [my character] was insecure.' Mistreating actors to influence their performance was a typical Kubrick tactic; he later marginalised Shelley Winters from the creative process on *Lolita* to emphasise the marginalisation of her character in the story, and invited the cast and crew of *A Clockwork Orange* to take turns spitting on Malcolm McDowell, thus giving him an appreciation of Alex's sociopathy. Marie Windsor noted that Kubrick tended to deal with actors on a one-to-one basis, so the cast would often not be aware of what each other had been coached to do. Sterling Hayden, for one, was impressed with Kubrick's methods. 'I have worked with few directors that good,' he later remembered. 'He's like the Russian documentarians who could put the same footage together five different ways, so it really didn't matter what the actors did – Stanley would know what to do with it.' He noted that this quality allowed Kubrick to be highly efficient, using almost everything he shot.

One can presume that Hayden did not, in retrospect, share the concern of his agent, Bill Schifrin, who believed that the non-linear structure of the film was incoherent and this failing would partly be attributed to his client. Schifrin muttered about a lawsuit (although given that the structure was unchanged from the script which Hayden had originally signed on to make, it is hard to see on what Schifrin would have based his case), and when others suggested to Kubrick and Harris that *The Killing* would work better as a chronological narrative, the pair started to doubt their initial conviction that the structure of White's novel would make an exciting film. They rented a studio in New York and produced an alternative, straightforward cut, but immediately realised that it was inferior to their original version; as Kubrick later said, 'It was the handling of time that may have made this more than just a good crime film.'

Harris and Kubrick presented the film to United Artists, who arranged a screening for head of production Max Youngstein. Youngstein's reaction was that the film was fine, that Harris-Kubrick had done an acceptable job, but he offered no further feedback. 'You have other producer-filmmaker teams,' Kubrick said. 'Where would you rate us with all of those people?' Youngstein's reply: 'Not far from the bottom.'

RECEPTION: *The Killing* opened on its own at one New York cinema on 20 May 1956; it was then assigned as supporting feature to the Robert Mitchum western *Bandido* (Richard Fleischer, 1956). *Variety* declared it 'sturdy fare for the action market, where it can be exploited for better than average returns' on 23 May 1956. The film 'soon settles into a tense and suspenseful vein which carries through to an unexpected and ironic windup. Hard-hitting and colorful performances point up strong values.' Thompson's grievance was doubtless exacerbated by reviews such as this, which gave the director full credit for the writing. 'Kubrick's direction of his own script is tight and fast-paced, a quality Lucien Ballard's top photography matches to lend particular fluidity of movement.'

Writing in the *New York Times*, AH Weiler called the film 'a sharp, black-and-white illustration of the theory that the odds are against both a daring gang who rob a race track and the bettors, to judge by the robbers' record "take" ', in a review on 21 May 1956. Although it 'is composed of familiar ingredients and it calls for fuller explanations, it evolves as a fairly diverting melodrama'. It was compared unfavourably with its key influence – 'The preparations of this coup are reminiscent but not nearly as imaginative as those of the classic, *The Asphalt Jungle*' – but nevertheless, 'Mr Kubrick has kept things moving at a lively clip.'

Time was one of the first to proclaim the significance of Kubrick's talent: '*The Killing* announces the arrival of a new boy wonder in a business that soon separates the men from the boys,' in a piece on 4 June 1956. 'Stanley Kubrick, in his third full-length picture, has shown more audacity with dialogue and camera than Hollywood has seen since the obstreperous Orson Welles went riding out of town on an exhibitors' poll.' At a time when budgets were soaring, it was further noted that he had 'made his entire movie for a price that would hardly pay for the lingerie in an Ava Gardner picture, with the result that *The Killing* seems likely to make a killing at the cash booths.'

In the UK it was released alongside a different Mitchum film, *Foreign Intrigue* (Sheldon Reynolds, 1956), and it was here that the critics really got excited. 'There are many new feature films which the critics are not invited to criticise,' wrote the *Manchester Guardian* on 28 July 1956. 'This is entirely understandable when the film is a bit of shoddy, only meant to fill an hour or so in a double-feature programme.' However, *The Killing* was thought to be in a different class. 'This film, which is now to be found as a humble "second feature" at the Dominion in Tottenham Court Road, the New Victoria, and the Gaumont circuit, is remarkable,' adding that it was 'a close and worthy cousin to' *The Asphalt Jungle*. '*The Killing* was written and directed by Stanley Kubrick, a young man who is certainly going to leave his mark on the American cinema.' Well spotted, sir. 'His only limitation (in the highly cinematic field of crime thrillers) would seem to be that, at present, his emphasis is a little too obvious and, therefore, too slow.'

Another critic who very probably had his perceptive review framed and hung on the wall of his office was Alan Brien. His *Evening Standard* review of 26 July 1956 stated that 'a brilliant thriller has been buried away as a second feature on the Gaumont circuit. I am glad to be able to open up the grave and declare the corpse still horribly alive and kicking.' Brien felt that 'The harsh newsreel photography gives a vivid and uncomfortable feeling of participation in this seedy underworld,' and offered the advice that 'Anybody who wishes to be in at what may be the birth of a new screen master cannot afford to miss a visit to the Dominion, Victoria or Gaumont north-west circuit this week.'

However, United Artists promoted *The Killing* poorly (and reacted angrily when Harris and Kubrick took out their own trade ads), and at one point MGM offered to buy it from UA in the belief that it could distribute the film more effectively. UA refused. In 1958, UA told Harris and Kubrick that the film had only made $30,000 against its $330,000 budget, and, if they were to finance *Lolita* (then intended as their next project), they would have to sell their 50 per cent share in *The Killing* to UA. Harris later noted that, once all potential profits on *The Killing* were due to UA, the film went into profit suspiciously quickly.

ASPECTS OF NOIR: Another word which is often bandied about in studies of film noir is 'fatalism': the notion that events are predetermined and that people are powerless to change or avert these events. The idea of a film which displays a fatalistic worldview is arguably a postmodern one, as the majority of films are indeed predetermined, worked out in advance. Rick Altman observes that this is particularly true of classical Hollywood cinema, with its tendency towards happy endings (and specifically certain types of happy ending): the narrative 'reasons backward', with the result that 'The end is made to *appear* as a function of the beginning in order better to disguise the fact that the beginning is actually a function of the ending.' A fatalistic worldview discards this approach; there is no need to disguise the fact that everything is leading towards the ending. A fatalistic character will often act as though aware that he is just a character in a movie, fulfilling a generic role. As noted under **The Killers**, films noirs often do this overtly by starting at the end of the story and then going back; as this often involves subjective narration from the main character, events often gain great significance in retrospect and are made to appear as portents of the narrator's ultimate doom (such as Neff's inability to hear his own footsteps in *Double Indemnity*).

The Killing is not constructed in flashback, because flashbacks must be initiated by a character within the narrative. This is fragmented narrative, which is a more self-conscious device than flashback. The flashback narrative of *The Killers* seems more natural because it is motivated by a single character – Reardon – who processes the information in the same order as the viewer. In *The Killing*, the cuts in time and space do not flow naturally out of the narrative itself and so make the viewer constantly aware of the guiding hands of the writer, director and editor. The addition of the omniscient narrator emphasises the self-consciousness of the device, but the contemporary viewer would have accepted such narration because of its use on numerous semi-documentary thrillers. This association creates another layer of fatalism, because there is always a degree of inevitability about how semi-documentaries will unfold: being true stories (or stories which pretend to be true), the criminals are always caught – because an open case does not make suitable subject matter. It is one of the staples of the genre that the crime is solved at the end, because this results in a satisfying plot. Yet the semi-documentary tended to focus around the forces of law and order and so fatalism was seen as a positive thing, an inevitability that the criminals are caught. Because *The Killing* follows a band of desperate, non-professional criminals, its fatalism is more downbeat and the meticulous detail with which the heist is planned seems tragically pointless.

In addition, because Kubrick contrasts these semi-documentary devices with stylised, self-conscious effects (such as the tracking shot which passes through walls), the viewer is aware of the film's artifice and this deepens the mood of fatalism: all the characters are being manoeuvred towards failure. Kubrick's use of the wide-angle lens, while not atypical of noir, is worthy of special note. In many noirs the lens is used to emphasise the graphic qualities of the image, but Kubrick's interest in them lies in the way that the lens does not draw attention to any particular aspect of the picture by keeping a large area of the frame in focus. Conventionally, a film camera tries to replicate the way that the eye works, focusing on a particular aspect of the frame: the viewer's eye is naturally drawn to whatever part(s) of the image are in sharpest focus. When no such detail is picked out by the camera, the viewer feels distanced; hence, this technique is partly responsible for Kubrick's 'detached' aesthetic, although his apparent misanthropy is another factor. (Other wide-angle enthusiasts include Robert Altman and the Coen brothers.) This produces a variety of effects in his films: in *A Clockwork Orange* and *Barry Lyndon*, it allows him to follow an unsympathetic protagonist without appearing to pass judgement, while in *The Shining* and *Full Metal Jacket* the camera observes violence as though not shocked by it. Not all viewers respond to the technique – some people just find that they don't care what happens to the characters – but many viewers find that the films' neutrality spurs them to strengthen their own reaction to what is happening (the violence perversely appears *more* shocking, for example, through not being expressed as such). In the case of *The Killing*, the finished film's distant, dispassionate observation of the characters adds to its fatalistic feel: the machinations of fate as depicted here do not favour any character over another.

AFTERLIFE: The film was an acknowledged influence on *Reservoir Dogs* (Quentin Tarantino, 1991), another straight-out-of-prison heist film with a non-linear narrative: in fact, *Reservoir Dogs* is essentially a melding of this film and the Hong Kong policier *City on Fire* (Ringo Lam, 1987). Tarantino claimed that he would have cast Sterling Hayden in the Harvey Keitel role, had he not been dead at the time. An even more overt homage followed: *23:58* (Pierre William-Glen, 1993), in which the Le Mans 24-hour motorcycle race is robbed by crooks who have used *The Killing* as the basis for their plan; they are pursued by a movie-buff policeman.

A remake announced by Warner Bros. in 1999 has thus far not materialised. As it would have starred Mel Gibson in the role of Johnny Clay, this is probably just as well.

AVAILABILITY: *The Killing* is out on Region 2 (17216DVD) and Region 1 DVD. The only extra is an original trailer.

The Wrong Man (1956)

Alfred Hitchcock's status as a noir director is controversial: some studies include him automatically while others only acknowledge his influence. Michael Walker's claim that 'his films tend to be seminal . . . rather than derivative and they have far more connections with each other than with any particular cycle or genre' seems logical to me, since, while it is beneficial to read Hitchcock's work alongside noir, he does not seem particularly in step with it (perhaps because he had much control over his own projects; note that Hawks, a director with a similar level of control, only made a noir – *The Big Sleep* – when obliged to do so by Warners). *The Wrong Man* is a good example, following a little after the heyday of the true-life 'semi-documentary' and subverting it. The level of police-procedural detail is present, but, rather than valorising the police, it is a harrowing illustration of how meticulously gathered evidence can still catch the wrong man and the process of proving him innocent can practically destroy his life. It is underlined by the true-story tag (publicity for the film challenged audiences to seek out the records of the case) and de-dramatised, lacking the aspect which is central to most 'wrong man' thrillers: the innocent man's search for the real culprit. The technique is quite unlike anything else in film noir. *Released on 22 December 1956*

Touch of Evil (1958)

Black and White – 95 mins 1958 release/108 mins 1976 release/111 mins 1998 release

Universal-International Presents
Touch of Evil
Screenplay by Orson Welles
Based on the Novel *Badge of Evil* by Whit Masterson
Director of Photography: Russell Metty, ASC
Art Direction: Alexander Golitzen and Robert Clatworthy
Set Decoration by Russell A Gausman and John P Austin
Sound: Lesley I Carey and Frank Wilkinson
Film Editors: Virgil Vogel, ACE and Aaron Stell, ACE
Gowns: Bill Thomas
Make-up: Bud Westmore
Assistant Director: Phil Bowles
Music: Henry Mancini
Music Supervision by Joseph Gershenson
Produced by Albert Zugsmith
Directed by Orson Welles

CAST: Charlton Heston (*Mike Vargas*), Janet Leigh (*Susan Vargas*), Orson Welles (*Hank Quinlan*), Joseph Calleia (*Pete Menzies*), Akim Tarkoff (*Uncle Joe Grandi*), Joanna Moore (*Marcia Linnekar*), Ray Collins (*DA Adair*), Dennis Weaver (*Motel Manager*), Valentin de Vargas ('*Pancho*'), Mort Mills (*Schwartz*), Victor Millan (*Manolo Sanchez*), Lalo Rios (*Risto*), Michael Sargent (*Pretty Boy*), Phil Harvey (*Blaine*), Joi Lansing (*Blonde*), Harry Shannon (*Chief Gould*) and guest stars Marlene Dietrich (*Tanya*), Zsa Zsa Gabor (*Nightclub Owner*)

SUMMARY: Mexican narcotics cop Mike Vargas is embarking on his honeymoon with American wife Susan in the border town of Los Robles, when he witnesses the explosion of a car which has just driven across the border. The victims are a wealthy businessman named Linnekar and a young lady companion. Mike attempts to help with the case, which is overseen by Detective Hank Quinlan. Mike is soon to prosecute a member of the Grandi crime family; as Susan heads back to the hotel, local crime boss Joe Grandi warns her that her husband should drop the case. Quinlan finds a suspect for the murder: Manolo Sanchez, a Mexican who wanted to marry Linnekar's daughter but knew that the older man would not allow it. Quinlan claims to have found dynamite in

Sanchez's apartment, but Mike realises that this evidence has been planted by Quinlan and sets out to prove it. Meanwhile, Quinlan and Grandi conspire to eliminate the Vargases by making them out to be drug addicts. The Grandis accost Susan at a motel and dope her up; Quinlan then murders Joe Grandi, intending for suspicion to fall upon Mike. However, Quinlan leaves his cane at the scene and it is found by his loyal colleague Pete Menzies, who reluctantly gives it to Mike. By this stage Mike has reason to believe that Quinlan has repeatedly fabricated evidence to gain convictions, and covertly records a conversation between Pete and Quinlan in which the latter admits to this. When Quinlan realises that he has been exposed he shoots Pete, who shoots back. They both die. Finally, it is revealed that Sanchez was responsible for the bombing after all.

DIRECTOR: Following *The Lady from Shanghai*, the fortunes of Orson Welles continued their downwards trend. He made a low-budget *Macbeth* (1948) for Republic which has found favour in retrospect, but was infamous at the time; he followed this by going to Europe (a necessity, as he owed a great deal of money to the IRS) to produce and direct *Othello* (1952), which took three years to make and won the Palme D'Or at Cannes. In between he made a celebrated acting turn in *The Third Man* (Carol Reed, 1949). In Spain Welles directed *Mr. Ardakin* (aka *Confidential Report*, 1955) and in Britain made a TV series called *The Orson Welles Sketch Book* (1955) and a stage version of *Moby Dick*. On returning to America, he put on a disastrous production of *King Lear* which ended his New York stage career, then directed a pilot for a TV anthology series called *The Fountain of Youth* (1958) before coming aboard *Touch of Evil*. After this Welles never directed in Hollywood again, but he did muster a trio of European works which are well regarded: a film of Franz Kafka's *The Trial* (1962), an adaptation of Falstaff's scenes from both parts of Shakespeare's *Henry IV* entitled *Chimes at Midnight* (1966) and a drama for French television, *The Immortal Story* (1968). His final film was the pseudo-documentary *F for Fake* (1973); he worked on other projects for the rest of his life, including a TV series called *The Magic Show*, but the onset of obesity prevented him from taking many acting roles. His final film work was voicing a malevolent robot planet in the animated feature *Transformers: The Movie* (Nelson Shin, 1985).

WRITER: 'Whit Masterson' was a pseudonym for two guys from San Diego called Robert Wade (born 1920) and William Miller (1920–61). They were better known for their collaborations under the name Wade Miller, the first of which was *Deadly Weapon* (1946). They used many

names, including the anagrams Will Daemer and Dale Wilmer; Whit
Masterson was the alias they generally used for police-procedural stories.
The partnership produced 33 novels, including *Kitten With a Whip*
(1959) and the popular Max Thursday detective series – the first of
which was filmed as the noir *Guilty Bystander* (Joseph Lerner, 1950).
Following Miller's death, Wade continued to write solo under the
Masterson name, writing a further thirteen novels.

DEVELOPMENT: Like any hardboiled cop thriller that sold well in the
1950s, the 'Whit Masterson' novel *Badge of Evil* (1956) was optioned by
Hollywood – in this case by Universal-International. Studio head Eddie
Muhl assigned its development to producer Albert Zugsmith, who
commissioned a script from Paul Monash.

There are two stories about how Welles ended up directing *Badge of
Evil*. One is that he was initially offered it only as an acting part, playing
the Quinlan role. 'I said "Maybe," ' Welles recalled later, 'and I was still
wondering whether I could afford *not* to make it when they called up
Chuck Heston.' Heston (see **CASTING**) had been sent the script by
Universal; he told the studio that he liked it, but wanted to know who
was directing before he signed on. Universal said that it had not found a
director for the project yet. Orson Welles was going to be in it, though.
'You know,' replied Heston, 'Orson Welles is a pretty good director.'
With word that Heston would do the movie if Welles directed, Universal
offered Welles his first opportunity to direct a Hollywood film in ten
years: such is the nature of star power. After some bargaining – Welles
wanted to be able to rewrite the script, and Universal agreed if he would
claim only an actor's fee – Welles was on board.

The other version is that Welles had just taken an acting role for
producer Albert Zugsmith in a film called *Man in the Shadow* (Jack
Arnold, 1957); he disliked the script, but needed the money. He
compulsively started to rewrite his own scenes without permission;
Zugsmith not only indulged this, but also asked Welles to join him in the
evenings after shooting and work on the next day's scenes. When the film
came to an end, Welles expressed an interest in directing something for
Zugsmith. The producer invited him to pick one from a pile of scripts.
'Which is the worst one?' asked Welles, and Zugsmith handed him
Badge of Evil. Confident that he could make a great movie out of a bad
script, Welles took it away and began work.

While the latter story is amusing and speaks volumes about Welles, it
rings less true than the former. When Heston first met Welles to discuss
the project, Welles was in the midst of rewrites, so the script Heston
originally received would have been the Monash draft. If Zugsmith
genuinely thought the script to be one of the worst he had, it seems

unlikely that Universal would have offered it to Heston. Also, offering Welles's Hollywood comeback to Heston might seem a risky move from Universal's point of view, implying that it was Heston's idea – either he asked for Welles to direct, or asked for the lead when he heard that Welles was directing. A way of combining the stories might be if Zugsmith had offered Welles a rewriting-and-acting role on *Badge of Evil*, reprising the kind of work Zugsmith had been impressed with on *Pay the Devil*. The script might then have been offered in its original form to Heston, who made his suggestion of Welles as director.

In any case the script was probably not that bad. Welles worked on it for three-and-a-half weeks and announced that he had come up with 'an entirely new story and script', but in truth he retained much of Monash's version, including scenes and dialogue which had not been in the novel. At some point the title changed to *Touch of Evil*, although Welles later claimed that this had been done by Universal between completion and release (see **RECEPTION**). Welles made a significant change by reversing the race relations between the central couple. In the novel and the Monash script, the cop is white American Mitch Holt, who marries a Mexican girl named Connie, but in Welles's version he became Miguel Vargas and his wife became Susan. Welles also moved the setting from southern California to the border with Mexico, a setting which became richer and more distinctive as Welles fleshed it out. Aside from this, Welles's main contribution was to give greater weight to his own role of Quinlan (even then, David Thomson notes that the celebrated description of Quinlan – 'a great detective . . . and a lousy cop' – appears in Monash's draft). But Welles emphasised his own contribution because he wanted to shake off his poor reputation in Hollywood; he wanted to be seen to be working hard and working well. He was putting more of himself into *Touch of Evil* than he had into his lacklustre *The Stranger* (1946), but aimed to do an equally professional job.

CASTING: Charlton Heston (born John Charles Carter, 1924) was largely a stage actor in the 1940s, but following a film of *Julius Caesar* (David Bradley, 1950) he starred in the noir *Dark City* (William Dieterle, 1950) and then *The Greatest Show on Earth* (Cecil B DeMille, 1952). His real breakthrough was the role of Moses in *The Ten Commandments* (Cecil B DeMille, 1956). Universal was delighted to get him on board *Touch of Evil*, and he worked for 7.5 per cent of the gross. Although *Touch of Evil* was not much of a success, Heston soon had another hit with *Ben-Hur* (William Wyler, 1959), which won him a Best Actor Oscar. This opened a historical phase in his career including *El Cid* (Anthony Mann, 1961) and *The Greatest Story Ever Told* (George Stevens, 1965), which gave way to a sci-fi phase – *Planet of the Apes*

(Franklin Schaffner, 1968) and *Soylent Green* (Richard Fleischer, 1973) – and a disaster-movie phase – *Airport 1975* (Jack Smight, 1974) and *Earthquake* (Mark Robson, 1974). Recently he has made fewer notable films and is better known as President of the National Rifle Association (he takes issue with the suggestion that this is incompatible with his work for civil rights in the 1960s).

Janet Leigh (1927–2004, born Jeanette Helen Morrison) had been acting since 1947, when her photograph had been passed on to MGM by one of the studio's former stars, Norma Shearer. Leigh's debut came in *The Romance of Rosy Ridge* (Roy Rowland, 1947), and her other MGM work includes the noir *Act of Violence* (Fred Zinnemann, 1949) as well as *Little Women* (Mervyn Le Roy, 1949). She married Universal's Tony Curtis in 1951 and often starred alongside him; one of their two children is the actor Jamie Lee Curtis. Leigh also made the noir *Rogue Cop* (Roy Rowland, 1954) prior to *Touch of Evil*. Leigh is best known for another film in which she is menaced in an isolated motel, *Psycho* (Alfred Hitchcock, 1960). She divorced Curtis in 1962 and took roles in *The Manchurian Candidate* (John Frankenheimer, 1962) and *Bye Bye Birdie* (George Sidney, 1963). Afterwards she increasingly worked in television, stepping back from cinema in the early 1970s – although she appeared alongside her daughter in *The Fog* (John Carpenter, 1980).

A couple of notable stars are uncredited: the police surgeon is played by Joseph Cotten (1905–94), one of the original Mercury Players and arguably the best. He debuted in Welles's *Citizen Kane* (1941) and played the lead in *The Magnificent Ambersons* (1942); he played disturbed killers in *Shadow of a Doubt* (Alfred Hitchcock, 1943) and *Niagara* (Henry Hathaway, 1953) and was acclaimed for his lead role in Carol Reed's British noir *The Third Man* (1949). Mercedes McCambridge (1916–2004), who plays one of the Grandis, had won the Best Supporting Actress Oscar for her debut, *All the King's Men* (Robert Rossen, 1949). Her appearance here was spur-of-the-moment, and Welles cut her hair himself. She played the voice of the demon in *The Exorcist* (William Friedkin, 1973). Similarly spontaneous was the appearance of Marlene Dietrich (1901–92), who had been a huge international star since making *The Blue Angel* (Josef von Sternberg, 1930) in her native Germany. Welles telephoned her the night before and asked if she had time to film a scene he had added to the script but not cast; Universal executives were amazed when this material turned up in the rushes, and decided to credit her (although this involved paying her more than the union-minimum she had agreed). Finally, there was Hungarian model/actress Zsa Zsa Gabor (born 1917), billed alongside Dietrich, whose most notable film role was *Moulin Rouge* (John Huston, 1952).

PRODUCTION: Welles's initial intention was to go to Mexico and shoot on the genuine border, but Universal vetoed this as too expensive (the film's budget was a modest $895,000) and ordered him to find somewhere closer to Los Angeles. Welles settled on Venice, a town south of the city that, to his delight, was falling into dereliction (it was authentically rough too: Janet Leigh was given a guard while filming in the flophouse used for the murder of Joe Grandi). He determined to reflect the setting's decay in himself as Quinlan. 'Orson Welles, at almost 20-stone, one of the heaviest actors in Hollywood, decided he was not weighty enough for the part of the fanatical detective in Universal-International's *Touch of Evil*,' declared contemporary publicity. Welles added an extra 60lb of padding, including a false stomach and hump. 'It's my weightiest role,' he joked. He also sported a false nose, bags under his eyes and an altered hairline – make-up which later came in useful to disguise the bruising he sustained after falling into a canal during production. He also sprained his wrist, ankle and knee, and had to use Quinlan's cane for real. When not on camera, his arm was in a splint. Occasionally Welles would amuse himself by turning up to parties still dressed as Quinlan (including one he threw for various Hollywood moguls, who told him how well he was looking).

Shooting began on 18 February 1957. Aware that Universal would be monitoring his activities, he started with a couple of simple inserts, demonstrating that he was doing things sensibly and economically. Then Welles and Metty worked out how the interrogation of Sanchez could be shot in an ambitious single take. This scene was originally scheduled for three days on-set: 'the action ranged through two rooms, a closet and bathroom, and . . . thirteen pages of dialogue,' Heston recalled. Welles spent hours plotting how to shoot it all with a crab dolly, time that was supposed to be spent getting the material in the can. 'It was quite a complex shot, with doors having to be pulled, walls having to be pulled aside – very intricate markings, inserts on the shoe box, and things like that.' The first take was at 4.30 p.m. and on the seventh or eighth attempt they got a print. Production wrapped for the day at 6 p.m. and Welles announced they were already two days ahead of schedule.

As well as Welles's injuries the company had to work around Leigh, who had broken her arm shortly before filming. Many of her scenes were shot with her wearing a cast, which was concealed from the camera. Aside from this the production was smooth by Welles's standards; it came close to disaster on 14 March as they tried to film the celebrated unbroken opening shot overnight, as aspects of the sequence kept going wrong (frustratingly, this would often be the guard towards the end of the shot, who fluffed his lines). With time for one more take before the sun came up, they carried it off. The rapid zoom on to the explosion that follows this sequence was achieved using a conventional zoom, then applying a process of skip-framing – hand-cutting alternate frames out of the film. On 2 April Welles finished the shoot full of confidence, telling friends and colleagues that Universal was pleased with the rushes and that he was confident of working at the studio again.

Welles spent around three months editing *Touch of Evil* before Universal viewed a rough cut on 22 July 1957. They were unhappy with how the film was progressing and handed the project over to Ernie Nims, a Universal executive who had worked as an editor. 'I could work forever on the editing of a film,' Welles told *Cahiers du Cinema* around the film's release. 'I don't know why it takes me so much time, but that has the effect of arousing the ire of the producers, who then take the film out of my hands.' Zugsmith has testified to Welles's indecision when editing, and the arguments that he would have with editors. Nims and staff editor Aaron Stell cut around fifteen minutes of material from the film and in November 1957 Universal engaged a staff director, Harry Keller, to shoot some extra scenes written by Frankie Coen to clarify the plot.

Welles would later protest at this having been done without his knowledge or any requests for his input, but sources at Universal claimed that Welles had dodged their contact. Certainly Welles did not make himself available; after handing over to Stell he went to Mexico to work on a film of *Don Quixote* (which he never finished), leaving a set of notes for Stell to follow, and while the reshoots were taking place he was acting in *The Long, Hot Summer* (Martin Ritt, 1958) for another studio. Welles attempted to discourage Heston and Leigh from further participation on the film. 'Unless the studio is stopped,' Welles wrote to Heston, 'they are going to wreck our picture – and I mean wreck it, because it is not the kind of one-two-three, ABC variety of commercial product that can be slightly wrecked.' For his own part Heston thought it better to work with the studio, and found Welles's attitude baffling. 'You can't leave a studio holding an unfinished film, surely not without talking to them,' he later recalled, noting that Welles 'was infinitely charming with his crew and actors, but I've seen him deliberately insult studio heads. Very dumb. Those are the guys with the *money*.'

On 3 December 1957, however, Welles settled into a screening room at Universal and viewed the latest cut of *Touch of Evil*, with the Keller scenes inserted. A memo written by Welles 'in the light of the decision to deny me permission to direct these scenes, to write the dialogue for them or to collaborate in that writing, or indeed even to be present during your discussions', dated 5 December, addressed to Edward I Muhl, Vice-President in charge of production at Universal-International, featured his detailed appraisal of this version. 'My effort has been to keep scrupulous care that this memo should avoid those wide and sweeping denunciations of your new material to which my own position naturally and sorely tempts me.'

Welles began, 'I assume that the music now backing the opening sequence of the picture is temporary.' Whether it was or not, the opening theme by Henry Mancini was not Welles's preference. His intention had been that we would hear diegetic music as the shot progressed, hearing different Latin American tunes from different sources, each one fading out to be replaced by another. He also noted, 'it's not clear where you have decided to place the credits'; he was opposed to having them placed over this opening shot, feeling that they dissipated the tension, but in the released version this was precisely where they ended up.

The early scene between Grandi and Susan provides a good example of where Welles's comments were justified. 'This scene is just exactly a thousand percent more effective played, as it was first arranged, in two parts, with a cutaway to the scene of the explosion between those two parts,' said Welles. In his absence the cutaway had been removed and the Grandi–Susan encounter was joined as a continuous scene, reflecting Universal's dislike of the movie's fragmented style. Welles asserted that this did not work logistically because 'There is no available footage for continuous action. As the editing now stands, the welding of these two parts has been managed with as much skill as the resources in actual film made possible.' However, Welles still found the solution – covering the gap with a shot of Pancho – wanting, and tried to express this in terms which would appeal to Muhl. 'When photography falls sharply below a particular standard, cameramen say that the scene shot is not "commercial." They do not, of course, mean that it is too "artistic" for the commercial market.' Rather, he meant that it was not of sufficient quality and considered the edit on this particular sequence in the same way: 'it is simply not commercial.' The change was not made.

'I note with distress that the shot of Vargas at the telephone has been blown up in such a way as to eliminate the blind woman in the foreground,' Welles went on to comment. 'She was not there by accident.' Without her presence, there seemed to be no reason why Vargas appeared uncomfortable when speaking on the telephone: Universal reinstated the shot as Welles had filmed it. In fact, Universal was by no means unreceptive to Welles's suggestions. About half of his comments were incorporated into the release print, usually those which related to plot logic; stylistic changes and ones relating to the emotional development of the characters tended to be ignored. An added scene between Mike and Susan in their hotel lobby led Welles to complain that it 'makes the later scene (one of my own), in which Susan packs and stamps out of her hotel room, completely arbitrary . . . The new lobby scene leaves our couple in a fairly warm relationship.' Welles believed that this scene, along with several other changes that had been made, came from a different concept of the story which was at odds with his own. 'In these opening stages,' he told Muhl, 'regardless of any question of individual taste, I'm convinced that one story (mine) or the other (yours) should be told. The attempt to combine them annuls the logic of both.' The lobby scene remained.

While Welles did not object to all of the new material ('I take pleasure in reporting my enthusiastic approval of the new scene between Schwartz and Vargas') and conceded that some clarification work had been necessary ('I believe that the criticism of my own, unfinished version of these opening reels was entirely justified and, as I told him, Ernie Nims made dramatic progress in reducing this confusion'), such comments were rare and Welles was clearly dissatisfied with the new cut. He wrote to Heston that his memo represented the 'minimum' changes necessary to make *Touch of Evil* work. 'It's my fear that [Universal's] execution of these changes will leave something to be desired, since they may be acting without much enthusiasm, but most importantly, because they will be working in great haste.' The existence of a substantially different preview version (see **AFTERLIFE**), produced between that viewed by Welles in December and the 93-minute release version, does suggest that the final edit of *Touch of Evil* was a muddled affair. Oddly the release print dropped much of the Keller material, which Universal had gone to such expense to shoot.

RECEPTION: The release of *Touch of Evil* seems to have been patchy. Some sources claim that it was released in February, and certainly some reviews appeared then. It opened in Los Angeles on 23 April 1958, with a New York release following on 21 May 1958, with no previews. Just as Columbia had done with *The Lady from Shanghai*, Universal-International released the film on the bottom half of a double bill (alongside *The Female Animal*, directed by – strangely enough – Harry Keller). 'Orson Welles is back at it,' observed *Variety* on 19 March 1958, 'playing himself as a writer-director-actor and turning out a picture, *Touch of Evil*, that smacks of brilliance but ultimately flounders in it.' Commercially, the film's problem was that it 'falls in no category – it's not a "big" picture nor is it in the exploitation category – and must depend solely on star names . . . but overall prospects look slim.' Ultimately, '*Touch of Evil* proves it takes more than good scenes to make a good picture.'

Regardless, Welles still had his fans. 'Thanks to Orson Welles, nobody, and we mean nobody, will nap during *Touch of Evil*, which opened yesterday at RKO theaters,' wrote Howard Thompson in the

New York Times the day after release. 'Any other competent director might have culled a pretty good, well-acted melodrama from such material, with the suspense dwindling as justice begins to triumph (as happens here).' Welles, armed with 'an obvious but brilliant bag of tricks', was said to operate his camera 'like a black-snake whip . . . he lashes the action right into the spectator's eye'. Thompson was highly enthusiastic about the film, describing it as 'like a wild, murky nightmare' but stressing that 'the lasting impression of this film is effect rather than substance, hence its real worth'. However, the reviewer did ask questions. 'Why would a villainous cop, having hoodwinked the taxpayers for some thirty years, suddenly buckle when a tourist calls his bluff?' Also, 'why, Mr. Heston, pick the toughest little town in North America for a honeymoon with a nice morsel like Miss Leigh?'

The situation in Britain was much the same. 'Critics have not been invited to review *Touch of Evil* . . . from which fact you are free to draw your own conclusions,' noted CA Lejeune in the *Observer* on 4 May 1958. 'I intend to go to see it as a paying customer, because I am always interested in the Welles eccentricities. In the meantime your comments are as good as mine.' Reviews appeared regardless. Philip Oakes had already reviewed the film way back on 1 February 1958 for the *Evening Standard*. 'Beneath the bulk of Orson Welles, the Boy Wonder is still trying to get out. The dazzling film technique, first shown in *Citizen Kane*, still flashes intermittently.' His summation was 'a bargain-basement display of the best and worst of Orson Welles. After a sharp and successful opening it blunders on into disjointed melodrama.' Oh, and, 'Welles, I should add, gives just about the hammiest performance of his career.'

'*Touch of Evil* may not be the best Welles, even as entertainment: like Graham Greene he has two levels, but has let the higher slide,' commented William Whitebait in the *New Statesman* on 10 May 1958. He found the film 'visually stunning, over-emphatic, muddled', but in contrast to Oakes he declared Welles's work in the Quinlan role 'a virtuoso performance, attended by all the story and camera tricks, that makes the film well worth seeing'. Welles took the trouble to answer this last review in a letter from Rome, which the *Statesman* printed on 24 May 1958. 'Sir – Without being quite so foolish as to set my name to that odious thing, "a reply to the critic", perhaps I may add a few oddments of information to Mr Whitebait's brief reference.' The letter is utterly characteristic of Welles, eliciting some sympathy but failing to give any reason why his audience should continue to indulge him. He all but abdicates responsibility for the film (even the name *Touch of Evil*: 'what a silly title, by the way; it's the first time I've heard it'). He deemed the film's incoherence 'understandable in the light of the wholesale re-editing of the film by the executive producer, a process of re-hashing in which I was forbidden to participate'. Welles also mentioned the additional scenes which he had not written or directed.

The director went on to address the more personal criticism that he was squandering his talent on genre movies. The Greene comparison was unfair: 'When Mr Greene finishes one of his "entertainments" he is immediately free to set his hand to more challenging enterprises. His typewriter is always available; my camera is not.' The desire to make the movie of one's choice was not enough to make it happen. 'The minimum kit is incredibly expensive, and one's opportunities to work with it are rather less numerous than might be supposed.' He noted, 'I can pretend to no special interest or aptitude' for the commercial crime picture, and stressed that he made such movies 'not "for the money" (I support myself as an actor) but because of a greedy need to exercise, in some way, the function of my choice: the function of director'. He was sombre in response to suggestions that the visuals were 'tricks' to distract the audience from the narrative. 'This is a language, not a bag of tricks.' The early years of widescreen had seen much unwieldy camerawork, leading Welles to ponder whether his own style, utilising black-and-white and smaller apertures (which he believed had the potential for greater vitality), was obsolete. 'If it is now a dead language . . . I must face the likelihood that I shall not again be able to put it to the service of any theme of my own choosing.'

ASPECTS OF NOIR: *Touch of Evil* takes place on the border in more ways than one, as it is frequently quoted as the final film noir of the classical period. It is possible to find others, but *Touch of Evil* does seem an appropriate end-point: the movement had been winding down for a few years, and in its atmosphere of corruption and decay there is a sense that the work of the movement is somehow finished. Noir's simultaneous movement towards realism and stylisation is demonstrated here, although the accent is more on the stylisation in a manner atypical of 1950s film noir. Location work was carried out in a genuinely run-down small town, and a sense of place is extremely important to the film. There's a huge amount of night-for-night shooting, as the film takes place over two nights and the day between, but the lighting does not glamorise the location as high-contrast lighting sometimes does (*Touch of Evil*'s lighting is more akin to a film like *Detour*, a style which some critics have dubbed 'film gris').

However, *Touch of Evil* is also one of the most stylised films noirs, repeatedly going against the classical style of establishing a comprehensible three-dimensional space out of two-dimensional images. There are many long takes: the famous opening one immediately creates a sense of self-consciousness (as John Blaser notes, 'our first question is not "What is going to happen?" but "How did he get the camera to do that?" ') and, while it establishes a sense of place, '[It] does not establish a clear sense of space,' according to Andrew Spicer, 'but rather a swirling, confused sequence of disconnected actions.' Long takes eliminate such conventions as the reaction shot, so the viewer is given less to respond to and feels distanced. Welles's use of wide-angle lenses has a similar effect, and also undermines the 'realism' of the location by distorting the edges of the frame and flattening the background. In the closing sequences the viewer is again prevented from making sense of the space, this time by the opposite technique of fast-cutting montage. There are also several ironic juxtapositions, such as when the camera lingers on the sign which reads 'Stop. Have you left anything?' after Quinlan has left his cane at the crime scene, and his pause beneath the bull's head run through with swords as he leaves Tanya's. Welles frequently leaves his own face shrouded in shadow and starts the film by shooting Quinlan from below (so he seems imposing), then later from above (so he seems vulnerable). 'Although . . . *Touch of Evil* does not exhaust the possibilities of the noir style,' says Spicer, 'its baroque expressionism is the culmination of its most powerful version, the one through which the cycle is now remembered.'

Furthermore, this is perhaps the ultimate example of filmmakers creating something stylish from lurid, pulpy source material – which is the case with a great many films noirs. The story of *Touch of Evil* is quite simple and not actually very interesting, but in the hectic telling it becomes obscured and overlaid with fascinating details. Arguably, Welles dents it too far out of shape in his portrayal of Quinlan, who is such a grotesque that it seems incredible nobody has ever queried his methods before; the film would work better if Quinlan was more unassuming and professional, as he was before Welles got his hands on the material. His true nature could have been suggested in the camerawork, which Welles does anyway, and the effect would have been more sinister (and would have given the film the ambiguity it seems to crave, such as when Sanchez is revealed to have been guilty all along). Ultimately, while the film is very much about Quinlan and his downfall, its most effective creation is an atmosphere of threat and confusion which clings to the border town like a layer of grime. This is very much a standard genre product whose game has been raised to compete with 'classier' pictures (which it did overseas, if not in the USA: *Touch of Evil* won the main prize at the 1958 Brussels film festival).

The end of the noir movement is very much linked to the divorcement of film production and exhibition and the death of the studio system, which was a gradual process roughly spanning the whole of the 1950s (see **BACKGROUND**). Although in many ways film noir was a 'subversive' movement in its eschewing of classical style and breaking of taboos, it was very much a product of the studio system which provided a guaranteed market for these films. As long as the genre-based plot was present, filmmakers could achieve a degree of freedom to do something interesting with the visuals or the narrative – although they were still usually under the watchful eye of the producer. However, by the end of the 1950s the majors were turning their backs on such genre product, concentrating on a smaller slate of pictures and trying to make each one distinctive from the competition (while not so unfamiliar as to scare away a mass audience, naturally). The initial period of divorcement offered greater freedom for noir filmmakers, partly because producers were focusing more than ever on their big-budget productions and left programme pictures to their own devices, but also because the lack of mid-range films being produced left a gap in the market which many B-picture producers and independents attempted to fill. Directors such as Joseph Lewis got the opportunity to produce lower-end A-pictures while retaining the sort of freedom enjoyed by B-picture directors like Edgar Ulmer. *The Big Combo* is a fine example, but its lack of success explains why the lower end of the market moved towards sci-fi, horror and other exploitable, lurid subjects aimed at the teenage audience (the drug-peddling Grandi gang of *Touch of Evil* seems to have walked in from one of these).

Furthermore, technological developments in the 1950s had helped to restrict certain types of film from being made. One of these, as Welles noted in his *New Statesman* letter, was the advent of widescreen formats. Not only did widescreen initially discourage stylisation of the image (as technology improved and filmmakers became more adept, this was less of a problem), but also there was an emphasis on spectacle in widescreen which noir narratives did not provide. The other main innovation was colour, and there are good reasons why black-and-white is so strongly associated with film noir: they are discussed under **The Night of the Hunter**. Welles always resisted colour, only ever making one colour production – *The Immortal Story* – and that was only because it was for television.

Of course, another explanation for the end of film noir was that there was no taste for it any more. One might argue that the mood of America lightened as the 1950s went on and the war seemed like a more distant memory, although this argument is based on a notion of the 1960s being more optimistic – in spite of race riots, the Cuban Missile Crisis, the assassination of JFK and the Vietnam War. Nevertheless, at some point in the 1970s filmmakers felt a need for the noir aesthetic once more (see **The Wider World of Film Noir**).

AFTERLIFE: In 1976 Universal located a 108-minute print of *Touch of Evil* in its archives. Hoping that this would attract attention from the New Hollywood generation whose appreciation for Welles was greater than anything he had enjoyed at the time, Universal put this print into circulation and later released it on video, billed as 'complete, uncut and restored'. However, this was not actually the 'original' Welles version at all; it was a preview version including some significant scenes which did not appear in the release print, but much of the extra footage was actually Keller's.

In 1998, working from restored prints of all available material and Welles's lengthy memo, a pseudo-director's cut was assembled by Walter Murch. Renowned as one of the best editors in the business, Murch's outstanding work can be seen in Francis Ford Coppola's *The Conversation* (1974), *The Godfather Part II* (1974) and *Apocalypse Now* (1979). Murch's version includes most of the footage from both previous versions, but drops certain shots and lines which Welles had objected to, plus the entire Keller-filmed lobby scene. Most of the Keller footage was left in as much of it had replaced Welles's scenes which no longer exist, but it was often re-edited following Welles's suggestions. The rendezvous of Vargas and Quinlan's cars (shot by Keller, which explains why Quinlan is mysteriously unseen) is a good example. Most notably, Murch removed the credits from the opening shot, instead letting them run over black at the end of the film, and replaced Mancini's music with a mix of diegetic sounds as Welles had intended.

This new version has been widely praised, although some have criticised it for cropping the picture to 1:1.85. However, this exercise does not seem to have cut any significant information from the frame or spoiled any compositions, suggesting that Welles was asked to frame for 1:1.85 (which was at that time replacing 1:1.33 as the standard ratio for films not using the more extreme widescreen formats which Welles disliked) but shoot 'full frame', to give the studio the option of either. Note that the opening credits on the original version fit neatly within the widescreen frame, strongly suggesting they were designed to be exhibited that way.

AVAILABILITY: The majority of home-video versions of *Touch of Evil* feature the preview version, but the 1998 Murch cut is regarded as the closest thing to a definitive version and the earlier cuts are increasingly hard to find (tracking down the 1958 release version is particularly difficult). The 1998 version is available on a Region 2 DVD (8207804) which also includes an original trailer.

Odds Against Tomorrow (1959)

Often regarded as the last noir of the 'classical' period, this heist story follows Johnny Ingram (Harry Belafonte) and Earl Slater (Robert Ryan) as they each take the decision to involve themselves in a bank job. The film hovers between noir and post-noir style; director Robert Wise had made several noirs including *Criminal Court* (1945), *Born to Kill* (1947), *The Set-Up* (1949), *The Captive City* (1951) and *I Want to Live!* (1958) and frequently makes use of extreme camera angles and unbalanced compositions. There's also a sense of fatalism that arises from the apparent ease of the heist: we know that *something* must go wrong or we would not be watching this. However, *Odds Against Tomorrow* reveals just how plot-driven classical noirs generally are: the heist is simple and its undoing is no less simple, tangentially caused by Slater's racist mistrust of Ingram, who is black. It takes fully half the film for both characters to decide that they want in on the job, and the heist itself is crammed into the last twenty minutes. At one point Slater notes, 'I don't mind the action, it's the waiting. I wasn't made to wait, and I been waiting all my life.' The script (by Nelson Gidding and the blacklisted Abraham Polonsky) works to keep the characters waiting. In classical Hollywood movies the majority of scenes have a clear purpose, but the plot of *Odds Against Tomorrow* develops slowly, prioritising character over action, and some scenes exist purely to postpone the ending, which creates greater tension when the heist scenes arrive. Other scenes are complete red herrings. All of these, and the sparseness of the dialogue, contribute to the naturalistic style of the film which feels more akin to the cinema of the 1960s. Wise went on to direct *The Sound of Music* (1965) and *Star Trek: The Motion Picture* (1979). *Released on 15 October 1959*

The Wider World of Film Noir

Brighton Rock (1947)

Following the American trend, Britain played host to its own film noir movement – although this did not fully emerge until after the war finished. Graham Greene, whose work had already spawned a noir adaptation in Hollywood in the form of *This Gun for Hire* (Alan Tuttle, 1942), was central to the British movement due to the psychological complexity with which he invested his crime stories. Like the American writers and filmmakers, he was influenced by French Poetic Realist films which had been much celebrated in Britain. The two best-known British noirs, *Brighton Rock* and *The Third Man* (see below), both originated with Greene: the latter was an original screenplay, the former an adaptation of his novel. In America the film was titled *Young Scarface*, reflecting its subject matter of a teenage crime boss, Pinkie (Richard Attenborough), who marries a waitress in order to provide himself with an alibi for murder, then decides to kill her as well. William Hartnell, here playing Dallow, previously appeared in one of the bleakest British noirs, the 'double jeopardy' thriller *Murder in Reverse* (Montgomery Tully, 1945) – which Andrew Spicer credits as the first British film to feature a femme fatale. *Released in December 1947*

The Third Man (1949)

Sometimes gathered up with studies of American film noir due to the presence of stars Joseph Cotten and Orson Welles, *The Third Man* was British made and has an overwhelmingly European atmosphere (although some of the funding came from American super-producer David O Selznick). Its post-war Vienna is divided into quarters, each overseen by a different Allied force, while its centre is a 'no man's land' space in which identity is fluid and morality is flexible. Into this space arrives American western novelist Holly Martins (Cotten), only to discover that the boyhood friend he came to see – Harry Lime – is dead. In searching for Lime's killer, Martins discovers more than he wanted to know. Directed by Carol Reed, whose other British noirs include *Odd Man Out* (1947) and *The Man Between* (1953), its impression of a world where the war has destroyed all certainties is emphasised by an extraordinary number of tilted shots. *Released on 3 September 1949*

Shoot the Pianist (1960)

Directed by French New Wave hero and influential film noir critic François Truffaut, *Shoot the Pianist* consciously references the movement from a distance and, as such, is arguably the first 'post-noir' – although the same year's *Breathless*, which Truffaut co-wrote with director Jean-Luc Godard and whose central character copies the attitude of Bogart, also has a claim. Truffaut himself described it as a 'respectful pastiche' of Hollywood genre movies but the film doesn't pastiche noir style as such, having more in common visually with Truffaut's debut *The Four Hundred Blows* (1959). The climactic gunfight seems deliberately to invert the noir tradition, employing high-contrast camerawork to shoot a daylight scene in a snowscape, and there's a direct reference to Hollywood's repression of nudity and sex. The influence from American noir is more thematic and structural. This is unsurprising, as it's adapted from the David Goodis novel *Down There* (1956); three of Goodis's other novels, *Dark Passage* (1946), *Nightfall* (1947) and *The Burglar* (1953) had already been adapted as part of Hollywood's noir cycle. Introverted hero Charlie (Charles Aznavour) is a bar-room piano player whom, it is revealed in flashback, was a well-known concert pianist under his real name of Edouart. Blaming himself for his wife's suicide, he withdrew into the urban nocturnal world; the fact that he is unrecognised here underlines the disconnection between the different milieus. After killing in self-defence (a scene which recalls Fritz Lang's *The Woman in the Window*) Charlie succumbs to fatalism, realising that, in spite of his promising future in music, he has been dragged down to the level of his criminal brothers. Although he is eventually able to return to his job at the bar, the film's events have left him more numb than ever. *Released on 25 November 1960*

Point Blank (1967)

Often cited as the start of Hollywood's second noir cycle (although some sources claim Jack Smight's *Harper*, released the previous year), *Point Blank* is a gangster revenge thriller following Walker (Lee Marvin – see **The Big Heat**) after the betrayal of his partner Reese (John Vernon), who shot Walker following a successful syndicate heist on the abandoned Alcatraz and absconded with $93,000. Although Walker's dogged pursuit of his money frequently explodes into violence, a code of conduct emerges over the course of the film; he does not set out to kill anybody (although Reese falls to his death while grappling with Walker on a balcony) and he never demands anything other than his $93,000. It is, therefore, an atypical revenge thriller because Walker doesn't want revenge; only what should have been his. However, when he finally gets an opportunity to take his money on Alactraz, Walker does not come forward and as the film ends where it began, the narrative is revealed as meaningless. Director John Boorman refashions the dreamlike, opiated aesthetic common to much left-field 1960s Hollywood cinema and makes it a noir style, going beyond the fragmented ordering of scenes of 'classical' noir to create fragmentation within scenes, so that the viewer is shuttled around in time and space without warning to massively disorientating effect. *Released on 30 August 1967*

Performance (1970)

In its depiction of a once-successful gangster who finds himself out of step with the world and suffers a crisis of identify, *Performance* is a left-field cousin of 1940s gangster noirs such as Raoul Walsh's *High Sierra* (1941) and *White Heat* (1948). It also sees the return of a Gothic sensibility to film noir as Chas (James Fox) hides out at a rambling town-house owned by reclusive rock star Turner (Mick Jagger), a space in which the identities of the two men become blurred until they are interchangeable. The title has multiple meanings but principally refers to the notion that we all play roles, and that there is nothing inherent that prevents us from playing the role of a criminal. Directed by Donald Cammell and Nicholas Roeg in the summer of 1968, release was delayed for two years because Warner Bros. was worried about how it might be received. It is not difficult to see why. *Released on 3 August 1970*

Get Carter (1971)

With its obsessive gangster seeker-hero, increasingly complex plot and downbeat resolution, *Get Carter* is one of the most noirish films to have been made anywhere since the 'classical' period. Director Mike Hodges makes the link explicit by depicting Jack Carter (Michael Caine) reading a copy of *Farewell, My Lovely* on his train journey to Newcastle, and the emphasis on young women being dragged into making pornography seems to draw upon the novel of *The Big Sleep*. However, Carter is more akin to Mike Hammer than Philip Marlowe: strictly adhering to a vigilante moral code, violent and driven by revenge, searching for whoever killed his brother. Hodges not only distances the viewer from this quest, but also renders it stunningly pointless by having Carter fall victim to an unidentified gunman mere seconds after he has brutally resolved the mystery. *Released on 3 March 1971*

The Long Goodbye (1973)

In the late 1960s there was a revival of Hollywood interest in private-eye stories, marked by the first Chandler adaptation on film in twenty years: *Marlowe* (Paul Bogart, 1969), a version of *The Little Sister*. James Garner (star of *The Rockford Files*) played the lead role, indicating the film's lean towards comedy, and it has been noted that, to permit the humour to emerge, the film did not construct a particularly threatening noir world for Marlowe. Four years later, Robert Altman's version of *The Long Goodbye* also updated and reworked Chandler, relocating the story in the early 1970s, but to more successful effect. Employing Leigh Brackett, scriptwriter of *The Big Sleep*, the film stayed true to the novel's plot but reinvented the character of Marlowe radically. Elliott Gould plays him as an anachronism in 1970s LA, a loser unable to assert himself. This was part of New Hollywood's 'modernist' approach, which revised standard Hollywood genres in order to examine America's myths about itself (as identified by critic John Cawelti). To viewers accustomed to Bogart's tougher portrayal this came as a shock, and the film was widely panned. It is, however, great. *Released on 7 March 1973*

The Conversation (1974)

One of the factors often identified as giving rise to 'classical' film noir was the uncertain atmosphere of wartime and post-war America; it is therefore unsurprising that the Watergate hearings of 1973–74 should have provoked a noir response, adopting classical noir's depiction of paranoia and corruption and broadening it to include the upper echelons of government, leaving the protagonist with no safe place to go. The whole of the USA becomes the noir world. Francis Ford Coppola's *The Conversation*, sandwiched between the first two *Godfather* films and consequently often forgotten, is one of the director's best: it concerns Harry Caul (Gene Hackman), an audio-surveillance expert who is shown as already mistrustful and withdrawn. He accepts an assignment to covertly record a conversation between a young couple and on the strength of something one of them says – 'He'd kill us if he had the chance' – becomes increasingly convinced that they are going to be killed. Coppola allows the seemingly objective nature of the audio tape to gain the audience's trust, but late on reveals that everything has been filtered through Harry's perceptions – and he has been listening to it the wrong way. The result is one of the most futile detective narratives in American cinema, as a vast enigma remains at the heart of the film. Its downbeat ending is possibly trumped, however, by *The Parallax View* (Alan J Paluka, 1974). *Released on 7 April 1974*

Chinatown (1974)

Other revisionist private-eye films of the early 1970s include *Klute* (Alan J Paluka, 1971), *Hickey and Boggs* (Robert Culp, 1972) and *Shamus* (Buzz Kulik, 1972), all playing upon the audience's expectations of such figures from 1940s films and undermining them by presenting such characters as ineffective. The best-known example is Roman Polanski's *Chinatown* which, in spite of its retro 1930s title sequence, does not pastiche earlier films but uses the character of Jake Gittes (Jack Nicholson) as a device to investigate how Los Angeles came to be the city it was in the 1970s. The scale of the case is therefore much greater than anything tackled by the 1930s pulp detectives, and greater than Gittes's usual lucrative matrimonial work. The plot more closely resembles those of the contemporary political thrillers, although it is unfolded in a Chandleresque manner. As Gittes is positioned, from the viewer's point of view, in the past, his ultimate failure seems inevitable as he is fighting to prevent the establishment of a Los Angeles which the viewer knows exists (loosely based on real events from 1908, it concerns the diversion of water into the San Fernando Valley to make it viable for development). John Huston (see **The Maltese Falcon**) turns up to give a grippingly repellent performance. *Released on 20 June 1974*

Taxi Driver (1976)

It is appropriate that Paul Schrader, whose 'Notes on Film Noir' was one of the most influential essays about the movement and which made a substantial contribution towards its recognition, should come to write the most obviously noir-influenced film of the 1970s. The most impressive aspect of his achievement is that it is clearly film noir, but is in no way a pastiche. Travis Bickle (Robert de Niro) is a returned war veteran not dissimilar to those seen in 'classical' noir, although his war was Vietnam. He is an emotionally detached loner, working night shifts at a taxi firm because he is unable to sleep; director Martin Scorsese shows the urban milieu as Travis sees it from his taxi, a shapeless, corrupt mass. This is at least partly an externalisation of Travis's feelings about himself. 'I saw the script as an attempt to take the European existential hero . . . and put him in an American context,' Schrader remarked. 'Travis's problem is the same as the existentialist hero's, that is, should I exist? But Travis doesn't understand that this is his problem, so he focuses it elsewhere . . . the self-destructive impulse . . . becomes outer-directed.' As Travis's killing spree is devoted to liberating teenage prostitute Iris (Jodie Foster), the film is able to create a 'happy' ending in which Travis is hailed as a hero and finds his way back into society,

which is more disturbing than most of the downbeat-for-the-sake-of-it
endings on New Hollywood films. *Released on 8 February 1976*

Body Heat (1981)

AKA *Double Indemnity* with sex scenes. Whereas the neo-noirs of the
1970s were part of a revisionist interrogation of old Hollywood genres,
questioning America's myths about itself, Andrew Spicer states that the
noirs of the 1980s, commencing with *Body Heat*, were part of a
reabsorption of film noir into mainstream culture: as a mode of
filmmaking it was recognisable enough to be exploited for its various
positive connotations. 'Although this commodification means that film
noir is no longer clearly an oppositional mode of film-making,' notes
Spicer, 'postmodern neo-noir retains the capacity, handled intelligently,
to engage with important issues.' Director Lawrence Kasdan stated that
Body Heat was an attempt to demonstrate that the slow death of 1960s
idealism was akin to what he believed post-war America must have felt
like, by placing someone of his own generation (Ned Racine, played by
William Hurt) in a *Double Indemnity* narrative. Criticisms of it as a
straight rip-off of the older film are unfair, as it only takes its model from
the Cain story – every detail of the plot is different. The most significant
'update' is that the femme fatale, Matty (Kathleen Turner), wins but
appears dissatisfied – as if everything she had been led to believe that she
wanted was not, in fact, what she wanted. It is true that the film does not
quite add enough, but its resurrection of the noir mode was significant
nevertheless. *Released on 28 August 1981*

Blade Runner (1982)

The depiction of a future in which anything may be an artificial
construct and perceptions can be easily manipulated was labelled
'cyberpunk' after William Gibson's 1984 novel *Neuromancer*, but the
most famous example is *Blade Runner*, released a couple of years earlier.
Cyberpunk texts often signal the postmodern nature of this future milieu
by referencing the style and details of other texts, and so *Blade Runner*'s
use of a noir protagonist – Deckard (Harrison Ford), a trench-coated
detective – to explore the science-fiction plot of rogue replicants
(artificial humans) marks it out as a lucid example. The narrative takes
on an existential dimension when Deckard starts a relationship with
another replicant, and doubt is cast on whether he himself is 'real' (and,
indeed, what it is to be 'real' at all). Other noir-related details: much of
the film was filmed on a redressed version of Old New York Street on the
Warner Bros. backlot, where street sequences in *The Maltese Falcon* and

The Big Sleep were shot; the appearance of Rachel (Sean Young) was based by director Ridley Scott on Rita Hayworth in *Gilda* (Charles Vidor, 1946); and Scott's intention had been to include a 'Chandleresque' (his phrase) voice-over, which was ultimately abandoned because they could not get the 'poetry' into it. It was replaced by a more prosaic, expository version which was much maligned by audiences and removed for the 1991 'director's cut' (which Scott actually had nothing to do with, but later approved). *Released on 15 June 1982*

Blood Simple (1984)

Joel and Ethan Coen's film debut is a testament to the continuing possibilities of noir as a low-budget mode. This independent production cost $1.5 million and, despite being a fairly unpretentious crime thriller, gained recognition on the art-house circuit for its inventive camerawork and reworking of James M Cain's tales of infidelity. Whereas many neo-noirs attempt a kind of colour chiaroscuro by the use of blue filters, *Blood Simple* swamps the frame with reds or yellows. The film is also a key example of 'country' noir, opting for a small-town setting over the urban milieu of most noirs and depicting its desert as an isolated, threatening space. A number of the Coens' later films are also neo-noirs, and what appear to be the most obvious examples are often more complex: *Miller's Crossing* (1990) is an homage to Dashiell Hammett, but of all the Coens' films comes closest to 'classical' Hollywood style. The minimalist visuals of *Fargo* (1996) suggest noir, but its plot is lucid and its camerawork attempts to suggest objectivity. *The Man Who Wasn't There* (2001) returns to Cain and is in black-and-white, but the Coens stressed that they had aimed for a low-contrast look in order to avoid noir pastiche. By contrast, *Barton Fink* (1991) is very noirish, plunging the title character into a world of chaos as he wakes up next to a corpse – possibly borrowed from *Deadline at Dawn* (Harold Clurman, 1946) – and striving for an air of ambiguity. *The Big Lebowski* (1998), meanwhile, is a Chandleresque trawl around Los Angeles which draws heavily upon *The Big Sleep*, but replaces Marlowe with ageing stoner Jeff 'The Dude' Lebowski. The idea that these characters are interchangeable is typical of postmodern noir. *Released on 7 September 1984*

Blue Velvet (1986)

As previously noted, the modern detective narrative has its origins in Gothic fiction: in *Blue Velvet*, David Lynch took it back there. Lynch's non-literal approach to narrative (his films are designed to resemble dreams) allows him to depict a very literal noir world, which seeker-hero Jeffrey (Kyle MacLachlan) enters at night and leaves during the day. He sets out to rescue Dorothy Valens (Isabella Rossellini), who has the none-more-noir occupation of nightclub singer, from the clutches of the vicious and unpredictable Frank Booth (Dennis Hopper), thus characterising the noir world as a place where people work out their repressed sexual impulses. Lynch's later *Mullholland Drive* (2001) is a wilfully intractable mystery story based in a Los Angeles which owes much to Raymond Chandler. Its indomitable seeker-heroine Betty Elms (Naomi Watts) helps amnesiac 'Rita' (Laura Elena Harring) – who can't remember her name, and names herself after a poster of Rita Hayworth in *Gilda* – to discover who she is. In accordance with generic conventions, Betty and 'Rita' fall in love: it is as though genre has transcended gender. *Released on 19 September 1986*

Angel Heart (1987)

Like *Blade Runner*, *Angel Heart* is a significant generic hybrid, mixing film noir and southern Gothic horror: it was based upon a novel called *Falling Angel* (1978) by William Hjortsberg which bore the cover quote, 'Raymond Chandler meets *The Exorcist*'. Director Alan Parker moved the novel's action back from 1959 to 1955 because '1955 for me still belonged to the 1940s. It allowed me to give an older look to the film.' This also aligned it closely with *Kiss Me Deadly* and the end of the hardboiled detective hero. The plot follows small-time detective Harry Angel (Mickey Rourke), hired by Louis Cyphere (Robert de Niro) to track down a man named Johnny Favourite. It transpires that Johnny was involved in Satanic rituals and stole the soul and memories of a young GI back from the war in order to save his own life. He had plastic surgery to make himself resemble this other man and has lived as him ever since. Harry discovers that the identity of that young man was . . . Harry Angel. The integration of noir themes is intelligently handled, with the post-war hero who cannot account for a missing period in his life, and the twist that the detective has been searching for himself was used in the Woolrich noir *Black Angel* (Roy William Neill, 1946) but here operates in conjunction with the horror genre trappings. The film was not a box-office success, but gained a cult following on home video. *Released on 6 March 1987*

The Grifters (1990)

The early 1990s saw a large upswing in the production of neo-noir, including a number of adaptations of the novels of Jim Thompson (see

The Killing), whose work tended to be too hardboiled for 1950s tastes. Stephen Frears's film of *The Grifters* is a typical example, with its heavy violence and overtones of incest. The plot concerns the relationship between small-time con artist Roy (John Cusack) and the more ambitious Myra (Annette Bening), disrupted by the reappearance of Roy's estranged mother Lily (Anjelica Huston). Both women are femmes fatales; Myra tries to tempt Roy away from his (relatively) safe existence on the borderline of the noir world, while Lily is not above seducing her son to prise his money away from him. This was one of several neo-noirs which tackled sexual themes which would not have been possible during the 'classical' period, such as *Basic Instinct* (Paul Verhoeven, 1991) and *Single White Female* (Barbet Schroeder, 1992). *Released on 5 December 1990*

Sonatine (1993)

Japanese writer/director/actor/children's TV presenter Takeshi Kitano (or 'Beat' Takeshi) is best known in the west for his gangster pictures, and *Sonatine* has a particularly existential bent and notable use of dream sequences that recalls 'classical' noir. A Yakuza gangster (Takeshi), sent to resolve a gang war, realises that he is being set up when some of his men are killed and he hides out at a beach house, planning his revenge while becoming increasingly convinced that there is no point to these power struggles. The gangster film is a popular and prolific genre in Japan, but Takeshi's work is considered some of the most accessible and a good starting point. Also of interest are the *Dirty Harry*-esque *Violent Cop* (1989 – Japanese title, *Sono otoko, kyobo ni tsuki*); *Boiling Point* (1990 – Japanese title, *3-4x jugatsu*); *Fireworks* (1997 – Japanese title, *Hana-bi*); and *Brother* (2000), his first English-language film, in which a Yakuza is exiled to the USA and settles in Los Angeles. *Released on 10 September 1993*

Pulp Fiction (1994)

Quentin Tarantino's *Reservoir Dogs* (1991) marked him out as a student of film noir (as he is of practically every other type of film), with elements stolen from *The Killing*, an ambiguity that arises from never being shown the heist itself, and a non-sequential narrative structure (note that this is different from flashback): plus Lawrence Tierney, the star of *Dillinger* (Max Nosseck, 1945). *Pulp Fiction*, as its title suggests, draws heavily upon the crime literature that gave rise to film noir, especially that of the 1950s: it has the feel of a compilation of short stories and scenes from hardboiled narratives but filtered through a number of other genres and narrative forms. Tarantino's critics claim that his films are merely a collection of references to other films and cultural artefacts, while his advocates (of whom the present writer is one) assert that his films are postmodern commentaries on the nature of genres and modes, putting genre characters in realistic situations, realistic characters in genre situations, and subverting both with the use of humour. However, Tarantino himself claims, 'I don't do neo-noir.' *Released on 14 October 1994*

The Last Seduction (1994)

When the straight-to-cable and straight-to-video market opened up in the 1980s, the low-budget 'exploitation' noir underwent a renaissance. Lacking star names or production values, such films often relied on sex and crime to sell themselves and the noir style not only accommodated this, but also disguised the cheapness of the product. In a study of B film noir, Arthur Lyons reckoned that around half of Showtime's TV movie output could be legitimately tagged as noir. While many of these films were obviously not of the highest quality, this practice did produce some films worthy of comparison with the best 'classical' noirs, such as *The Last Seduction*. This tightly plotted reworking of *Double Indemnity* trumped the earlier *Body Heat*, using the femme-fatale figure of Bridget Gregory (Linda Fiorentino) to critique yuppie culture. She profits from business deals both above and below the law, and the same ethos leads her to have her husband murdered. As the husband is equally avaricious, Bridget's negative qualities are not characterised as feminine and so the film avoids misogyny. Furthermore, Bridget is permitted to win and shows no remorse – these are the games that are played in her society, and she is frighteningly good at them. Directed by John Dahl, the film was judged worthy of a theatrical release. *Released on 26 October 1994*

The Usual Suspects (1995)

As noted under *The Killers*, *The Usual Suspects* would not have worked in the 'classical' era – it would have been thought of as 'cheating' – and therefore demonstrates the wide dissemination of postmodern attitudes. The film is mostly told in flashback by Verbal Kint (Kevin Spacey), recounting how he and four colleagues were set up by the near-mythical crime lord Keyser Soze. At the end of the story the police place their interpretation upon events, suggesting that Keaton (Gabriel Byrne) was Soze – yet the audience is then shown that Verbal has invented many of the story's details, leaving them with the impression that it may be mostly true or mostly untrue. The audience reaction to this revelation was positive, enjoying the elaborate construction of the twist rather than feeling frustration at having followed a story which has now been discredited – demonstrating recognition that Verbal's story and the wider story of his interrogation are both fictions, and neither is more valid than the other. *Released on 19 July 1995*

L.A. Confidential (1997)

A flipside to the police-procedural thrillers of the late 1940s and early 1950s – which it acknowledges via the presence of the fictional *Dragnet*-like TV series *Badge of Honour* – *L.A. Confidential* is based upon a novel by one of the most notable modern noir novelists, James Ellroy (his status is perhaps only equalled by Elmore Leonard). Although there is close attention to the details of police work and the workings of the department, the film employs those details to demonstrate how the diligent, morally upstanding work of Ed Exley (Guy Pearce) is abused by his corrupt superiors to cover up their illegal activities. The complexity of the plot creates an impression of a system which is difficult to fight because it is so difficult to pull into view; in the end Ed resorts to murder, pragmatically using the whole affair to advance his own career. *Released on 19 September 1997*

Memento (2000)

Memento features perhaps the most extreme use imaginable of two noir devices, the fragmented narrative and the amnesiac hero. Leonard Shelby (Guy Pearce) is a former insurance investigator (shades of *Double Indemnity* and *The Killers*) who, through a combination of head injury and the trauma of his wife's murder, has no short-term memory. He searches for her killer, using post-it notes and Polaroid photographs in lieu of a memory and tattooing clues on his body so that he cannot lose them. The scenes are arranged in reverse order, beginning with Shelby killing Teddy (Joe Pantoliano) and working backwards to establish why Shelby came to believe that Teddy was the murderer. The two devices work in tandem, as each scene lasts roughly as long as Shelby's memory can hold information, and so, although all the movie's subsequent scenes have already happened to him, he cannot remember them and so has no advantage over the audience. While events do eventually form a coherent pattern, the audience is left with more doubts about who killed Shelby's wife than at the start – it may have been Teddy; it may have been somebody else entirely; it may even have been Shelby himself. Furthermore, Shelby will forget killing Teddy in a matter of minutes, rendering his catharsis redundant and opening up the possibility that he may go on to hunt down another suspect and kill him. There is also a possibility that this has already happened. Director Christopher Nolan went on to make *Batman Begins* (2005). *Released on 11 October 2000*

Oldboy (2003)

This South Korean film by director Park Chan-wook makes use of the paranoid noir style, as Oh Dae-su (Choi Mik-sin) is abruptly accosted and imprisoned for fifteen years with only a TV set for company and no explanation for his plight. Then, just as abruptly, he is released and given five days to unravel the mystery behind his ordeal, experiencing a typically noir switch from victim-hero to seeker-hero (and back again). When Lee Woo-jin (Yu Ji-tae) appears halfway through and reveals that he is responsible, the whole thing appears to be a pointless game – but the film pulls the plot threads back around to make horrific sense of everything. The film's violence is on a par with Renaissance tragedy (people sending each other severed hands in boxes, that sort of thing) and, once seen, it is certainly never forgotten. *Released on 21 November 2003*

Index of Quotations

Introduction

2   'there are only half . . .' Frank Capra, quoted in *Hollywood Cinema* by Richard Maltby

2   'values the personality of . . .' Andrew Sarris, quoted in *Hollywood Cinema* by Richard Maltby

Stranger on the Third Floor

8   'and was deeply impressed . . .' Lee S Marcus, quoted in the *Stranger on the Third Floor* publicity notes

10   'The advance work saves . . .' Boris Ingster, quoted in the *Stranger on the Third Floor* publicity notes

11   'I was supposed to . . .' Margaret Tallichet, quoted in the *Stranger on the Third Floor* publicity notes

11   'LET'S BE FRANK! This . . .' *Stranger on the Third Floor* publicity notes

11   'They haven't done right . . .' Review of *Stranger on the Third Floor* in *Variety*, 4 September 1940

11   'When the first film . . .' Andy Klein, quoted in *The Film Noir Reader* edited by Alain Silver and James Ursini

12   'American critics have always . . .' Paul Schrader, 'Notes on Film Noir', reprinted in *The Film Noir Reader* edited by Alain Silver and James Ursini

12   'Film noir is not . . .' Paul Schrader, 'Notes on Film Noir', reprinted in *The Film Noir Reader* edited by Alain Silver and James Ursini

12   'film noir is not . . .' Michael Walker, 'Film Noir: An Introduction' in *The Movie Book of Film Noir*

12   'high cultural capital . . . connotations . . .' Andrew Spicer, *Film Noir*

12   'is normally understood in . . .' Richard Maltby, *Hollywood Cinema*

13   'The issue of whether . . .' Michael Walker, 'Film Noir: An Introduction' in *The Movie Book of Film Noir*

14   'a fearful sense of . . .' Chris Baldick, *The Oxford Book of Gothic Tales*

The Maltese Falcon

21 'I must take my . . .' John Huston, quoted in *Bogart* by AM Sperber and Eric Lax

22 'Don't try to get . . .' Hal Wallis, quoted in *Bogart* by AM Sperber and Eric Lax

23 'This method of "designing" . . .' Publicity for *The Maltese Falcon*, quoted in *Bogart* by AM Sperber and Eric Lax

23 'I attempted to transpose . . .' John Huston, quoted in *Bogart* by AM Sperber and Eric Lax

23 'There was the understanding . . .' Meta Wilde Carpenter, *A Loving Gentleman: The Love Story of William Faulkner and Meta Carpenter*

24 'shut us up and . . .' Mary Astor, quoted in *Bogart* by AM Sperber and Eric Lax

24 'the audience knows no . . .' John Huston, quoted in *Bogart* by AM Sperber and Eric Lax

24 'silent and disinterested . . .' Publicity for *The Maltese Falcon*, quoted in *Bogart* by AM Sperber and Eric Lax

24 'Bogart . . . has adopted a . . .' Hal Wallis, quoted in *Bogart* by AM Sperber and Eric Lax

24 'He was forever surprising . . .' John Huston, quoted in *Bogart* by AM Sperber and Eric Lax

25 'Why be so clever . . .' Jack Warner, quoted in *Bogart* by AM Sperber and Eric Lax

25 'in the Warner projection . . .' Review of *The Maltese Falcon* in the *Motion Picture Herald*, 4 October 1941

25 'One of the best . . .' Review of *The Maltese Falcon* in *Variety*, 1 October 1941

25 'The Warners have been . . .' Bosley Crowther, review of *The Maltese Falcon* in the *New York Times*, 4 October 1941

26 '*The Maltese Falcon* has . . .' William Whitebait, review of *The Maltese Falcon* in the *New Statesman*, 20 June 1942

26 'the most interesting and . . .' Dilys Powell, review of *The Maltese Falcon* in *The Sunday Times*, 21 June 1942

26 'prefers balanced, low-contrast lighting . . .' John Blaser, 'The Outer Limits of Film Noir' (http://www.lib.berkley.edu/MRC/noir/ol-all.html)

27   'If I could beat . . .' Arthur Conan Doyle, 'The Final Problem'

27   'finds that the process . . .' John Cawelti, *Adventure, Mystery and Romance*

27   'As [the detective] unravels . . .' Michael Walker, 'Film Noir: Introduction' in *The Movie Book of Film Noir*

28   'is his first and . . .' John Blaser, 'The Outer Limits of Film Noir' (http://www.lib.berkley.edu/MRC/noir/ol-all.html)

28   'By the late thirties . . .' AM Sperber and Eric Lax, *Bogart*

28   'an embattled man equally at . . .' AM Sperber and Eric Lax, *Bogart*

29   'The last of the . . .' Publicity notes for *The Maltese Falcon*

29   'Sam Spade is not . . .' John Blaser, 'The Outer Limits of Film Noir' (http://www.lib.berkley.edu/MRC/noir/ol-all.html)

29   'It would almost seem . . .' John Huston, quoted in 'Huston Blasts Colorizing', *Variety*, 19 November 1986

Phantom Lady
31   'works particularly well for . . .' Michael Walker, 'Robert Siodmak' in *The Movie Book of Film Noir*

Double Indemnity
34   'Look, do you know James . . .' Joseph Sistrom, quoted by Billy Wilder in an interview with Robert Porfirio, published in *Film Noir Reader 3*

34   'Certainly. He wrote *Postman* . . .' Billy Wilder, interview with Robert Porfirio, published in *Film Noir Reader 3*

34   'Well, we don't have . . .' Joseph Sistrom, quoted by Billy Wilder in an interview with Robert Porfirio, published in *Film Noir Reader 3*

34   'Terrific. It's not as . . .' Billy Wilder, interview with Robert Porfirio, published in *Film Noir Reader 3*

34   'He is every kind . . .' Raymond Chandler, letter to his publisher, sourced from http://www.kirjasto.sci.fi/jmcain.htm

35   'bad-tempered – kind of . . .' Billy Wilder, quoted in '10 Shades of Noir' in *Images* issue 2 (http://www.imagesjournal.com/issue02/infocus/double.htm)

35   'I was a lot . . .' Billy Wilder, quoted in *Nobody's Perfect* by Charlotte Chandler

35   'We worked well. We . . .' Billy Wilder, quoted in '10 Shades of Noir' in *Images*

36   'Working with Billy Wilder . . .' Raymond Chandler, quoted in
      Cinema Texas Program Notes by Louis Black, 1978

36   'Don't fall for that . . .' Billy Wilder, quoted in *Billy Wilder in
      Hollywood* by Maurice Zolotow

36   'I tried up and . . .' Billy Wilder, interview with Robert Porfirio,
      published in *Film Noir Reader 3*

36   'That's when we knew . . .' Billy Wilder, quoted in *Cinema Texas
      Program Notes* by Louis Black

36   'He volunteered to do . . .' Billy Wilder, interview with Robert
      Porfirio, published in *Film Noir Reader 3*

37   'I could have turned . . .' Fred MacMurray, quoted in the publicity
      notes for *Double Indemnity*

37   'I realized that I . . .' Barbara Stanwyck, quoted in 'Barbara
      Stanwyck and *Double Indemnity*' by Michael Mills
      (http://www.moderntimes.com/palace/palace_di.htm)

37   'He used the right . . .' Fred MacMurray, quoted in the publicity
      notes for *Double Indemnity*

38   'She was as good . . .' Billy Wilder, quoted in 'Barbara Stanwyck
      and *Double Indemnity*' by Michael Mills

38   'I debated accepting it . . .' Edward G Robinson, quoted on
      www.imdb.com

38   'Keep it quiet, fellows . . .' Billy Wilder, quoted in the publicity
      notes for *Double Indemnity*

39   'I had always visualised . . .' Barbara Stanwyck, quoted in the
      publicity notes for *Double Indemnity*

39   'I wanted to make . . .' Billy Wilder, quoted in 'Barbara Stanwyck
      and *Double Indemnity*' by Michael Mills

39   'We hired Barbara Stanwyck . . .' Buddy DeSylva, quoted in
      'Barbara Stanwyck and *Double Indemnity*' by Michael Mills

39   'Fortunately it did not . . .' Billy Wilder, interview with Robert
      Porfirio, published in *Film Noir Reader 3*

39   'The film was shot . . .' John Seitz, quoted in 'Barbara Stanwyck
      and *Double Indemnity*' by Michael Mills

40   'We were delighted with . . .' Billy Wilder, interview with Robert
      Porfirio, published in *Film Noir Reader 3*

40   'one of the two best . . .' Billy Wilder, quoted in *Cinema Texas
      Program Notes* by Louis Black

40   'I never look at . . .' Billy Wilder, quoted in 'Barbara Stanwyck and
      Double Indemnity' by Michael Mills

40   'certain boxoffice insurance . . .' Review of *Double Indemnity* in *Variety*, 26 April 1944

40   'The cooling system in . . .' Bosley Crowther, review of *Double Indemnity* in the *New York Times*, 7 September 1944

41   '*Double Indemnity* is quite . . .' James Agee, review of *Double Indemnity* in *The Nation*, 14 October 1944

41   'the nature of its . . .' John Lardner, review of *Double Indemnity* in *The New Yorker*, 16 September 1944

41   'one of those cynical . . .' Campbell Dixon, 'A Brilliant New Thriller' in the *Daily Telegraph*, 18 September 1944

41   'the heyday of the . . .' Edgar Anstey, review of *Double Indemnity* in the *Spectator*, 22 September 1944

41   'Good murders on the . . .' William Whitebait, review of *Double Indemnity* in the *New Statesman*, 23 September 1944

42   'is among the oldest . . .' Janey Place, 'Women in Film Noir' in *Women in Film Noir*

43   'it is only occasionally in . . .' Michael Walker, 'Film Noir: An Introduction' in *The Movie Book of Film Noir*

44   'the lack of excitement . . .' Janey Place, 'Women in Film Noir' in *Women in Film Noir*

44   'the theme of looking . . .' Martha Wolfenstein and Nathan Leites, quoted in *Hollywood Cinema* by Richard Maltby

44   'Her importance to the . . .' Andrew Spicer, *Film Noir*

44   'the fact that a work . . .' Andrew Britton, 'Betrayed by Rita Hayworth: Misogyny in *The Lady from Shanghai*' in *The Movie Book of Film Noir*

45   'Since Paramount's *Double Indemnity* . . .' Article in the *Daily News*, 6 December 1945

45   'Can you believe that . . .' Billy Wilder, quoted in *Nobody's Perfect* by Charlotte Chandler

The Woman in the Window
46   'you know as well . . .' Fritz Lang, quoted in *Fritz Lang in America* by Peter Bogdanovich

Murder, My Sweet
49   'It struck me that . . .' Raymond Chandler, from *Selected Letters of Raymond Chandler*

50 'good, gritty movie.' Adrian Scott, quoted in *Raymond Chandler on Screen: His Novels into Film* by Stephen Pendo

50 'too narrative, too aimless . . .' John Paxton, quoted in *Raymond Chandler on Screen: His Novels into Film* by Stephen Pendo

51 'I was on my . . .' Edward Dmytryk, quoted in *Film Noir Reader 3* edited by Robert Porfirio, Alain Silver and James Ursini

51 'Could you use Dick . . .' Charles M Koerner, quoted by Edward Dmytryk in *It's a Hell of a Life But Not a Bad Living*

51 'believed that musicals were . . .' Edward Dmytryk, *It's a Hell of a Life But Not a Bad Living*

51 'figured it would be . . .' Dick Powell, quoted in *Raymond Chandler on Screen: His Novels into Film* by Stephen Pendo

52 'The budget, instead of . . .' Edward Dmytryk, quoted in *Film Noir Reader 3* edited by Robert Porfirio, Alain Silver and James Ursini

52 'I felt Powell was . . .' Edward Dmytryk, *It's a Hell of a Life But Not a Bad Living*

52 'the best of all . . .' Edward Dmytryk, quoted in *Film Noir Reader 3* edited by Robert Porfirio, Alain Silver and James Ursini

53 'So Dick walked in . . .' Edward Dmytryk, *It's a Hell of a Life But Not a Bad Living*

53 'We put Powell on . . .' Edward Dmytryk, *It's a Hell of a Life But Not a Bad Living*

54 'produced, previewed, and even . . .' John Paxton, quoted in *Raymond Chandler on Screen: His Novels into Film* by Stephen Pendo

54 'They released it as . . .' Edward Dmytryk, quoted in *Film Noir Reader 3* edited by Robert Porfirio, Alain Silver and James Ursini

54 'considered the book . . .' Raymond Chandler, quoted in *Raymond Chandler on Screen: His Novels into Film* by Stephen Pendo

54 'as good a piece . . .' Review of *Murder, My Sweet* in *Time*, 14 December 1944

54 'as smart as it . . .' Review of *Murder, My Sweet* in *Variety*, 14 March 1945

54 'Murder and assorted violence . . .' Bosley Crowther, review of *Murder, My Sweet* in the *New York Times*, 9 March 1945

55 'Some of the poetry . . .' Dilys Powell, review of *Murder, My Sweet* in *The Sunday Times*, 15 April 1945

55 'belongs in the same . . .' William Whitebait, review of *Murder, My Sweet* in the *New Statesman*, 21 April 1945

55   'As for that style . . .' Edward Dmytryk, quoted in *Film Noir Reader 3* edited by Robert Porfirio, Alain Silver and James Ursini

56   'Columbia's noirs specialized in . . .' Andrew Spicer, *Film Noir*

57   'Anybody who says they . . .' Joseph Lewis, quoted in *Film Noir Reader 3* edited by Robert Porfirio, Alain Silver and James Ursini

57   'RKO developed the quintessential . . .' Robert Porfirio in *Film Noir: An Encyclopaedic Reference to the American Style* edited by Alain Silver and Elizabeth Ward

58   'A cameraman contributes what . . .' Edward Dmytryk, quoted in *Film Noir Reader 3* edited by Robert Porfirio, Alain Silver and James Ursini

59   'There's no question that . . .' Edward Dmytryk, quoted in *Film Noir Reader 3* edited by Robert Porfirio, Alain Silver and James Ursini

Detour

62   'At that time I . . .' Edgar G Ulmer, quoted in *Who the Devil Made It* by Peter Bogdanovich

64   'For days, [Tom] Neal . . .' Publicity notes for *Detour*

64   'Most of my PRC . . .' Edgar G Ulmer, quoted in *Who the Devil Made It* by Peter Bogdanovich

64   'I had a perfect . . .' Edgar G Ulmer, quoted in *Who the Devil Made It* by Peter Bogdanovich

65   'Based on a novel . . .' Review of *Detour* in *Variety*, 23 January 1946

65   'No-one noticed its existence . . .' Andrew Britton, 'Detour' in *The Movie Book of Film Noir*

66   'It had a nice . . .' Edgar G Ulmer, quoted in *Who the Devil Made It* by Peter Bogdanovich

The Postman Always Rings Twice

70   'It was a real chore . . .' Tay Garnett, quoted in *Halliwell's Film & Video Guide* edited by John Walker

The Big Sleep

73   'Hawks read the book . . .' Leigh Brackett, quoted in *Backstory 2* by Pat McGilligan

73   'She wrote that like . . .' Howard Hawks, quoted in *Backstory 2* by Pat McGilligan

74   'We ought to have . . .' Jack Warner, quoted by Howard Hawks in
      Who the Devil Made It by Peter Bogdanovich

74   'Yes, a little like . . .' Howard Hawks, quoted in *Who the Devil
      Made It* by Peter Bogdanovich

74   'I had been writing . . .' Leigh Brackett, quoted in *Backstory 2* by
      Pat McGilligan

74   'I have worked out . . .' William Faulkner, quoted by Leigh
      Brackett in *Backstory 2* by Pat McGilligan

74   'Don't monkey around with . . .' Howard Hawks, quoted in *Who
      the Devil Made It* by Peter Bogdanovich

74   'I never saw what . . .' Leigh Brackett, quoted in *Backstory 2* by Pat
      McGilligan

75   'It was the sort . . .' Meta Wilde, quoted in *Bogart* by AM Sperber
      and Eric Lax

75   'I think everybody got . . .' Leigh Brackett, quoted in *Backstory 2*
      by Pat McGilligan

75   'Dammit I didn't know . . .' Raymond Chandler, quoted in *Bogart*
      by AM Sperber and Eric Lax

77   'I said I'd respect . . .' Lauren Bacall, quoted in *Bogart* by AM
      Sperber and Eric Lax

77   'On a Hawks film . . .' Leigh Brackett, quoted in *Backstory 2* by
      Pat McGilligan

77   'I had a deal . . .' Howard Hawks, quoted in *Who the Devil Made
      It* by Peter Bogdanovich

77   'The girl who played . . .' Raymond Chandler, quoted in *The Big
      Sleep* by David Thomson

77   'Do you know what . . .' Regis Toomey, quoted in *Bogart* by AM
      Sperber and Eric Lax

78   'It was necessary for . . .' Eric Stacey, quoted in *Bogart* by AM
      Sperber and Eric Lax

79   'Bacall [is] about a hundred . . .' Jack Warner, quoted in *The Big
      Sleep* by David Thomson

79   'three or four additional . . .' Charlie Feldman, quoted in *The Big
      Sleep* by David Thomson

79   'It was during the . . .' Howard Hawks, quoted in *Who the Devil
      Made It* by Peter Bogdanovich

79   'Miss Bacall comes through . . .' Review of *The Big Sleep* in
      Variety, 14 August 1946

79   'If somebody had only . . .' Bosley Crowther, review of *The Big Sleep* in the *New York Times*, 24 August 1946

80   '*The Big Sleep* would . . .' Manny Farber, review of *The Big Sleep* in the *New Republic*, 23 September 1946

80   'Film titles become increasingly . . .' Review of *The Big Sleep* in the *Evening Standard*, 29 September 1946

80   'Miss Lauren Bacall gives . . .' Review of *The Big Sleep* in *The Times*, 30 September 1946

80   'You will realize what . . .' Raymond Chandler, quoted in *Bogart* by AM Sperber and Eric Lax

81   'brutal . . . sinister . . . a new . . .' James Agee, quoted in *Raymond Chandler on Screen: His Novels into Film* by Stephen Pendo

81   'could claim to, in . . .' Review of *The Big Sleep* in the *Spectator*, 11 October 1946

81   'I'm all for your . . .' Raymond Chandler, quoted in *The Big Sleep* by David Thomson

81   'visually, it displays none . . .' Michael Walker, '*The Big Sleep*: Howard Hawks and Film Noir' in *The Movie Book of Film Noir*

82   'a virulently anti-Semitic conservative . . .' Andrew Spicer, *Film Noir*

83   'the camera pointing at . . .' Michael Walker, '*The Big Sleep*: Howard Hawks and Film Noir' in *The Movie Book of Film Noir*

The Killers
87   'fully half the gang . . .' Mark Hellinger, quoted in *Burt Lancaster: An American Life* by Kate Buford

88   'You ought to go . . .' Ernest Hemingway, 'The Killers'

88   'He had been a . . .' Ernest Hemingway, 'The Killers'

89   'I was the cheapest . . .' Burt Lancaster, quoted in *Burt Lancaster: An American Life* by Kate Buford

90   'Under the usual studio . . .' Mark Hellinger, quoted in '*The Killers*: Teamwork on Film Production' by Herb Lightman in *American Cinematographer*, December 1946

91   'a style which he . . .' Herb Lightman, '*The Killers*: Teamwork on Film Production'

91   'The lighting set-ups were . . .' Woody Bredell, quoted in '*The Killers*: Teamwork on Film Production' by Herb Lightman

91   'The audience can't see . . .' Anonymous cast member, quoted in '*The Killers*: Teamwork on Film Production' by Herb Lightman

91   'We had no elaborate . . .' Woody Bredell, quoted in '*The Killers*: Teamwork on Film Production' by Herb Lightman

91   'In modern production it . . .' Robert Siodmak, quoted in '*The Killers*: Teamwork on Film Production' by Herb Lightman

92   'I didn't have to . . .' Burt Lancaster, quoted in *Burt Lancaster: The Terrible-Tempered Charmer* by Michael Munn

92   'We had a good . . .' Mark Hellinger, quoted in '*The Killers*: Teamwork on Film Production' by Herb Lightman

92   'It might be a . . .' Internal memo at Universal, quoted in *Burt Lancaster: An American Life* by Kate Buford

92   'the best screen adaptation . . .' Ernest Hemingway, quoted in '*The Killers*: Teamwork on Film Production' by Herb Lightman

92   'does not enhance the . . .' Bosley Crowther, review of *The Killers* in the *New York Times*, 29 August 1946

92   'all pieced together neatly . . .' Review of *The Killers* in *Variety*, 7 August 1946

93   'Hollywood has so frequently . . .' John McNulty, review of *The Killers* in *The New Yorker*, 7 September 1946

93   'Though there is a . . .' Manny Farber, review of *The Killers* in the *New Republic*, 30 September 1946

93   'This is undoubtedly exciting . . .' Patrick Kirwan, review of *The Killers* in the *Evening Standard*, 18 November 1946

93   'Does it mean anything . . .' Campbell Dixon, review of *The Killers* in the *Daily Telegraph*, 18 November 1946

93   'Played with a grim . . .' Review of *The Killers* in the *Daily Herald*, 15 November 1946

93   'Whoever went to the . . .' D Marshman, article for *Life*, 25 August 1947

94   'tried to create a sort . . .' Robert Siodmak, quoted in 'Robert Siodmak' by Michael Walker in *The Movie Book of Film Noir*

96   'the camera has conspired . . .' Seymour Chatman, 'The Cinematic Narrator' in *Film Theory and Criticism*

96   'although Nick can describe . . .' Michael Walker, 'Robert Siodmak' in *The Movie Book of Film Noir*

Out of the Past

101 'I wrote six pictures . . .' Daniel Mainwaring, from 'Screenwriter Daniel Mainwaring Discusses *Out of the Past*' by Tom Flinn in *Velvet Light Trap*, Fall 1973

101 'Howard Hughes dropped my . . .' Daniel Mainwaring, from 'Screenwriter Daniel Mainwaring Discusses *Out of the Past*' by Tom Flinn

101 'I wanted to get . . .' Daniel Mainwaring, from 'Screenwriter Daniel Mainwaring Discusses *Out of the Past*' by Tom Flinn

102 'basically . . . the same, although . . .' Daniel Mainwaring, from 'Screenwriter Daniel Mainwaring Discusses *Out of the Past*' by Tom Flinn

102 'When I finished the . . .' Daniel Mainwaring, from 'Screenwriter Daniel Mainwaring Discusses *Out of the Past*' by Tom Flinn

103 'Gosh, I must be . . .' Robert Mitchum, quoted in the publicity notes for *Out of the Past*

103 'I was learning to . . .' Jane Greer, quoted on www.imdb.com

103 'It was a great . . .' Jane Greer, quoted in *Robert Mitchum: 'Baby, I Don't Care'* by Lee Server

104 'He walked in on . . .' Paul Valentine, quoted in *Robert Mitchum: 'Baby, I Don't Care'* by Lee Server

104 'He smoked marijuana all . . .' Daniel Mainwaring, from 'Screenwriter Daniel Mainwaring Discusses *Out of the Past*' by Tom Flinn

104 'We all went a . . .' Paul Valentine, quoted in *Robert Mitchum: 'Baby, I Don't Care'* by Lee Server

105 'I think we lost . . .' Robert Mitchum, quoted in *Cinema Texas Program Notes* by Louis Black

105 'Jacques Tourneur's direction was . . .' Jane Greer, quoted in *American Cinematographer* volume 65 issue 3, March 1984

105 'Zzjjane, do you know . . .' Jacques Tourneur, quoted by Jane Greer in *Robert Mitchum: 'Baby, I Don't Care'* by Lee Server

105 'it would have worked . . .' Jane Greer, quoted in *Robert Mitchum: 'Baby, I Don't Care'* by Lee Server

105 'Any time I find . . .' Nicholas Musuraca, quoted in *American Cinematographer* volume 65 issue 3, March 1984

105 'It was so dark . . .' Jane Greer, quoted in *Robert Mitchum: 'Baby, I Don't Care'* by Lee Server

105 'It was a hoot . . .' Jane Greer, quoted in *Robert Mitchum: 'Baby, I Don't Care'* by Lee Server

106 'one of the finest . . .' Samuel Beetley, quoted in *American Cinematographer* volume 65 issue 3, March 1984

106 'didn't like *Out of* . . .' Daniel Mainwaring, from 'Screenwriter Daniel Mainwaring Discusses *Out of the Past*' by Tom Flinn

106 'There have been double- . . .' Bosley Crowther, review of *Out of the Past* in the *New York Times*, 14 November 1947

106 'sturdy film fodder for . . .' Review of *Out of the Past* in *Variety*, 19 November 1947

107 'Conventional private-eye melodrama . . .' James Agee, review of *Out of the Past* in *The Nation*, 24 April 1948

107 'I rather liked this . . .' Review of *Out of the Past* in the *Daily Herald*, 4 December 1947

107 'I couldn't make head . . .' Review of *Out of the Past* in the *Daily Graphic*, 19 December 1947

107 'Several critics have expressed . . .' Richard Winnington, review of *Out of the Past* in the *Chronicle*, 20 December 1947

108 'symbolically homeless, its . . .' Andrew Spicer, *Film Noir*

108 'Bridgeport and its environs . . .' Leighton Grist, 'Out of the Past' in *The Movie Book of Film Noir*

109 'the reactionary ethnic coding . . .' Jim Kitses, *Gun Crazy*

The Lady from Shanghai

112 'to prove to the . . .' Orson Welles, quoted in 'The Sea Was Full of Sharks' in *Kabinet* issue 11 (http://www.kabinet.org/words/issue11/lady1.html)

114 'I could play the . . .' Letter from Orson Welles to William Castle, quoted in *Rosebud* by David Thomson

114 'I was lucky to . . .' Orson Welles, quoted by Peter Bogdanovich on the *Lady from Shanghai* DVD

115 'Of course he loved . . .' Orson Welles, quoted by Peter Bogdanovich on the *Lady from Shanghai* DVD

115 'Because I can't fire . . .' Harry Cohn, quoted by Peter Bogdanovich on the *Lady from Shanghai* DVD

116 'Yes . . . you could even . . .' Orson Welles, quoted by Peter Bogdanovich on the *Lady from Shanghai* DVD

117 'Good morning! This is . . .' Orson Welles, quoted by Peter Bogdanovich on the *Lady from Shanghai* DVD

117 'the dive is treated . . .' Letter from Orson Welles to Harry Cohn, quoted in 'The Sea Was Full of Sharks' in *Kabinet* issue 11 (http://www.kabinet.org/words/issue11/lady3.html)

117 'If the lab had . . .' Letter from Orson Welles to Harry Cohn, quoted in 'The Sea Was Full of Sharks' in *Kabinet* issue 11 (http://www.kabinet.org/words/issue11/lady3.html)

118 'Even a minor work . . .' Review of *The Lady from Shanghai* in *The Times*, 8 March 1948

118 'Orson Welles has stated . . .' Richard Winnington, review of *The Lady from Shanghai* in the *Chronicle*, 8 March 1948

118 'For all his airs . . .' Review of *The Lady from Shanghai* in *Time and Tide*, 13 March 1948

119 'Tension is recklessly permitted . . .' Bosley Crowther, review of *The Lady from Shanghai* in the *New York Times*, 10 June 1948

119 'It's exploitable and has . . .' Review of *The Lady from Shanghai* in *Variety*, 14 April 1948

119 'Columbia's *The Lady from* . . .' George H Spiers, review of *The Lady from Shanghai* in the *Motion Picture Herald*, 17 April 1948

120 'behavioural histories of individuals . . .' David Punter, *The Literature of Terror*

120 'doubles, mirrors and the . . .' Fred Botting, *Gothic*

120 'delights in complications of . . .' David Punter, *The Literature of Terror*

121 'combines elements of both . . .' Andrew Britton, 'Betrayed by Rita Hayworth: Misogyny in *The Lady from Shanghai*' in *The Movie Book of Film Noir*

121 'Gothic texts do not . . .' Catherine Spooner, *Fashioning Gothic Bodies*

122 'The narrative seems not . . .' Andrew Spicer, *Film Noir*

Force of Evil

124 'However appalled I was . . .' Abraham Polonsky, interview with William Pechter in *Film Quarterly* No.3, Vol XV, Spring 1962

125 'affiliated with from five . . .' 'Report on the Communist "Peace" Offensive – A Campaign to Disarm and Defeat the United States', Committee on Un-American Activities, U.S. House of Representatives, 82nd Congress, House report No. 378, April 1, 1951

125 '*Body and Soul* made . . .' Abraham Polonsky, quoted in 'If You Don't Get Killed It's a Lucky Day' by Lee Server in *The Big Book of Noir*

125 'I'd like to direct . . .' Abraham Polonsky, quoted in *He Ran All the Way: The Life of John Garfield* by Robert Nott

125 'Okay, go ahead. But . . .' Bob Roberts, quoted in *He Ran All the Way: The Life of John Garfield* by Robert Nott

126 'Melodrama was a term . . .' Richard Maltby, *Hollywood Cinema*

126 'I knew that was . . .' Abraham Polonsky, quoted in 'If You Don't Get Killed It's a Lucky Day' by Lee Server in *The Big Book of Noir*

126 'It had an allegory . . .' Abraham Polonsky, interview with William Pechter in *Film Quarterly*

126 'The book had a . . .' Abraham Polonsky, quoted in *The Director's Event: Interviews with Five American Film-Makers* by Eric Sherman and Martin Rubin

126 'What he wrote was . . .' Abraham Polonsky, quoted in *The Director's Event* by Eric Sherman and Martin Rubin

126 'I no longer remember . . .' Abraham Polonsky, interview with William Pechter in *Film Quarterly*

127 'It was necessary for . . .' Abraham Polonsky, quoted in *The Director's Event* by Eric Sherman and Martin Rubin

127 'Adapting a book to . . .' Abraham Polonsky, interview with William Pechter in *Film Quarterly*

127 'No. But the babble . . .' Abraham Polonsky, interview with William Pechter in *Film Quarterly*

127 'It was a mixture . . .' Abraham Polonsky, quoted in *The Director's Event* by Eric Sherman and Martin Rubin

128 'He defended his streetboy's . . .' Abraham Polonsky, interview with William Pechter in *Film Quarterly*

128 'She was brought to . . .' Abraham Polonsky, interview with William Pechter in *Film Quarterly*

128 'We had that big . . .' Abraham Polonsky, quoted in *The Director's Event* by Eric Sherman and Martin Rubin

129 'Of course, you die . . .' Abraham Polonsky, quoted in *The Director's Event* by Eric Sherman and Martin Rubin

129 'Abe, I just don't . . .' John Garfield, quoted in *He Ran All the Way: The Life of John Garfield* by Robert Nott

129 'Just think of him . . .' Abraham Polonsky, quoted in *He Ran All the Way: The Life of John Garfield* by Robert Nott

130 'There was nobody upstairs . . .' Abraham Polonsky, quoted in *He Ran All the Way: The Life of John Garfield* by Robert Nott

130 'I originally had a . . .' Abraham Polonsky, quoted in *The Director's Event* by Eric Sherman and Martin Rubin

130 'the blacklist took the . . .' Abraham Polonsky, interview with William Pechter in *Film Quarterly*

130 'It got lost in . . .' Abraham Polonsky, interview with William Pechter in *Film Quarterly*

130 'It may be said . . .' Bosley Crowther, review of *Force of Evil* in the *New York Times*, 27 December 1948

131 '*Force of Evil* fails . . .' Review of *Force of Evil* in *Variety*, 29 December 1948

131 'I find the second . . .' Dilys Powell, review of *Force of Evil* in *The Sunday Times*, 24 April 1949

131 'An efficiently made and . . .' Review of *Force of Evil* in the *National Chronicle*, 28 April 1949

133 'Ideologically, they are the . . .' Michael Walker, 'Film Noir: Introduction' in *The Movie Book of Film Noir*

133 'their politics were more . . .' Andrew Spicer, *Film Noir*

133 'If we take it that . . .' Michael Walker, 'Film Noir: Introduction' in *The Movie Book of Film Noir*

134 'I moved to California . . .' James M Cain, *The Five Great Novels of James M Cain*

134 'even worse . . . he felt . . .' Abraham Polonsky, quoted in *The Director's Event* by Eric Sherman and Martin Rubin

135 'The numbers racket . . . was . . .' Martin Scorsese, *Scorsese on Scorsese* edited by David Thompson and Ian Christie

Gun Crazy

138 'We know what'll . . .' Maurice King, quoted in *Gun Crazy* by Jim Kitses

139 'has never forgiven . . .' Joseph Lewis, quoted in *Who the Devil Made It* by Peter Bogdanovich

139 'Politics didn't enter into . . .' Frank King, quoted in *Dalton Trumbo* by Bruce Cook

139 'A lot of independents . . .' Dalton Trumbo, quoted in *Dalton Trumbo* by Bruce Cook

139 'There was no big . . .' Frank King, quoted in *Dalton Trumbo* by Bruce Cook

139 'a very worrisome . . .' Censors' report, quoted in *Gun Crazy* by Jim Kitses

141 'I wanted to have . . .' Joseph Lewis, quoted in *Film Noir Reader 3* edited by Robert Porfirio, Alain Silver and James Ursini

141 'just a brilliantly executed . . .' Joseph Lewis, quoted in *Who the Devil Made It* by Peter Bogdanovich

141 'some protection shots, merely . . .' Censors' report, quoted in *Gun Crazy* by Jim Kitses

142 'So when she shoots . . .' Joseph Lewis, quoted in *Gun Crazy* by Jim Kitses

142 'I didn't know what . . .' Joseph Lewis, quoted in *Who the Devil Made It* by Peter Bogdanovich

142 'Now, when we see . . .' Joseph Lewis, quoted in *Who the Devil Made It* by Peter Bogdanovich

142 'They were going to . . .' Joseph Lewis, quoted in *Who the Devil Made It* by Peter Bogdanovich

143 'two little fill lights . . .' Joseph Lewis, quoted in *Who the Devil Made It* by Peter Bogdanovich

143 'Now, you know the . . .' Joseph Lewis, quoted in *Who the Devil Made It* by Peter Bogdanovich

143 'Dramatically I wanted to . . .' Joseph Lewis, quoted in *Film Noir Reader 3* edited by Robert Porfirio, Alain Silver and James Ursini

143 'Shoot ending (alt.) of . . .' *Gun Crazy* shooting script, quoted in *Gun Crazy* by Jim Kitses

143 'Yes and no . . .' Censors' report, quoted in *Gun Crazy* by Jim Kitses

144 'Just after we made . . .' Joseph Lewis, quoted in *Film Noir Reader 3* edited by Robert Porfirio, Alain Silver and James Ursini

144 'You cannot give it . . .' Joseph Lewis, quoted in *Who the Devil Made It* by Peter Bogdanovich

144 '*Gun Crazy* comes to . . .' Review of *Gun Crazy* in *Variety*, 2 November 1949

144 'The film was not . . .' Joseph Lewis, quoted in *Film Noir Reader 3* edited by Robert Porfirio, Alain Silver and James Ursini

145 'Even with some adroit . . .' Howard Thompson, review of *Gun Crazy* in the *New York Times*, 25 August 1950

145 'Not five years out . . .' Review of *Gun Crazy* in the *Observer*, 23 July 1950

145 'One could dismiss the . . .' Dilys Powell, review of *Gun Crazy* in *The Sunday Times*, 23 July 1950

145 'The only success that . . .' Joseph Lewis, quoted in *Who the Devil Made It* by Peter Bogdanovich

145 'I'm here at the . . .' Billy Wilder, quoted by Joseph Lewis in *Who the Devil Made It* by Peter Bogdanovich

145 'Billy, I promised I . . .' Joseph Lewis, quoted in *Who the Devil Made It* by Peter Bogdanovich

145 'No, we had an . . .' Billy Wilder, quoted by Joseph Lewis in *Who the Devil Made It* by Peter Bogdanovich

145 'Billy, I'm sorry. It's . . .' Joseph Lewis, quoted in *Who the Devil Made It* by Peter Bogdanovich

146 'It is through the . . .' Richard Maltby, *Hollywood Cinema*

146 'The thrill of the . . .' Ian Leong, Mike Sell and Kelly Thomas, 'Mad Love, Mobile Homes, and Dysfunctional Dicks' in *The Road Movie Book*

146 'Unlike other fugitive couples . . .' Alain Silver and James Ursini, *Film Noir*

147 'the action sequences are . . .' Ian Leong, Mike Sell and Kelly Thomas, 'Mad Love, Mobile Homes, and Dysfunctional Dicks' in *The Road Movie Book*

Sunset Boulevard

151 'Silent picture star commits . . .' Billy Wilder, quoted in *On Sunset Boulevard* by Ed Sikov

151 'We kept going back . . .' Billy Wilder, interview with David Gritten for the *Mail on Sunday*, 11 July 1993

151 'Brackett and I had . . .' Billy Wilder, quoted in *Nobody's Perfect* by Charlotte Chandler

151 'We would work on . . .' Billy Wilder, interview with David Gritten for the *Mail on Sunday*, 11 July 1993

152 '*Sunset Boulevard* came about . . .' Charles Brackett, quoted in *Written for the Screen* by Donald Deschner

152 'with some star who's . . .' Billy Wilder, interview with David Gritten for the *Mail on Sunday*, 11 July 1993

152 'At first we saw . . .' Charles Brackett, quoted in *Written for the Screen* by Donald Deschner

152 'The night shot where . . .' Billy Wilder, quoted in *On Sunset Boulevard* by Ed Sikov

152 'This is the first . . .' *Sunset Boulevard* screenplay, quoted in *On Sunset Boulevard* by Ed Sikov

152 'I thought it might be . . .' Gloria Swanson, quoted in *Nobody's Perfect* by Charlotte Chandler

152 'Each day, we would . . .' Gloria Swanson, quoted in *Nobody's Perfect* by Charlotte Chandler

153 'Mae, for example, lived . . .' George Cukor, quoted in *Nobody's Perfect* by Charlotte Chandler

153 'I knew she wanted . . .' George Cukor, quoted in *Nobody's Perfect* by Charlotte Chandler

153 'If they ask you . . .' George Cukor, quoted by Gloria Swanson, quoted in *Nobody's Perfect* by Charlotte Chandler

153 'If my career had . . .' Gloria Swanson, quoted in *Nobody's Perfect* by Charlotte Chandler

153 'one of the great . . .' Billy Wilder, quoted in *Nobody's Perfect* by Charlotte Chandler

154 'she wasn't exactly objective . . .' Billy Wilder, quoted in *Nobody's Perfect* by Charlotte Chandler

154 'Bill was very much . . .' Billy Wilder, quoted in *Nobody's Perfect* by Charlotte Chandler

154 'That was beautiful, a . . .' Billy Wilder, quoted in *Nobody's Perfect* by Charlotte Chandler

155 'but Louella knew quite . . .' Billy Wilder, interview with David Gritten for the *Mail on Sunday*, 11 July 1993

155 'I was never worried . . .' Billy Wilder, interview with David Gritten for the *Mail on Sunday*, 11 July 1993

155 'Johnny, keep it out . . .' Billy Wilder, quoted in *On Sunset Boulevard* by Ed Sikov

156 'I remember he came . . .' Nancy Olson, quoted in *Nobody's Perfect* by Charlotte Chandler

156 'She was so right . . .' Billy Wilder, quoted in *Nobody's Perfect* by Charlotte Chandler

156 'It was a brilliant . . .' Gloria Swanson, *Swanson on Swanson*

156 'Just sold an original . . .' *Sunset Boulevard* screenplay, quoted in *On Sunset Boulevard* by Ed Sikov

157 'If only every picture . . .' Billy Wilder, quoted in *Nobody's Perfect* by Charlotte Chandler

157 'There are about six . . .' Billy Wilder, quoted in *Nobody's Perfect* by Charlotte Chandler

157 'We tested it with . . .' Billy Wilder, quoted in *Nobody's Perfect* by Charlotte Chandler

158 '*Sunset Boulevard* was the . . .' Nancy Olson, quoted in *Nobody's Perfect* by Charlotte Chandler

158 'You have disgraced the . . .' Louis B Mayer, quoted on www.imdb.com

158 'For audiences who remember . . .' James D Ivers, review of *Sunset Boulevard* in the *Motion Picture Herald*, 22 April 1950

158 'Because it is tied . . .' Review of *Sunset Boulevard* in *Variety*, 19 April 1950

158 '*Sunset Boulevard* is by . . .' Thomas M Pryor, review of *Sunset Boulevard* in the *New York Times*, 11 August 1950

159 'a pretentious slice of . . .' Philip Hornburger, review of *Sunset Boulevard* in the *New Yorker*, 19 August 1950

159 '*Sunset Boulevard* is the . . .' Dilys Powell, review of *Sunset Boulevard* in *The Sunday Times*, 20 August 1950

159 'In a cynically adoring . . .' William Whitebait, review of *Sunset Boulevard* in the *New Statesman*, 26 August 1950

160 'then and now, real . . .' Charles Brackett, quoted in *Swanson on Swanson* by Gloria Swanson

160 'the history of Hollywood . . .' Richard Maltby, *Hollywood Cinema*

161 'I'd had a very . . .' Gloria Swanson, quoted in *Nobody's Perfect* by Charlotte Chandler

The Big Heat
166 'I wouldn't touch anything . . .' William P McGivern, *The Big Heat*

166 '*The Big Heat*, which . . .' Fritz Lang, *Columbia News Service*, 1 February 1953

167 'Lang said he had . . .' William P McGivern, quoted in *Fritz Lang* by Patrick McGilligan

168 'The more the audience . . .' Fritz Lang, quoted in *Fritz Lang* by Patrick McGilligan

169 'show your back all . . .' Fritz Lang, quoted in *Suicide Blonde: The Life of Gloria Grahame* by Vincent Curcio

169 'I dote on death . . .' Gloria Grahame, quoted in *Suicide Blonde: The Life of Gloria Grahame* by Vincent Curcio

169 'You should underline the . . .' Jerry Wald, quoted in *The Big Heat* by Colin McArthur

169 'The coffee business was . . .' Fritz Lang, quoted in *Fritz Lang in America* by Peter Bogdanovich

170 'It is not the . . .' William P McGivern, quoted in *Fritz Lang* by Patrick McGilligan

170 'Columbia has a taut . . .' Review of *The Big Heat* in *Variety*, 23 September 1953

170 'Say this for Fritz . . .' Bosley Crowther, review of *The Big Heat* in the *New York Times*, 15 October 1953

170 '*The Big Heat*, like . . .' Review of *The Big Heat* in *Time*, 2 November 1953

170 'Fritz Lang's gangster film . . .' Dilys Powell, in *The Sunday Times*, 9 May 1954

170 'In its stereotypical way . . .' Review of *The Big Heat* in *Monthly Film Bulletin*, April 1954

171 'Considered at the time . . .' Review of *The Big Heat* in *Halliwell's Film & Video Guide*

171 'audiences had been shown . . .' Andrew Spicer, *Film Noir*

172 'In one way, that's . . .' Fritz Lang, quoted in *Fritz Lang in America* by Peter Bogdanovich

The Big Combo

174 'In the '40s the . . .' Philip Yordan, quoted in *Gun Crazy* by Jim Kitses

176 'We had cast Jack Palance . . .' Joseph Lewis, quoted in *Who the Devil Made It* by Peter Bogdanovich

177 'This man was, unfortunately . . .' Joseph Lewis, quoted in *Film Noir Reader 3* edited by Robert Porfirio, Alain Silver and James Ursini

178 'Then how do you . . .' Joseph Lewis, quoted in *Who the Devil Made It* by Peter Bogdanovich

178 'Well, we'll just go . . .' Jean Wallace, quoted by Joseph Lewis in *Who the Devil Made It* by Peter Bogdanovich

178 'No, Jean, you must . . .' Joseph Lewis, quoted in *Who the Devil Made It* by Peter Bogdanovich

178 'How *dare* you? Why . . .' Jean Wallace, quoted by Joseph Lewis in *Who the Devil Made It* by Peter Bogdanovich

178 'I know what you . . .' Jean Wallace, quoted by Joseph Lewis in *Who the Devil Made It* by Peter Bogdanovich

178 'I think she was . . .' Joseph Lewis, quoted in *Who the Devil Made It* by Peter Bogdanovich

178 'How dare you shoot . . .' Cornel Wilde, quoted by Joseph Lewis in *Who the Devil Made It* by Peter Bogdanovich

178 'What did I do . . .' Joseph Lewis, quoted in *Who the Devil Made It* by Peter Bogdanovich

178 'This filth of showing . . .' Anonymous censor, quoted by Joseph Lewis in *Who the Devil Made It* by Peter Bogdanovich

178 'This wasn't my intention . . .' Joseph Lewis, quoted in *Who the Devil Made It* by Peter Bogdanovich

178 'How the hell do . . .' Joseph Lewis, quoted in *Film Noir Reader 3* edited by Robert Porfirio, Alain Silver and James Ursini

178 'You supply me with . . .' Joseph Lewis, quoted in *Who the Devil Made It* by Peter Bogdanovich

179 'They wanted us to . . .' Joseph Lewis, quoted in *Joseph H Lewis: Overview, Interview, and Filmography* by Francis M Nevins

179 'I had a heart . . .' Joseph Lewis, quoted in *Joseph H Lewis: Overview, Interview, and Filmography* by Francis M Nevins

179 'This is another saga . . .' Review of *The Big Combo* in *Variety*, 16 February 1955

179 '*The Big Combo* isn't . . .' Howard Thompson, review of *The Big Combo* in the *New York Times*, 26 March 1955

180 'Although some cuts have . . .' Review of *The Big Combo* in *Monthly Film Bulletin*, February 1956

181 'The private eye continues . . .' Jonathan Buchsbaum, 'Tame Wolves and Phoney Claims: Paranoia and Film Noir' in *The Movie Book of Film Noir*

181 'a more metaphorical meaning . . .' Jonathan Buchsbaum, 'Tame Wolves and Phoney Claims: Paranoia and Film Noir' in *The Movie Book of Film Noir*

183 'in any erotic rivalry . . .' Eve Kosofsky Sedgwick, *Between Men: English Literature and Male Homosocial Desire*

183 'The end of the . . .' Chris Hugo, '*The Big Combo*: Production Conditions and the Film Text' in *The Movie Book of Film Noir*

Kiss Me Deadly

187 'I regret having accepted . . .' Robert Aldrich, interview with Francois Truffaut for *Cahiers du Cinema*, November 1956

187 'provided [Saville] would let . . .' Robert Aldrich, quoted in *The Films and Career of Robert Aldrich* by Eugene L Miller Jr and Edwin T Arnold

187 'you lessen the enemy . . .' Robert Aldrich, quoted in *What Ever Happened to Robert Aldrich?* by Alain Silver and James Ursini

187 '[Aldrich] gave me the . . .' AI Bezzerides, quoted in *The Big Book of Noir* edited by Lee Server

187 'The original book . . .' Robert Aldrich, quoted in *The Celluloid Muse* by Charles Highham

188 'make every scene, every . . .' AI Bezzerides, quoted in *The Big Book of Noir* edited by Lee Server

188 'That devilish box . . .' Robert Aldrich, quoted in *The Celluloid Muse* by Charles Highham

188 'I just put Bezzerides's . . . ' Robert Aldrich, quoted in *Robert Aldrich: Interviews* edited by Eugene L Miller Jr and Edwin T Arnold

188 'about the hidden meanings . . .' AI Bezzerides, quoted in *The Big Book of Noir* edited by Lee Server

188 'Those characters fit those . . .' AI Bezzerides, quoted in *The Big Book of Noir* edited by Lee Server

189 'I thought he was . . .' Robert Aldrich, quoted in *Robert Aldrich: Interviews* edited by Eugene L Miller Jr and Edwin T Arnold

189 'a quickie movie, a . . .' Gaby Rodgers, interview with Wes Clark (http://wesclark.com/ubn/gaby_rodgers.html)

190 'On *Kiss Me Deadly* . . .' Robert Aldrich, quoted in *Robert Aldrich: Interviews* edited by Eugene L Miller Jr and Edwin T Arnold

190 'I rented a tiny . . .' Robert Aldrich, interview with Francois Truffaut for *Cahiers du Cinema*, November 1956

190 'It has a direct . . .' Robert Aldrich, quoted in *What Ever Happened to Robert Aldrich?* by Alain Silver and James Ursini

190 'Va-va-voom was Nick . . .' Robert Aldrich, quoted in *Robert Aldrich: Interviews* edited by Eugene L Miller Jr and Edwin T Arnold

190 'We worked a long . . .' Robert Aldrich, quoted in *The Celluloid Muse* by Charles Highham

191 'a lovely man, jolly . . .' Gaby Rodgers, interview with Wes Clark (http://wesclark.com/ubn/gaby_rodgers.html)

191 'The camera focuses first . . .' Robert Aldrich, quoted in *The Films and Career of Robert Aldrich* by Eugene L Miller Jr and Edwin T Arnold

191 'a movie of action . . .' Robert Aldrich, quoted by J Hoberman in an article for *Village Voice*, 15 March 1994

191 'springs . . . from subhuman thinking . . .' 'Sex and Violence "Justified" ' in *America: The National Catholic Weekly Review*, 5 March 1955

191 'there certainly could not . . .' Robert Aldrich, quoted in *The Films and Career of Robert Aldrich* by Eugene L Miller Jr and Edwin T Arnold

191 'Mickey Spillane's name must be . . .' Memo from United Artists, quoted on www.imdb.com

191 'most people in America . . .' Robert Aldrich, quoted in *The Films and Career of Robert Aldrich* by Eugene L Miller Jr and Edwin T Arnold

192 'The ingredients that sell . . .' Review of *Kiss Me Deadly* in *Variety*, 20 April 1955

192 'I don't like any of . . .' Mickey Spillane, interview with Michael Carson for *Crime Time* (http://www.crimetime.co.uk/interviews/mickeyspillane.html)

192 'The censor has excised . . .' Review of *Kiss Me Deadly* in *Monthly Film Bulletin*, August 1955

193 'I had a career . . .' Robert Aldrich, quoted in 'Robert Aldrich says, "Life is Worth Living" ' by John Calendo in *Andy Warhol's Interview* issue 3, August 1973

193 'I couldn't believe what . . .' AI Bezzerides, quoted in *The Big Book of Noir* edited by Lee Server

193 'Here it is, the . . .' Claude Chabrol, review of *Kiss Me Deadly* in *Cahiers du Cinema* issue 54

193 'No, I like the . . .' Robert Aldrich, quoted in *Robert Aldrich: Interviews* edited by Eugene L Miller Jr and Edwin T Arnold

193 'once you got outside . . .' Robert Aldrich, quoted in *Robert Aldrich: Interviews* edited by Eugene L Miller Jr and Edwin T Arnold

194 'when I asked my . . .' Robert Aldrich, interview with Francois Truffaut for *Cahiers du Cinema*, November 1956

194 'What they have done . . .' Edward Gallafent, 'Kiss Me Deadly' in *The Movie Book of Film Noir*

195 'the city of the . . .' Andrew Spicer, *Film Noir*

196 'I have never seen . . .' Robert Aldrich, quoted in 'The Kiss Me Mangled Mystery' by Glenn Erikson in *Images* issue 3 (www.imagesjournal.com/issue3/features/kmd1.htm)

196 'By dwelling on Hammer's . . .' Glenn Erikson, 'The Kiss Me Mangled Mystery' in *Images*

The Night of the Hunter

199 'I was drinking in . . .' Davis Grubb, quoted in *The Night of the Hunter* by Simon Callow

200 'Hollywood has been looking . . .' Charles Laughton, quoted in *The Night of the Hunter* by Simon Callow

200 'absolutely anti-religious in the . . .' Paul Gregory, quoted in *The Night of the Hunter* by Simon Callow

200 'I had been filming . . .' Davis Grubb, quoted in *The Night of the Hunter* by Simon Callow

200 'My dear Dave, the . . .' Charles Laughton, quoted in *The Night of the Hunter* by Simon Callow

200 'Charles wouldn't come near . . .' Paul Gregory, quoted in *The Night of the Hunter* by Simon Callow

201 'a fairy-story, really a . . .' Charles Laughton, quoted in *The Night of the Hunter* by Simon Callow

201 'I'm fascinated, and about . . .' James Agee, quoted in *The Night of the Hunter* by Simon Callow

201 'My feeling was, and . . .' James Agee, quoted in *The Night of the Hunter* by Simon Callow

201 'We do not feel . . .' Paul Gregory, quoted in *The Night of the Hunter* by Simon Callow

202 'I got three expressions . . .' Robert Mitchum, quoted on www.imdb.com

202 'All the tough talk is . . .' Charles Laughton, quoted on www.imdb.com

202 'I fell in love . . .' Charles Laughton, quoted in *The Night of the Hunter* by Simon Callow

203 'In these scenes, you . . .' Charles Laughton, quoted in *The Night of the Hunter* by Simon Callow

203 'It was designed from . . .' Stanley Cortez, quoted in *The Night of the Hunter* by Simon Callow

203 'He was a sort . . .' Robert Mitchum, quoted in *The Night of the Hunter* by Simon Callow

204 'I knew what Charles . . .' Robert Mitchum, quoted in *The Night of the Hunter* by Simon Callow

204 'Moving from Ford to . . .' Peter Graves, quoted in *The Night of the Hunter* by Simon Callow

204 'When I tell people . . .' Stanley Cortez, quoted in *The Night of the Hunter* by Simon Callow

204 'Despite all efforts of . . .' Publicity notes for *The Night of the Hunter*

205 'Golden! What do I . . .' Charles Laughton, quoted in *The Night of the Hunter* by Simon Callow

205 'The one thing Laughton . . .' Robert Golden, quoted in *The Night of the Hunter* by Simon Callow

205 'The relentless terror of . . .' Review of *The Night of the Hunter* in *Variety*, 20 July 1955

205 'The trenchant and troubling . . .' Bosley Crowther, review of *The Night of the Hunter* in the *New York Times*, 20 September 1955

206 'a fairly eclectic item . . .' John McCurtew, review of *The Night of the Hunter* in *The New Yorker*, 8 October 1955

206 'His subject is nothing . . .' CA Lejeune, review of *The Night of the Hunter* in the *Observer*, 27 November 1955

206 'I have not the . . .' Dilys Powell, review of *The Night of the Hunter* in *The Sunday Times*, 27 November 1955

206 'Robert Mitchum can't carry . . .' Harris Deans, review of *The Night of the Hunter* in the *Sunday Dispatch*, 27 November 1955

207 'For the best part . . .' Richard Maltby, *Hollywood Cinema*

207 'Colors objectify their subjects . . .' Scott McCloud, *Understanding Comics*

207 'enables us to portray . . .' Natalie Kalmus, quoted in *Hollywood Cinema* by Richard Maltby

207 'In the 1940s, a . . .' Richard Maltby, *Hollywood Cinema*

208 'When [Laughton] saw the . . .' Stanley Cortez, quoted in *The Night of the Hunter* by Simon Callow

210 'to graft avant-garde techniques . . .' Andrew Spicer, *Film Noir*

The Killing
215 'We hired Thompson *because* . . .' James B Harris, quoted in *Kubrick: A Biography* by John Baxter

215 'I wonder whether there . . .' Sterling Hayden, quoted on www.imdb.com

217 'There was an air . . .' James B Harris, quoted in *Stanley Kubrick: A Film Odyssey* by Gene D Phillips

217 'I kept waiting for . . .' Coleen Gray, quoted in 'What They Say About Stanley Kubrick' by Peter Bogdanovich, the *New York Times*, 4 July 1999

218 'I have worked with . . .' Sterling Hayden, quoted in *Stanley Kubrick: A Film Odyssey* by Gene D Phillips

218 'It was the handling . . .' Stanley Kubrick, quoted in *Stanley Kubrick: A Film Odyssey* by Gene D Phillips

218 'You have other producer-filmmaker . . .' and 'Not far from the bottom . . .' Kubrick and Youngstein, quoted by James B Harris in 'Stanley Kubrick: A Cinematic Odyssey', *Premiere*, August 1999

218 'sturdy fare for the . . .' Review of *The Killing* in *Variety*, 23 May 1956

219 'a sharp, black-and-white . . .' AH Weiler, review of *The Killing* in the *New York Times*, 21 May 1956

219 '*The Killing* announces the . . .' Review of *The Killing* in *Time*, 4 June 1956

219 'There are many new . . .' Review of *The Killing* in the *Manchester Guardian*, 28 July 1956

219 'a brilliant thriller has . . .' Alan Brien, review of *The Killing* in the *Evening Standard*, 26 July 1956

220 'reasons backward . . . The end is . . .' Rick Altman, 'Dickens, Griffith, and Film Theory Today,' in *Classical Hollywood Narrative: The Paradigm Wars*

The Wrong Man
222 'his films tend to . . .' Michael Walker, 'Film Noir: Introduction' in *The Movie Book of Film Noir*

Touch of Evil
225 'I said "Maybe," and . . .' Orson Welles, quoted in *Rosebud* by David Thomson

225 'You know, Orson Welles . . .' Charlton Heston, quoted in *Rosebud* by David Thomson

225 'Which is the worst . . .' Orson Welles, quoted in *Rosebud* by David Thomson

226 'an entirely new story . . .' Orson Welles, quoted in *Rosebud* by David Thomson

228 'Orson Welles, at almost . . .' Publicity notes for *Touch of Evil*

228 'the action ranged through . . .' Charlton Heston, quoted in *Rosebud* by David Thomson

229 'I could work forever . . .' Orson Welles, interviewed for *Cahiers du Cinema*, quoted on www.wellesnet.com

229 'Unless the studio is . . .' Orson Welles, letter to Charlton Heston, quoted in *Rosebud* by David Thomson

229 'You can't leave a . . .' Charlton Heston, quoted in *Rosebud* by David Thomson

229 'in the light of . . .' Orson Welles, memo to Edward I Muhl, 5 December 1957, sourced from www.wellesnet.com/touch_ memo1.htm

230 'I assume that the . . .' Orson Welles, memo to Edward I Muhl

230 'This scene is just . . .' Orson Welles, memo to Edward I Muhl

230 'I note with distress . . .' Orson Welles, memo to Edward I Muhl

231 'I take pleasure in . . .' Orson Welles, memo to Edward I Muhl

231 'It's my fear that . . .' Orson Welles, quoted in *Rosebud* by David Thomson

231 'Orson Welles is back . . .' Review of *Touch of Evil* in *Variety*, 19 March 1958

231 'Thanks to Orson Welles . . .' Howard Thompson, review of *Touch of Evil* in the *New York Times*, 22 May 1958

232 'Critics have not been . . .' CA Lejeune, review of *Touch of Evil* in the *Observer*, 4 May 1958

232 'Beneath the bulk of . . .' Philip Oakes, review of *Touch of Evil* in the *Evening Standard*, 1 February 1958

232 '*Touch of Evil* may . . .' William Whitebait, review of *Touch of Evil* in the *New Statesman*, 10 May 1958

232 'Sir – Without being quite . . .' Orson Welles, letter to the *New Statesman*, 24 May 1958

233 'When Mr Greene finishes . . .' Orson Welles, letter to the *New Statesman*, 24 May 1958

234 'our first question is . . .' John Blaser, 'The Outer Limits of Film Noir' (http://www.lib.berkley.edu/MRC/noir/ol-all.html)

234 '[It] does not establish . . .' Andrew Spicer, *Film Noir*

The Wider World of Film Noir
243 'I saw the script . . .' Paul Schrader, quoted in *Hollywood Cinema* by Richard Maltby

244 'Although this commodification means . . .' Andrew Spicer, *Film Noir*

246 '1955 for me still . . .' Alan Parker, quoted in 'Past Perfect: *Angel Heart*' by Steve O'Brien in *SFX* issue 127, February 2005

Bibliography

Books

Baldick, Chris (ed.), *The Oxford Book of Gothic Tales*, Oxford University Press, Oxford, 1992

Baxter, John, *Kubrick: A Biography*, HarperCollins, London, 1997

Bogdanovich, Peter, *Fritz Lang in America*, Studio Vista, London, 1967

Bogdanovich, Peter, *Who the Devil Made It*, Alfred A. Knopf, New York, 1997

Botting, Fred, *Gothic*, Routledge, London, 1996

Braudy, Leo & Cohen, Marshall, *Film Theory and Criticism*, Oxford University Press, New York, 1999

Buford, Kate, *Burt Lancaster: An American Life*, Aurum, London, 2000

Cain, James M, *The Five Great Novels of James M. Cain*, Picador, London, 1985

Callow, Simon, *The Night of the Hunter*, BFI Publishing, London, 2000

Cameron, Ian (ed.), *The Movie Book of Film Noir*, Studio Vista, London, 1992

Carpenter, Meta Wilde & Borsten, Orin, *A Loving Gentleman: The Love Story of William Faulkner and Meta Carpenter*, Simon & Schuster, New York, 1976

Cawelti, John, *Adventure, Mystery and Romance: Formula Stories as Art and Popular Culture*, University of Chicago Press, Chicago, 1976

Chandler, Charlotte, *Nobody's Perfect: Billy Wilder, A Personal Biography*, Simon and Schuster, New York, 2002

Chandler, Raymond, *The Big Sleep and Other Novels*, Penguin Classics, Harmondsworth, 2000

Chandler, Raymond, *Selected Letters of Raymond Chandler*, edited by Frank MacShane, Columbia University Press, New York, 1981

Clarke, James, *Ridley Scott*, Virgin, London, 2002

Cohan, Steven & Hark, Ina Rae (eds.), *The Road Movie Book*, Routledge, New York, 1997

Cook, Bruce, *Dalton Trumbo*, Scribner, New York, 1977

Curcio, Vincent, *Suicide Blonde: The Life of Gloria Grahame*, William Morrow, New York, 1989

Deschner, Donald, *Written for the Screen*

Dmytryk, Edward, *It's a Hell of a Life But Not a Bad Living*, Times Books, New York, 1978

Doyle, Arthur Conan, *Sherlock Holmes: The Short Stories*, Paragon, London, 1995

Gaines, Jane (ed.), *Classical Hollywood Narrative: The Paradigm Wars*, Duke University Press, Durham, 1992

Gorman, Ed, Greenberg, Martin H & Server, Lee (eds.), *The Big Book of Noir*, Carroll & Graf, New York, 1998

Halliwell, Leslie and Walker, John (ed.), *Halliwell's Film & Video Guide 2003*, HarperCollins Entertainment, London, 2002

Hammett, Dashiell, *The Four Great Novels*, Picador, London, 1982

Highham, Charles, *The Celluloid Muse*, Henry Regnery, Chicago, 1969

Hiney, Tom, *Raymond Chandler: A Biography*, Chatto & Windus, London, 1997

Hughes, David, *The Complete Kubrick*, Virgin, London, 2000

Kaplan, E Ann, *Women in Film Noir*, BFI Publishing, London, 1978

Karney, Robyn (ed.), *Cinema Year By Year 1894–2002*, Dorling Kindersley, London, 2002

Kitses, Jim, *Gun Crazy*, BFI Publishing, London, 2000

Maltby, Richard, *Hollywood Cinema*, Blackwell, Oxford, 1995

McArthur, Colin, *The Big Heat*, BFI Publishing, London, 1992

McCloud, Scott, *Understanding Comics*, HarperPerennial, New York, 1994

McGilligan, Pat, *Backstory 2: Interviews with Screenwriters of the 1940s and 1950s*, University of California Press, 1991

McGilligan, Patrick, *Fritz Lang: The Nature of the Beast*, Faber and Faber, London, 1997

McGivern, William P, *The Big Heat*, Magna Print Books, London, 1990

Miller Jr, Eugene L & Arnold, Edwin T, *The Films and Career of Robert Aldrich*, University of Tennessee Press, Knoxville, 1986

Miller Jr, Eugene L & Arnold, Edwin T (eds.), *Robert Aldrich: Interviews*, University of Mississippi Press, Jackson, 2004

Munn, Michael, *Burt Lancaster: The Terrible-Tempered Charmer*, Robson Books, London, 1995

Nevins, Francis M, *Joseph H Lewis: Overview, Interview, and Filmography*, Scarecrow Press, Maryland, 1998

Nott, Robert, *He Ran All the Way: The Life of John Garfield*, Limelight Editions, New York, 2003

Pendo, Stephen, *Raymond Chandler on Screen: His Novels into Film*, Scarecrow Press, Metuchen, 1976

Phillips, Gene D, *Stanley Kubrick: A Film Odyssey*, Popular Library, New York, 1977

Punter, David, *The Literature of Terror: The Gothic Tradition*, Longman, Harlow, 1996

Sedgwick, Eve Kosofsky, *Between Men: English Literature and Male Homosocial Desire*, Columbia University Press, New York, 1985

Sennett, Robert S, *Hollywood Hoopla*, Billboard, New York, 1998

Server, Lee, *Robert Mitchum: 'Baby, I Don't Care'*, Faber and Faber, London, 2001

Sherman, Eric & Rubin, Martin, *The Director's Event: Interviews with Five American Film-Makers*, Athenum, New York, 1970

Sikov, Ed, *On Sunset Boulevard: The Life and Times of Billy Wilder*, Hyperion, New York, 1998

Silver, Alain & Ward, Elizabeth (eds.), *Film Noir: An Encyclopaedic Reference to the American Style*, Overlook Press, New York, 1980

Silver, Alain & Ursini, James *What Ever Happened to Robert Aldrich?*, Limelight, New York, 1995

Silver, Alain & Ursini, James (eds.), *The Film Noir Reader*, Limelight, New York, 1996

Silver, Alain, Ursini, James & Porfirio, Robert (eds.), *Film Noir Reader 3*, Limelight Editions, New York, 2002

Silver, Alain & Ursini, James, *Film Noir*, Taschen, London, 2004

Sperber, AM & Lax, Eric, *Bogart*, Phoenix, London, 1997

Spicer, Andrew, *Film Noir*, Longman, Harlow, 2002

Spooner, Catherine, *Fashioning Gothic Bodies*, University of Manchester Press, Manchester, 2004

Swanson, Gloria, *Swanson on Swanson*, Random House, New York, 1980

Thompson, David & Christie, Ian, *Scorsese on Scorsese*, Faber and Faber, London, 1996

Thomson, David, *Rosebud: The Story of Orson Welles*, Abacus, London, 1997

Thomson, David, *The Big Sleep*, BFI Publishing, London, 1997

Zolotow, Maurice, *Billy Wilder in Hollywood*, GP Putnam's Sons, New York, 1977

Articles and Short Stories

Agee, James, review of *Double Indemnity* in *The Nation*, 14 October 1944

Agee, James, review of *Out of the Past* in *The Nation*, 24 April 1948

Anderson, Jeffrey M, 'Detour: Ulmer's B-Movie Masterpiece' (http://www.combustiblecelluloid.com/detour.shtml)

Anonymous, publicity notes for *Stranger on the Third Floor*, 1940

Anonymous, review of *Stranger on the Third Floor* in *Variety*, 4 September 1940

Anonymous, publicity notes for *The Maltese Falcon*, 1941

Anonymous, review of *The Maltese Falcon* in *Variety*, 1 October 1941

Anonymous, review of *The Maltese Falcon* in the *Motion Picture Herald*, 4 October 1941

Anonymous, publicity notes for *Double Indemnity*, 1944

Anonymous, review of *Double Indemnity* in *Variety*, 26 April 1944

Anonymous, review of *Murder, My Sweet* in *Time*, 14 December 1944

Anonymous, review of *Murder, My Sweet* in *Variety*, 14 March 1945

Anonymous, article in the *Daily News*, 6 December 1945

Anonymous, publicity notes for *Detour*, 1945

Anonymous, review of *Detour* in *Variety*, 23 January 1946

Anonymous, review of *The Killers* in *Variety*, 7 August 1946

Anonymous, review of *The Big Sleep* in *Variety*, 14 August 1946

Anonymous, review of *The Big Sleep* in the *Evening Standard*, 29 September 1946

Anonymous, review of *The Big Sleep* in *The Times*, 30 September 1946

Anonymous, review of *The Big Sleep* in the *Spectator*, 11 October 1946

Anonymous, review of *The Killers* in the *Daily Herald*, 15 November 1946

Anonymous, publicity notes for *Out of the Past*, 1947

Anonymous, review of *Out of the Past* in *Variety*, 19 November 1947

Anonymous, review of *Out of the Past* in the *Daily Herald*, 4 December 1947

Anonymous, review of *Out of the Past* in the *Daily Graphic*, 19 December 1947

Anonymous, review of *The Lady from Shanghai* in *The Times*, 8 March 1948

Anonymous, review of *The Lady from Shanghai* in *Time and Tide*, 13 March 1948

Anonymous, review of *The Lady from Shanghai* in *Variety*, 14 April 1948

Anonymous, review of *Force of Evil* in *Variety*, 29 December 1948

Anonymous, review of *Force of Evil* in the *National Chronicle*, 28 April 1949

Anonymous, review of *Gun Crazy* in *Variety*, 2 November 1949

Anonymous, review of *Sunset Boulevard* in *Variety*, 19 April 1950

Anonymous, review of *Gun Crazy* in the *Observer*, 23 July 1950

Anonymous, 'Report on the Communist "Peace" Offensive – A Campaign to Disarm and Defeat the United States', Committee on Un-American Activities, U.S. House of Representatives, 82nd Congress, House report No. 378, April 1, 1951

Anonymous, article on *The Big Heat* in the *Columbia News Service*, 1 February 1953

Anonymous, review of *The Big Heat* in *Variety*, 23 September 1953

Anonymous, review of *The Big Heat* in *Time*, 2 November 1953

Anonymous, review of *The Big Heat* in *Monthly Film Bulletin*, April 1954

Anonymous, review of *The Big Combo* in *Variety*, 13 February 1955

Anonymous, 'Sex and Violence "Justified" ' in *America: The National Catholic Weekly Review*, 5 March 1955

Anonymous, review of *Kiss Me Deadly* in *Variety*, 20 April 1955

Anonymous, review of *The Night of the Hunter* in *Variety*, 20 July 1955

Anonymous, review of *Kiss Me Deadly* in *Monthly Film Bulletin*, August 1955

Anonymous, review of *The Big Combo* in *Monthly Film Bulletin*, February 1956

Anonymous, review of *The Killing* in *Variety*, 20 May 1956

Anonymous, review of *The Killing* in *Time*, 4 June 1956

Anonymous, review of *The Killing* in the *Guardian*, 28 July 1956

Anonymous, publicity notes for *Touch of Evil*, 1958

Anonymous, review of *Touch of Evil* in *Variety*, 19 March 1958

Anonymous, 'Out of the Past' in *American Cinematographer* volume 65 issue 3, March 1984

Anonymous, 'Huston Blasts Colorizing', *Variety*, 19 November 1986

Anstey, Edgar, review of *Double Indemnity* in the *Spectator*, 22 September 1944

Black, Louis, 'Double Indemnity', *Cinema Texas Program Notes*, 1978

Black, Louis, 'Out of the Past', *Cinema Texas Program Notes*, 1978

Blaser, John, 'The Outer Limits of Film Noir' (http://www.lib.berkley.edu/MRC/noir/ol-all.html)

Bogdanovich, Peter, 'What They Say About Stanley Kubrick', the *New York Times*, 4 July 1999

Brien, Alan, review of *The Killing* in the *Evening Standard*, 26 July 1956

Calendo, John, 'Robert Aldrich says, "Life is Worth Living" ' in *Andy Warhol's Interview* issue 3, August 1973

Carson, Michael, interview with Mickey Spillane for *Crime Time* (http://www.crimetime.co.uk/interviews/mickeyspillane.html)

Chabrol, Claude, review of *Kiss Me Deadly* in *Cahiers du Cinema* issue 54

Chandler, Raymond, letter to his publisher, sourced from http://www.kirjasto.sci.fi/jmcain.htm

Clark, Wes, 'My Interview with Gaby Rodgers' (http://wesclark.com/ubn/gaby_rodgers.html)

Crowther, Bosley, review of *The Maltese Falcon* in the *New York Times*, 4 October 1941

Crowther, Bosley, review of *Double Indemnity* in the *New York Times*, 7 September 1944

Crowther, Bosley, review of *Murder, My Sweet* in the *New York Times*, 9 March 1945

Crowther, Bosley, review of *The Big Sleep* in the *New York Times*, 24 August 1946

Crowther, Bosley, review of *The Killers* in the *New York Times*, 29 August 1946

Crowther, Bosley, review of *Out of the Past* in the *New York Times*, 14 November 1947

Crowther, Bosley, review of *The Lady from Shanghai* in the *New York Times*, 10 June 1948

Crowther, Bosley, review of *Force of Evil* in the *New York Times*, 27 December 1948

Crowther, Bosley, review of *The Big Heat* in the *New York Times*, 15 October 1953

Crowther, Bosley, review of *The Night of the Hunter* in the *New York Times*, 20 September 1955

Deans, Harris, review of *The Night of the Hunter* in the *Sunday Dispatch*, 27 November 1955

Dixon, Campbell, 'A Brilliant New Thriller' in the *Daily Telegraph*, 18 September 1944

Dixon, Campbell, review of *The Killers* in the *Daily Telegraph*, 18 November 1946

Erikson, Glenn, 'The Kiss Me Mangled Mystery' in *Images* issue 3 (www.imagesjournal.com/issue3/features/kmd1.htm)

Farber, Manny, review of *The Big Sleep* in the *New Republic*, 23 September 1946

Farber, Manny, review of *The Killers* in the *New Republic*, 30 September 1946

Flinn, Tom, 'Screenwriter Daniel Mainwaring Discusses *Out of the Past*' in *Velvet Light Trap*, Fall 1973

Frazer, Bryant, 'Gun Crazy' for *Deep Focus* (http://www.deep-focus.com/flicker/guncrazy.html)

Gritten, David, interview with Billy Wilder for the *Mail on Sunday*, 11 July 1993

Grost, Michael E, 'A Guide to Classic Mystery and Detection' (http://members.aol.com/MG4273/classics.htm)

Hagopian, Kevin Jack, '10 Shades of Noir' in *Images* issue 2 (www.imagesjournal.com/issue02/infocus.htm)

Harris, James B, 'Stanley Kubrick: A Cinematic Odyssey', *Premiere*, August 1999

Hemingway, Ernest, 'The Killers', 1927 (http://www.shortstory.by.ru/hemingway/killers/)

Hoberman, J, article on *Kiss Me Deadly* for *Village Voice*, 15 March 1994

Hornburger, Philip, review of *Sunset Boulevard* in *The New Yorker*, 19 August 1950

Ivers, James D, review of *Sunset Boulevard* in the *Motion Picture Herald*, 22 April 1950

Kirwan, Patrick, review of *The Killers* in the *Evening Standard*, 18 November 1946

Lardner, John, review of *Double Indemnity* in *The New Yorker*, 16 September 1944

Lejeune, CA, review of *The Night of the Hunter* in the *Observer*, 27 November 1955

Lejeune, CA, review of *Touch of Evil* in the *Observer*, 4 May 1958

Lightman, Herb, '*The Killers*: Teamwork on Film Production' in *American Cinematographer*, December 1946

Marling, William, *Hard-Boiled Fiction*, Case Western Reserve University (http://www.cwru.edu/artsci/engl/marling/hardboiled/index.html)

Marshman, D, article for *Life*, 25 August 1947

Martin, Adrian, 'Violently Happy: *Gun Crazy*' in *Senses of Cinema* (http://www.sensesofcinema.com/contents/00/10/guncrazy.html)

McCurtew, John, review of *The Night of the Hunter* in *The New Yorker*, 8 October 1955

McNulty, John, review of *The Killers* in *The New Yorker*, 7 September 1946

Mills, Michael, 'Barbara Stanwyck and *Double Indemnity*' in *Modern Times* (http://www.moderntimes.com/palace/palace_di.htm)

Morris, Gary, review of *Detour* for *Images* issue 9 (http://www.imagesjournal.com/issue09/reviews/detour/)

Oakes, Philip, review of *Touch of Evil* in the *Evening Standard*, 1 February 1958

O'Brien, Steve, 'Past Perfect: *Angel Heart*', *SFX* issue 127, February 2005

Pechter, William, interview with Abraham Polonsky in *Film Quarterly* No. 3, Vol XV, Spring 1962

Polan, Dana, 'Detour' for *Senses of Cinema* (http://www.ensesofcinema.com/contents/cteq/02/21/detour.html)

Powell, Dilys, review of *The Maltese Falcon* in *The Sunday Times*, 21 June 1942

Powell, Dilys, review of *Murder, My Sweet* in *The Sunday Times*, 15 April 1945

Powell, Dilys, review of *Force of Evil* in *The Sunday Times*, 24 April 1949

Powell, Dilys, review of *Gun Crazy* in *The Sunday Times*, 23 July 1950

Powell, Dilys, review of *Sunset Boulevard* in *The Sunday Times*, 20 August 1950

Powell, Dilys, review of *The Big Heat* in *The Sunday Times*, 9 May 1954

Powell, Dilys, review of *The Night of the Hunter* in *The Sunday Times*, 27 November 1955

Powell, Dilys, review of *Touch of Evil* in *The Sunday Times*, 4 May 1958

Pryor, Thomas M, review of *Sunset Boulevard* in the *New York Times*, 11 August 1950

Richards, Brad, 'The Sea Was Full of Sharks' in *Kabinet* issue 11 (http://www.kabinet.org/words/issue11/lady1.html)

Shepler, Michael, 'Hollywood Red: The Life of Abraham Polonsky' in *Political Affairs Magazine* (http://www.politicalaffairs.net/article/view/66/1/22)

Spiers, George H, review of *The Lady from Shanghai* in the *Motion Picture Herald*, 17 April 1948

Swierczynski, Duane, 'This Here's A Stick-Up' (http://www.allanguthrie.co.uk/4/Lets_Book_Em.htm)

Thompson, Howard, review of *Gun Crazy* in the *New York Times*, 25 August 1950

Thompson, Howard, review of *The Big Combo* in the *New York Times*, 26 March 1955

Thompson, Howard, review of *Touch of Evil* in the *New York Times*, 22 May 1958

Truffaut, Francois, interview with Robert Aldrich for *Cahiers du Cinema*, November 1956

Weiler, AH, review of *The Killing* in the *New York Times*, 21 May 1956

Welles, Orson, memo to Edward I. Muhl, 5 December 1957, sourced from www.wellesnet.com/touch_memo1.htm

Welles, Orson, letter to the *New Statesman*, 24 May 1958

Weston, Robert, 'Detour' in Film Monthly (http://www.filmmonthly.com/Noir/Articles/Detour/Detour.html)

Whitebait, William, review of *The Maltese Falcon* in the *New Statesman*, 20 June 1942

Whitebait, William, review of *Double Indemnity* in the *New Statesman*, 23 September 1944

Whitebait, William, review of *Murder, My Sweet* in the *New Statesman*, 21 April 1945

Whitebait, William, review of *Sunset Boulevard* in the *New Statesman*, 26 August 1950

Whitebait, William, review of *Touch of Evil* in the *New Statesman*, 10 May 1958

Winnington, Richard, review of *Out of the Past* in the *Chronicle*, 20 December 1947

Picture Credits

The following pictures are from the Kobal Collection:
Page 2 (bottom) courtesy of Producers' Releasing Corporation/The
Kobal Collection; Page 4 (bottom) courtesy of MGM/The Kobal
Collection; Page 5 (bottom) courtesy of Paramount/The Kobal
Collection; Page 7 (top) courtesy of United Artists/The Kobal Collection;
Page 7 (bottom) courtesy of United Artists/The Kobal Collection
The following pictures are from the Ronald Grant Archive:
Page 1 (top) and Page 3 (top) courtesy of Warner Bros.; Page 1 (bottom)
courtesy of Paramount Pictures; Page 2 (top) courtesy of RKO; Page 3
(bottom) courtesy of Universal Pictures; Page 4 (top) courtesy of RKO;
Page 5 (top) courtesy of Pioneer Pictures; Page 6 (top) courtesy of
Columbia Pictures; Page 6 (bottom) courtesy of Allied Artists; Page 8
(top) courtesy of Harris/Kubrick Productions; Page 8 (bottom) courtesy
of Universal International

Index

Across the Pacific 29
Agee, James 41, 81, 107, 199–200, 201
Aldrich, Robert 128–129, 172, 185–197
Allied Artists 175
Altman, Rick 220
Altman, Robert 165, 221, 242
Alton, John 177, 179
American Cinematographer 91
Anders, Glenn 115
Andrews, Dana 46, 141
Angel Face 162–163
Angel Heart 246
Angels With Dirty Faces 60
Anstey, Edgar 41
Apology For Murder 45
Arthur, Robert 169, 170
Asphalt Jungle, The 133, 215, 219
Associates and Aldrich production company 185–186
Astor, Mary 22, 23–24, 26, 29
Atlantic Monthly 36
Attenborough, Richard 239
auteurism 2
Aznavour, Charles 240

B-movies 6, 65–69, 235
Bacall, Lauren 74, 75–80, 103
Badge of Evil (book) 225
Badlands 147
Baldick, Chris 14–15
Ballard, Lucien 217, 219
Barnes, George 129
Barry Lyndon 221
Barton Fink 160, 245
Beetley, Samuel 106
Belafonte, Harry 237
Bening, Annette 247
Bennett, Joan 45, 46
Bezzerides, Al 186, 187, 188, 193, 194, 196–197
Bicycle Thief, The 132
Big Combo, The 172, 173–183, 216, 235
Big Heat, The 56, 163–172, 194
Big Lebowski, The 245
Big Sleep, The (book) 241
Big Sleep, The 23, 34, 44, 56, 70–84, 222, 245, 245
black and white vs colour 207–210, 235
Black Angel 246
Black Bird, The 29

Blade Runner 1, 244–245
Blanke, Henry 23
Blaser, John 26, 29, 234
Blind Alley 16
Blood Simple 1, 110, 245
Blue Velvet 1, 110, 245–246
Body and Soul 125, 127, 128
Body Heat 45, 244, 248
Boehm, Sydney 165–166, 170
Bogart, Humphrey 21–22, 24, 26, 28–29, 51, 53, 74, 75–81, 102, 149, 161, 175
Bogart, Paul 242
Bogdanovich, Peter 46, 122
Bonnie and Clyde 146, 147, 148
Boorman, John 241
Botting, Fred 120
Brackett, Charles 33, 34, 150–153, 155, 157
Brackett, Leigh 73, 74, 75, 77, 242
Brahm, John 97
Brando, Jocelyn 168–169
Brassai, Gilberte 15
Breathless 240
Bredell, Woody 91
Breen, Joseph 34, 35–36, 82
Bridges, Jeff 110
Brien, Alan 219–220
Brighton Rock 239
Britton, Andrew 44–45, 65, 121
Brown, Hilyard 203
Bruce, Sally Jane 203
Buchsbaum, Jonathan 180–182
Build My Gallows High (book) 101
Busch, Niven 70
Byrne, Gabriel 248

Cabinet of Dr Caligari, The 13, 116
Cagney, James 28, 126
Cahiers du Cinéma 193, 229
Cain, James M 14, 33–35, 40, 59, 70, 101–102, 134, 181, 245
Caine, Michael 241
California locations 133–134
Callow, Simon 200
cameras 16, 57
Cammell, Donald 241
Capra, Frank 2, 37, 155
Carné, Marcel 14
Carter, Milt 203
Casablanca 60, 75
Cassavetes, John 97

Castle, William 113, 114
Cat People 57, 100, 105
Catholic Legion of Decency 191, 192
Cawelti, John 27, 242
Chabrol, Claude 193
Chandler, Raymond 14, 28, 34–36, 39, 40,
    43, 48–49, 54, 72, 74, 75, 77, 80–81, 98,
    181, 242, 246
Chapin, Billy 203
Chatman, Seymour 96
Chinatown 243
Choi Mik-sin 250
Chronicle 107, 118
Citizen Kane 12, 56–57, 95, 112, 114–115,
    118, 155, 227
Clark, Pat 79
Clay Pigeon, The 109
Clean Break 213, 214
Clift, Montgomery 153
Clockwork Orange, A 213, 218, 221
Cobb, Lee J 128
Coen, Frankie 229
Coen brothers 245
Cohn, Harry 113, 114, 115, 116–118
Collins, Joan 84
Collins, Wilkie 14
colour vs black and white 207–210, 235
Columbia 5, 6, 56, 113, 166, 167, 168
Communism 15, 125, 161, 215
Confidential Agent 79
Conrad, William 29, 90
Conte, Richard 176–177, 178
Conversation, The 1, 242
Cook, Elisha Jr 9, 23, 29, 76, 80, 216
Cooper, Maxine 189
Coppola, Francis Ford 242
Cornered 171
Cortez, Stanley 203, 204, 208
Cotten, Joseph 227, 239
'country' noir 107–108, 245
'crab dollies' 16, 228
Crawford, Joan 59
Cregar, Laird 30
crime fiction 14
Criminal Code, The 15
Crowther, Bosley 25–26, 40–41, 54–55,
    79–80, 92, 106, 119, 130–131, 170,
    191, 192, 205–206
Cry of the City 133, 176, 202
Cukor, George 152–153
Cummins, Peggy 140, 143, 145
Curtis, Alan 31
Curtis, Tony 227
Curtiz, Michael 59–60

Cusack, John 247
cyberpunk 244

Dahl, John 248
Daily Graphic 107
Daily Herald 93, 107
Daily News 45
Daily Telegraph 41, 93
Dall, John 140–141, 143
Dangerous Female 20
Dark Mirror, The 94
Davis, Bette 20, 21, 167
De Corsia, Ted 115, 177, 216
De Niro, Robert 243, 246
Deadly is the Female 135, 144
Del Ruth, Roy 20
DeMille, Cecil B 153, 155, 156–157
Dennis, Nick 190
DeSylva, Buddy 39
detective characters 3, 14, 26–27, 95–97,
    195–196
Detour 43, 60–69, 95, 134, 147, 233
Deutsch, Adolph 25
Deutsch, Armand 151
Dickinson, Angie 97
Dieterle, William 20
Dietrich, Marlene 227
Dillinger 138, 174–175, 247
Dimendberg, Edward 110
Directors Guild of America 186
Dixon, Campbell 41, 93
Dmytryck, Edward 48, 50–55, 58–59, 102
D.O.A. 14, 90, 148
'docu-noir' films 56, 131–135, 147, 221
Double Indemnity 3, 12, 32–45, 49, 56, 70,
    72, 82, 94, 95, 134, 150, 160, 181, 220,
    244, 248
Douglas, Kirk 103–104, 105, 107, 138
Dozier, Bill 101, 106
Dragnet (TV series) 133, 155
Drier, Hans 30–31
Duff, William 101, 102
Dureya, Dan 46

Eastmancolor 207
Easy Rider 146
Ellroy, James 249
Enterprise Studios 125, 127, 130
Epstein, Philip 79
Erikson, Glenn 196–197
Erikson, Todd 12
Evans, Ray 155
Evening Standard 80, 93, 219, 232
existentialism 15–16, 243

Experiment Perilous 55
Expressionism 13, 15, 31, 54, 58–59, 82, 96, 107, 122, 133, 165, 209–210

Falling Angel (book) 246
Farber, Manny 80, 83, 93
Farewell, My Lovely (book) 34, 49, 241
Farewell My Lovely (film) 202
Fargo 245
fatalism 220
Faulkner, William 72–73, 74–75
Fedora 162
Feldman, Charlie 79
Fellig, Arthur H 15
femme fatale characters 3, 14, 42–44, 60, 97, 121, 160, 163, 239, 244, 247, 248
Fenton, Frank 102
Fight Club 96
film noir
    country or city settings 107–108, 195, 245
    definitions 11–13
    misogyny 44–45, 69
    'neo-noir' 12
    paranoid noir 14
Final Twist, The 14, 34
Fiorentino, Linda 248
flashback narratives 94–98, 181, 220–221
Fleischer, Richard 162
Flynn, Errol 115–116
Force of Evil 123–135, 185, 216
Ford, Glenn 69, 167, 169, 170
Ford, Harrison 244
Ford, John 116, 204
Foreign Intrigue 219
Forever Amber 140
Foster, Jodie 243
Fox, Edward 84
Fox, James 241
Foy, Brian 65–66
France
    film noir 12
    Poetic Realism 13–14, 239
    reception of *Kiss Me Deadly* 193
Frank, Nino 12
Frears, Stephen 247
Freud, Sigmund 180, 181
Fromkess, Leon 62
Full Metal Jacket 221
Furthman, Jules 73, 75

Gabor, Zsa Zsa 227
Gallafent, Edward 194
gangster films 15, 81, 127, 134–135
Gardner, Ava 89, 90, 92

Garfield, John 51, 70, 125, 127–128, 129–130, 131
Garner, James 242
Garnett, Tay 70
General Teleradio 56
Gentleman's Agreement 128
Get Carter 241
Getty, J Paul 156
Getty, Mary 156
Gibson, Mel 222
Gidding, Nelson 237
Gilda 44–45, 56, 69, 109, 110, 114, 117, 118, 167, 171, 245, 246
Gish, Lilian 202–203
Godard, Jean-Luc 240
Godfrey, Peter 78
Goebbels, Joseph 164
Goldberg, Molly 124
Goldsmith, Martin 62–63
Gomez, Thomas 128, 130
'good-bad girl' character 44
Goodis, David 240
Gordon, Robert 203, 205
Gothic romance 14–15, 94, 120–122, 245, 246
Gould, Elliott 242
Grable, Betty 30
Grahame, Gloria 149, 161, 167–168, 169, 170
Graves, Peter 203, 204
Gray, Coleen 216, 217–218
Greene, Graham 30, 232, 233, 239
Greenstreet, Sydney 22–23, 29
Greer, Jane 101, 103, 105–107, 110
Gregory, Paul 200, 201, 203, 205, 206
Griffith, DW 201, 202
Grifters, The 246–247
Grist, Leighton 108
Grubb, David 199, 200, 204, 205
Gun Crazy 109, 133, 135–148
Guncrazy 148

Hackford, Taylor 110
Hackman, Gene 242
Hammett, Dashiell 14, 19–20, 23, 27, 29, 245
Harper 240
Harris, James B 214, 215, 217
Harris-Kubrick Pictures 214
Hartnell, William 239
Hathaway, Henry 132, 133
Hawks, Howard 20, 72–79, 81–83, 112, 222
Hawks, Nancy Gross 'Slim' 76
Hayden, Sterling 133, 215–216, 218, 222

Hays, Will 82
Hayworth, Rita 69, 113–114, 116–119, 167, 245, 246
He Walked By Night 132–133, 154–155
Head, Edith 39
Hellinger, Mark 87, 88–93, 94, 132
Hemingway, Ernest 86, 87, 92
Herald Examiner 169
Herald Tribune 191
Heston, Charlton 225–229, 231
Hickey and Boggs 243
Hickox, Sid 79
High Sierra 21, 28, 148, 176
Hitchcock, Alfred 132, 146, 222
Hjortsberg, William 246
Hodges, Mike 241
Holden, William 153–154, 157, 158, 162
Hollywood
    film noir 12–13
    New Hollywood cinema 135, 236, 242
    studio system 5–7, 175, 234–235
    Sunset Boulevard 159–162
    violence in films 171–172
Holmes, Sherlock 27
Homes, Geoffrey *see* Mainwaring, Daniel
'homme fatal' character 60, 161
homosexuality 180, 183
Hopper, Dennis 246
Hopper, Edward 15, 129
Hopper, Hedda 155
Hornburger, Philip 158–159
horror movies 15
House on 92nd Street, The 132
House Un-American Activities Committee (HUAC) 15, 19, 22, 48, 125, 127–128, 137, 139, 155, 161, 166, 193, 215
Houseman, John 81, 112
Howard, Cy 169
Hughes, Howard 101, 103
Hugo, Chris 175, 183
Humberstone, Bruce 30
Hunter, Ian McLellan 138
Hurt, William 244
Huston, Anjelica 247
Huston, John 19–26, 28, 29, 87, 94, 175, 243
Huston, Virginia 107

I Am a Fugitive from a Chain Gang 15
I Wake Up Screaming 30, 76
If I Die Before I Wake (book) 112, 113, 122
In a Lonely Place 56, 149, 161, 167, 172
Ingster, Boris 8, 10, 11
'investigative' narrative 95
It's a Wonderful Life 43, 167

Ivers, James D 158

Jagger, Mick 241
Jurow, Martin 88, 128

Kalmus, Natalie 207
Kantor, MacKinlay 137–140, 141
Kasdan, Lawrence 244
Kaufman, Millard 137, 140
Keaton, Buster 155
Kefauver Commission 192
Keller, Harry 229, 231, 236
Key Largo 12, 19, 76, 128
Killer's Kiss 210, 212, 214
Killers, The 15, 29, 84–97, 132, 162, 168
Killing, The 1, 76, 133, 210–222, 247
King, Frank 138, 139
King, Herman 138
King, Maurice 138
King, Sherwood 112–113
Kirwan, Patrick 93
Kiss Me Deadly 172, 184–197
Kitses, Jim 109
Klein, Andy 11
Klute 243
Knudsen, Peggy 79
Koerner, Charles M 50, 51, 52, 56
Krasner, Milton 46
Kubrick, Stanley 212–222

L.A. Confidential 249
Ladd, Alan 30, 31
Lady from Shanghai, The 14, 45, 65, 110–122, 177, 216, 231
Lady in the Lake, The 98
Laemmle, Carl 61
Lake, Veronica 30, 31
Lancaster, Burt 88–89, 90–92, 93, 104
Lang, Fritz 15, 45–46, 61, 161, 164–172
Lardner, John 41
Lasky's production company 155
Last Seduction, The 248
Last Tycoon, The 160
Last Will of Dr Mabuse, The 13
Laughton, Charles 198–206, 208
Laura 12, 46, 163
Lawrence, Viola 117
Lawton, Charles 116
Lax, Eric 28
Lazslo, Ernie 190
Leachman, Cloris 189
Lederer, Charles 112–113, 114
Leigh, Janet 227, 228, 229
Leites, Nathan 44

Lejeune, CA 206, 232
Leong, Ian 146, 147
Leopard Man, The 57, 100
Lerner, Max 93
Let Us Live! 16
Levene, Sam 90
Lewis, Joseph H 57, 136–137, 140–145,
   174–179, 235
Lewis, Matthew 120
Lewton, Val 57, 58
Library of Congress National Film Registry 69
Life magazine 94, 103
lighting 16–17, 26, 58, 67, 81, 91, 105
Livingston, Jay 155
Lloyd Webber, Andrew 162
location filming 132, 133–134, 233
Locket, The 97–98
Lolita 218, 220
Long Goodbye, The 242
Lorre, Peter 9, 17, 22, 33
Lost Weekend, The 150, 153
'lying flashbacks' 96
Lynch, David 245–246
Lyons, Arthur 16, 248

M 13, 61, 164
MacDonald, Edmund 64
MacLachlan, Kyle 246
MacMurray, Fred 36–37, 40, 43, 153
Magnificent Ambersons, The 112, 117, 227
Mainwaring, Daniel 100–102, 104, 106
Maltby, Richard 12, 82, 126, 160, 172,
   207–208
Maltese Falcon, The 3, 9, 12, 15, 17–30, 43,
   56, 75, 81, 101, 102, 110, 195, 244
*Man Who Searched For His Own Murderer,
   The* 148
Man Who Wasn't There, The 1, 245
Manchester Guardian 219
Mancini, Henry 230
Mann, Anthony 212
Marcus, Lee S 8
Markle, Fletcher 113, 114
Marlowe 242
Marshman, D 94
Marshman, DM 151, 152, 157
Marvin, Lee 97, 168, 240
Masterson, Whit 224–225
Maté, Rudolph 116, 148
Mature, Victor 30
Mayer, Louis B 56, 158, 174
Mazurki, Mike 53
McCambridge, Mercedes 227
McCarthy, Joseph 15, 193

McCloud, Scott 207
McCready, George 69
McCurtew, John 206
McDowell, Malcolm 218
McGivern, William P 165, 166, 167, 170
McGraw, Charles 162
McGuire, John 9
McNulty, John 93
Meeker, Ralph 189, 192
'melodramas' 125–126
Memento 249–250
Methot, Mayo 77, 78
Metro-Goldwyn-Mayer 5, 34, 56, 70, 130,
   131, 136, 139, 144, 220
Metty, Russell 228
Mildred Pierce 14, 59–60, 73
Miller, William 224–225
Miller's Crossing 245
Mills, John 84
misogyny 44–45, 69
Mitchum, Robert 59, 84, 97, 101, 102–107,
   110, 162, 201–202, 203–204, 205–206
Monash, Paul 225–226
Monogram 6, 138, 175
Montgomery, Robert 98
Monthly Film Bulletin 170–171, 180, 192
Mooney, Martin 62, 63
Morris, Wayne 89
Motion Picture Herald 25, 119, 158
Muhl, Eddie 225, 229, 230, 231
Mulholland Drive 1, 246
Murch, Walter 236
Murder in Reverse 239
Murder, My Sweet 12, 15, 34, 43–44, 46–59,
   72, 94, 95, 181, 195
Murnau, FW 54
Musuraca, Nicholas 9–10, 11, 98, 105, 107,
   165

Naked City, The 132
Narrow Margin, The 162, 216
Nation, The 41, 107
National Chronicle 131
Nazism 164, 167
Neal, Tom 63, 64
Neal, Tom Jr 69
Negri, Pola 153
New Hollywood cinema 135, 242
New Republic 80, 93
New Statesman 26, 41–42, 55, 159, 232, 235
New York locations 133–134
New York Times 25, 40–41, 54, 79–80, 92,
   106, 119, 130–131, 145, 158, 170, 171,
   179, 191, 192, 205, 219, 232

New Yorker, The 41, 93, 158, 206
Nicholson, Jack 243
Night of the Hunter, The 197–210
Nilsson, Anna Q 155
Nims, Ernie 229, 231
Nolan, Christopher 250
Not as a Stranger 206

Oakes, Philip 232
O'Brien, Edmond 89–90, 148
Observer, The 145, 206, 232
Odds Against Tomorrow 237
Oldboy 250
Olivier, Laurence 176
Olson, Nancy 154, 155–156, 158
O'Shea, Oscar 10
Out of the Past 15, 44, 99–110, 133, 134, 201

Palance, Jack 176
Pantoliano, Joe 249
Parallax View, The 242
Paramount Pictures 5, 33, 35–37, 40, 45, 49,
    56, 72, 124, 151, 155
paranoia 180–183
Park Chan-wook 250
Parker, Alan 246
Parklane Productions 187
Parsons, Louella 155
Partos, Frank 8
Patrick, Lee 29
Paul Gregory Productions 200
Paxton, John 49, 50, 51, 54
Pearce, Guy 249
Pearson, Beatrice 128, 130
Peck, Gregory 141
Performance 241
Phantom Lady 31, 86, 95, 128, 181
photography 15, 56–57, 91, 129, 177,
    228–229, 233, 234, 237
Pickford, Mary 153
Place, Janey 42, 44
Player, The 160
PM magazine 93
Poe, Edgar Allen 120
Poetic Realism 13–14, 82, 239
Point Blank 240–241
Polanski, Roman 243
Polonsky, Abraham 124–131, 134, 185, 237
Porfirio, Robert 57–58
Postman Always Rings Twice, The (book) 14,
    33, 34
Postman Always Rings Twice, The (film) 56,
    70, 127, 162–163
'poverty row' studios 6, 66, 69, 175

Powell, Dick 36, 48, 51, 52–53, 54, 55, 102
Powell, Dilys 26, 55, 131, 145, 159, 170, 206
PRC (Producers Releasing Corporation) 6,
    61, 62, 65, 66
Preminger, Otto 46, 163
Price, Vincent 46
Production Code 15, 28, 34, 35–36, 42, 43,
    45, 49, 68, 82, 88, 139, 141–142, 143,
    178, 191
Pryor, Thomas M 158
psychoanalysis 15, 180–181, 183
Pulp Fiction 197, 247–248
Punter, David 120

Queen Kelly 156

Radcliffe, Anne 120
Raft, George 21–22, 36
Raines, Ella 31
Ray, Nicholas 149
Reagan, Ronald 97
realism 209, 233
Rebecca 15
Reed, Carol 239
Reed, Oliver 84
Repo Man 197
Republic film company 6
Reservoir Dogs 183, 222, 247
Richards, Dick 59
Ridgely, John 78
Rio 16
RKO 5, 8, 9, 11, 15, 48, 49, 50, 55–56,
    57–58, 100, 101, 103–106, 112
road movies 67–68, 146–148
Roberts, Bob 125
Robinson, Edward G 28, 38, 45, 176
Rochemont, Louis de 132
Rodgers, Gaby 189–190, 191
Roeg, Nicholas 241
Roemheld, Heinz 117
Rome, Open City 132
Rooney, Mickey 89
Rosa, Miklos 97
Rossellini, Isabella 246
Rourke, Mickey 246
Ruskin, Harry 70
Ryan, Robert 237

Samson and Delilah 156
Sanders, Terry and Denis 204
Sandford, Erskine 115
Sarris, Andrew 2, 59
Satan Met a Lady 20
Savage, Ann 45, 63, 64

Saville, Victor 187
Scarlet Street 82, 165
Schaefer, George 56
Schary, Dore 106
Schifrin, Bill 218
Schilling, Gus 115
Schoenfeld, Bernard 31
Schrader, Paul 12, 243
Schumann, Walter 203
Scorsese, Martin 135, 243
Scott, Adrian 49, 50, 51
Scott, Ridley 245
Sedgwick, Eve Kosofsky 183
'seeker-hero' characters 26–27, 95, 147, 148
'seeker-heroine' characters 31
Segal, George 29
Seitz, John 31, 39, 155, 156
Sell, Mike 146, 147
Shadow of a Doubt 132
Shamus 243
Shannon, Harry 115
Shearer, Norma 227
Shining, The 221
Shirley, Anne 52
Shoot the Pianist 240
Siegel, Don 97
Sikov, Ed 162
Silver, Alain 146
Silver, Arthur 78
Silver Screen 169
Simenon, Georges 14
Simmons, Jean 162
Sinatra, Frank 89, 214
Singer, Alexander 217
Singin' in the Rain 160
Siodmak, Robert 31, 85–86, 90–92, 94, 133, 148
Sistrom, Joseph 34, 35
Skolsky, Sidney 156
Sloane, Everett 114–115, 119
Small, Eddie 144
Smeight, Jack 45, 240
Sonatine 247
Spacey, Kevin 248
Spartacus 138
Spectator, The 41, 81
Sperber, A M 28
Spicer, Andrew 12–13, 44, 55, 56, 82, 108, 109, 122, 133, 171, 195, 210, 234, 239, 244
Spiegel, Sam 112, 113, 185
Spiers, George H 119
Spillane, Mickey 186–188, 190, 191, 192, 193, 195

Spiral Staircase, The 94, 121
Spooner, Catherine 121
Stacey, Eric 78
Stage Fright 96
Stanwyck, Barbara 37–38, 39, 40, 153
Star is Born, A 160
Stell, Aaron 229
Stewart, James 84
Stranger on the Third Floor 7–17, 57, 65, 94
Strangers on a Train 12
Street, The 13
'street films' 13
Street of Chance 56
Stroheim, Erich von 154, 156, 162
studio system 5, 65, 175, 210, 234–235
Sunday Times, The 26, 55, 131, 145, 159, 170, 206
Sunset Boulevard 43, 149–162
Swanson, Gloria 152, 153, 155, 156, 158, 161–162

Takeshi Kitano 247
Tallichet, Margaret 9, 10–11
Tarantino, Quentin 222, 247–248
Tarkovsky, Andrei 97
Taxi Driver 1, 243–244
Technicolor 207
Thelma and Louise 146, 147
They Live By Night 146, 148
Thin Man, The 19–20
Third Man, The 227, 239
This Gun For Hire 30–31, 56
Thomas, Kelly 146, 147
Thompson, Howard 145, 179, 231–232
Thompson, Jim 213, 214–215, 219, 246–247
Thomson, David 226
Tierney, Gene 46
Tierney, Lawrence 247
Tiffany film company 6
Time 54, 170, 219
Time and Tide 118–119
Times, The 80, 118
To Have and Have Not 72, 73, 74, 75, 88
Todd, Richard 84
Toland, Gregg 56–57
Toomey, Regis 77–78
Totter, Audrey 98
Touch of Evil 15, 209, 223–236
Tourneur, Jacques 57, 100, 102, 104–107
Trevor, Claire 51–52
Truffaut, François 187, 193, 194, 240
Trumbo, Dalton 137–140, 143
Tucker's People (book) 125, 126
Tufts, Sonny 89

Turner, Kathleen 244
Turner, Lana 70
Turner, Ted 29
Tuttle, Frank 31
Twentieth Century Fox 5, 21–22, 30, 56, 125, 132

Ubijtsi 97
Ulmer, Edgar G 61–66, 69, 235
United Artists 5–6, 55, 138, 144, 153, 156, 187, 191, 200, 205, 212, 214, 217, 220
Universal 5, 6, 15, 31, 56, 57, 87, 132, 225, 226, 228, 236
urban milieu of noir 107–110, 195
Ursini, James 146
Usual Suspects, The 96, 248–249

Valentine, Paul 104
Van Cleef, Lee 177
Vanishing Point 146, 147
Variety 11, 25, 40, 54, 65, 79, 92–93, 106–107, 119, 131, 144, 170, 179, 192, 205, 218–219, 231
Veiller, Anthony 86–87, 93
Vera Cruz 185, 191
Vernon, John 240
Vickers, Martha 77, 78
'victim-heroes' 42–43, 95, 148
Vidor, Charles 69
violence 171–172, 179–180, 188, 191, 192
Vogue 81

Wade, Robert 224–225
Wald, Jerry 166, 169
Walker, Joseph 116
Walker, Michael 12, 14, 27, 31, 42, 81, 83, 96, 97, 133, 222
Wallace, Jean 175–176, 178
Wallis, Hal B 23, 24, 25, 26, 88, 103
Walpole, Horace 122
War Production Board 16
Ward, Rachel 110
Warner, HB 155
Warner, Jack L 23, 25, 73, 74, 75, 78
Warner Bros 5, 19, 20, 21–22, 24, 29, 56, 74, 77, 176, 241
Watergate 242
Watts, Naomi 246

Webb, Jack 154–155
Weiler, AH 219
Welles, Orson 2, 3, 56–57, 58, 112–119, 122, 209, 219, 224–236, 239
West, Mae 152–153
West, Nathaniel 8–9
What Price Hollywood? 159
White, Lionel 213
Whitebait, William 26, 41–42, 55, 159, 232
wide-angle lenses 221, 234
widescreen formats 235
Wild, Harry 58
Wilde, Cornel 175–176, 178
Wilde, Meta 23, 75
Wilder, Billy 33–40, 43, 45, 49, 145, 150–162, 175
Williams, Wade 69
Windsor, Marie 128, 162, 216, 218
Winner, Michael 84
Winnington, Richard 107, 118
Winters, Shelley 202, 203, 218
Wise, Robert 112, 237
Wolfenstein, Martha 44
Wolfert, Ira 125, 126
Woman in the Window, The 12, 44, 45–46, 55, 165, 240
women's role in noir 121–122
  femme fatale characters 3, 14, 42–44, 60, 97, 121, 160, 163, 239, 244, 247, 248
  misogyny 44–45, 69
  'seeker-heroine' characters 31
Woods, James 110
Woolrich, Cornell 14, 31, 57, 137, 181, 246
World War II 16, 171–172
Wright, Tenny 78
Wrong Man, The 222
Wyler, William 175

xenophobia 109–110

Yordan, Philip 174–175
You Only Live Once 146, 165
Young, Sean 245
Youngstein, Max 218
Yu Ji-tae 250

Zanuck, Darryl 132
Zugsmith, Albert 225–226, 229